THE OXFORD HISTORY OF THE BRITISH EMPIRE

COMPANION SERIES

THE OXFORD HISTORY OF THE BRITISH EMPIRE

Volume I. *The Origins of Empire*
EDITED BY Nicholas Canny

Volume II. *The Eighteenth Century*
EDITED BY P. J. Marshall

Volume III. *The Nineteenth Century*
EDITED BY Andrew Porter

Volume IV. *The Twentieth Century*
EDITED BY Judith M. Brown and Wm. Roger Louis

Volume V. *Historiography*
EDITED BY Robin W. Winks

THE OXFORD HISTORY OF THE BRITISH EMPIRE

COMPANION SERIES

Wm. Roger Louis, CBE, D. Litt., FBA

*Kerr Professor of English History and Culture, University of Texas, Austin
and Honorary Fellow of St Antony's College, Oxford*

EDITOR-IN-CHIEF

Canada and the British Empire

Phillip Buckner

*Senior Research Fellow,
Institute of Commonwealth
Studies*

EDITOR

OXFORD

UNIVERSITY PRESS

OXFORD
UNIVERSITY PRESS

Great Clarendon Street, Oxford OX2 6DP

Oxford University Press is a department of the University of Oxford.
It furthers the University's objective of excellence in research, scholarship,
and education by publishing worldwide in

Oxford New York

Auckland Cape Town Dar es Salaam Hong Kong Karachi
Kuala Lumpur Madrid Melbourne Mexico City Nairobi
New Delhi Shanghai Taipei Toronto

With offices in

Argentina Austria Brazil Chile Czech Republic France Greece
Guatemala Hungary Italy Japan Poland Portugal Singapore
South Korea Switzerland Thailand Turkey Ukraine Vietnam

Oxford is a registered trade mark of Oxford University Press
in the UK and in certain other countries

Published in the United States
by Oxford University Press Inc., New York

British Library Cataloguing in Publication Data

Data available

Library of Congress Cataloging in Publication Data

Buckner, Phillip A. (Phillip Alfred), 1942-
Canada and the British Empire / Phillip Buckner.
p. cm.—(The Oxford history of the British Empire companion series)
Includes index.
ISBN 978-0-19-927164-1
1. Canada—Relations—Great Britain. 2. Great Britain—Relations—Canada.
3. Canada—Civilization—British influences. 4. Canada—
History. 5. Great Britain—Colonies—America. I. Title.
F1029.5.G7B83 2008
327.71041—dc22   2007033476

Typeset by Laserwords Private Limited, Chennai, India
Printed in Great Britain
on acid-free paper by
Biddles Ltd, King's Lynn, Norfolk

ISBN 978-0-19-927164-1

1 3 5 7 9 10 8 6 4 2

FOREWORD

The purpose of the five volumes of the Oxford History of the British Empire was to provide a comprehensive survey of the Empire from its beginning to end, to explore the meaning of British imperialism for the ruled as will as the rulers, and to study the significance of the British Empire as a theme in world history. The volumes in the Companion Series carry forward this purpose. They purpose themes that could not be covered adequately in the main series while incorporating recent research and providing fresh interpretations of significant topics.

Wm. Roger Louis

Preface

In the twentieth century there have been two major multi-volume, multi-authored histories of the British Empire. The first was the *Cambridge History of the British Empire*, published by Cambridge University Press in nine volumes between 1929 and 1959; the second was the five-volume *Oxford History of the British Empire* published by Oxford University Press in 1998–9. Both series reflected the dominant themes in Imperial history at the time when they were written. The *Cambridge History* focused heavily on the self-governing Dominions and on India. A separate volume was devoted to Canada, as seemed befitting the oldest and largest of the Dominions, and the history of the settler colonies featured heavily in the three general volumes in the series. The tone of the Cambridge series was Whiggish, romanticized, and triumphalist, extolling the benefits that Imperial expansion had brought both to the colonizers and the colonized. Written in a very different age, the *Oxford History* reflected a very different perspective. It presented a more nuanced and far more critical assessment of the impact of British Imperial expansion around the globe and of the legacies of that Empire. Moreover, the balance of the *Oxford History* was very different. In the *Cambridge History* only the history of the Dominions and of India were examined in separate volumes; the remainder of the British possessions were dealt with in one volume on the 'dependent empire'. In the *Oxford History* the Dominions were given less preferential treatment and much greater attention was paid to Britain's African and Asian colonies. Even those parts of the world considered to be part of Britain's 'informal empire' were treated in more detail in the volumes on the nineteenth and twentieth centuries than the colonies of settlement in Canada and Australasia. To an extent this shift of emphasis was inevitable and probably necessary but from a Canadian perspective, the shift was too decisive. This companion volume to the *Oxford History of the British Empire* seeks to remedy that problem by giving a more detailed account of Canada and the British Empire, one that presents a Canadian perspective on the history of Canada's long participation in the British Empire.

This volume is not meant to be a history of Canada, and many aspects of Canadian history are discussed only in passing. The focus is on Canada's relations with the British Empire, but not in a narrowly constitutional way. Of course, constitutions mattered since they established the boundaries and rules of the relationship between Britain and its colonies. But in Canada's case (and in Australia's and New Zealand's) the Imperial relationship was based upon more than a set of constitutional agreements. It reflected the sense of common identity between Britons at home and Britons abroad, a sense of belonging to what has been described as a wider 'British World'. The relationship between Britain and the Dominions was often described in kinship terms, as one between a mother and her daughters and in the twentieth century as one between sister nations. In Canada's case, this description reflected a basic reality, that the Dominion of Canada was largely the creation of the huge wave of British migration that flowed into the British North American colonies after 1815, and that was reinforced by successive waves in the twentieth century. Without the arrival of the Loyalists in the 1780s there probably would have been no British colonies in North America (save perhaps Newfoundland) to preserve, but it was a century and a half of large-scale British migration that created the emotional bonds that endured until the Empire began to disintegrate in the 1950s and 1960s.

The premise of this volume is that the history of Canada cannot be understood without placing its evolution in an Imperial context. There was a time when this generalization was assumed to be true on both sides of the Atlantic, but this is no longer the case. Chapter 1—the Introduction to the volume—examines how Imperial historiography and Canadian historiography diverged in the period after the Second World War and why the two historiographies gradually lost interest in one another. Chapters 2 to 6 give a chronological narrative of the nature of the Imperial connection and of the attitude of Canadians to the Imperial relationship from the foundation of the first British bases in Canada in the early seventeenth century until the patriation of the Canadian constitution in 1982. Chapter 7 focuses on Newfoundland during the period when it was a somewhat anomalous Dominion between 1869, when it rejected Confederation, and 1949, when it reluctantly joined Canada. Chapters 8 and 9 examine British migration to British North America and to Canada. Chapter 10 describes the ambivalent way in which Canada's largest cultural minority, the French Canadians, perceived the Imperial relationship and Chapter 11 focuses on the attitudes of Canada's Aboriginal people or First Nations, who were dispossessed of most of their land and resources by the European newcomers. Chapter 12 focuses on gender, in particular on the ways in which Canadian women perceived and reacted to the Imperial connection. Chapter 13 examines the economic relationship between Britain and Canada and Chapter 14 the role of Imperial law and legal structures, which, along with the parliamentary and monarchical system of government, remain the most enduring legacies of the British Empire in Canada.

There are a number of themes that are touched upon, but not adequately dealt with, in this volume. We would have liked to include chapters on the attitude of the non-British, non-French immigrants who made their home in Canada—including the large number of American immigrants—towards the Empire, on working-class attitudes, on the connection between religion and Empire, and on the critics of Empire. We would have liked to be able to include a chapter on Canadians in Britain and on Canada's relationship with the other Dominions, though both would have been difficult to write given the state of current scholarship. More could have been said about how Imperial policy toward Canada was made and how British policy makers viewed events in Canada, two central themes in much of the older scholarship on Canada's relationship with the Empire. More could also have been said about the cultural links between Britain and Canada that persist in an attenuated form to the present. But in a volume this limited in length some very hard choices had to be made. For the same reason the documentation had to be kept to a minimum and lengthy references to the sources avoided. Even the select bibliographies attached to the various chapters had to be strictly limited to a few titles.

It will quickly become clear to any reader that the volume reflects a Canadian perspective on Canada's relationship with the British Empire. Almost all of the authors are Canadian citizens and teach or did teach for many years at a Canadian university. The two who are not Canadian, one Scottish and one American, have written extensively about Canada. Like the companion volume on Australia, this volume embodies a different vision of Empire from that embodied in the five-volume *Oxford History*. This vision is captured in the title of the companion volume on Australia—*Australia's Empire*—much more clearly than in the rather pedestrian title of this volume. The British Empire (as the *Cambridge History* for all its faults recognized) was unique among the European empires because it created a series of far-flung colonies, dominated by British migrants and their descendants, that became independent in all but name but remained voluntarily part of the Empire and helped to reshape it into the British Commonwealth of Nations. Indeed, the terms colony and colonial are somewhat misleading in referring to the self-governing colonies of the British Empire. They imply subordination and inferiority, but the British migrants who carved out colonies overseas were not prepared to accept subordination to a remote Imperial authority for very long after settler dominance was firmly established and the majority of the colonists (a word carrying less scorn than colonials) did not view themselves as inferior to the kith and kin they had left behind in Britain. They demanded and received institutions of self-government that gave them the power to determine their own destiny.

The tendency of many Imperial historians (and few of the authors of this volume would define themselves as Imperial historians) is to look at the Empire from the centre outwards, to view Britain as the core and the rest of the Empire as a series of frontiers or peripheries. But this model is misleading. Historians of the First British Empire have largely abandoned it. Increasingly they accept that the relationship between the colonists in the pre-1783 Empire was a 'negotiated' one, that only broke down when the Imperial government sought unilaterally to impose new and unpopular policies on the Thirteen Colonies after 1763. In the aftermath of the American Revolution the Imperial government lacked the will to impose authoritarian constitutions on the colonies that were left in British North America. Within a short period of time all of the British North American colonies were given representative Assemblies directly elected upon a comparatively broad franchise (except for Newfoundland which had to wait until 1832). The Colonial Office, established in 1801, was not designed to shape events in the settler colonies; it was essentially a regulatory body, designed to respond to events overseas. As in the first British Empire, the initiative lay in the hands of local authority structures which were increasingly dominated by the settler communities rather than by Imperial officials appointed from London. Canadian historians used to emphasize the crucial part that Canada played in the evolution of the doctrine of responsible government, a doctrine that became a rallying cry among British colonists everywhere. There is still considerable merit in that argument, for without the grant of responsible government in the 1840s, the larger British North American colonies and in due course the Australasian colonies would probably have left the Empire. Certainly the loyalty of generations of Canadians was predicated on the assumption that they would be free to run their own domestic affairs and that they would decide how far they would follow British leadership internationally. The last vestiges of Imperial control were not formally removed until the passing of the Statute of Westminster in 1931, but long before 1931 Imperial power rested upon the consent of the governed in Canada and in the other colonies dominated by settler communities.

Close economic ties helped to strengthen the ties between the mother country and the Dominions, but they were never the crucial factor in maintaining loyalty to the Empire. Indeed, as Doug McCalla argues in Chapter 13 of this volume, the role of Imperial policies in the economic development of Canada has probably been overemphasized both by Imperial and by Canadian historians. What the Empire did provide was a secure political, military, and diplomatic framework within which Canada could develop and evolve into an increasingly self-conscious and mature nation. Canadians did seek a national identity, but the English-Canadian majority sought it within the framework of the British Empire. Canadians frequently disliked specific Imperial policies and even more frequently complained that their concerns were not adequately understood in London, but they participated in the Empire voluntarily and for the most part enthusiastically. There was no straightforward transition from colony to nation because generations of English Canadians defined themselves as British as well as Canadian, at least until it became apparent in the 1950s and 1960s that the Empire's days were numbered. Even then it was with a great deal of reluctance that the English-Canadian majority abandoned their Imperial loyalties and sought to redefine their national identity in purely Canadian terms. It is this complex story that this volume addresses.

PHILLIP BUCKNER

Contents

List of Contributors

Phillip Buckner (Ph.D., University of London) is a Professor Emeritus in the Department of History of the University of New Brunswick and a senior research fellow at the Institute of Commonwealth Studies at the University of London. He is the author of *The Transition to Responsible Government: British Policy in British North America, 1815–50* and editor of *Canada and the End of Empire* and *Canada and the British World*.

J. M. Bumsted (Ph.D., Brown) is a member of the History Department and a fellow of St John's College at the University of Manitoba. His recent publications include *Fur Trade Wars: The Founding of Western Canada* and *Trials and Tribulations: The Red River Settlement and the Emergence of Manitoba 1811–70*.

Sarah Carter (Ph.D., Manitoba) holds the H. M. Tory Chair in the Department of History and Classics and the School of Native Studies at the University of Alberta. Her publications include *Aboriginal People and Colonizers of Western Canada to 1900*, *Capturing Women: The Manipulation of Cultural Imagery in Canada's Prairie West*, and *Lost Harvests: Prairie Indian Reserve Farmers and Government Policy*.

Colin M. Coates (Ph.D., York University, Toronto) holds the Canada Research Chair in Canadian Cultural Landscapes at Glendon College, York University. He is the author of *The Metamorphoses of Landscape and Community in Early Quebec* and co-author with Cecilia Morgan of *Heroines and History: Representations of Madeleine de Verchères and Laura Secord*.

Elizabeth Jane Errington (Ph.D., Queen's University, Kingston) is a Professor of History at the Royal Military College of Canada and Queen's University. She is the author of *The Lion, the Eagle and Upper Canada* and *Wives and Mothers, School Mistresses and Scullery Maids*.

Philip Girard (Ph.D., Dalhousie) is Professor of Law, History, and Canadian Studies at Dalhousie University. He is the author of *Bora Laskin: Bringing Law to Life* and co-editor (with Jim Phillips and Barry Cahill) of *The Supreme Court of Nova Scotia, 1754–2004: From Imperial Bastion to Provincial Oracle*.

Marjory Harper (Ph.D., Aberdeen) is a Reader in History at the University of Aberdeen. Her recent publications include *Adventurers and Exiles: The Great Scottish Exodus* and *Emigrant Homecomings: The Return Movement of Emigrants, 1600–2000*. She has been commissioned (along with Stephen Constantine) to write an OHBE volume on *Migrants and Settlers in the Empire and Commonwealth*.

James K. Hiller (Ph.D., Cambridge) is University Research Professor in the History Department at Memorial University, St John's, Newfoundland. He has written extensively on the history of Newfoundland and Labrador, and has co-authored a history of Atlantic Canada.

Douglas McCalla (D.Phil., Oxford) has been Canada Research Chair in Rural History at the University of Guelph since 2002. His publications include *Planting the Province: The Economic History of Upper Canada, 1784–1870*.

Elizabeth Mancke (Ph.D., Johns Hopkins) is a member of the Department of History at the University of Akron. She is the author of *The Fault Lines of Empire: Political Differentiation in Massachusetts and Nova Scotia, ca 1760–1830* and co-editor (with Carole Shammas) of *The Creation of the British Atlantic World*.

Adele Perry (Ph.D., York University, Toronto) holds the Canada Research Chair in Western Canadian Social History at the University of Manitoba. Her publications include *On the Edge of Empire: Gender, Race, and the Making of British Columbia*.

John G. Reid (Ph.D., University of New Brunswick) is a member of the Department of History at St Mary's University, Halifax, Nova Scotia. His publications include *Acadia, Maine, and New Scotland: Marginal Colonies in the Seventeenth Century*, *The New England Knight: Sir William Phips, 1651–1695*, and (with five co-authors) *The 'Conquest' of Acadia, 1710: Imperial, Colonial, and Aboriginal Constructions*.

John Herd Thompson (Ph.D. Queen's University, Kingston) teaches in the History Department and the Canadian Studies Program at Duke University. He contributed two volumes to the *Illustrated History of Canada* series published by OUP Canada, *Forging the Prairie West* and (with Patricia E. Roy) *British Columbia: Land of Promises*, and co-authored (with Stephen Randall) *Canada and the United States: Ambivalent Allies*.

Maps

1

Introduction: Canada and the British Empire

Phillip Buckner

In a groundbreaking article published in 1954 J. M. S. Careless divided English-Canadian historians into three distinct schools of interpretation. The first group, whom he termed 'the Britannic, or Blood is Thicker than Water School', were those nineteenth- and early twentieth-century historians who focused 'on the emergence of a new Britannic community within the empire, a part of one imperial organism, whose people enjoyed the British institutions of their forefathers and were worthy members of that indefinable company, the "British race" '. In 'the young twentieth century', a second school developed, who 'viewed the imperial tie more critically' and whom Careless dubbed the 'School of Political Nationhood'. Careless saw two phases in the evolution of this school. The first was 'favourably disposed to things British', but 'gradually a watershed was being crossed' and the second phase focused primarily on the quest for autonomy by authors 'less friendly to British influences', whose motto 'might well have been "A Canadian Citizen I will die" '. This group was succeeded in turn by 'the Environmental School, or North Americans All', who stressed that 'Canadian institutions were not simply British but in their own way as American as those of the United States'. Careless was critical of the 'North Americans All', because of their 'tendency to overvalue the influence of native North American forces and the material environment, and a tendency to undervalue forces transferred from Europe and the non-material environment: that of ideas, traditions, and institutions'. Careless's own preference was for a 'qualified version of environmentalism—metropolitanism', which placed urban communities rather than the frontier at 'the centre of the stage' and which recognized the continuing importance of Canada's long and close relationship with Britain.[1]

Careless's article provided the basic framework of English-Canadian historiography, used today even by those who no longer accept the central importance of

---

[1] J. M. S. Careless, 'Frontierism, Metropolitanism, and Canadian History', *Canadian Historical Review*, 35 (1954), pp. 1–21.

the Imperial connection in the history of Canada.[2] It also marked a watershed in the writing of Canadian history far greater than the one that Careless described between the early and later proponents of 'Political Nationhood'. Like most English-Canadian nationalists of his generation, Careless saw Canada as more British than American in its 'ideas, traditions, and institutions', but in the aftermath of the Second World War all racist ideologies had been thoroughly discredited and Careless undoubtedly found language referring to race distasteful. Thus he emphasized the importance of metropolitan links—particularly the commercial, intellectual, and institutional links—with Britain and ridiculed the idea of belonging to 'that indefinable company, the "British race"'. Of course, all racial definitions are by their very nature confused and arbitrary since they lack any scientific basis. Most nineteenth- and early twentieth-century Canadians tended to conflate race and ethnicity (itself a slippery term) and to use race, nation, and people as if they were synonymous. And those who used the term 'British race' fluctuated between a circumscribed ethnic definition that focused on ancestry in the United Kingdom and a broader but still subjective cultural definition that could be extended to include at least some of those who adopted 'British' values and 'British' culture.

This confusion was compounded by the fact that most English Canadians who described themselves as British also defined themselves as Canadian. In its original usage *Canadien* was adopted by the permanent residents of New France to distinguish themselves as a cultural group within the French Empire and, after 1763, as a cultural group within the British Empire. In the nineteenth century English-speaking Canadians also began to refer to themselves as Canadians, particularly after the creation of the Dominion of Canada in 1867. But the meaning of the term was ambiguous. In the late nineteenth century its usage increasingly signalled the evolution of a territorially based civic nationalism, but Canadian could also be used as the marker of a more limited ethnic identity. While French Canadians referred to themselves as French Canadians and to the English-speaking majority as English Canadians, the latter normally referred to themselves simply as Canadians. Only 'other' Canadians were described as hyphenated Canadians. The implication was that the true Canadian was British ethnically, and depending on the context English Canadians tended to define themselves as either British or Canadian without much distinction. Indeed, until the passing of the Canadian Citizenship Act of 1946 there was legally no such thing as a Canadian, only a British subject resident in Canada. Even after the passing of the 1946 Act, English Canadians remained British subjects and they retained the sense of belonging to an extended British family (a term increasingly preferred to the word 'race'). The distinction between a civic nationalism (which

---

[2] See, for example, Carl Berger, *The Writing of Canadian History: Aspects of English-Canadian Historical Writing since 1900* (Toronto, 1986) and Doug Owram, 'Canada and the Empire', *Oxford History of the British Empire*, vol. V (Oxford, 1999), pp. 146–62.

is territorially based) and an ethnic nationalism (which is based on ancestry) remained blurred. Only gradually in the period after the 1950s did most English Canadians abandon the earlier ethnic definition of Canada as a 'British' nation, though even today it lingers on in a somewhat muted and disguised form in parts of Canada where a significant proportion of the population can trace their ethnic origins to the United Kingdom.

Maurice Careless was only 27 in 1946 and it is reasonably safe to assume that he welcomed the passage of the Canadian Citizenship Act and that he never referred to himself as a member of the 'British race' or even as British. Like most liberal nationalists, he approved of the creation of a more clearly (if still ambiguously) defined civic nationalism. Moreover, Careless was also eager to heal the divisions that had developed between English Canadians and French Canadians during the Second World War by emphasizing their common citizenship and their shared historical experience and de-emphasizing the distinct ethnic origins and distinctive histories of Canada's two largest ethnic groups. In this too he was typical of post-war liberal nationalists. This theme can be seen clearly in Careless's *Canada: A Story of Challenge*, first published in 1953 but which went through many editions and was widely used in schools and universities across the country. The book opens with a lengthy description of the land which Canadians inhabit and which is seen as their shared patrimony. Careless stresses the importance of migration from the British Isles, the struggle for responsible government, and Canada's continuing ties with Britain and the Empire-Commonwealth, but ethnic identities are downplayed and the emphasis is on the ability of Canadians to work together to create a new nation and a new national identity that would gradually erode the ethnic loyalties of earlier generations of Canadians. Increasingly these would be the themes stressed by English-Canadian historians in the 1950s, 1960s, and 1970s as they sought to come to terms with the end of Empire and to redefine the nature of the Canadian identity. In the early twenty-first century, when it remains uncertain—after two referenda—whether Quebec will remain within Canada, it is surely time to re-examine these assumptions. We may find offensive and undesirable the racist and ethnic assumptions held by earlier generations of Canadians but we should not dismiss those assumptions (however irrational and confused) as unimportant or irrelevant. If we are to understand how Canadians defined themselves in the past, we have to abandon the nationalist teleology that underpinned the studies of Careless and his successors who saw the evolution of a Canadian civic nationalism as an inevitable and natural progression as Canada shook off its colonial status. English Canadians and French Canadians do have a shared history but they have traditionally formed two distinct societies with very different historical roots. Put crudely, these societies were the creation of two very different imperial projects and two very different patterns of European migration.

French Canada's foundations lay in the first period of European colonization from the sixteenth to the eighteenth century. The total number of Europeans who migrated to the Americas in this period was somewhere around 1.5 million. The vast majority were young, single, and male and most were probably involuntary migrants who crossed the Atlantic as convicts, as soldiers, or as indentured servants. Over time a native-born European population slowly took root, but there was considerable miscegenation between European males and non-European women and in most parts of the Americas the Indigenous peoples and imported African slaves outnumbered the Europeans and their descendants. New France was something of an anomaly. There were relatively few Indigenous people along the banks of the St Lawrence River and an economy based upon subsistence agriculture, the fur trade, and the fisheries could support only a small number of slaves. New France also attracted relatively few European migrants and they were drawn (particularly the small number of female migrants) from an extremely limited range of places in France, mainly during the middle decades of the seventeenth century. Particularly after New France became part of the British Empire in 1763, the French-Canadian population grew largely (though never entirely) through natural increase, creating one of the most homogeneous population groups in the Americas. The core of the French-Canadian community was concentrated in the area that is today the province of Quebec, where the descendants of the original French settlers still form over three-quarters of the population. Not surprisingly, they have a strong sense of being part of a distinctive national community.

English Canada on the other hand was primarily a product of the second period of European migration between 1815 and 1914 when an estimated 44 million people emigrated from Europe, 10 million from the British Isles alone. The colonies that remained under British control on the northern half of the North American continent after 1783 attracted only small numbers of migrants before 1815, mainly from the United States, and the total population of European origin in British North America in 1815 was only around 500,000, a majority of them French speaking. Migration from the British Isles began on a substantial scale after 1815. About 60 per cent of the British migrants between 1815 and 1914 went to the United States, but Canada, Australia, and New Zealand received most of the rest. Moreover, unlike the United States, during the nineteenth century the British settler colonies received comparatively few migrants from other European sources. In British North America the British born and their immediate descendants formed the majority of the population within a few decades after 1815 and by 1901 60 per cent of the population of Canada was defined by the census as of British origin and 30 per cent of French origin. After 1900 Canada did attract immigrants from a much wider range of sources. Canadian history textbooks usually emphasize that between 1901 and 1914 over a million non-British immigrants came to Canada from Europe and Asia. What they do not tend to emphasize is that the number of immigrants from the British Isles was even larger. In every census until 1941 people of British origin formed a majority of the Canadian population and a majority in all of the provinces except Quebec, which was home to most of the 30 per cent of the population of French origin. Even as late as 1971, after a quarter-century of heavy non-British migration, people of British origin still formed 45 per cent of the Canadian population and a clear majority of the population outside Quebec, though increasingly not in Canada's rapidly growing urban centres. Of course, Canada has always been a poly-ethnic society in the sense that there have always been ethnic minorities (some fairly substantial ones after 1900) but numbers—as French Canadians have always been aware—do matter.

Not everyone shared the imperial vision of the British immigrants and their descendants—not even all of the British immigrants and their descendants. But most of the American immigrants were descended from earlier British immigrants to the Thirteen Colonies and they could define (or redefine in some cases) themselves as British. Some of the non-British immigrants quickly integrated into the British majority (which was not all that difficult if you were white and Protestant). Others sought to preserve their cultural distinctiveness and resisted in varying degrees the cultural hegemony of the British-Canadian majority.[3] But so long as those who self-consciously defined themselves as 'British' formed a majority of the population and held a disproportionate share of economic and political power, it makes much more sense to see Canada as essentially a 'British' nation that included a number of ethnic minorities rather than as a modern, multicultural society that recognizes, accepts, and even promotes cultural diversity. And that is precisely how the English-Canadian majority continued to view Canada even in the 1950s—as a British nation with one large ethnic minority that was guaranteed specific rights in the federal Parliament and courts and in the province of Quebec, where that ethnic minority formed the majority. Both biculturalism and multiculturalism only began to take hold on the English-Canadian imagination in the 1960s and 1970s, as English Canadians gradually came to terms with the unravelling of the British connection, the 'Quiet Revolution' in Quebec, and the impact of the huge wave of post-war migration from continental Europe, Asia, and the Caribbean.

Defining Canada as a British nation did not prevent English Canadians from developing an overlapping sense of North American or Canadian identity. Even prior to Confederation the British population in the British North American colonies increasingly referred to themselves collectively as British Americans. They saw themselves as provincial Britons, claiming on the basis of ethnic descent the right to self-governing institutions similar to those possessed by the metropolitan British, a cry which came to be summed up in the phrase 'responsible government' (a term taken from the Durham Report of 1839). By the 1860s the British North American colonies were already largely self-governing in their domestic affairs, and in 1867 British Americans created the Dominion

[3] See, for example, Patricia K. Wood, *Nationalism from the Margins: Italians in Alberta and British Columbia* (Montreal and Kingston, 2002).

of Canada, a larger British colony with imperial ambitions of its own—in particular, to spread across the continent before the Americans beat them to it. As George Brown accurately pointed out, the British Commonwealth of Nations was not merely 'an association of states', it was also 'an association of empires', which in Canada's case included even in 1953 (when Brown made the comment) a vast northern territory, inhabited largely by Indigenous peoples but run by a bureaucracy appointed and controlled from Ottawa.[4]

After 1867 English Canadians rapidly developed a sense of loyalty to the country they had created and a sense of being a member of a distinct British-Canadian community. For most of the British immigrants the idea that one could be both British and something else was easy to accept since they were already British and something else. They were English, Irish, Scottish, or Welsh. As John MacKenzie has pointed out, the 'sub-nationalisms of the United Kingdom' survived and flourished within the British Empire. MacKenzie argues that the Empire 'was more notable in preserving a plurality of British identities than in welding together a common imperial tradition'.[5] Yet in the neo-Britains created overseas in the nineteenth century in Canada, Australia, and New Zealand, immigrants from different parts of the British Isles mingled and intermarried, and among their descendants the sense of a common British identity grew stronger than in the British Isles. Britishness did not preclude multiple overlapping identities and one could remain English, Irish, Scottish, and Welsh while becoming British and Canadian, but over time it was the latter loyalties that were increasingly central in the way most English Canadians thought of themselves.

Seen as a commitment to certain institutions (most notably the monarchy and the parliamentary system) and a sense of values (including the rule of law, the freedom of the individual, the sanctity of private property, and some vague and rather ill-defined notions about duty and fair play), Britishness was a flexible identity compatible with a range of other non-British identities. Not all Britons either at home or in the settlement colonies accepted this flexible and relatively benign definition. 'British' could be defined more narrowly to exclude those whose ethnic origins were not in the British Isles and even some whose origins were (such as Irish Catholics). But the meaning of Britishness was open to negotiation and renegotiation. By the early twentieth century only the more extreme members of ultra-Protestant organizations in Canada, such as the Orange Order, would have denied the right of Irish Catholics to be defined as British. People of northern European origin with an 'Anglo-Saxon' and Protestant heritage were fairly easily assimilated into the 'British' population as honorary Britons until the First World War temporarily turned the Germans into

---

[4] George W. Brown, *Canada in the Making* (Toronto, 1953), p. 136.
[5] John M. MacKenzie, 'Empire and National Identities: The Case of Scotland', *Transactions of the Royal Historical Society*, 6th ser., 8 (1998), p. 230.

enemy aliens. The colour of one's skin was a more difficult barrier to overcome. Blacks in Canada defined themselves as British and praised Britain as the home of the anti-slavery movement but they were still treated as second-class Britons. Native peoples were offered the full rights of British subjects but only if they cut themselves off from their native culture and became 'civilized'. The Canadian government went to great lengths to ensure that the number of immigrants from the Indian subcontinent to Canada was severely restricted, despite the fact that they were already British subjects. But even though the definition of Britishness was contested and unstable, the idea that Canada was essentially a British nation was not open for debate among the English-Canadian majority until well after the Second World War.

French Canadians had to negotiate a place for themselves within this British nation and they frequently complained that English Canadians had two conflicting loyalties—to Canada and to Britain—whereas French Canadians had only one—to Canada. This glosses over the fact that most French Canadians saw themselves as part of a distinctive and self-conscious national community within the Canadian Confederation. They viewed (and to a considerable extent still do view) Canada as composed of two ethnic cores, a French-Canadian core based in Quebec and an English-Canadian core in the rest of the country. Historically French Canadians were not the champions of multiculturalism. They did not welcome the large-scale emigration of Europeans from south and central Europe or of Asians into Canada. Indeed, until quite recently they were probably less tolerant of ethnic and cultural diversity than English Canadians. Their vision of Canada rested upon a belief in what has been described as 'arm's length racial cohabitation'.[6] On this basis, French Canadians saw no difficulty in having an overlapping loyalty to Canada and to the concept of a French-Canadian nation. Only in the 1960s did French Canadians begin to redefine themselves in a way—as Québécois—that made this overlapping loyalty more problematic.

It has become axiomatic among many Canadian historians that the nationalism of earlier generations of English Canadians was somehow incomplete or immature and therefore inauthentic. Historians seek to find the moment when English Canadians abandoned their loyalty to Britain and British institutions and finally became true Canadians. Although no one today would make the same argument about Italian Canadians or Ukrainian Canadians or Chinese Canadians, the dual national loyalties of generations of Canadians of British origin seem suspect, even to their descendants. Of course, British Canadians did not suffer the cultural schizophrenia frequently experienced by other immigrants.[7] Until 1946 they had only one nationality; they were British subjects whether they lived in Britain or

---

[6] Alan Gordon, *Making Public Pasts: The Contested Terrain of Montreal's Public Memories, 1891–1930* (Montreal and Kingston, 2001), p. 79.

[7] See Deryck M. Schreuder, 'Introduction: Exhuming an Empire', in Deryck M. Schreuder and Stuart Ward (eds), *Australia's Empire* (Oxford, 2008).

in Canada, and those British subjects who lived in Canada (and in the other Dominions) had a shared sense of history, culture, and ethnicity with those who lived in the 'mother country'. But the fact that the connection of English Canadians with their ancestral homeland persisted over several generations does not mean that they viewed Canada as merely an overseas projection of Britain. The majority of English-speaking Canadians saw themselves in the nineteenth century as British Americans and in the first half of the twentieth century as British Canadians. They had been born and wished to die as British subjects but they realized that they were British with a difference. In some respects they thought of themselves as Better Britons, living in a land that offered greater economic potential, that avoided the rigid class distinctions of the mother country, and that produced healthier and stronger men and women. In 1910 the British-born Canadian journalist Arthur Hawkes declared: 'But if this country has got any great contribution to make in the future of the Empire (and I am an Imperialist through and through) it is going to be made because we can show the Old Country that we can raise better men here than she can send us, and it is being done every day.'[8]

This sense of superiority coexisted alongside an almost uncritical admiration for British culture and institutions, but English Canadians did not see themselves as second-hand Englishmen, even if that is how French Canadians (and Americans) perceived them. The desire for a rigidly hierarchical Empire that mimicked the class system of the 'mother country', as described by David Cannadine in his recent book on Ornamentalism, was not a vision of Empire that most English Canadians shared.[9] Indeed, those who showed excessive reverence for everything British often faced ridicule. In the 1820s the English-born Henry John Boulton found himself taunted by the other members of the Upper Canadian elite and even by his own Canadian-born wife 'with being a prejudiced Englishman'.[10] During the first half of the nineteenth century relatively few British migrants and their descendants made their way across the Atlantic to the place that they still referred to as 'home' or the 'old Country' and most of them were drawn from the colonial elites. Their reactions varied widely. For some—like Boulton—the sense of exile, of living in a provincial backwater, was painful. For many others, while a visit to the 'mother country' reinforced their sense of admiration for Imperial culture, it also strengthened their sense of the advantages of living in Canada.

There were no barriers—other than financial ones—to prevent British immigrants to Canada from returning 'home' or to prevent their Canadian-born

---

[8] Quoted in J. C. Hopkins (ed.), *The Empire Club of Canada: Speeches, 1910–11* (Toronto, 1912), pp. 110–16.

[9] See David Cannadine, *Ornamentalism: How the British Saw their Empire* (London, 2001), esp. chap. 3.

[10] Quoted in Phillip A. Buckner, *The Transition to Responsible Government: British Policy in British North America, 1815–50* (Westport, Conn., 1985), p. 99.

descendants from immigrating to the United Kingdom. During the late nineteenth and early twentieth centuries a growing number did so, as the Canadian upper class became more wealthy, as the cost of transatlantic fares fell, and as steamships made the journey less dangerous and infinitely more comfortable. It is often assumed that migrants from the settler colonies occupied an in-between status within the United Kingdom, not quite foreign but not fully British either. But this is to confuse issues of social class and of ethnicity. There is no convincing evidence that migrants from Canada found it difficult to be accepted within the provincial subcultures from which they or their forebears had migrated, and in upper-class London society they were treated little differently from any other provincial Britons. Most Canadian migrants seem to have integrated (or re-integrated) into British society fairly easily but they did not necessarily occupy the same social rank as they had in Canada where wealth was more equally distributed and where even the very rich were much less wealthy than their British counterparts. Those Canadians who did come to Britain with a substantial fortune rose to positions of prominence. Some—such as the Scottish-born railway baron Lord Strathcona and the Canadian-born newspaper baron Lord Beaverbrook—ended up in the House of Lords. A small number also entered the House of Commons, such as the radical John Arthur Roebuck in the 1830s and the well-known Canadian author Thomas Chandler Haliburton in 1859. Between 1900 and 1950 there were twenty-nine MPs in the British House of Commons who had been born in Canada and at least another seven who had spent lengthy periods of time there; twenty-one of them were elected as Conservatives, ten as Liberals (before the Liberal Party went into rapid decline), three as Socialists, and two as Irish Nationalists.[11] In 1920 the British Cabinet included three ministers who had been born in Canada. Tens of thousands of Britons who had been born or who had spent part of their lives in Canada occupied less exalted positions. Tens of thousands more returned for more limited periods, for professional or commercial reasons, to visit branches of the family that had not emigrated or the places from which their forebears had migrated. Both world wars brought even larger numbers of Canadians into contact with British society. These visits 'home' reinforced the sense that English Canadians had of themselves as members of an extended Imperial family whose lives had grown apart but who still shared a common ancestry and a commitment to a common sense of values. In this sense for generations of English Canadians blood was indeed thicker than water and they did feel themselves to belong to that indefinable company—the 'British race'.

Until the 1950s the vast majority of English-speaking historians in Canada were British-born or Canadian-born but of British ethnic ancestry and few of them doubted that Canada should remain 'a Britannic community within the

---

[11] See J. M. McEwan, 'Canadians at Westminster, 1900–1950', *Dalhousie Review*, 43 (1963), pp. 522–38.

Empire'. The question was on what terms? Prior to the First World War there was a division between those who advocated some form of Imperial federation and those who wanted equality of status in a decentralized Imperial structure. Those who believed in Imperial federation—and there were never all that many of them—wanted Canada to play a larger role in running the Empire and were prepared to accept some limitations on Canadian autonomy, but even the most extreme proponent of Imperial federation did not argue that Canada should surrender entire control over its domestic affairs to a federal Parliament based in the United Kingdom. On the other hand, most English-Canadian liberal nationalists, while they wanted autonomy for Canada, also wanted Canada to remain within the British Empire. After the First World War the decentralists carried the day, but the majority even of the 'extreme autonomists' were, as Sir John Willison—a prominent Imperial federationist—admitted in 1923, 'as devoted to the British Empire as those of us who take my view of the situation'.[12] A desire for autonomy did not imply in most cases a desire to break the imperial tie. Indeed, the autonomists argued that decentralization would have the reverse effect, that it would strengthen the emotional bonds between Britain and the neo-Britains overseas and strengthen—not weaken—English-Canadians' loyalty to the Empire.

Even during the inter-war years there were comparatively few English-Canadian historians who were not committed to Canada's continued membership in the Empire, so long as it was an Empire of self-governing Dominions. In his 1954 article Careless pointed out that there was no sharp break between the 'Britannic' and the 'Political Nationhood' schools of historians. In fact, the 'watershed' that he saw being crossed in the inter-war years was somewhat illusory. Few of those historians whom he placed in the 'A Canadian Citizen I will Die' camp wanted to abandon their status as British subjects or Canada to abandon its place as a partner nation in the British Commonwealth of Nations. The most obvious exception was O. D. Skelton, who became Undersecretary of State of the Canadian Department of External Affairs in 1925. Disillusioned by the South African War and the First World War, Skelton never doubted that Canada should remain a British nation, but he did believe that it was time for a parting of the ways with the British Empire and that Canada should remain neutral in 1939. Skelton's anti-imperial views were, however, not shared by most English-Canadian historians, not even by that quintessential liberal nationalist J. W. Dafoe. In three lectures delivered at Columbia in 1935, Dafoe accepted that Canada was an 'American Nation', but he stressed that the roots of liberty and a tradition of self-government in both Canada and the United States lay in the British Isles. Dafoe believed that the Dominions must have absolute equality of status with the United Kingdom, but he also believed that Canadian

---

[12] Quoted in A. H. U. Colquhoun, *Press, Politics and People: The Life and Letters of Sir John Willison* (Toronto, 1935), p. 215.

autonomy did not preclude 'a permanent alliance of British nations dedicated to the cause of civilization and progress'.[13] *Canada Fights: An American Democracy at War*, which Dafoe edited in 1941, declared that Canada is 'a British nation' and warned against reading into Canadian nationhood 'the false deduction that it meant desertion of the Empire'.[14] Careless found it difficult to find many scholars to place in his 'Canadian Citizen' camp: A. G. Dewey, R. MacGregor Dawson, G. P. Glazebrook, and R. H. Soward might be considered 'affiliates' but none of them, Careless admitted, were 'eager nationalists'. In fact, all of them were closer to Dafoe than they were to Skelton in their attitude toward the Empire. Even many of those whom Careless defined as 'North Americans All' are rather uneasily described as anti-British. Some of them—such as A. R. M. Lower—did not want Canada to follow British leadership into another world war, but continued to believe in the formative influence of British institutions and British liberal-democratic values in the creation of the Canadian nation. Like Dafoe, many of them believed that both Canada and the United States shared a common British heritage and looked forward to a Churchillan alliance of the English-speaking nations rather than a dramatic break with the Empire and Canada's absorption into the United States.

Indeed, continentalism had limited purchase among Canadian historians during the inter-war years, even though it was strongly promoted (at least by some of the authors) in the twenty-five-volume series on American–Canadian relations sponsored by the Carnegie Endowment for International Peace and published by Yale University Press between 1936 and 1945. The Carnegie series was primarily the work of a number of Canadian-born academics, who had been trained in or who ended up teaching in the United States. Those Canadians who had made their careers in the United States were particularly receptive to an approach that emphasized the shared history of Canada and the United States and portrayed the international border as an artificial barrier between Canadians and Americans. Not all of the volumes in the series reflected these views. A number of the detailed studies of American–Canadian relations focused on the long history of conflict that had led to the establishment of the border; several of the volumes sought to place American–Canadian relations into a larger transatlantic framework (including J. B. Brebner's concluding volume in 1945 on *The North Atlantic Triangle*); and several of the volumes (notably those by Harold Innis and Donald Creighton) rejected the essential premises of the continentalist approach. In 1972 Carl Berger concluded that history 'has not

[13] Dafoe to G. M. Wrong, 16 Oct. 1916, quoted in Paul Phillips, *Britain's Past in Canada* (Vancouver, 1989), p. 58.
[14] John W. Dafoe (ed.), *Canada Fights: An American Democracy at War* (New York, 1941), pp. 30, 182. The book, written for an American audience, was the work of Percy Corbett of McGill and five prominent Canadian journalists, Grant Dexter, Bruce Hutchison, George W. Ferguson, B. T. Richardson, and Dafoe, who edited the contributions into an integrated narrative for which the authors took collective responsibility.

been kind' to the vision that lay behind the series, for the 'majority of Canadian historians have never forgotten that Canada's past had to be seen in an imperial perspective' and that 'it had to answer the question of how Canada survived as an independent state in North America'.[15]

Ironically, by the time that Berger penned his comments about the Carnegie series fewer and fewer historians were concerned with placing Canadian history into an Imperial perspective. Partly this was because in the 1950s and 1960s there was a revolution in the way in which Imperial history was studied and taught. Until the 1950s most Imperial historians continued to insist that the British Empire was fundamentally different from the other European empires. The 'British peoples', Nicholas Mansergh declared, 'did not believe in colonial rule itself. They believed in the government of men by themselves; and because of that faith in self-government as a stage necessary for the bringing of backward peoples to political maturity but of its very nature transient.'[16] Mansergh was one of the last Imperial historians to talk of the British 'peoples' and to believe that the term 'British' could not be restricted to the inhabitants of the British Isles. He was also one of the last to emphasize the importance of constitutional history. Yet, until the 1950s, virtually every major Imperial historian shared his perspective, whether they lived in Britain or in one of the self-governing Dominions. These historians did not see themselves as apologists for Empire (though most, in fact, were) and they could be critical of specific Imperial policies but the doctrine of Imperial trusteeship, however inadequately acted upon, seemed a sufficient justification for the possession of a vast dependent empire that had not yet (at least in their eyes) reached a level of maturity that merited independence. In the aftermath of the Second World War, however, the Empire did not look as durable as it had in the past and it was increasingly evident that Imperial trusteeship had done little to prevent the exploitation and to improve the quality of life of Britain's African, Asian, and Caribbean subjects. A growing number of younger scholars began to reassess British Imperial history far more critically. In Canada, for example, in 1959 A. P. Thornton produced his witty and cynical study of *The Imperial Idea and its Enemies: A Study in British Power*. But the most important of the post-war publications was undoubtedly an article published in 1953 by Ronald Robinson and John Gallagher on the 'Imperialism of Free Trade'.[17] Like Thornton, Robinson and Gallagher were deeply sceptical of the whole notion of Imperial trusteeship. Primarily interested in explaining the rise and decline of Britain as a world power (an understandable preoccupation at a

---

[15] Carl C. Berger, 'Internationalism, Continentalism, and the Writing of History: Comments on the Carnegie Series on the Relations of Canada and the United States', in Richard A. Preston (ed.), *The Influence of the United States in Canadian Development* (Durham, NC, 1972), pp. 50–51.

[16] Nicholas Mansergh, *Survey of the British Commonwealth* (London, 1952), III, p. 6.

[17] John Gallagher and Ronald Robinson, 'The Imperialism of Free Trade', *Economic History Review*, 2nd ser., 6 (1953), pp. 1–15.

time when Britain was clearly in decline), they were more interested in a history of British imperialism than in a history of the British Empire.

This is not simply a question of semantics. Until the 1950s most Imperial historians had started from the implicit assumption that the Empire consisted of three distinct components. The first was the United Kingdom and the self-governing Dominions established overseas by British emigrants in Canada, Newfoundland, Australia, and New Zealand. South Africa and Ireland after 1921 were included—somewhat more ambiguously—in this group. The second was India, where the British monarch was also an emperor. The third consisted of a vast series of dependencies, none of them self-governing (though some had more representative forms of government than others), varying enormously in their geopolitical significance, and composed largely of non-British peoples. In the minds of earlier Imperial historians the first component consisted of the 'British' Empire proper now transformed into the British Commonwealth of Nations. The other components were seen as merely Imperial possessions, though the more liberal Imperial historians believed that in time the larger dependencies like India might achieve Dominion status. Robinson and Gallagher rejected this division. They did not believe that a study of British power could be limited to those territories over which Britain exercised some kind of formal control and they had little sympathy with those who believed in an inner imperial core of partner or sister nations whose loyalty was founded upon bonds of kinship. Robinson, in particular, insisted that settler colonies were 'profitable economic satellites' whose 'political collaboration' with the mother country 'stemmed largely from economic dependence'.[18] He was scornful of Sir John Seeley (whom he dismissed as a Latin professor but 'no imperial historian') for 'insisting that the home islanders and the colonists belonged to the same imperial nation (Australian 'Diggers' and Canadian lumberjacks were as much a part of it as the ratepayers of Kent or Cumberland)'.[19] The fact that not all Canadians were lumberjacks and that those who were might well have relatives in Kent or Cumberland passed Robinson by, partly because he was not interested in the phenomenon of migration, he understood little about the mentality of those who lived in the settler colonies, and he blew out of all proportion Canada's dependence on British trade and capital.

The struggle for responsible government, the evolution of the colonies of settlement into self-governing Dominions, and the transition of the Empire into the British Commonwealth of Nations had been central themes in the older historiography, and the role of Canada had been seen as central in these developments. But constitutional history fell into particular disfavour and few

---

[18] Ronald E. Robinson, 'Conclusion', in Clarence B. Davis and Kenneth E. Wilburn, Jr. (eds), *Railway Imperialism* (Westport, Conn., 1991), pp. 175–16, 179.

[19] Robinson, 'Oxford in Imperial Historiography', in E. T. Williams, A. F. Madden, and D. K. Fieldhouse (eds), *Oxford and the Idea of Commonwealth* (London, 1982), p. 32.

Imperial historians continued to write it.[20] Those who did sought to debunk
the significance that had been placed on such landmarks as the Durham Report.
The focus of the new Imperial history was not upon what was distinctive about the
British Empire—the creation of a series of settler communities that had acquired
virtual independence without seeking to break their ties with Britain—but
upon the similarities between Britain and the other European empires. The
new Imperial historians viewed colonies as simply strategic or commercial assets,
whether the population consisted of British colonists or indigenous peoples.
Looking at the past from the perspective of the era of decolonization, they
stressed the fragility of Britain's hold over its vast empire and the marginal
impact of the Empire upon British culture and society. Robinson and Gallagher
and their many disciples did emphasize that Imperial expansion was frequently
triggered by events on the periphery and they were concerned with the ways
in which Indigenous peoples around the globe responded to British Imperial
expansion through a mixture of collaboration and resistance, but the new Imperial
historiography was metropolitan centred and it denied the central importance
of the settler colonies to how the British viewed their Empire. Not surprisingly,
given these emphases, Imperial history came to be seen within Canada as a
subfield in British history or of European expansion into the 'third world', of
limited relevance to Canadian historians. Whereas Canadian and Imperial history
had once been seen as intertwined and interconnected, they were now seen as
two entirely different fields of study.

During the past few decades the focus of Imperial history has gradually shifted
direction again. A growing volume of work—associated particularly with the
Studies in Imperial History series edited by John MacKenzie for Manchester
University Press and with feminist scholars such as Catherine Hall and Antoinette
Burton—has emphasized the extent to which the culture of metropolitan Britain
was shaped by the fact that the British ruled over a vast territorial empire composed
largely of non-British peoples. The focus of these studies—particularly those
by Hall and Burton—is very clearly upon metropolitan culture and upon the
persistence in post-imperial Britain of racial attitudes shaped by the Imperial
legacy. Very limited attention is paid to attitudes within Britain towards the
settler colonies or to the role of Empire in shaping similar attitudes within the
settler colonies themselves. The other emphasis of recent Imperial scholarship has
been an attempt to re-examine events within the colonies from the perspective of
the colonized. In Africa and Asia this has meant attempting to construct histories
that incorporate the rich pre-colonial histories of these societies and to show
the negative impact of imperialism on their economic and social development.
Initially these studies were concerned to legitimize the new states that were
created by nationalist uprisings against British rule, but in the 1980s and 1990s

---

[20] See Robert Holland, 'Britain, Commonwealth and the End of Empire', in Vernon Bogdanor,
(ed.), *The British Constitution in the Twentieth Century* (Oxford, 2003), pp. 631–61.

a rather simplistic and uncritical view of the national liberation movements was replaced by an emphasis on 'histories from below', which focused on the role of subaltern groups and the complex relationship between collaboration and resistance at the grassroots level. The implication of these studies was that the creation of a truly postcolonial society (in this context postcolonial is never hyphenated) has to involve much more than a simple transfer of power from one elite to another.

For a settler colony like Canada postcolonialism is an approach of limited utility, even if defined merely as the process by which a former colony attempts to emancipate itself from its lingering ties with the Empire. By the late nineteenth century the Dominion of Canada was largely self-governing and after 1931 any limitations that Canadians accepted on their autonomy continued only so long as Canadians were prepared to accept them. In the 1960s Canada did begin to shed the symbolic vestiges of the Imperial relationship, but this is more accurately described as a process of de-dominionization rather than decolonization.[21] Even this process remains incomplete. Canada retains a foreign monarch as its head of state, for while it is true that Elizabeth II is legally Queen of Canada in her own right, no Canadian would accept as their constitutional monarch anyone who was not also the King or Queen of England. There will be no Charles III of Canada if there is no Charles III of the United Kingdom and perhaps not even then. Partly because the office of Governor-General has been successfully Canadianized and partly because constitutional reform is very difficult to achieve given the divisions between Quebec and the rest of Canada, the creation of a Canadian Republic does not seem a pressing issue to most Canadians. Queen Elizabeth II is not unpopular in most of English Canada and a constitutional monarchy is still seen by many Canadians as one of the key institutions, like the parliamentary system and responsible government, distinguishing Canada from the United States. Even if the British monarch were replaced by an elected or appointed head of state who was Canadian, the Canadian system of government would remain monarchical in all its essential features. But if Canadians retain some Imperial institutions, it is not because of some lingering colonial cringe, for Canadians no longer see Britain as a role model. Indeed, in every important respect Canada is now a post-imperial society. It is not, however, a postcolonial society for the colonizers have not been replaced by the colonized.

There is a long tradition among French-Canadian historians, which goes back to François-Xavier Garneau (who was writing in reaction to the Durham Report), of presenting the French Canadians as a colonized people, forced to become part and to remain part of the British Empire against their will. In the past few decades this tradition has gained renewed strength. Nationalist historians in Quebec were much influenced by decolonization movements in

---

[21] The term 'De-Dominionisation' was coined by the Australian scholar Jim Davidson. See his 'De-Dominionisation Revisited', *Australian Journal of Politics and History*, 51 (2005), pp. 108–13.

African and Asia and they began to argue that Quebec had been prevented
from becoming a 'normal' postcolonial society by its incorporation within
the British Empire. The post-war Quebec historians adopted as their heroes
those who struggled against Imperial oppression—Louis-Joseph Papineau and
the *Patriotes* of 1837 and Louis Riel (whose 1885 rebellion is viewed far
more favourably now than it was by contemporary French Canadians). From
Garneau on, French-Canadian historians had stressed that the *Canadiens* were
a distinctive people with a distinctive national identity based upon their shared
ethnicity. The new historiography subtly began to emphasize the evolution of a
territorially based civic nationalism in Quebec. From this perspective Quebec's
history has been a continuous struggle against its colonial status that will remain
incomplete until Quebec achieves sovereignty and joins the other nations in
the New World created by European colonization.[22] Of course, this argument
overlooks a number of awkward facts. French Canadians are themselves, after all,
descended from European colonizers and the emphasis on a territorially defined
Quebec nationalism rather than an ethnically defined *Canadien* nationalism
based primarily but not exclusively in Quebec is a relatively recent phenomenon.

Moreover, the degree of oppression suffered under British rule should be put
into perspective. The French-Canadian population in the St Lawrence valley
were not cruelly removed from their ancestral land like the Acadians of Nova
Scotia and, because they came from a European culture, they were not for long
denied the basic rights of British subjects. In 1774 a legal system was created that
was designed not to exclude the French-Canadian population but to integrate
them, and the result was the creation of a hybrid legal system that blended French
and English civil law and that persists to the present in Quebec. In 1791 the
colony of Lower Canada was created and was given representative institutions,
which the French-Canadian majority in the colony quickly came to dominate.
French Canadians did not simply resist British rule; they sought to harness
British institutions for their own ends and with considerable success. In one sense
the rebellions of 1837–8 took place not because French Canadians had been
denied power but because they had been able to use their dominant position in
the Assembly to accumulate power. By the mid-1830s the Assembly controlled
most of the colony's finances and was whittling away at the independence of the
executive and legislative councils. The *Patriote* majority in the Assembly used
their control over colonial finances to confront—foolishly as it turned out—the
Imperial government by refusing to vote any supplies until all their demands
were met and by rejecting any efforts at compromise. The *Patriote* movement
can legitimately be seen as an anti-colonial national liberation movement and it
may be that its leaders were liberal and republican in their sentiments and drew
their inspiration from the United States. But the rebellions of 1837–8 received
very little support from the British or even the Irish minority in the colony and

---

[22] See Gérard Bouchard, *Genèse des nations et cultures du Nouveau Monde* (Montreal, 2000).

whatever the rhetoric of their leaders, those French Canadians who took up arms did so largely out of a sense of ethnic solidarity. One of the underlying factors behind the rebellion was a growing concern over the rapid influx of British immigrants into Lower Canada, which threatened in the long run to undermine the dominance of the French-Canadian majority. If successful, the rebellions would have created a nation-state defined in ethnic terms and one of the first measures that this state would have imposed would have been a series of controls over the flow of British migrants into the province to reinforce and guarantee that Quebec would have a French-Canadian majority.

As a result of the rebellions, there was repression, and self-governing institutions were temporarily suspended in Lower Canada from 1838 until 1841, but the Imperial government never doubted that French Canadians would have to be given the same representative institutions as British subjects in the neighbouring colonies. After 1841 the French-Canadian political elite quickly learned how to manipulate the politics of the United Province of Canada to protect their distinctive culture and they were able to ensure that Confederation in 1867 created a federal system with one province in which the French Canadians formed a substantial majority. French Canadians became partners—unequal partners perhaps—with English Canadians in the creation of a Canadian empire that stretched 'from sea unto sea'. French Canadians continued to chafe at the limitations upon Canadian autonomy that membership in the British Empire involved. They were alienated by the determination of the English-Canadian majority to participate in the South African War and to impose conscription in both world wars. But except during the First World War they were well represented in every federal Cabinet and determined who exercised political power within Quebec. The debate over the impact of the Conquest continues unabated in Quebec but whatever else it did or did not do, the Conquest did not turn the French Canadians into a powerless minority ruled by an alien people.

To see English Canadians as the colonized is even more nonsensical. English-Canadian historians tended to treat imperialism and colonization as if they were two separate phenomena. This is not a distinction likely to be accepted by the Aboriginal peoples who were dispossessed of their land and resources by waves of British immigrants and their descendants in what John Weaver has described as the greatest land grab in history.[23] Indeed, colonization is one of the most ruthless forms of imperialism; its impact may not be fatal for the survival of native cultures, but it is largely irreversible in those settler colonies where the native peoples came to form but a small minority of the population and are unlikely ever to regain the control that they once had over their land and their lives. Canadian historians (both English and French) used to see the spread of European civilization as natural, inevitable, and even progressive. No Canadian

[23] John C. Weaver, *The Great Land Rush and the Making of the Modern World, 1650–1900* (Montreal and Kingston, 2003).

historian would use such terms today. Ironically there is, however, a tendency to stress that the British immigrants who came to Canada were themselves victims, oppressed peoples who were forced to emigrate to escape abject poverty. Of course, there were periods when this was true, but the Great Irish Famine and the Highland Clearances were exceptional events. As Eric Richards points out in his recent study of *Britannia's Children*, British migration was not 'a series of mass exoduses of the desperate'. Most British emigrants had access to some (even if limited) capital and they emigrated because they believed that the new worlds opened up by Imperial expansion had created better opportunities for men of limited means than existed within Britain. British emigrants were not 'blameless in the expansion of the diaspora, simply the passive tools of their capitalist and imperial masters'; they were, in fact, 'an engine of empire and its expansion'.[24] That is how the emigrants to the settler colonies and their immediate descendants perceived themselves. But just as it has now become fashionable to have a convict ancestor in Australia, so in Canada it has become fashionable to see one's forebears as destitute Britons carried across the Atlantic in a tide of inhumanity, thus relieving them of direct responsibility for the dispossession of the native peoples. To read most recent histories of Canada, it would be easy to conclude—quite erroneously—that English Canadians were more reluctant imperialists than those who lived at the heart of the Empire. This is not only bad history, but it enables Canadians to avoid having to face up to the fact that their forebears were active—not passive—imperialists and to take some responsibility for the plight of Canada's Indigenous peoples.

The flight from Empire in English Canada began in the late 1950s and the 1960s when the Imperial relationship moved to the centre of Canadian politics and became a partisan issue, as the Liberal Party under Lester Pearson and Pierre Elliott Trudeau began to remove the lingering symbols of the British connection, partly in the hope that this policy would weaken the rapidly growing separatist movement in Quebec. But de-dominionization was vehemently opposed by the Conservative Party led by John Diefenbaker and by conservative historians such as Donald Creighton and W. L. Morton, who argued that Canada was being turned into a dependency of the United States. Their anti-Americanism struck a chord with many young Canadians in the 1960s but not their conservatism and not their defence of the Imperial connection. Canadian universities expanded dramatically during the 1960s and so did the number of historians teaching Canadian history. Although a majority of the professional English-Canadian historians were still of British ethnic origin, their ethnic ties with Britain were increasingly remote and a growing minority had parents who were not British in origin. The overwhelming majority of men and of the substantial number of women who began teaching Canadian history in the 1960s and 1970s had

---

[24] Eric Richards, *Britannia's Children: Emigration from England, Scotland, Wales, and Ireland since 1600* (London, 2004), pp., 286, 288, 291, 303.

received their graduate training neither in British nor in American universities but in Canadian. They did not identify themselves as British or British Canadian but simply as Canadian. Their interests were very different from those of the elderly, white middle-class males who had previously dominated the profession. They were more interested in social history, in gender history, in working-class history, in ethnic history, and in regional and local history than their predecessors. All of these themes had an imperial dimension but it was not central to the agenda of those who wished to focus on the more 'limited identities' of Canadians. Indeed, the new historians viewed with some scepticism the idea of a national narrative that placed the British Empire and the British in Canada (or in what became the preferred term those of Anglo-Celtic origin) at the centre of events.

Moreover, in the 1960s imperialism of any kind became unacceptable. This was partly due to the impact of the Vietnam War. It was also due to the transformation of the British Commonwealth into a Commonwealth composed of a majority of African and Asian nations, some of which had achieved independence through resistance and armed struggle. Arnold Smith, a Canadian who served as the first Secretary General of the Commonwealth, 'observed in speeches in various parts of the world that so far from being a ghost of Empire, the Commonwealth was largely the creation of the leaders of successful national liberation movements. I added that the first of these was Sir John Macdonald.'[25] This was, to put it mildly, a somewhat flawed interpretation of Canadian history, but a popular one among those who did not want Canada to be identified as an 'imperialist' nation. Imperial history continued to be studied by those who could not avoid it, by those interested in international relations, by military historians (since most of the wars in which Canada had been involved were Imperial wars), and by those interested in native studies. But it had little appeal to most 'limited identity' historians, who wished to write history from the 'bottom up' and to focus on the dispossessed and the underprivileged, on those who had been neglected by earlier historians. These were necessary and legitimate goals in a post-imperial society and resulted in a broader and more comprehensive national history. But something was also lost in the process. Early feminist historians were attempting to show the discrimination from which generations of Canadian women had suffered; they were not particularly interested in examining the role women (and not just conservative women) had played in the promotion of Imperial ideals. Early working-class historians sought to show that the Canadian working class had its own cultural institutions and identity; they were not particularly interested in stressing that this working-class tradition was often racist and usually pro-imperial. Ethnic historians wished to focus on the neglected 'others'; they were less interested in the 'Anglo-Celtic' majority (even the term 'British' was

---

[25] Arnold Cantwell Smith, 'Britain and Canada in the Wider World: The Commonwealth', in David Dilks, (ed.), *Britain and Canada: A Colloquium Held at Leeds October, 1979* (London, 1980), p. 46.

shunned). Many social historians were greatly influenced by some variant of Marxist or socialist ideology. The most popular paradigm they used was a crude social control model that emphasized the degree to which the 'Anglo-Celtic' elite was able to manipulate the masses. Imperialism was simply another instrument for that purpose. Over time the historiography in all these areas became more sophisticated and less ideologically driven. Feminist historians in particular were greatly influenced by an international literature that stressed the complicity of white women in the imperial project. Some historians of the Canadian Irish, of other ethnic minorities, and of the Canadian working class have begun to accept that imperialism had a great deal of popular support among the groups they are studying and not just with the Anglo-Celtic Protestant elite. But such concessions are reluctantly made. Most Canadian historians continue to believe that Canadian participation in the Empire was an elite preoccupation and that the support for the Empire did not have deep roots in Canadian soil.

This volume essentially refutes that proposition. It should not be necessary to stress that the authors of this volume are not part of a new breed of Imperial apologists. There are no disciples of Donald Creighton among us. Indeed, it is time to abandon the notion that to be interested in Imperial history you have to be an anti-modernist, an admirer of the British class system, and a British race patriot. Most English-Canadian imperialists were not anti-modernists and had very mixed feelings about the British class system. Most of them certainly were British race patriots but the privileged place occupied by British immigrants and their descendants in Canada was always indefensible and fortunately has long since been eroded. But no one is served by the collective historical amnesia which denies that Canada was for nearly two centuries a predominantly British nation and claims that Canadians were unenthusiastic imperialists. We may disagree over the extent to which Canada was influenced and shaped by its long membership of the British Empire and its close relationship with Britain. Indeed, the authors who contributed to this volume did and do disagree over these issues. But we all do agree that the Empire mattered.

SELECT BIBLIOGRAPHY

CARL BERGER, *The Writing of Canadian History: Aspects of English-Canadian Historical Writing since 1900* (Toronto, 1986).

CARL BRIDGE and KENT FEDOROWICH, (eds), *The British World: Diaspora, Culture, and Identity* (London, 2003).

PHILLIP BUCKNER, 'Was there a "British" Empire?, *The Oxford History of the British Empire* from a Canadian Perspective', *Acadiensis*, 32/1 (Autumn 2002), pp. 110–28.

———— 'Whatever happened to the British Empire?, *Journal of the Canadian Historical Association*, 4(1993), pp. 3–32.

———— and R. DOUGLAS FRANCIS, *Canada and the British World: Culture, Migration and Identity* (Vancouver, 2006).

J. M. S. CARELESS, 'Frontierism, Metropolitanism, and Canadian History', *Canadian Historical Review*, 35 (1954), pp. 1–21.

ERIC RICHARDS, *Britannia's Children: Emigration from England, Scotland, Wales, and Ireland since 1600* (London, 2004).

ROBIN W. WINKS, *The Oxford History of the British Empire*, vol. V: *Historiography* (Oxford, 1999).

2

From Global Processes to Continental Strategies: The Emergence of British North America to 1783

John G. Reid and Elizabeth Mancke

The British North America that took shape following the Treaty of Paris in 1783 was no mere incidental creation of the rebellion of the Thirteen Colonies. Rather, its origins can be found in the global processes set in train by European expansion in the sixteenth and seventeenth centuries. By 1783 this British North America had colonial populations in some areas, but its foundations had been established by commerce more than by colonization. Across its vast expanses Europeans were a minority and often in competition with one another, and imperial representatives had long negotiated to create and preserve accommodations among diverse commercial and strategic interests, among contending imperial systems, and between British and non-British inhabitants. The results were long-lasting. In the 1780s British commitments expanded rapidly. Colonial settlements multiplied along the Atlantic littoral, on the upper St Lawrence, and along the north shores of the Great Lakes. Continental outreach soon extended to the Pacific, fuelled both by the legacy of the French regime with its Montreal-based networks of trade and by the inland expansion of the Hudson's Bay Company (HBC) after 1763. Yet only gradually, as the nineteenth century proceeded, would these colonial and continental enterprises seriously challenge the maritime, commercial, and cross-cultural considerations that had defined British Imperial strategies in the early modern era.

The European origins of this system emerged first in the Newfoundland fishery and may have been pre-Columbian, an outreach of fishermen to new North Atlantic fishing grounds that complemented the more southerly expansion of Iberians to the Atlantic islands, Africa, and eventually the Americas and Asia. From its earliest days, English involvement in the fishery had been informed by the merchant networks that financed global expansion and by the international competition for overseas empires. West Country merchants operated fleets out of ports such as Barnstaple, Bideford, Dartmouth, and Plymouth, but had investment links to merchant networks in London and Bristol that in turn were investing in commerce to Asia, Africa, and the Caribbean, as well as exploration for a northern passage to Asia. European wars after 1580 allowed English and French interests to gain ascendancy in the fishery, as they attacked Spanish and Portuguese vessels, and as Philip II of Spain requisitioned commercial shipping for his military ventures. In negotiating the end of these wars, the joint Spanish–Portuguese Crown (1580–1640) refused to acknowledge the overseas advances of France and England in the Treaty of Vervins (1598) and the Treaty of London (1604), respectively. James I, however, was so confident that Spain could not defend a claim to the fishery that he granted the area to the Newfoundland Company in 1610 'without doing wrong to any other prince or state' because it was 'so vacant' that 'they cannot justly pretend any sovereignty or right thereto'.[1]

For the next 150 years, commercial interests in the fishery and later the fur trade, not the development of colonial societies, established the foundations of British claims in the northern half of North America. While the English, and later the British, state did not invest directly in either trade, it provided an increasingly elaborate infrastructure of diplomacy, legislative sanction, and naval protection within which both could flourish, and under which incipient colonial societies could be established.

For England, the fishery assumed great importance domestically and internationally because of the capital involved and the employment and training it generated. When London commercial interests attempted to insinuate themselves into the fishery through the organization of the Newfoundland Company, they encountered the political strength of West Country merchants who protested this infringement on their ancient pursuits to both Whitehall and Westminster. Plans to colonize the island, they feared, would create locally based authorities that could restrict access to fishing grounds and shore resources for fishermen who came seasonally. After protracted political discussions in England, Charles I issued the 'Western Charter' in 1634, which guaranteed the right of all English subjects to fish in Newfoundland waters, legitimized the tradition of the first ship's master in a harbour—the 'admiral'—taking responsibility for maintaining order for the season, and allowed for civil and

---

[1] Ralph Pastore, 'The Sixteenth Century: Aboriginal Peoples and European Contact', in Phillip A. Buckner and John G. Reid, (eds), *The Atlantic Region to Confederation: A History* (Toronto, 1994), pp. 22–39; John Mannion and Selma Barkham, 'The 16th Century Fishery', in R. Cole Harris, (ed.), *Historical Atlas of Canada* (Toronto, 1987), I, plate 22; Kenneth R. Andrews, *Trade, Plunder, and Settlement: Maritime Enterprise and the Genesis of the British Empire, 1480–1630* (Cambridge, 1984), esp. pp. 41–63; Samuel Lucas, *Charters of the Old English Colonies in America with an Introduction and Notes* (London, 1850), p. 1; Elizabeth Mancke, 'Negotiating an Empire: Britain and its Overseas Peripheries, c.1550–1780', in Christine Daniels and Michael V. Kennedy, (eds), *Negotiated Empires: Centers and Peripheries in the Americas, 1500–1820* (New York, 2002), p. 237.

criminal disputes arising in Newfoundland to be adjudicated in West Country courts.[2]

Yet contestations over Newfoundland's resources did not abate. While various English-based interests became ever more committed to protecting their concerns against other contenders, including an emerging settler population, both economic and military rationales could be advanced in favour of residency on a modest scale. The first Anglo-Dutch War (1652–4) exposed the vulnerability of fishing vessels and shore installations to enemy attacks, and the English navy began providing convoys to and from Newfoundland. As much as naval strategists could argue that the Newfoundland fishery was a nursery for seamen, and that settlements should be discouraged so as to keep these men residents of England, the need to demonstrate and protect English occupation of the island was also clear. French competition later in the century contributed to the termination of the Western Charter and the 1699 passage of the Newfoundland Act, or King William's Act as it was known in Newfoundland, which permitted land grants to settlers with pre-1685 claims. Settlement in Newfoundland had become increasing viable as colonists in New England and later the mid-Atlantic colonies produced agricultural surpluses that they traded from Newfoundland to Barbados. Newfoundland fish exported to southern Europe in freight vessels known as 'sack ships', moreover, could be traded for necessary English imports of commodities such as wine.[3]

The intensification of metropolitan oversight of the Newfoundland fishery in the second half of the seventeenth century reflected, in part, a more widespread intensification of overseas expansion and international competition. Spain finally acknowledged England's American claims in the 1667 Treaty of Madrid in exchange for reining in pirates. Louis XIV began extending direct royal authority over French overseas claims in the 1660s, and consolidated the North American holdings as New France with a royally appointed Governor-General and an Intendant, both of whom resided in Quebec. In Newfoundland, the French built Plaisance on the south coast as a centre for administration of the fishery and a site of year-round settlement. In Canada, the French began rebuilding the fur trade after the devastation of the native wars of the 1640s and 1650s, which had included the destruction of Huronia.[4]

---

[2] Gillian T. Cell, *English Enterprise in Newfoundland, 1577–1660* (Toronto, 1969), pp. 53–80, 99–100, 112–17; Keith Matthews, *Lectures on the History of Newfoundland, 1500–1830* (St John's, 1988), pp. 54–65.

[3] Peter E. Pope, *Fish into Wine: The Newfoundland Plantation in the Seventeenth Century* (Chapel Hill, NC, 2004); Matthews, *Lectures*, pp. 71–88; C. Grant Head, *Eighteenth Century Newfoundland: A Geographer's Perspective* (Toronto, 1976), pp. 30–62.

[4] Frances G. Davenport, *European Treaties Bearing on the History of the United States and its Dependencies*, 4 vols. (Washington, DC, 1917–37), vol. II, pp. 329–46; W. J. Eccles, *France in America* (rev. edn East Lansing, Mich., 1990), pp. 63–94; Elizabeth Mancke and John G. Reid, 'Elites, States, and the Imperial Contest for Acadia', in John G. Reid et al., *The 'Conquest' of Acadia: 1710:*

In England, the restoration of the monarchy in 1660 was accompanied by renewed overseas ventures: the Royal African Company and the Carolina proprietors received charters in 1663, and in 1664 an English naval fleet took New Netherland from the Dutch and renamed it New York. In 1670 a group of courtiers asked for a charter to prosecute the fur trade as the HBC, with a claim to all the lands in the Hudson Bay watershed, named Rupert's Land after the king's cousin Prince Rupert. Behind that English venture were two disaffected Frenchmen, Pierre-Esprit Radisson and Médard Chouart Des Groseillers, who had made an exploratory journey to Lake Superior in 1659-60 and returned with furs they had acquired without a licence. French officials confiscated the furs, and in anger Radisson and Des Groseillers approached English courtiers, an example of how elite co-option crossed national boundaries.[5]

By the 1690s, London merchants had assumed the management of the HBC fur trade, which proved to be a sump for capital rather than a well for wealth for its first half-century. Prices for furs soared in the 1680s, plummeted in the 1690s, and then stabilized. Warehouses and lodgings for employees had to be built along the bay, two-year supplies of trade goods and provisions had to be maintained in case the annual ship did not arrive, careful records had to be kept to coordinate the purchase of trade goods in Europe and their sale in North America, and the release of furs on European markets had to be carefully regulated to avoid oversupply and price collapses. The Nine Years War (1689–97) and the War of the Spanish Succession (1702–13) further complicated the Company's survival. French naval forces sailing from Quebec under the command of Pierre Le Moyne d'Iberville attacked English settlements in Newfoundland, as well as capturing HBC forts. By 1713, the HBC held only Fort Albany in James Bay, but through its connections to Whitehall, most notably the Duke of Marlborough, British negotiators at the congress in Utrecht undertook the defence of the Company's interest and persuaded the French to acknowledge British claims to the Hudson Bay watershed and to vacate York Fort.[6]

In the 1713 Treaty of Utrecht, Britain significantly consolidated its claims in North America. In addition to acknowledging British claims to Rupert's Land, France conceded British sovereignty over Newfoundland and agreed to evacuate Plaisance, though the French retained shore rights to much of the northern and western parts of the island. During the war, British forces also took Port Royal, the French administrative centre of Acadia. In the peace negotiations, the

---

Imperial, Colonial, and Aboriginal Constructions (Toronto, 2004), pp. 25–47; James Pritchard, *In Search of Empire: The French in the Americas, 1670–1730* (Cambridge, 2004).

  [5] E. E. Rich, *The History of the Hudson's Bay Company, 1670–1870*, 2 vols. (London, 1958–59), vol. I, pp. 21–35.

  [6] Elizabeth Mancke, *A Company of Businessmen: The Hudson's Bay Comp and Long-Distance Trade, 1670–1730* (Winnipeg, 1988); Rich, *History*, vol. I, pp. 238–49, 301–6, 327–54, 368–92, 416–26; Pritchard, *In Search of Empire*, pp. 341–55.

French agreed to give up Acadia, although they kept Île Saint-Jean (renamed Prince Edward Island in 1799) and Cape Breton, where they built Louisbourg as a new administrative centre for the fishery and a North American base for the French navy. The British restored the name Nova Scotia, in lieu of Acadia, in recognition of Sir William Alexander's Scottish attempts at colonization during the 1620s and 1630s, and renamed Port Royal as Annapolis Royal in honour of Queen Anne.[7]

The importance of Nova Scotia, Newfoundland, and Rupert's Land in the negotiations for the Treaty of Utrecht (1713)—and the lack of comparable negotiations over British territories further south in North America—is testimony to how the patterns of development in these territories were shaped by global processes of expansion in ways that other British North American territories were not. The direct competition with the French, the lack of British settler populations with recognized rights of self-government, the absence of significant environmental change, and the influence of metropolitan-based commercial interests set these areas apart.

The years of war from 1689 to 1713 also brought about major changes in the structures of power within Britain that had transatlantic implications. The overthrow of James VII and II, and the crowning of William and Mary, followed by the 1707 Union of the Kingdoms with a single British Parliament in Westminster, contributed to the coalescence of state power within Britain. The Treasury's creation of a fiscal system to manage the public debt, much of it derived from fighting two costly wars, further undergirded British state power. In 1696, William III established the Lords Commissioners of Trade and Plantations (commonly known as the Board of Trade) as a permanent committee of the Privy Council. Its formation helped to regularize some British practices overseas, such as the use of common law, while at the same time it curbed the earlier Stuart practice of delegating overseas governance to prominent men such as William Penn. The importance of the Royal Navy to Britain's military strategies also had transatlantic impacts. Parliament passed legislation that safeguarded naval stores on ungranted land in North America and helped to redefine Crown lands as state lands.[8]

The years of war had diminished Spain's power both within Europe and compared to its overseas competitors, particularly Britain and France. While Britain had bested France in the War of the Spanish Succession and garnered substantial territorial concessions, France remained a formidable imperial competitor. The founding of Louisiana in 1699 and the building of Louisbourg after the Treaty of Utrecht demonstrated France's ability to define North American

---

[7] John G. Reid, '1686–1720: Imperial Intrusions', in Buckner and Reid, *Atlantic Region to Confederation*, pp. 93–103.

[8] Elizabeth Mancke, 'Another British America: A Canadian Model for the Early Modern British Empire', *Journal of Imperial and Commonwealth History*, 25 (1997), pp. 1–36.

territory and establish alliances with Indigenous nations. The war's reconfiguration of power both in Europe and overseas brought nearly three decades of peace between the Treaty of Utrecht and the War of the Austrian Succession (1740–8). During those years, European settlements and commerce in the Americas coalesced and grew, whether fishing outports in Newfoundland, Acadian villages in Nova Scotia, Canadian farms along the St Lawrence, New England towns, Virginia plantations, or port cities from Boston, Massachusetts, to Kingston, Jamaica. At the same time, Aboriginal military power and territorial control remained substantial outside the denser areas of settlement. Other than in Newfoundland, where the strategic retreat of the Beothuk produced a geographical separation between Aboriginal and non-Aboriginal populations, all areas north and west of New England remained subject to Aboriginal power or influence.[9]

It was partly for this reason that the conquest of Acadia proved to be an ambiguous, contested, and repeatedly renegotiated achievement. British control of Acadia/Nova Scotia was largely illusory, and implicitly, if not explicitly, challenged by the Aboriginal peoples, the French, and the Acadians. The problems of colonial governance centred on the weakness of the British presence vis-à-vis non-British peoples, and the continuing necessity for imperial officials to behave for London's benefit as if they were exerting control while in reality maintaining negotiated relationships. The British population at Annapolis Royal (including the garrison) and at Canso (where it fluctuated with the fishing season) numbered only a few hundred, while the Aboriginal nations counted over 4,000, and the Acadians grew in numbers from some 2,500 in 1713 to upwards of 10,000 by mid-century.[10]

Furthermore, the extent of the French concessions at Utrecht was contested. Not only did the treaty leave delineation of the Hudson Bay territory for later consideration, but also it defined Acadia only by its 'ancient limits', which were themselves contested. With no agreed version of the boundaries, the British contended that Acadia/Nova Scotia included the territory of the modern New Brunswick and extended south-westward to the Penobscot River, the northeastern boundary of Massachusetts's claim to Maine. The French argued that the ceded lands included, at most, peninsular Acadia east of the Isthmus of Chignecto. Although there were different versions of the French claim, all of them implied a substantial territorial separation between British claims to New England and Nova Scotia.[11]

---

[9] Emerson W. Baker and John G. Reid, 'Amerindian Power in the Early Modern Northeast: A Reappraisal', *William and Mary Quarterly*, 3rd ser. 61 (2004), pp. 77–106.

[10] Reid et al., *'Conquest' of Acadia*, p. ix.

[11] Baker and Reid, 'Amerindian Power in the Early Modern Northeast', pp. 93–6; John G. Reid, 'Imperialism, Diplomacies, and the Conquest of Acadia', in Reid et al., *'Conquest' of Acadia*, pp. 102–6; G. F. G. Stanley, *New France: The Last Phase, 1744–1760* (Toronto, 1968), pp. 70–1.

While the dispute over the territorial definition of Acadia heightened the possibility of future French–British conflict, the outcome of the treaty failed to reflect reality in a deeper sense. As was true of much of north-eastern North America in the early modern period, the areas that European statesmen divided between France and Britain—increasingly claiming legitimacy based on long-ago voyages of discovery—were not effectively under the control of either French or British subjects. Rather the Mi'kmaq and Wulstukwiuk (Maliseet), the Aboriginal inhabitants, retained the initiative throughout what were known to the British and French, respectively, as the colonies of Nova Scotia and Île Royale. In Île Royale—a term that referred geographically to Cape Breton Island, but for administrative purposes included Île Saint-Jean—the French established a militarily impressive presence at the fortified town of Louisbourg, but it was underpinned by negotiated relationships between French Governors and the Mi'kmaq leaders they hosted at annual meetings.[12]

A Mi'kmaq delegation made diplomatic overtures to the British at Annapolis Royal soon after the 1710 conquest of Acadia. Although the immediate results were inconclusive and did not forestall the emergence of a troubled relationship, the Aboriginal approach signalled the terms under which they would tolerate a British presence on their lands. As during earlier imperial regimes at Port Royal—French, English, and Scottish—Aboriginal leaders were willing to accept some European settlers in exchange for trade and alliance, provided that Aboriginal diplomatic protocols were respected and that Europeans confined themselves to areas where their presence was acceptable. Breach of these conditions would lead to quick and effective military rebuke by Aboriginal forces.[13]

Whitehall was not oblivious to the need for harmonious relations with non-British inhabitants. Governor Richard Philipps was instructed in 1719 to enter into treaty negotiations so that Aboriginal inhabitants 'may be induced by degrees not only to be good neighbors to our subjects but likewise themselves to become good subjects to us', and to encourage intermarriage between British male settlers and Aboriginal women by making 50-acre land grants on privileged terms. Yet the Imperial view, that there existed a colony of Nova Scotia covering a substantial territory, inherently conflicted with the Aboriginal view that toleration was being extended only to a limited British occupation of small areas of Mi'kma'ki and Wulstukwik. An important phase of treaty making between 1725 and 1728 kept the peace for some time, but tensions remained and were prone to develop into hostility at times of British–French warfare,

---

[12] George Rawlyk, '1720–1744: Cod, Louisbourg, and the Acadians', in Buckner and Reid, *Atlantic Region to Confederation*, pp. 107–24; William C. Wicken, *Mi'kmaq Treaties on Trial: History, Land, and Donald Marshall Junior* (Toronto, 2002), pp. 51–2.

[13] John G. Reid, '*Pax Britannica* or *Pax Indigena*? Planter Nova Scotia and Competing Strategies of Pacification', *Canadian Historical Review*, 85 (2004), pp. 669–92; Wicken, *Mi'kmaq Treaties*, pp. 99–117.

as between 1744 and 1748. Although Aboriginal forces were never subservient to the French, setting limits to British encroachments could readily become a common cause.[14]

In Nova Scotia, the British confronted further complications with the Acadians. The settlement of French colonists in the seventeenth century, primarily on or near marshland around the Bay of Fundy, resulted in the foundation of a series of Acadian communities, with economies based on marshland agriculture, fishing, fur trading, and illegal trade with New Englanders. While the initial number of settlers was small, substantial rates of natural increase raised the population total to some 2,500 by the early eighteenth century. The Acadian communities were unmilitarized, even resisting organization into militia units for the defence of pre-Conquest Acadia. They generated almost all the wealth of the non-Aboriginal economy of Nova Scotia. They also recognized and respected the terms of Aboriginal territorial control. Their economic and demographic importance presented difficulties for both French and British Imperial administrators. For some years after the Treaty of Utrecht, French officials repeatedly invited these seasoned colonists to resettle on Île Royale, but few accepted the offer. British officials faced the challenge of establishing some semblance of British authority over Acadians who had no pressing reason to recognize it.[15]

The Acadians presented British officials at Annapolis Royal with the dilemma of how to come to terms with a population that was French and Catholic, and yet occupied a central position in the agricultural economy of the new Nova Scotia. Efforts to induce Acadians to subscribe to an oath of allegiance initially had poor results. Although Acadians were far from monolithic in their approaches to the British regime—there were Anglophiles and Francophiles, as well as a substantial proportion whose preference was to stay out of British–French quarrels altogether—only a few were willing to take the oath. Most were swayed by concerns over the possibilities of being forced to fight against French forces in a future war, of incurring Mi'kmaq enmity caused by British expansion, or of compromising their Catholicism by swearing allegiance to the head of the Church of England. Acadian leaders argued that as a non-military people, it was unnecessary for their compatriots to take any oath. Finally, in 1729–30, Governor Philipps—an absentee Governor for most of

[14] Leonard W. Labaree, ed., *Royal Instructions to British Governors, 1670–1776*, 2 vols. (1935; New York, 1967), vol. II, pp. 469–70; Stephen E. Patterson, '1744–1763: Colonial Wars and Aboriginal Peoples', in Buckner and Reid, *Atlantic Region to Confederation*, pp. 125–7; Wicken, *Mi'kmaq Treaties*, pp. 99–139.

[15] Andrew Hill Clark, *Acadia: The Geography of Early Nova Scotia to 1760* (Madison, 1968), pp. 86–261; Naomi E. S. Griffiths, *The Contexts of Acadian History, 1686–1784* (Kingston and Montreal, 1992); Griffiths, *From Migrant to Acadian: A North American Border People, 1604–1755* (Kingston and Montreal, 2005); Julian Gwyn, *Excessive Expectations: Maritime Commerce and the Economic Development of Nova Scotia, 1740–1870* (Kingston and Montreal, 1998), pp. 16–17.

his lengthy term—persuaded a large number of Acadian heads of families to take a qualified oath that reputedly safeguarded their Catholic beliefs and ruled out military service. On this basis, the Acadians became known as 'the Neutral French'. Francophile Acadians warned, however, that such neutrality was unpredictable and might not hold in time of war. During the war of 1744–8, Acadians took a minimal role, despite New England troops' protests that Acadians had aided the French at the 1747 Battle of Grand Pré. The conditional oath of allegiance was symbolic of a negotiated arrangement between Annapolis Royal and the Acadians, one that generally held firm to the end of the 1740s.[16]

In eighteenth-century Newfoundland, ethnic divisions etched themselves more deeply into the landscape. The expansion of the European fishery prompted the Beothuk to move north towards Notre Dame Bay and then increasingly into the interior. Although this strategy of withdrawal worked effectively well into the eighteenth century, an ensuing reduction in the Beothuks' ecological base resulted in dietary deficiencies, which in combination with the toll of European-introduced diseases and attacks by hostile settlers contributed to increasing distress and the eventual extinction of the Beothuk in the late 1820s. On the south coast of Newfoundland, Mi'kmaq sojourners and residents maintained another Aboriginal presence. Journeys across the Cabot Strait may have brought Mi'kmaq hunters to Newfoundland as early as the sixteenth century, although firm indications of residence come substantially later. Despite France's evacuation of its Newfoundland settlements under the Treaty of Utrecht, French coastal rights on the north coast from Bonavista to Port-au-Choix—the 'French Shore'—were periodically renegotiated after major wars until finally surrendered in 1904.[17]

In British-controlled harbours along the east coast of Newfoundland from the Avalon Peninsula to Bonavista, the resident population expanded and diversified; by 1720 it had reached 3,000 and it doubled again by mid-century. A sharp increase in the numbers of Irish migrants was the most striking change over seventeenth-century patterns of settlement and migration, in which the English—disproportionately drawn from the West Country—predominated. The Irish, insignificant at the time of the Treaty of Utrecht, were approaching parity with English settlers by 1770. Ethnicity also reflected social class. 'Planters'—residents who acted as intermediaries for English-based merchants in hiring fishers and managing the summer fishing season, some of whom become

---

[16] Maurice Basque, 'The Third Acadia: Political Adaptation and Societal Change', in Reid et al., *'Conquest' of Acadia*, pp. 155–77; Geoffrey Plank, *An Unsettled Conquest: The British Campaign against the Peoples of Acadia* (Philadelphia, 2001), pp. 87–121.

[17] Charles A. Martijn, ed., *Les Micmacs et la mer* (Montreal, 1986); Ralph Pastore, 'The Collapse of the Beothuk World', *Acadiensis*, 19/1 (1989), pp. 52–71 and *The Newfoundland Micmacs: A History of their Traditional Life* ([St John's], 1978); Frederic F. Thompson, *The French Shore Problem in Newfoundland: An Imperial Study* (Toronto, 1961).

small-scale merchants themselves—were overwhelmingly English and Protestant. 'Servants' or 'fishermen', employed as wage labourers, were increasingly and soon predominantly Irish Catholics. Young men continued to dominate Newfoundland's population. Most were seasonal, but many were residents in the sense that they stayed for a sufficient period of years to accumulate a small amount of capital from their wages. Few expected to live out their lives in Newfoundland, but in the eighteenth century the immigration of young Irish women seeking domestic employment encouraged a gradual shift to a pattern of lifetime residency.[18]

Governance in Newfoundland evolved significantly during the early eighteenth century. Although King William's Act in 1699 recognized settlement, the emerging Imperial state remained ambivalent about the value of a resident population, and not until 1832 did it authorize an Assembly on the island. For many years from the early nineteenth century onwards, contemporary observers of Newfoundland and later historians lamented the island's supposed institutional weakness and portrayed government by the Royal Navy and the fishing admirals as primitive and chaotic. Recent analysis, however, offers a more nuanced portrayal. Between 1699 and 1729, the fishing admirals administered justice, and their decisions could be appealed to the naval commodore detailed to Newfoundland for the fishing season. In the 1720s, prominent residents began establishing their own courts, and in response the Privy Council approved a plan to commission the naval commodore as the seasonal civilian Governor with the right to appoint magistrates and justices of the peace who could convene courts year round. This decision inaugurated a distinctive legal and administrative system that combined civil and naval authority. Unlike the governmental institutions in any of the other British American territories, Newfoundland was a society in which the active presence of the imperial state in the guise of the Royal Navy provided an effective, albeit authoritarian, system of governance that was well adapted to preserving the social authority of employers over the fishing servants.[19]

In Rupert's Land, the decades of peace following the Treaty of Utrecht allowed the HBC to capitalize on its investments in long-distance trade, and in 1718 it paid its first annual dividend. To winnow profits from the trade, it learned how to coordinate and link two trading systems at its bayside forts: a British-dominated system provided the transatlantic connection, while a native-dominated system stretched deep into the interior of North America. In most years, two ships would sail from Gravesend no later than 25 May so that they could return in one sailing season rather than winter on the bay. In the eighteenth century ships began stopping at Stromness in the Orkney Islands where the company

---

[18] Jerry Bannister, *The Rule of the Admirals: Law, Custom, and Naval Government in Newfoundland, 1699–1832* (Toronto, 2003), pp. 7–10; Head, *Eighteenth Century Newfoundland*, p. 85.

[19] Bannister, *Rule of the Admirals*, p. 133, and *passim*.

hired labourers who soon numerically dominated the British residents at the forts.[20]

In North America, the HBC relied heavily on native expertise and labour. Bayside forts, sited at the termini of riverine transportation systems, encouraged the establishment of nearby Cree communities. Native hunters and fishers helped provision the forts, and native women made a range of items such as moccasins and snowshoes for company employees. Many native women and HBC men formed conjugal unions according to 'the custom of the country', and their offspring constituted an increasingly distinct social group of 'mixed bloods', the HBC equivalent of the Métis communities that developed in the French fur trade. Native middlemen traders prosecuted the fur trade in the interior of the continent, transporting European manufactures to distant native nations and furs to the bayside forts. For the most part the HBC eschewed inland expansion as long as it could, partly to avoid the expense and difficulty of building and supplying inland forts, and partly to stay out of native conflicts. By the 1730s, however, French *coureurs de bois* were intercepting furs that native traders had previously carried down to Fort Albany. Pierre de La Vérendrye and his sons had travelled as far north-west as Lake Winnipeg and the Saskatchewan River system.[21]

Demographic and economic growth in Nova Scotia, Newfoundland, and Rupert's Land during the decades of peace aggravated old points of Anglo-French contention within North America, as well as creating new ones. French and New England fishermen sparred over control of the fishing grounds off Canso, Nova Scotia. New England merchants actively traded at Louisbourg, yet worried about the growth of French power in the North Atlantic. The undefined boundary between Nova Scotia and Canada became an increasingly tendentious issue. French fur traders siphoned off high-value furs from the HBC. These tensions in the northerly portions of North America mirrored similar points of tension between various European overseas empires, whether in the slave-trading forts of West Africa, in the spice and cloth markets of Asia, or on the sugar islands in the West Indies. Fighting finally erupted in 1739 in the Caribbean between the British and Spanish and became the overseas prelude to the War of the Austrian Succession.

Although many observers had anticipated the resumption of global-scale European war in the 1740s, few residents of the Americas were prepared for it. In earlier wars, relatively isolated outposts had been particularly vulnerable to attacks. Examples include York Fort on Hudson Bay, Port Royal in Acadia, and St John's,

---

[20] Rich, *History*, pp. 91, 461; Jennifer S. H. Brown, *Strangers in Blood: Fur Trade Company Families in Indian Country* (Vancouver, 1980), pp. 27–9.

[21] Brown, *Strangers in Blood*, pp. 52–80; Sylvia Van Kirk, *Many Tender Ties: Women in Fur-Trade Society, 1670–1870* (Winnipeg, 1980), pp. 53–73; Conrad E. Heidenrich and Françoise Noël, 'Trade and Empire, 1697–1739', and 'France Secures the Interior, 1740–1755', in Harris, (ed.), *Historical Atlas of Canada*, vol. I, plates 39 and 40.

Newfoundland. During the 1730s, the HBC devised various plans to protect its forts. In Nova Scotia, the British kept military detachments at Annapolis Royal and Canso. In 1744, a French force leaving from Louisbourg took Canso but failed to take Annapolis Royal. The following year, the governments of New England, led by Massachusetts and Governor William Shirley, mobilized colonial troops for the audacious plan of taking Louisbourg, which surrendered in June after a seven-week siege. Elsewhere the war went badly for the British and they went to the negotiating tables at Aix-la-Chapelle having little to bargain with except Louisbourg. The French and British agreed in the treaty (1748) to return their overseas possessions to *status quo ante bellum*, demonstrated most graphically with the exchange of Louisbourg for Madras in India. This exchange of territory in North America for territory in Asia symbolized the global perspective that European power brokers had assumed in their competition for empire.[22]

Despite the return to *status quo ante bellum* for territorial possessions, Britain's *post bellum* strategies of war and imperial governance were not status quo. Nova Scotia, Newfoundland, and Rupert's Land were particularly affected for three reasons: the fishery was commercially significant for both France and Britain; the waters between Nova Scotia and Newfoundland provided the French access to the St Lawrence River and Canada; and Rupert's Land was an enormous territory in the heart of the continent that still promised access to a North-west Passage, as well as the fur trade. In anticipation of another war for empire, British metropolitan officials implemented new programmes in 1748 and 1749, including an unprecedented militarization of north-eastern North America.[23]

For Nova Scotia, Parliament voted moneys in 1748 to build a new North Atlantic naval base on Chebucto Bay, Nova Scotia, as well as move the capital of the colony to this site and name it Halifax after the Earl of Halifax, President of the Board of Trade. The next year the new Governor, Edward Cornwallis, arrived with 2,500 British settlers. Meanwhile, a British agent was in continental Europe recruiting foreign Protestant settlers for Nova Scotia, a plan designed to dilute the influence of the Catholic Acadians; those settlers began arriving in 1750. Annapolis Royal, no longer the colony's headquarters, was strengthened, but across the Bay of Fundy at the mouth of the St John River the French responded by refortifying an abandoned fort. They built another, Fort Beauséjour, on the west side of the Missiguash River on the Isthmus of Chignecto, which they claimed was the boundary between Nova Scotia and Canada. In response, the British built Fort Lawrence on the east side of the river, scarcely a cannon shot away.[24]

[22] Patterson, '1744–1763', pp. 125–55.
[23] Jack P. Greene, ' "A Posture of Hostility": A Reconsideration of Some Aspects of the Origins of the American Revolution', *Proceedings of the American Antiquarian Society*, 87 (1977), pp. 27–68.
[24] Patterson, '1744–1763', pp. 127–34.

Newfoundland felt corresponding pressures, and fortification in St John's ranged from the reconstruction of Fort William during the War of the Austrian Succession to the beginning of work on Forts Amherst and Townshend on the eve of the American Revolution. Always a pressing concern in this era, however, was reform of governance. It coincided with an increased involvement of the Admiralty both in the formulation of criminal justice policy for Britain and in imperial expansion. In 1749, Captain George Brydges Rodney, the Governor for the season, began an overhaul of Newfoundland's judicial system. He initiated the local recording of judicial decisions in the 'Colonial Secretary's Letterbook', which became critical in defining customary law for the island. It was subsequently used to record civil contracts of various kinds. Prior to Rodney's reforms, the Navy's presence had been confined largely to St John's, but in 1749 he used his gubernatorial powers to commission naval officers as civil magistrates and sent them to all the major outports. Rather than the navy providing primarily courts of appeal, these floating surrogate courts, instead of the fishing admirals' courts, increasingly heard most cases.[25]

Meanwhile in Britain, merchants and imperial visionaries found common cause in criticizing the HBC. The former wanted the Company's monopoly revoked and the fur trade opened, while the latter, particularly Sir Arthur Dobbs, were concerned about French encroachments in Rupert's Land, the Company's seeming negligence in exploring for a North West Passage, and its extreme secretiveness. The Admiralty sent an expedition to search for the North West Passage in 1741 and a privately funded expedition followed in 1746. Dobbs wrote a highly negative *Account of Hudson's Bay* (1745), followed by other accounts of the Company and of the high likelihood of a North West Passage. A petition campaign by merchants from throughout Britain finally prompted Parliament to convene an inquiry in 1749 to consider the legitimacy of the HBC's monopoly control of the fur trade in Rupert's Land. The conclusion reached by the inquiry, as captured in a newspaper report, was that the trade needed permanent 'forts and settlements [that] must be supported either by exclusive companies, or at the publick expence'.[26]

One of the striking characteristics of these metropolitan initiatives for Nova Scotia, Newfoundland, and Rupert's Land was the greater coordination among branches of the British government—particularly the Board of Trade, the Admiralty, the Board of Ordnance, and Parliament—in shaping policy and appropriating moneys for colonial governance, settlement, exploration, and military preparedness. That coordination represented a consolidation of the Imperial state and the privileging of imperial over colonial concerns, a development that

---

[25] Bannister, *Rule of the Admirals*, pp. 108–12.

[26] Glyndwr Williams, 'The Hudson's Bay Company and its Critics in the Eighteenth Century', *Transactions of the Royal Historical Society*, 5th ser., 20 (1970), p. 163.

in the short run proved devastating to the Acadians and contributed to the sundering of the Empire in the 1770s and 1780s.

Nowhere in North America were Anglo-French hostilities considered more likely than in Nova Scotia and neighbouring Île Royale. The building of Halifax made the colony a focal point for naval vigilance throughout the Atlantic basin, while the new emphasis on military preparedness, both in the colony and in the broader British Atlantic world, created tensions with Aboriginal and Acadian populations. The Mi'kmaq protested Britain's unauthorized annexation of Chebucto harbour as a settlement area, and Anglo-Mi'kmaq hostilities persisted intermittently despite the negotiation of a treaty in 1752. Acadians faced competing pressures from French and British Imperial officials, each side hoping—largely in vain—to enlist active Acadian allegiance to its cause. The outbreak of fighting between French and British troops in the Ohio River valley in 1754 provided justification for the military establishment in Halifax to storm Fort Beauséjour in the following year. A surprisingly speedy French surrender encouraged the British regime in Halifax to demand a complete and immediate oath of allegiance from all Acadians. If they resisted, a victorious British army—composed mainly of New Englanders—was available to provide coercion. When Acadian leaders refused the unqualified oath, Governor Charles Lawrence ordered the deportation of the entire Acadian population of some 14,000. Approximately half were deported in 1755 and deposited in British seaports from New Hampshire to Georgia. Many Acadians took refuge in remote areas of Nova Scotia or on Île Saint-Jean. The British defeat of the French at Louisbourg in 1758 led to another round of Acadian deportations, but this time some were sent to France and French colonies. By the end of the Seven Years War only about 1,500 Acadians remained in the old Acadia. Some returned, but others went to Louisiana where they became the Cajuns.[27]

The Acadian deportation, despite its execution from a position of military strength, worked against British ambitions for creating a secure and prosperous colony of Nova Scotia. Its economic costs were devastatingly high: productive fields remained untended; dykes were left unrepaired; thousands of houses succumbed to flames; livestock was either killed or taken away. In 1760, New England settlers began the task of rebuilding the devastated agrarian economy, but in 1767 their numbers on the former farms of the Acadians were only about 4,600 (including some English and Irish immigrants), far fewer than the pre-1755 population.[28]

Peaceful British relations with the Mi'kmaq and Wulstukwiuk nations remained critical to the tenability of Nova Scotia. Treaties signed in 1760 and 1761 muted tensions, but as had been true of earlier treaties, British and

[27] Griffiths, *Contexts*.
[28] Gwyn, *Excessive Expectations*, pp. 25–7; Nova Scotia Census 1767, Nova Scotia Archives and Records Management, RG 1, vol. 443, No. 1.

Aboriginal understandings of their import differed. Did they represent the triumph of British Imperial rule or did they represent an extension of Aboriginal toleration to an expanded British presence on their lands? In the short run the latter was the more realistic assessment given the continued Aboriginal military power. British installations were vulnerable to raiding warfare and New England settlers remained pocketed in isolated townships. Friction continued intermittently throughout the 1760s and 1770s; it would take more settlers for the British claims of regional control to gain practical ascendancy over Aboriginal claims.[29]

The formal declaration of war between Britain and France in 1756 was preceded by a number of French military successes: they defeated the British in the Ohio River valley; they successfully reinforced Louisbourg in 1755; and in India their victories in battle at least matched those of the British. The French entered the war at an advantage and in 1757 enhanced it with the capture of Fort William Henry on the Hudson River–Lake Champlain corridor between New York and Canada. That year, the British shifted their military strategy and decided to expend all necessary resources to win the war. Henceforth they would strike at the strong points of France's overseas presence and not at its weak flanks. In 1758, 15,000 British sailors and soldiers transported in 150 ships took Louisbourg after an extended siege. The following year the largest military force ever assembled in North America took Quebec, and in 1760 French officers in Montreal—unable to resupply their troops—surrendered to the British, effectively ending the French colonial presence in North America. In the Caribbean, British troops took Martinique and Guadeloupe. When the Spanish entered the war in 1762, the British seized Havana and Manila. By contrast, the French seizure of St John's, Newfoundland, in the same year was quickly reversed. Meanwhile in India, British troops made gains against both French and Indian armies, and in 1765 the East India Company was granted the *diwani* of Bengal by the Mughal emperor.[30]

Britain's wartime triumphs engendered sobering peacetime challenges. A crushing and potentially destabilizing public debt had to be funded. Newly acquired colonies had to be governed, and in North America approximately 70,000 Canadians had to be accommodated. Dozens of Aboriginal nations suddenly found themselves in territory now claimed by Britain. New territories had to be defended and funds secured to cover the cost. Finally, the role of colonists in implementing any of these changes had to be considered. Many of these problems had modest antecedents in Nova Scotia, Newfoundland, and Rupert's Land at earlier imperial junctures. In Nova Scotia and Rupert's Land, non-British subjects had long been a majority and the British a minority, and

---

[29] Reid, '*Pax Britannica* or *Pax Indigena*'.
[30] Fred Anderson, *Crucible of War: The Seven Years' War and the Fate of Empire in British North America, 1754–1766* (New York, 2000).

in both places the minority status of Britons and their defensive vulnerabilities had constrained the expansion of settlements. The HBC built Henley House 150 miles into the interior from Fort Albany, but in 1755 the post was abandoned after an attack by disaffected Aboriginal traders. Newfoundland outports were difficult to defend and were raided repeatedly by the French up until 1762. All three areas had come under parliamentary oversight in the first half of the eighteenth century, with varying involvement by other branches of the metropolitan government, particularly the Admiralty. The post-1763 imperial turn was not incremental and sector specific, however, but empire-wide.

The first serious conflict came from Aboriginal nations newly incorporated into the British Empire and high-handedly treated by Jeffery Amherst, British military commander in North America. In 1763 an alliance led by the Ottawa chief Pontiac and the Delaware prophet Neolin launched attacks against British-occupied forts around the Great Lakes, providing graphic evidence that the Aboriginal allies of the French would not conform easily to the implications of the Treaty of Paris. On 7 October 1763, the King-in-Council issued the proclamation usually known as the Royal Proclamation of 1763, which addressed many issues concerning the new non-British residents of the expanded Empire. Most specific to Pontiac's War, it reserved the territory west of the Appalachian Mountains for native inhabitants and severely restricted its alienation. The instructions to Quebec's Governors enjoined them—as earlier in Nova Scotia—to pursue a negotiated relationship with the 'several nations and tribes of Indians', so as to bring them gradually to the status of subjects of the Crown. While these instructions did not prevent all land encroachments or obviate periodic tensions, they did signal that negotiation, not armed coercion, was the preferred method of securing the frontiers of Imperial expansion.[31]

The Proclamation of 1763 also addressed other issues crucial to the future of the British presence in North America. It placed the coast of Labrador, along with Anticosti and the Magdalen Islands, under the authority of the Governor of Newfoundland. It established governments in the newly acquired colonies of Canada (renamed as the province of Quebec), East and West Florida, and Grenada. Quebec, defined to include the St Lawrence and Ottawa valleys and surrounding areas but not the fur trade territories of the Great Lakes, was to have an elected Assembly and the benefits of English law. Successive Governors, most notably Guy Carleton, considered this model unworkable because *Canadiens* as Catholics could not hold public office and the adoption of English common law would disrupt contractual relations among upwards of 70,000 *Canadiens* ranging from landholding, to marriages, to inheritance, to labour contracts. Furthermore, Catholicism technically precluded jury service, thus excluding *Canadiens* from a

---

[31] Richard White, *The Middle Ground: Indians, Empires, and Republics in the Great Lakes Region, 1650–1815* (Cambridge, 1991), pp. 269–314; Labaree, *Royal Instructions*, vol. II. pp. 478–80.

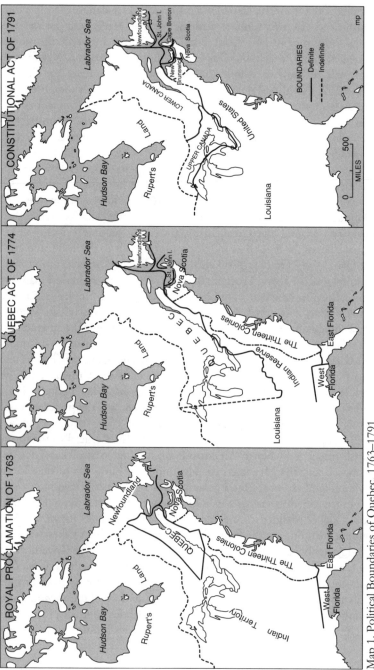

ROYAL PROCLAMATION OF 1763

Labrador Sea

Hudson Bay

Rupert's Land

Newfoundland

Nova Scotia

QUEBEC

Indian Territory

The Thirteen Colonies

West Florida

East Florida

QUEBEC ACT OF 1774

Labrador Sea

Hudson Bay

Rupert's Land

Newfoundland

St. John I.

Nova Scotia

Q U E B E C

Louisiana

Indian Reserve

The Thirteen Colonies

West Florida

East Florida

CONSTITUTIONAL ACT OF 1791

Labrador Sea

Hudson Bay

Rupert's Land

Newfoundland

St. John I.

Cape Breton

New Brunswick

Nova Scotia

LOWER CANADA

UPPER CANADA

United States

Louisiana

BOUNDARIES

Definite
Indefinite

0   500

MILES

mp

Map 1. Political Boundaries of Quebec, 1763–1791

fundamental element of English justice. Although incoming British merchants, frequently associated with the fur trade, pressed for the full implementation of the Proclamation's model of government, the reality was that negotiation would prevail. In 1774 Parliament codified these accommodations in the Quebec Act. It recognized French civil law, including the perpetuation of seigneurial landholding, but English law would prevail in criminal cases. Catholics could hold public office and the Catholic Church could collect tithes, used in large part to fund social services. The colony would not have an Assembly, but would be governed by the Governor and Executive Council. Quebec's boundaries were extended south to the Ohio River and west to the Mississippi River, thereby bringing the *Canadiens* and Métis living in the *pays d'en haut* within the jurisdiction of Quebec.[32]

For the HBC, the French defeat offered the false promise of an end to encroachments in Rupert's Land. The Montreal-based trade, however, was not dismantled after 1763. British merchants, with Scots predominating, took over the trade and they were every bit as aggressive as their French predecessors, if not more so. The Montreal traders pushed north-west around Lake Winnipeg, travelled west along the Saskatchewan River system, even though they were on lands included in the HBC charter, and by 1778 had crossed into the Arctic watershed. This aggressive expansion finally forced the HBC to end its 'sleep by the frozen sea' and to begin establishing inland posts in the 1770s.[33]

The Seven Years War and Britain's capture of Manila in the Philippines in 1762 helped to weaken Spain's exclusionary claims to the Pacific Ocean, which the Russian penetration of Alaska had already challenged directly. In the 1760s and 1770s, the French and British governments found numerous reasons to sponsor exploratory expeditions in the Pacific: to observe the transit of Venus from Tahiti; to search for Austral-Asia, the theoretical counterpart of Asia in the southern hemisphere; and to find the Pacific entrance to the equally mythical North West Passage. Not incidentally, the HBC allowed scientists sponsored by the Royal Society to observe the transit of Venus from Fort Churchill, and gave the Admiralty geographic information about Rupert's Land when it prepared for James Cook's last voyage to the Pacific, which left England in 1776, the same year that thirteen colonies declared their independence. Among that expedition's significant landfalls was Nootka Sound on the coast of Vancouver Island, where western Europeans got their first glimpse of the highly lucrative, but short-lived, trade in sea otter pelts. Reports from the expedition unleashed a race for the Pacific, both by maritime routes and across North America from Montreal.

[32] Hilda Neatby, *Quebec: The Revolutionary Age, 1760–1791* (Toronto, 1966), pp. 9–10, 15–16, 45–8, 125–41.
[33] D. Wayne Moodie et al., 'Competition and Consolidation, 1760–1825', in Harris, (ed.), *Historical Atlas of Canada*, vol. I, plate 61.

In 1793, an overland expedition leaving from Montreal and led by Alexander Mackenzie reached the Pacific.[34]

The outbreak of fighting between British regulars and New England militias on 17 April 1775 made clear that some British Americans considered the recent changes in imperial governance worthy of armed conflict. The American Revolution, like the preceding wars of the late seventeenth and eighteenth centuries, drew in people from throughout the world. Although residents of Nova Scotia, the Island of St John (separated from Nova Scotia in 1769 and renamed Prince Edward Island in 1799), Newfoundland, Quebec, and Rupert's Land tended to remain loyal members of the Empire, the conflict still unsettled and transformed their lives. Troop movements, disruptions in shipping, rerouting of the provisioning trades, and privateering caused upheaval, privation, and loss of life and property in settlements all along the Atlantic littoral. For the British, the two colonies of greatest concern were Quebec and Nova Scotia, the former because it shared a long border with the rebelling colonies and the latter because of the large number of former New Englanders who lived there.[35]

Quebec was the one loyal colony against which the Continental Congress authorized and financed an offensive campaign, partly because the revolutionaries thought the *Canadiens* might want to be independent of their British overlords, partly because control of the St Lawrence and Great Lakes provided access to the interior of the continent. In the autumn of 1775, two American armies marched towards Quebec, one up the Hudson River–Lake Champlain corridor, the other up the Kennebec River in Maine. The first army took Montreal in December and then met the second army outside Quebec to begin an abortive winter siege of the city. When British resupply ships arrived in the spring, the American armies, depleted by disease, death, and desertion, returned home. *Canadiens* were ambivalent members of the British Empire but, for most, any misgivings were insufficient to prompt rebellion. Governor Frederick Haldimand, who took over from Carleton in 1777, worked assiduously to maintain the loyalty of merchants in the fur trade, Aboriginal nations, and colonists, only to have the British turn over the southern portion of Quebec to the Americans in the 1783 Treaty of Paris.[36]

Nova Scotia saw one small military campaign on its soil, the unsuccessful attempt by a small force led by Jonathan Eddy to storm Fort Cumberland, the former Fort Beauséjour. Planters, Wulstukwiuk, and Acadians were among Eddy's force of less than one hundred. Their failure confirmed Nova Scotia, like the Island of St John, as a Loyalist colony. Although some Planters professed

---

[34] Glyndwr Williams, 'The Pacific: Exploration and Exploitation', in P. J. Marshall, (ed.), *The Oxford History of the British Empire*, vol. II: *The Eighteenth Century* (Oxford, 1998), pp. 552–75.

[35] Elizabeth Mancke, 'The American Revolution in Canada', in Jack P. Greene and J. R. Pole, eds., *A Companion to the American Revolution* (Oxford, 2000), pp. 503–10.

[36] Gustave Lanctôt, *Le Canada et la révolution américaine* (Montreal, 1965); G. F. G. Stanley, *Canada Invaded, 1775–1776* (Toronto, 1973).

neutrality in the conflict, the military power of Halifax limited their assertiveness, while their numbers were countered by those Nova Scotians who enlisted in Loyalist regiments.[37]

Although the formal conclusion of the second Treaty of Paris took place only in 1783, the outpouring of Loyalist refugees—principally from the port of New York—was well under way by the end of 1782. Two years of the Loyalist migration brought some 35,000 refugees to the Maritime colonies, where they not only established the autonomous colonies of New Brunswick and Cape Breton but also spread into many hitherto uncolonized areas of the region, beginning a process of thorough environmental change that had destructive results for the outnumbered Aboriginal population. Other Loyalist refugees settled in the western part of the province of Quebec, notably along the north shore of Lake Ontario and in the Eastern Townships. Although their numbers were smaller and their Loyalism often indistinguishable from an acquisitive hunger for land, these migrants not only established another nodal point for English-speaking settlement in the original province, but also formed the nucleus of settlement in the future Upper Canada.[38]

The Loyalist migration, by making the northern British North America more like the former colonies of settlement further south, contributed to a more continental orientation. So, in a different way, did the competing western movements of the HBC and the North West Company, their strategies now directed towards the Pacific Northwest. In these contexts, British North America—now the only British North America rather than a northern British North America essentially distinct from a more southerly counterpart—had moved from its formation through the play of global forces on a variety of North American areas and their Aboriginal inhabitants, to a more continental focus. Administratively, however, it was not one entity but a series of entities. Despite the new continental strategies, British North America continued to be part of a global empire—along with, particularly, portions of the Caribbean and of India—and shaped by its concerns. Ideologically, the continental focus never had the purchase on British North Americans that it did on the United States. British North America, moreover, was still characterized by an inherent ethnic diversity, and the continuing role of Aboriginal power—even though now severely eroded in some places. Negotiated imperialism persisted. Thus, while British North America had made a transition from global processes to continental strategies, there were enough continuities to make it clear that although the northern British North America of the earlier eighteenth century had been modified, it nevertheless continued in its evolving form.

---

[37] Ernest Clarke, *The Siege of Fort Cumberland, 1776: An Episode in the American Revolution* (Montreal and Kingston, 1995); J. M. Bumsted, *Understanding the Loyalists* (Sackville, 1986), p. 47.

[38] Ann Gorman Condon, '1783–1800: Loyalist Arrival, Acadian Return, Imperial Reform', in Buckner and Reid, *Atlantic Region to Confederation*, pp. 183–209; Jane Errington, *The Lion, the Eagle, and Upper Canada: A Developing Colonial Ideology* (Montreal and Kingston, 1987).

SELECT BIBLIOGRAPHY

FRED ANDERSON, *The Crucible of War: The Seven Years' War and the Fate of Empire in British North America, 1754–1766* (New York, 2000).

JERRY BANNISTER, *The Rule of the Admirals: Law, Custom, and Naval Government in Newfoundland, 1699–1832* (Toronto, 2003).

N. E. S. GRIFFITHS, *From Migrant to Acadian: A North American Border People, 1604–1755* (Montreal and Kingston, 2005).

RONNIE-GILLES LEBLANC, (ed.), *Du Grand Dérangement à la Déportation: nouvelles perspectives historiques* (Moncton, 2005).

GEOFFREY PLANK, *An Unsettled Conquest: The British Campaign against the Peoples of Acadia* (Philadelphia, 2001).

PETER E. POPE, *Fish into Wine: The Newfoundland Plantation in the Seventeenth Century* (Chapel Hill, NC, 2004).

JOHN G. REID et al., *The 'Conquest' of Acadia: 1710: Imperial, Colonial, and Aboriginal Constructions* (Toronto, 2004).

3

The Consolidation of British North America, 1783–1860

J. M. Bumsted

At the end of the American Revolution what remained of British America consisted of various centres of ethnic settlement, mainly in the north-eastern part of the continent, separated from one another culturally and geographically, demonstrating little political cohesion, and only loosely connected to Great Britain.[1] By 1860, the colonies in the eastern half of British America had been transformed into comparatively densely settled provinces with increasingly sophisticated economies. All the original provinces had achieved responsible government under the Imperial umbrella. The relationship of the British American provinces with the British Empire had passed through a number of stages, but in 1860 the Imperial connection remained unquestioned, at least among the English-speaking inhabitants of British America, who increasingly saw themselves as 'British' rather than English or Scots or Irish or some other nationality. But exactly what that Britishness meant was open to interpretation. It certainly did not mean a slavish acceptance of British authority. At the same time that effusions of loyalty were at their height, the largest of the developed provinces—Canada—had already begun to exhibit signs of continental expansionism, seeking to annex unorganized territory on its western boundary in its own interests. Such expansionism would require British assistance and support in the short run, but implied the possibility of a longer-term autonomy, particularly when combined with an internal expansion of state activity not controlled by the Colonial Office, talk of the national unification of the various jurisdictions, and the desire of the British to limit their liabilities in the New World. The result was the emergence of a tension in British America between a centripetal loyalty to the existing British Empire and a centrifugal series of other forces at work. The other forces tended chiefly to autonomy rather than towards a closer connection with the United States.[2]

---

[1] See J. M. Bumsted, 'The Cultural Landscape of Early Canada', in Bernard Bailyn and Philip D. Morgan, eds., *Strangers within the Realm: Cultural Margins of the First British Empire* (Chapel Hill, NC, 1991), pp. 363–92.

[2] For another view of the Imperial implications of 1783–1860, see Chap. 4 in this volume.

Great Britain lost the military struggle for the thirteen rebellious colonies in 1781, when Lord Cornwallis surrendered at Yorktown. The war had been expensive and lacking in great victories, and public opinion would probably not have permitted its continuation. Extrication from the lost cause at minimal cost involved the negotiation of a peace treaty with the United States, finally signed at Paris in 1783. The new ministry made the peace by sacrificing most of Britain's commitments to its American supporters, particularly to the Loyalists and the Aboriginal peoples. While the peace negotiations continued, Loyalist refugees and soldiers began the process of resettlement within what remained to Great Britain in the New World, from Nova Scotia to Quebec to Florida to the Caribbean area. Ultimately perhaps just over half of the Loyalists would settle in what would become Canada. Cape Breton and the Island of St John received about 1,000 each. Perhaps 35,000 arrived initially in Nova Scotia (including over 5,000 blacks) and about 10,000 (including 3,000 Aboriginals) in Quebec. The resettlement cost the British millions of pounds in removal costs and eventual compensation. The loyal colonies of the American empire received a publicly supported injection of English-speaking colonists grounded in American culture, although not all newcomers necessarily fitted the specification. As recent studies of the Loyalist population have emphasized, relatively large numbers of the newcomers were Aboriginals, blacks, women, relatively recent arrivals to America from the British Isles and Germany, and German mercenaries.[3]

The combination of the Treaty of Paris and Loyalist resettlement had completely transformed British America. Instead of being marginal jurisdictions, the few provinces remaining to Britain took on a new importance. A first round of Imperial reorganization took place in 1784. Cape Breton was recognized as a separate jurisdiction (without an assembly), and both it and the Island of St John were placed under the authority of the Governor of Nova Scotia. Continual controversy between Loyalist newcomers and the government of Nova Scotia resulted in the creation of New Brunswick as a distinct and separate colony, one that the Loyalists could dominate and that was designed to serve as a model of what men and women of loyalty could produce; a number of prominent Loyalist leaders were awarded official positions in the administration. For Newfoundland, still not yet given official colonial status, 1784 was also a critical year. By agreement between the British government and the Vatican, James O'Donnell arrived as Prefect Apostolic, the first officially recognized Roman Catholic priest on the island.

---

[3] For detailed studies dealing with the composition of the Loyalists, see Janice Potter-MacKinnon, *While the Women Only Wept: Loyalist Refugee Women* (Montreal and Kingston, 1993); Neil MacKinnon, *This Unfriendly Soil: The Loyalist Experience in Nova Scotia, 1783–1791* (Montreal and Kingston, 1986); James St G. Walker, *The Black Loyalists: The Search for a Promised Land in Nova Scotia and Sierra Leone, 1783–1870* (Toronto, 1992); Hazel C. Mathews, *The Mark of Honour* (Toronto, 1965).

The British were prepared to permit their loyal colonies to take the place of the Americans in the old transatlantic commercial networks, if they could fill the American role, especially in the West Indies. As it turned out, surpluses for trade were slow to develop, and the British quickly learned that political independence did not affect the American willingness for commerce. The United States rapidly resumed its old place as Britain's most important New World trading partner. Anglo-American relations were fraught with tensions, however, some left over from the treaty of separation. Particularly uneasy was the situation along the western boundary between the United States and British America, where the aspirations of various Aboriginal peoples for autonomy further complicated matters.

The arrival of the Loyalists saw the reinforcement of existing liberal political and constitutional ideas in the remaining loyal British colonies. The newcomers were familiar with assemblies and their employment in constitutional battles with the office-holding factions in the various provinces. The process of resettlement itself provided grounds for political conflict, as factions of Loyalists fought against the entrenched interests of the pre-Loyalists as well as with one another. The flow of Americans did not end in the 1780s, but was constant until the War of 1812. The ready availability of cheap land in the Canadas, especially in Upper Canada, meant that American settlers moving west often moved there rather than to the states of the Ohio valley. In all colonies the main targets of opposition were established elite groups of office holders and their privileges, as well as the concept of a close connection between the Anglican Church and the government. The principal rhetoric employed was the standard 'country party' line developed in England and imported into the American colonies before the rebellion. 'Country' opposition feared centralization of power and sought to defend traditional liberties and rights against what were regarded as corrupt and self-serving official factions sheltering under the power of the colonial Governor, his council, and the Established Church. The Loyalists in Quebec joined the English-speaking merchants in demanding an elected assembly and more English law.

Two years after the creation of new governments, Guy Carleton, now Lord Dorchester, was given a commission as Governor-General over all of Britain's North American provinces as well as one as Governor of Quebec. Dorchester could exercise actual power in a province only when on its soil, but he was obviously intended to provide a new unity, especially in military matters, in what remained of Britain's American empire. His instructions suggested that many routine items of business in the several provinces could be conducted through him and without reference to the mother country.[4] That sense of unity and

---

[4] See the instructions to Carleton reprinted at Adam Shortt and Arthur G. Doughty, (eds), *Documents Relating to the Constitutional History of Canada, 1759–1791* (2nd edn, Ottawa, 1918), Part II, pp. 813–37.

autonomy was subsequently lost when Britain decided by the Constitutional Act of 1791 to divide Quebec into Upper and Lower Canada, and to give each an Assembly. This parliamentary legislation was intended to resolve the demands of the Loyalists in the western part of Quebec for their own government as well as to create a jurisdiction in which the *Canadiens* could be granted an Assembly.[5] The creation of elected Assemblies in the Canadas was not intended, any more than in the Maritimes, to produce either democracy or autonomy from Great Britain. Representative government was to provide some measure of local control over government. In the short run, it certainly produced Imperial decentralization. Athough the franchise everywhere was restricted principally to adult male property holders, most adult males possessed enough property to vote. While women were not formally excluded from voting until the 1830s and 1840s, few did so. It was also intended that the executive government would be controlled by colonial Governors, who were appointed by and were responsible to the London authorities. Both Canadas were given appointed Legislative Councils, and in most colonies certain revenues were set aside for the Crown through the establishment of Crown and Clergy Reserves. The customs revenues collected at Quebec formed the major source of income for the governments of both Canadas until, after a lengthy dispute, they were placed under the control of the Assemblies in 1831. The Clergy Reserves also became a bone of political contention, particularly in Upper Canada, where one-seventh of the land was set aside as reserves. The other Protestant denominations challenged the preference given to the Church of England, and the failure by the Church of England to develop the reserved lands interfered with settlement.

Our understanding of the formal structure of the early post-revolutionary Imperial system has not changed appreciably since Helen Taft Manning published her *British Colonial Government after the American Revolution, 1782–1820* (New Haven, 1933) almost three-quarters of a century ago. Before 1820, colonial administrations were dominated by an appointed elite, consisting of a small number of officials, usually chosen by the Governor although sometimes appointed by the British government (after 1801 the Colonial Office), who ran the province and who served as the Governor's executive council. Those officials received substantial annual salaries and often had access to extensive fees. Assemblies were regularly elected, but had limited control over either financial matters or the government itself. Occasionally a legislator would temporarily emerge to oppose the Governor or government, but there was initially no concerted opposition. Critics like James Glenie in New Brunswick, William Cottnam Tonge in Nova Scotia, and Robert Thorpe in Upper Canada were outspoken political gadflies with little support among their colleagues. By 1810, however, nascent political parties were emerging in several provinces, and the Assemblies were beginning to recognize that if they could acquire control over

[5] Hilda Neatby, *Quebec: The Revolutionary Age, 1760–1791* (Toronto, 1966), pp. 249–63.

budgets and finances, they could aspire to run the governments themselves.[6] One major colonial development of these years not considered by Manning was the transfer to and codification of English law and legal institutions in most of the colonies of British America; only Lower Canada retained parts of its French legal heritage.[7]

There were some obvious points of friction among Britain, its North American provinces (the label 'British North America' had no official standing and was not often employed until well into the nineteenth century), and the newly independent United States. One was in the territory west of the Appalachians and south of the Great Lakes, which the British had ceded to the Americans in 1783 as part of the price of a quick peace, without a second thought for treaty and other commitments to the Aboriginal inhabitants of the region. A new understanding of the dynamics of this territory has been one of the principal developments of scholarship on this period in both Canada and the United States over the past quarter-century.[8] The primary result of the new work has been to underline the extent to which the Aboriginal peoples had their own agendas, including a quest for internal unity to make possible a concerted defence against American expansionism and racism. The British authorities may have facilitated the local inhabitants for their own reasons, but the American War Hawks (and subsequent American historians) were quite wrong in placing the responsibility for trouble in this region squarely on the shoulders of Great Britain. At the same time, it is quite true that the British were prepared to support the creation of a confederate state proposed after 1805 by the Shawnee leaders Tenskwatawa ('The Prophet', so-called because of his visions about native unity) and his brother Tecumseh. Another area of friction between Britain and the United States was on the high seas, where the British both blockaded European seaports after 1806 and continually violated what the United States regarded as its rights as a neutral nation. It would be this issue that would ultimately lead to war.

The subsequent War of 1812 has developed a reputation as the 'Neglected War', and this may well be the case in terms of popular consciousness in the United States. The war has never been ignored or forgotten in Canada, however, and it has certainly never been neglected by historians and academics in either nation. The War of 1812 also has the reputation of being the war that nobody won, as well as being the war for which both sides (especially the United States

---

[6] Virtually the only general analysis of Canadian politics in this period is provided by Gordon Stewart in his *The Origins of Canadian Politics: A Comparative Approach* (Vancouver, 1986), although John Garner's *The Franchise and Politics in British North America, 1755–1867* (Toronto, 1969) is much more important than its title might suggest.

[7] See Chap. 14 in this volume.

[8] Robert Allen, *His Majesty's Indian Allies: British Indian Policy in the Defence of Canada, 1774–1815* (Toronto, 1992); Colin G. Calloway, *Crown and Calumet: British–Indian Relations, 1783–1815* (Norman, Okla, 1987); Gregory Evans Dowd, *A Spirited Resistance: The North American Indian Struggle for Unity, 1745–1815* (Baltimore, 1992); Richard White, *The Middle Ground: Indians, Empires, and Republics in the Great Lakes Region, 1650–1815* (New York, 1991).

and Canada) claim victory. Indeed, this war involved an extremely intricate set of protagonists within protagonists. The British fought it as a sideshow to the main event, which was the European war with Napoleon. The Americans thought they were confronting British might, when in truth they were fighting mainly the British colonies in Canada, reinforced by relatively small numbers of British regular troops and naval vessels. The First Nations, with no state of their own, fought chiefly on the British side.

The major military front on land occurred in the Canadas, invaded by a series of badly led American armies between 1812 and 1814. The Americans expected their former compatriots living north of the border to support them, and just enough did so to vindicate those who had warned against permitting American settlement.[9] The Canadian authorities adopted repressive measures against American collaborators, but generally did a good job of avoiding unnecessary witch-hunts during the period of emergency.[10] The loyalty question would not become an open political issue until after the war was over when it would emerge as the 'Alien Question'. American armies were thrust back through the major entry points: the Detroit–Windsor corridor, the Niagara peninsula, and Lake Champlain. Well-led British regulars were assisted by militiamen from both the Canadas and by a number of Aboriginal allies. The Upper Canadians came out of the war convinced that their militia had won the war virtually single-handed. This 'militia myth' contributed to the emergence of an Upper Canadian identity through the middle years of the nineteenth century.[11] Lower Canada provided more support for the British cause, including soldiers, than anyone had expected. Nevertheless, the British regulars did the bulk of the fighting. A minor sideshow occurred in the west in 1812, when *Canadien* voyageurs captured and held Fort Michilimackinac on western Lake Huron.

The naval war was fought on several fronts. The first and best-known front was on the Great Lakes, especially Lake Ontario, where both sides built substantial navies from scratch and fought to a standstill from 1812 to 1814.[12] The Atlantic Ocean front consisted of a handful of legendary set battles between individual American and British naval vessels—which the Americans typically won—and a considerable quantity of prize taking, both by the British navy and by privateers on both sides. The British probably won the war of the prizes. Atlantic Canada's privateers were, the latest study insists, 'well capitalized, law-abiding,

[9] George Sheppard, *Plunder, Profit, and Paroles: A Social History of the War of 1812 in Upper Canada,* (Montreal and Kingston, 1994).

[10] Paul Romney and Barry Wright, 'State Trials and Security Proceedings in Upper Canada during the War of 1812', in F. M. Greenwood and Barry Wright, eds., *Canadian State Trials: Law, Politics & Security Measures, 1608–1837* (Toronto, 1996).

[11] David Mills, *The Idea of Loyalty in Upper Canada, 1784–1850* (Montreal and Kingston, 1988).

[12] Robert Malcolmson, *Lords of the Lake: The Naval War on Lake Ontario, 1812–1814* (Toronto, 1998).

business-like, generally well-behaved, and moderately successful'.[13] They made a substantial economic contribution to their communities, and helped keep the economies of Nova Scotia and New Brunswick humming during the conflict.

Because the *status quo ante bellum* was so quickly restored in 1814, the temptation is to regard the War of 1812 as one without much impact. Nothing could be further from the truth, especially from the British–American standpoint. One area clearly affected was the domestic politics of Upper Canada. To earlier notions of loyalty to the British Crown of the revolutionary war period was added a fresh ideological stream born of the War of 1812. The Tory leadership of Upper Canada became persuaded that the province had been in great danger, as much from the political machinations of American residents as from the external activities of American soldiers. The Tories came out of the war convinced of the necessity of the simultaneous suppression of American-style political opposition and the maintenance of British cultural hegemony, by force if necessary. This belief would control Upper Canadian Toryism for several generations.[14] The influence of American culture was held at bay, or even reduced. The reform opposition in Upper Canada would by the 1830s develop its own version of loyalty, stressing the need for an emphasis on the British rights of the people to restore a constitutional balance to the province.

The War of 1812 also had substantial implications for the Aboriginal peoples, particularly those living in the old 'Middle Ground' of the Great Lakes. A treaty article called for a return to the Aboriginal peoples of 'possessions, right and privileges' that they enjoyed in 1811, but this clause was never implemented by the American government. Instead, many of the Aboriginal peoples reluctantly came to terms with the Americans, while others retreated further west to continue a doomed resistance to the encroachment of settlement.

In the short run, the war resolved a number of potentially contentious issues and prepared the way for what could have been a new era of Anglo-American cooperation. The two nations in the Rush–Bagot Agreement of 1817 agreed to limit the size and number of naval armaments on the Great Lakes, an understanding which, from the British perspective, was motivated entirely by the need for economy. A similar sense of saving money led Britain in 1818 to negotiate with the Americans a compromise understanding about the western boundary as far as the Rocky Mountains. British America was the chief beneficiary of these understandings. But these pacific moves did not resolve British suspicions of the United States. The drive for economy was broken as early as 1819, when

---

[13] Faye Margaret Kert, *Prize and Prejudice: Privateering and Naval Prize in Atlantic Canada in the War of 1812* (St John's, 1997), p. 155.

[14] Mills, *The Idea of Loyalty in Upper Canada*; S. F. Wise, 'The Origins of Anti-Americanism in Canada', *Fourth Seminar on Canadian–American Relations at Assumption University of Windsor* (Windsor, 1962); Paul Romney, 'Re-inventing Upper Canada: American Immigrants, Upper Canadian History, English Law, and the Alien Question', in Roger Hall et al., (eds), *Patterns of the Past: Interpreting Ontario's History* (Toronto, 1988).

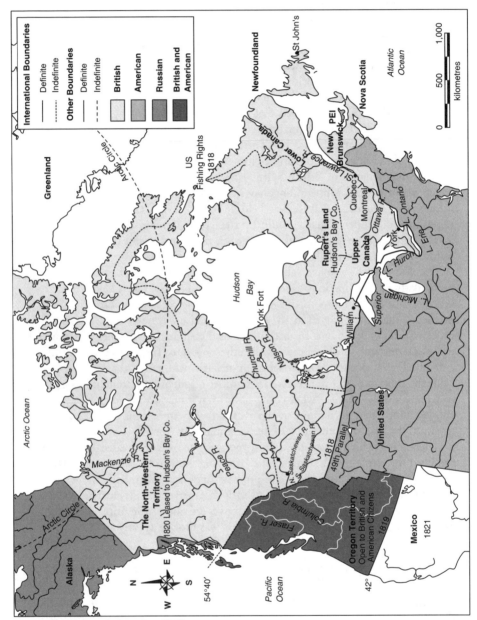

Map 2. British North America, 1825

the Duke of Wellington supported the insistence of the new Governor-General of British America, the Duke of Richmond, that defending the colonies was still necessary. The decision was made that year to increase the number of soldiers garrisoned in British America to 5,000 regulars and to improve land fortifications and military communications.[15] The army itself in that year began a canal between Lake Ontario and Ottawa. The Rideau Canal was conceived purely in terms of military communication and was not deep enough for most commercial vessels. Nevertheless, the British invested more than £1 million sterling in its construction, and between 1825 and 1843 dispersed another £1.5 million on fortifications and communication projects.[16] Much of this money was used to hire construction workers and buy local building materials. After 1828 the British naval presence was also beefed up. Military garrisons—there were sixteen fortified posts in British America in 1840—were important parts of their local communities.[17] They not only brought money into the local economy, but made significant contributions to the cultural and social life of the community. Some of these contributions, such as the introduction of British sports like ice hockey, curling, and cricket, were positive. Others, such as the drinking establishments and prostitution that grew up around a military post, were less so.

The British government's direct financial expenditure in British America between 1783 and 1860 is difficult to calculate precisely but can be conservatively estimated as in excess of £7–8 million sterling. The British government paid pensions to military officers from the wars against the French onwards, for example, and those pensions could be collected by their widows until their deaths; it also provided over £1 million in compensation for Loyalists; and it paid the civil list of several colonies. In addition, before the duties on colonial wheat were abolished by the British Parliament in 1846 and on colonial timber in 1849, the British Isles provided a preferential market for colonial raw materials, especially timber and grain. Most British political economists opposed such mercantilism, and its maintenance had little to do with the colonial situation and much to do with politics at home. Nevertheless, the British authorities generally saw British America as an underdeveloped responsibility—the most common metaphor was one of mother and child—that required maternal nursing. The other side of economic expenditure, of course, was a certain amount of deliberate political dependency that continued until the late 1830s.

The administrative decentralization of British America has to some considerable extent been replicated in its historiography, which tends to focus at the

[15] Kenneth Bourne, *Britain and the Balance of Power in North America, 1815–1908* (Berkeley and Los Angeles, 1967).

[16] George Raudzens, *The British Ordnance Department and Canada's Canals, 1815–1855* (Waterloo, 1979).

[17] Elinor Kyte Senior, *British Regulars in Montreal: An Imperial Garrison, 1832–1854* (Montreal, 1981).

provincial level. As a result the structural similarities of political conflict through-out the colonies have tended to be downplayed in favour of their provincial exceptionalisms and the assumption that all colonies were like Upper Canada. But after 1820 political critics emerged in every colony to challenge the official factions. Every colony had its own negative label for the faction that had long dom-inated its government. In Upper Canada they were called 'the Family Compact', in Lower Canada the 'Chateau Clique', in Nova Scotia 'the System', in Prince Edward Island 'the Cabal'. These factions were not completely unified either in make-up or in policy. They frequently added new members from within their colony, and tended to divide over such issues as development and commercial pol-icy, as well as over the extent to which political support should be extended to the Governor who headed the colonial administration. Not all members of the official factions in the English-speaking colonies were members of the Church of England or supported it blindly. Not all members of the government in Lower Canada were of British origin. The new generation of critics (they liked to call themselves reformers) were more energetic than their predecessors, and were often more willing to employ popular opinion in their opposition. More ideological similar-ities existed across the colonies than might have been imagined. Like the official factions, reform was not monolithic. It broke into several main camps with much overlap among them. One camp of reformers represented the radicals; the other consisted of various factions with more moderate voices, which in Upper Canada included former Americans. In Upper Canada, the government had attempted after the War of 1812 to limit the access of Americans to British citizenship. This so-called 'Alien Question' played into other issues. Many of the members of the evangelical sects so critical of the Church of England were former Americans, and they would play a prominent role in the rebellions of 1837 and 1838.

The three most visible radical reformers were William Lyon Mackenzie of Upper Canada, Louis-Joseph Papineau of Lower Canada, and William Cooper of Prince Edward Island; Joseph Howe of Nova Scotia was sometimes but not consistently a radical. Although the first three came from very different social origins, they were all outspoken agrarians who idealized the 'independent cultivator of the soil' and condemned the commercial and merchant classes for being in league with (or identical to) the official faction. All three had an abiding belief in equality of conditions and a hostility to expensive public improvements by the state. Much of their ideology, which matured only after 1830, came from two distinct sources. One was British liberalism, with its emphasis on free trade and the mechanism of the marketplace. The other was Jacksonian democracy, with its 'equal agrarianism' and its belief in the natural wisdom of the people, a natural aristocracy among mankind, and the desirability of rotation in office to allow everyone a chance to govern.[18] According to Louis-Joseph Papineau, the aristocratic nature of the existing political constitution was inconsistent with the

[18] John William Ward, *Andrew Jackson: Symbol for an Age* (New York, 1966).

democratic nature of the social constitution in the Canadas. Papineau sometimes fitted quite uneasily with such rhetoric, since he was a seigneur who did not support the abolition of the seigneurial system, but he was like the democratic American slaveholder in being able to hold seemingly inconsistent positions (one political, the other socio-economic) simultaneously. In many ways the radical reformers got most of the publicity, but were not always very successful in dealing with the colonial official factions, in convincing the electorate to support them, or in persuading the British government to sympathize with their demands. One of the reasons for violence in 1837 was because the radicals were losing ground to more moderate voices and to successful political management by the governors, who reflected a new Imperial policy of conciliation after 1830.

While the conflict between the official factions and the reformers as played out in the various legislatures was an important part of the political dynamic, over the past half-century Canadian historians have increasingly come to realize not only the complexities of the conflict but that it was only a part of the political story. The legislative struggle occurred simultaneously on several levels, and changed over time. On one level the early dynamic between official factions and critics before 1830 sometimes suggested the 'court–country' confrontation of the mother country of an earlier period. The official factions tended to form around the Governor at the capital city, while the opposition tended to be based in the outlying districts and was reflected in the Assemblies as the only place where the countryside could find any political leverage. In the 1830s the struggle began more to suggest a political contest between nascent political parties roughly divided between 'conservatives' and 'liberals'. The ideological issues dividing these groups were many, including development strategies and attitudes toward the use of the law and the state to deal with dissent.

At the same time, the official factions did not consist solely of office holders resistant to any and all change. They co-opted political opposition wherever possible, remaking the Legislative Councils in the process, and usually had some considerable interest in public improvements (canals, banks, roads) that would be beneficial to the commercial classes of the colony. Under pressure from the Colonial Office, they surrendered the revenues in dispute between the Assemblies and themselves, particularly those from the lease and sale of Crown lands, and they limited the special treatment shown to the Church of England. It was the sensitivity of the official factions, not always at the provincial level, to public criticism that led them frequently to employ the British Tory concept of 'seditious libel' against those who opposed them. Joseph Howe won a famous victory against charges of seditious libel by the magistrates of Halifax in 1835 by persuading a jury that he had spoken nothing but the truth, but the victory was personal rather than precedent making.[19] At the same time, the majority

---

[19] F. Murray Greenwood and Barry Wright, eds., *Canadian State Trials: Law, Politics and Security Measures, 1608–1837* (Toronto, 1996), especially the article on Joseph Howe's trial.

of reformers extolled the glories of the English constitution and its supposed entrenchment of British rights and liberties. Moderate reformers like Robert Baldwin in Upper Canada or Joseph Howe in Nova Scotia did not wish to eliminate the Imperial connection; instead they wanted to employ it to obtain a colonial constitution that more closely resembled that of the mother country; the principal complaint of moderates was that the rights of Englishmen had not been fully extended to North America.

Legislative and even electoral politics, restricted as these usually were to adult males of European ancestry, were only the tip of the political iceberg. The development of the common law was also an important if unheralded part of the political process. Since the courts and the justice system could often be weapons in the hands of the elite, the judicial system was an important component of the body politic. Rioting and public violence were usually not random outbursts, but had some form and objective.[20] Curiously enough, much of the violence was orchestrated by the anti-reform forces. Perhaps the best-known example was the 1826 'Types Riot' in which a mob destroyed the printing office of William Lyon Mackenzie's *Colonial Advocate*.[21] Members of the Orange Order were frequently employed at election time to cause trouble to the reformers. The farmers in the countryside and the disenfranchised had their own agendas and acted their own parts in the political process. Even the disenfranchised often found their own way to participate in politics. One was through popular religion, typically of the evangelical variety.[22] The forces that Deacon (later Bishop) John Strachan battled in his defence of the Anglican establishment in Upper Canada did not always manifest themselves in elections. Many dissenters, religious and otherwise, found some voice through the process of petitioning, which was in Upper Canada in the 1830s designed more to influence the British government than the local authorities.[23] The most important expression of popular political sentiment was, of course, in various sorts of resistance to authority. In the 1790s the spill-over of the French Revolution had led to public rioting in Lower Canada on several occasions.[24] After 1800 sporadic outbreaks of rioting occurred, none of them extensive; the people did not often challenge the authorities. When they did challenge the system, British Americans had a number of models upon

[20] Rusty Bitterman, 'Women and the Escheat Movement: The Politics of Everyday Life on Prince Edward Island', in Janet Guildford and Suzanne Morton, eds., *Separate Spheres: Women's Worlds in the 19th-Century Maritimes* (Fredericton, 1994).

[21] George Romney, 'Upper Canada in the 1820s', in Greenwood and Wright, (eds), *State Trials*, pp. 505–21.

[22] See, for example, Nancy Christie, '"In Times of Democratic Rage and Delusion": Popular Religion and the Challenge to the Established Order, 1760–1815', in G. A. Rawlyk, (ed.), *The Canadian Protestant Experience 1760 to 1990* (Burlington, 1990).

[23] Carol Wilton, *Popular Politics and Political Culture in Upper Canada, 1800–1850* (Montreal and Kingston, 2000).

[24] F. Murray Greenwood, *Legacies of Fear: Law and Politics in Quebec in the Era of the French Revolution* (Toronto, 1993).

which they could draw, including the American and French Revolutions, the Constitutional movement in Britain at the end of the eighteenth century, the Irish Nationalists, Captain Swing, and Chartism.

In 1837 both Upper and Lower Canada experienced outbursts of public violence and resistance to authority exceeding anything that had gone before in British America. The course of events suggested that there were at least two different sorts of resistances at work, combining into rebellion, especially in Lower Canada. One resistance was middle class in origin and based in the capital cities. It was headed by the radical leaders of the reformist political parties in the Assemblies, men like William Lyon Mackenzie and Louis-Joseph Papineau, and employed the contemporary rhetoric of the assembly confrontation with the governors' parties. This was the classic resistance so much studied by Canadian historians before the 1960s. The other was popular in origin and based in the rural areas. It was more interested in economic grievances, class issues, and land reform, particularly of the seigneurial system.[25] The two resistances came more or less together in 1837, first in Lower Canada and then in Upper Canada. That they did not more closely cooperate was partly because politics in Lower Canada was by 1837 increasingly conducted along ethnic lines. The *Patriote* party had lost most of its British supporters, and one of its goals was a government—if not a state—with a *Canadien* majority.

The radical political reformers led the way, but quickly left the country when the government employed the military and were replaced by armed farmers with their own set of grievances. The Assembly leaders were probably not really revolutionaries but merely frustrated liberals in a hurry. The extent of popular involvement in the 1837 uprisings is unclear, but much of it was clearly motivated by a form of *Canadien* nationalism. It was in any case quickly and easily suppressed by the authorities. The 1838 resistance was on one level—especially in Lower Canada—more grass roots in origin, but in both provinces involved large numbers of invaders from the United States, not all of them exiles from the Canadas. The growing fear of war with the United States over these border incursions permitted by the American government led to a substantial increase in British military strength in North America at the end of the 1830s. By early 1840 there were nearly 11,500 British regulars in Canada, and the size of the naval establishment had been nearly doubled. The 1838 uprising was also easily but even more brutally put down. In both years, the governments of the Canadas let the reform leaders get away—usually to the United States—and concentrated

---

[25] Allan Greer, *The Patriots and the People: The Rebellion of 1837 in Rural Lower Canada* (Toronto, 1993); Donald Salée, 'Revolutionary Political Thought, the Persistence of the Old Order, and the Problem of Power in an Ancien Régime Colonial Society: Ideological Perspectives of Lower Canada, 1827–1828', *British Journal of Canadian Studies*, 3 (1988); Colin Read, *The Rising in Western Upper Canada, 1837–1838: The Duncombe Revolt and After* (Toronto, 1982); Colin Duquemin, *Niagara Rebels: The Niagara Frontier in the Upper Canadian Rebellion, 1837–1838* (St Catherines, 2001).

on prosecuting the rank-and-file ordinary people who had become caught up in the rebellions. Although, in the classic account of the political development of Canada, the rebellions led to parliamentary democracy, recent studies have emphasized that, at least in the short run, what they first produced were criminal trials for treason and other offences against the state, many conducted at the expense of the British tradition of justice.[26] In Upper Canada, rebels were permitted by law to petition for pardons, thus implicitly acknowledging their guilt. Most, although not all, petitioners were released.

The rebellion trials suggest how widespread was the resistance, if not the numbers involved or the extent of the commitment of the rebels. In Upper Canada trials occurred at Toronto, Hamilton, and London in response to the 1837 troubles, and at Niagara and Kingston after the 1838 incidents. Almost 400 individuals were put on trial in Upper Canada, most of them for high treason. Over 300 were convicted, and twenty were eventually executed. In Lower Canada those arrested in 1837 were dealt with by Lord Durham without trial. In response to the 1838 uprisings, 753 were arrested, nearly 200 were tried by general court martial in Montreal, 99 were sentenced to death, and twelve were eventually executed. Most of those convicted in both provinces were not executed, but were instead transported to Australia, although a few were banished and some were released on bail. One of the effects of the legal prosecutions was to reduce further American influence in the Canadas.

Early in 1838 Lord Durham was appointed Governor-General of British America with a commission to investigate the causes of the crisis in the Canadas. Durham has become a somewhat ambiguous figure in Canadian historiography. For more than a century one of the heroes of the British Empire in Canada, he was credited with the ideas of both responsible government and federalism through the publication of his famous 1839 Report to the British Parliament.[27] More recent studies have emphasized other factors, such as the importance of the political conflicts of the 1840s, in achieving responsible government, and the shift in Imperial attitudes (and British public opinion) towards the settlement colonies in the late 1830s, while attempting to rehabilitate him from charges of intellectual muddleheadedness.[28] Durham was dispatched to British America partly to get him out of the way of the government headed by Viscount Melbourne, although the ministry wanted a reformer of impeccable credentials to do the job. In Canada, Durham resolved the problem of Lower Canada's political prisoners by

[26] F. Murray Greenwood and Barry Wright, (eds), *Rebellion and Invasion in the Canadas, 1837–1839: Canadian State Trials,* vol. II (Toronto, 2002).

[27] Sir Charles P. Lucas, (ed.), *Lord Durham's Report on the Affairs of British North America*, 3 vols. (Oxford, 1912).

[28] Phillip A. Buckner, *The Transition to Responsible Government: British Policy in British North America, 1815–1850* (Westport, Conn., 1985); Peter Burroughs, (ed.), *British Attitudes towards Canada, 1822–1849* (Scarborough, 1971); Janet Ajzenstat, *The Political Thought of Lord Durham* (Montreal and Kingston, 1988).

exiling a number to Bermuda without trial, prohibiting others who had escaped to the United States from returning, and amnestying almost everybody else. This decision was popular if illegal. When Durham's methods, which ignored the rule of law being emphasized by both colonial and British governments, were repudiated by the ministry, Durham announced his resignation in October.[29] He was back in London on 7 December 1838, submitting his famous Report on 31 January 1839. A chronic sufferer from tuberculosis, he died a year later.

The Report made two major recommendations. The first was that the internal government of the colonies be placed 'in the hands of the colonists themselves'. This recommendation certainly bought into the major ideas of the moderate reformers, and had been pressed upon Durham by Robert and William Warren Baldwin in meetings in Upper Canada in 1838. Whether Durham deserves full credit for the constitutional arrangements of parliamentary democracy that ultimately emerged in British America is another matter. He mistakenly believed that the appointed Governors could remain political leaders in the legislatures by the judicious use of patronage and brokerism, as they had in the 1830s. The chief issue of the politics of the 1840s was the question of whether the party that held a majority in the Assembly would be allowed to control the composition of the government and the distribution of patronage. It was the insistence of the tandem of Robert Baldwin and Louis-Hippolyte La Fontaine on the need for an independent executive based solely on the Assembly that finally won the day.

The final collapse of mercantilism in Great Britain in the same time period certainly helped reorient the traditional relationship between mother country and colonies in North America. While the repeal caused a short-term economic panic in British America, producers and merchants alike soon adjusted to the changing conditions. Perhaps more important to British America than the loss of a protected market was the British decision to seek entente with the United States. In 1842 the Webster–Ashburton Treaty settled the long-standing dispute over the border between Maine and New Brunswick. In 1846 another unsettled border on the Pacific coast was resolved in the Oregon Boundary Treaty, which responded to American sabre rattling by giving the Americans most of what they wanted: a continuation of the border on the continent between British and American territory across the Rocky Mountains at the 49th parallel, although the British got the southern tip of Vancouver Island. Britain had decided that it did not wish to face increased military expenditures to defend British America.

In 1848, Governor-General Lord Elgin stepped aside from party politics when he accepted a party government headed by Louis-Hippolyte La Fontaine and Robert Baldwin, and he sealed his subordinate position in April 1849 when he signed the Rebellion Losses Act, which indemnified those Lower Canadians who had suffered losses in the recent upheavals. By this time, the

---

[29] Jean-Marie Fecteau, ' "This Ultimate Resource": Martial Law and State Repression in Lower Canada, 1837–8', in Greenwood and Wright, (eds), *Canadian State Trials*, vol. II, pp. 207–48.

refomers had already won the battle in Nova Scotia for a system of party government, and the other provinces soon followed. Prince Edward Island was granted responsible government in 1851; New Brunswick achieved it in 1854. After a period with a unicameral legislature composed of elected and appointed members, introduced because the Colonial Office thought Newfoundland both different and less mature politically than other colonies, Newfoundland finally achieved responsible government in 1855. Responsible government was not totally autonomous government. The degree of self-government in each colony was negotiated between the imperial and colonial authorities. The United Province of Canada gained control over tariff policy only in 1858–9 when it introduced a partially protective tariff over the appeals of British manufacturers to the Imperial government. In Prince Edward Island the Imperial government refused to allow the Assembly to resolve the Land Question through compulsory purchase of land from the private proprietors, and in Newfoundland the Imperial government reserved the French Shore as its responsibility well into the twentieth century. Moreover, the British government still controlled military defence and relationships with foreign states, and was still in full Imperial control of the west—Vancouver Island, British Columbia, Red River, and the Hudson's Bay Company territories. Control over Aboriginal policy was transferred to the colonies only in 1860. Responsible government was not automatically given to new colonies. When Vancouver Island and British Columbia were merged in 1866, the British denied the new province a totally elected assembly and instituted a partly elected, partly appointed Legislative Council. Responsible government became a demand of the Confederation movement on the west coast. The Red River Settlement never had an elected assembly, although the local movement resisting Canada in 1869–70 led by Louis Riel demanded one as its 'right'.

The other leading recommendation made by Durham was more immediately and directly translated into policy. It was also far more contentious. In the most notorious passage of his Report, Durham had written: 'I had expected to find a contest between a government and a people. I found two nations warring in the bosom of a single state: I found a struggle not of principles, but of races.'[30] Durham may have overstated the case, but his sense of ethnic struggle was not entirely misguided. His solution was to put the two groups under a single government and to allow assimilation to the dominant culture (which he assumed to be the British one) to take effect. 'I entertain no doubts as to the national character which must be given to Lower Canada', he wrote, 'it must be that of the British Empire; that of the majority of the population of British America; that of the great race which must, in the lapse of no long period of time, be predominant over the whole North American Continent.'[31] The insistence on assimilation was in the context of the time a classic expression of liberalism, maintaining as it did that the French Canadians must be liberated

[30] Lucas, *Lord Durham's Report*, vol. II, p. 16.   [31] Ibid., p. 146.

from their parochialism and narrow traditionalism and allowed to flourish in the mainstream of modern life.[32] Whether the French Canadians could be easily assimilated was another matter. In any event, the result was the union of the Canadas by Act of Parliament in July 1840, to take effect in 1841. This union was a legislative union (as had been the union of England and Scotland in 1707) but the constitutional situation of the United Province of Canada remained complicated and even controversial. Members of the legislature were still disagreeing about it in the debates over Confederation in 1865. Certain aspects of administration, including law, education, and language, continued to operate separately in the two unofficial sections of Canada (now called Canada East and Canada West). The union did produce assimilative pressures but it also allowed French-Canadian nationalism and the Catholic Church to flourish.[33] How popular the union was in French Canada is another matter. Certainly in 1865 the need to allow French Canada its own separate province was argued quite strenuously within Canada East.

The union of the Canadas and the development of responsible government facilitated the development and elaboration of a different kind of state. Its growth was not particularly associated with any of the great political-philosophical 'isms' of the nineteenth century, including either 'imperialism' or 'anti-imperialism', but because this development occurred mainly outside traditional Imperial structures it could help reinforce centrifugal trends away from the Empire in the various provinces of British America. Whether it actually did so is another matter. This new entity gradually took over new functions, created new sorts of administrative structures (including a new professional bureaucracy to replace the colonial officials who had previously kept the system functioning), and even acquired some new coercive capabilities. The earlier concentration of Canadian historians upon the achievement of responsible government and political autonomy from Britain has helped disguise the importance of this new development, which was to some extent a logical result of the introduction into the United Province of Canada and later elsewhere of the principle that money bills could only be introduced by the government but was also a result of a new mood in British America. Similar tendencies occurred in every colony in British America, but nowhere on the American continent was the pattern so clear as in Canada.

Part of what was happening was the emergence of a new thinking, in both Europe and America, to replace the older liberalism of the first part of the nineteenth century. The new climate of opinion was in part humanitarian, as people everywhere sought to deal with the increasingly obvious deleterious effects of economic change, industrialism, and urbanization, especially for the poor. To some extent the new ideas reflected the ways in which the middle classes had

---

[32] Ajzenstat, *The Political Thought of Lord Durham.*
[33] Jacques Monet, *The Last Cannon Shot: A Study of French-Canadian Nationalism, 1837–50* (Toronto, 1969).

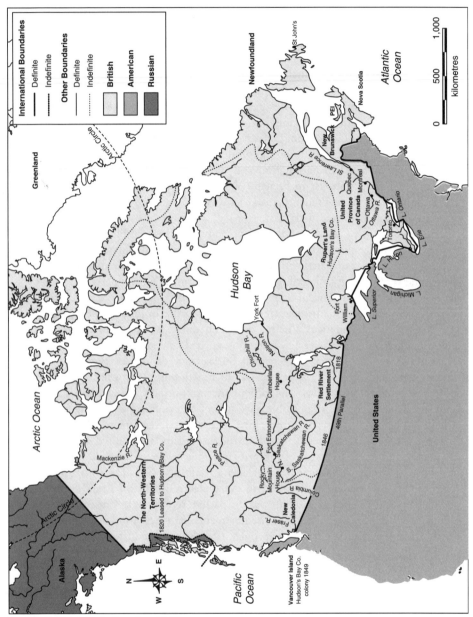

Map 3. British North America, 1849

been admitted to—or had seized—power. It was also much more rigorously interventionist and regulatory than liberalism had ever been, frequently motivated by fear for the consequences should the poor rise up. In British America, the propertied classes had a recent illustration of what could go wrong in the rebellions of 1837–8. Whether the creation of the administrative state was a deliberately coordinated and totally conscious action, fully supported by rhetoric, is disputable. Whether it deliberately espoused 'social control', coercive interventions by dominant classes to continue power, is equally disputable. Canadian historians have not been much attracted by theory building. What could not be doubted, however, was that state activity greatly increased everywhere after 1840.

Signs of the new administrative state were to be found in all sectors of Canadian life, often in imitation of British developments. Until the late 1830s, law enforcement was in the hands of local magistrates and constables, backed by the British military. The rebellions of 1837–8 in Lower Canada encouraged the creation of a mounted police force in that province. In 1839 the Rural Police of Lower Canada was established, based upon the Irish Constabulary, to deal with the countryside. Gradually the model of Sir Robert Peel's London Metropolitan Police (the 'bobbies' or the 'peelers') was introduced into various urban centres across British America. By the 1850s policing had become less a matter of suppressing rebellion and more one of managing the troublesome elements of society through positive action that was intended to be reformist in nature.[34] Another area of state growth occurred in the increase of public provisions made for orphans, the poor, the criminal, and the mentally disturbed. Large public buildings—typically huge piles of grey stone with few windows—were now constructed to house these unfortunates and isolate them from the outside world.[35] Asylums and prisons developed together. Both sought to give the state complete control over those housed within them. They represented an acceptance of the extension of public responsibility for the unfortunate, but also an extension of new long-term coercive powers by the state. The Canadian government spent most of its scientific budget on the Geological Survey of Canada, founded in 1842 to uncover the great mineral wealth of the province.[36]

In many respects, changes in educational policy and practice both exemplified and facilitated the administrative growth that occurred not only in Canada, but in all the provinces of British America. An elementary general education came increasingly to be viewed as the best way of preparing people for useful

[34] Allan Greer, 'The Birth of the Police in Canada', in Allan Greer and Ian Radforth, (eds), *Colonial Leviathan: State Formation in Mid-Nineteenth-Century Canada* (Toronto, 1992), pp. 17–49.

[35] Revealing examples of the construction similarities of asylums and prisons may be found in *Memorandum of the Board of Inspectors of Asylums and Prisons &c &c* (Quebec, 1860).

[36] Morris Zaslow, *Reading the Rocks: The Story of the Geological Survey of Canada, 1842–1972* (Ottawa, 1975).

lives, but before 1840 public education everywhere was limited and sporadic. The transformation occurred first in Canada West in the 1840s with the Irish educational system serving as an important model. The School Act of 1843 introduced an arrangement of state grants supervised by local school inspectors responsible to a central education office. Legislation drafted by Egerton Ryerson became a new School Act in 1846. It not only improved the inspection arrangement but created the first Normal Schools to train teachers. The principle of free public elementary education for all children was gradually extended across British America, developing independently in the Maritime colonies in the 1850s and in conscious imitation of Canada in British Columbia in the 1860s. These schools taught a version of historical development that stressed British America as an extension of Britain and saw British American culture (such as literature) as a branch of British accomplishment. They were funded by general local property assessments, with school inspections to ensure local compliance to central authority. The inspection system was extended into other areas, helping to improve state authority.[37]

As the state grew stronger and more efficient, the government of the United Province of Canada began to think in terms of acquiring and governing the vast areas to the west managed by the Hudson's Bay Company. In retrospect, what is probably most surprising about what happened to the region of North America stretching from north of Georgian Bay to the Pacific Slope is how rapidly and suddenly it became integrated into British America. By the time of the American Rebellion, fur traders operating out of Quebec had moved overland into the Hudson Bay drainage basin, and were competing with the trading posts of the Hudson's Bay Company for the best furs. By 1800 a series of amalgamations among the Quebec traders had produced a dominant fur-trading company—the North West Company—which controlled the bulk of the western trade.[38] The Hudson's Bay Company had attempted to fight back under the new ownership of the family of Thomas Douglas, Fifth Earl of Selkirk, who in 1811 received a grant of 116,000 square miles from the HBC and began to plan a settlement at the junction of the Red and Assiniboine rivers. Selkirk was an imperialist in both thought and deed. He was the first political economist to argue seriously for the advantages of British emigration to British America, and his strategies in the west were always influenced by the need to keep the region British. Curiously enough, the British government rejected organized Imperial expansion into the west, at the time of Selkirk or later. Selkirk's settlement, never recognized by the Colonial Office, became caught in the conflict between the two fur-trading companies. The result was considerable violence, a series of bitterly fought law cases, and in 1821 the merger of the two companies—with British approval—into a new

---

[37] Bruce Curtis, 'Class Culture and Administration: Educational Inspection in Canada West', in Greer and Radforth, (eds), *Colonial Leviathan*, pp. 103–33.
[38] See J. M. Bumsted, *Fur Trade Wars: The Founding of Western Canada* (Winnipeg, 1999).

Hudson's Bay Company. This new company administered the entire British west before 1848 on behalf of the British Empire, which maintained a hands-off attitude, until Britain was forced into establishing Vancouver Island as a formal colony.

Vancouver Island was located 'on the edge of Empire', but its overwhelmingly male population and its disparaging attitude towards local First Nations made it typical of Britain's Imperial outposts in the Victorian era.[39] Indeed, the entire western half of British America in 1849 fitted more neatly into the new British Empire of simultaneously exploited and protected Aboriginals than it did into the older one of European settlement. At this point, the Red River Settlement was virtually the only concentration of population west of Georgian Bay, most of whom were of mixed descent.[40] Such a situation would not last long. Intensely class-conscious and afraid, the European colonists who came to Vancouver Island insisted that the Aboriginal people should be 'speedily coerced'. In 1857 gold was discovered on the mainland, along the Thompson and Fraser rivers. The amount of gold easily accessible was quite small by California standards, and the ensuing rush was a pale imitation of the earlier American one. But Governor James Douglas used the appearance of hundreds of gold seekers from the United States to justify a takeover of the mainland to prevent American annexation. The British government was forced to rush through parliamentary legislation establishing the mainland colony of British Columbia in August 1858.

Meanwhile, a major parliamentary inquiry was held in 1857 on the future of the prairies. The resulting report was sympathetic to the Hudson's Bay Company's administration of the local Aboriginal peoples, but recognized 'the growing desire of our Canadian fellow-subjects that the means of extension and regular settlement should be afforded to them over a portion of this territory; the necessity of providing suitably for the administration of the affairs of Vancouver's Island, and the present condition of the settlement which has been formed on the Red River'.[41] This recommendation was confirmed not long thereafter by the reports of two scientific expeditions to the region, one sponsored by the Royal Geographical Society and the other by the Canadian government. Both expeditions insisted that large portions of the prairies were highly suitable for agricultural settlement. They helped provide a scientific justification for a new Imperial policy of transferring control of the west to the existing colonies already established on the eastern half of the continent.[42]

---

[39] Adele Perry, *On the Edge of Empire: Gender, Race, and the Making of British Columbia, 1849–1871* (Toronto, 2001).

[40] See J. M. Bumsted, *Trials and Tribulations: The Red River Settlement and the Emergence of Manitoba, 1811–1870* (Winnipeg, 2003).

[41] *Report from the Select Committee on the Hudson's Bay Company* (London, 1857), pp. iii–iv.

[42] Suzanne Zeller, *Inventing Canada: Early Victorian Science and the Idea of a Transcontinental Nation* (Toronto, 1987).

Between 1815 and the 1860s nearly 2 million residents of the British Isles sailed to British North America as part of a larger exodus to the United States and other British settlement colonies (such as South Africa, Australia, and New Zealand). Not all of these 2 million remained permanently in British America. Many moved on to the United States (while some unknown number left the United States for British America), and others returned again to Britain. But the newcomers from the British Isles constituted a large proportion of the population of British America in 1860. Many of these people left the British Isles defining themselves as English, Irish, Scottish, or Welsh, although increasing numbers, at least outside Catholic Ireland, would also have seen themselves as British at the time of their migration.[43] Their experiences in British America provided impetus to further assimilation into a British identity, as they were forced to live together with people other than those of their own nation and were no longer exposed solely to a narrowly national perception of their homeland. At the same time, many British Americans retained a strong sense of their national origins, often celebrating them and frequently fighting with one another in their name. We do not yet have a detailed understanding for this period of any of these identity processes: of becoming British, of retaining an Old World nationality, or of the beginning of the invention of a new one. Some British Americans, like Joseph Howe, wanted the colonies represented in the Imperial Parliament. Others, like the former Irish Nationalist D'Arcy McGee, called for a 'new nationality' through 'the speedy and secure establishment of the Canadian Nationality'.[44] Still others were already envisioning the ultimate creation of a new nation from sea to sea. Few of those calling for a change of nationhood or national identity before 1860 had worked through the implications for the Imperial relationship of such new visions, any more than the Fathers of Confederation would do in the 1860s. Canadian nationality would be somehow inseparably entwined with Imperial enthusiasm and loyalty until after the Great War.

By 1860 the Empire in Canada was able consciously to take advantage of Queen Victoria and the royal family as symbols of unity. The celebrations in Toronto in 1854 and 1855 for the Queen's birthday had seen thousands from the outlying areas journey by railroad to the metropolis, and on 23 July 1860 His Royal Highness the Prince of Wales landed at St John's, Newfoundland, to begin a two-month tour of British America.[45] The tour probably marked the height of Imperial enthusiasm in the colonies, and was easily the most important single collective event in British America before Confederation, for the Prince was greeted with rapturous enthusiasm everywhere by enormous crowds. A short visit to the United States helped briefly seal Anglo-American amity. Within months,

---

[43] Linda Colley, *Britons: Forging the Nation, 1707–1837* (New Haven, 1992).
[44] *New Era*, 19 Jan. 1858.
[45] Ian Radforth, *Royal Spectacle: The 1860 Visit of the Prince of Wales to Canada and the United States* (Toronto, 2004).

however, the United States began coming apart, and the political situation in British America quickly became destabilized. A new era had arrived.

SELECT BIBLIOGRAPHY

PHILLIP A. BUCKNER, *The Transition to Responsible Government: British Policy in British North America, 1815–50* (London, 1985).

F. MURRAY GREENWOOD and BARRY WRIGHT, (eds), *Canadian State Trials: Law, Politics & Security Measures, 1608–1837* (Toronto, 1996).

ALLAN GREER, *The Patriots and the People: The Rebellion of 1837 in Rural Lower Canada* (Toronto, 1993).

―――― and IAN RADFORTH, (eds), *Colonial Leviathan: State Formation in Mid-Nineteenth-Century Canada* (Toronto, 1992).

NEIL MACKINNON, *This Unfriendly Soil: The Loyalist Experience in Nova Scotia, 1783–1791* (Montreal, 1986).

ADELE PERRY, *On the Edge of Empire: Gender, Race, and the Making of British Columbia, 1849–1871* (Toronto, 2001).

GEORGE SHEPPARD, *Plunder, Profit, and Paroles: A Social History of the War of 1812 in Upper Canada* (Montreal, 1994).

RICHARD WHITE, *The Middle Ground: Indians, Empires, and Republics in the Great Lakes Region, 1650–1815* (New York, 1991).

CAROL WILTON, *Popular Politics and Political Culture in Upper Canada, 1800–1850* (Montreal, 2000).

4

The Creation of the Dominion of Canada, 1860–1901

Phillip Buckner

In 1860 the Prince of Wales (the future Edward VII) made the first official royal tour to the British North American colonies. In 1901 his son, the Duke of Cornwall (the future George V), made an even lengthier official tour across the Dominion of Canada. Much had obviously changed in the intervening years. The scattered British North American colonies had (with the exception of Newfoundland) joined in a federal union. The vast areas of the west previously under the control of the Hudson's Bay Company had been acquired by the new Dominion and opposition to federal expansion from the Indigenous peoples had been largely subdued. One new province—Manitoba—had been created and two others—Saskatchewan and Alberta—were rapidly taking shape. By 1901 British Columbia was connected to the rest of Canada by the Canadian Pacific Railway (CPR). Canada had grown slowly, but its population had still climbed from 3.1 million in 1861 to 5.3 million in 1901 and the flow of outmigration to the United States had been partly stemmed by the programme of tariff protection introduced by the Conservative government in 1879. The Conservatives described this programme as the National Policy and successfully defended it in the election of 1891 against the Liberal policy of unrestricted reciprocity with the United States. After 1891 the Liberals abandoned their opposition to the National Policy and, when they came to power in 1896, effectively governed little differently from the Conservatives previously. The Liberals took office as the Canadian economy entered a period of rapid growth. Canadians entered the twentieth century increasingly self-confident about their nation's future and determined to play a more important part in world affairs.

Not surprisingly, Canadian historians have interpreted this period in heroic nationalist terms. John A. Macdonald has been immortalized as the archetypal Canadian nationalist, the National Policy has been endorsed as the foundation of a successful national economy, and the CPR described as part of the 'national dream'. There is limited room for the British Empire in this interpretation and most recent histories of Canada seem to assume that even in the late nineteenth century the Imperial connection was already a relatively insignificant legacy of the past that Canadians would shake off as soon as it became apparent that the costs outweighed the benefits. Yet the reception accorded the Duke of Cornwall casts considerable doubt upon this rather simplistic nationalist interpretation.[1] Much had indeed changed between 1860 and 1901 but what had not changed was the enthusiasm with which Canadians—particularly but not exclusively Canadians of British origin—welcomed the heir to the throne. The notion that Imperial enthusiasm waned as Canadian nationalism waxed is simply not borne out by the evidence. If anything, Imperial enthusiasm and Canadian nationalism both grew stronger during this period, one feeding off the other.

Although the Confederation movement of the 1860s was born out of a variety of motives, anti-imperialism was not one of them. The most important pressure for union was the American Civil War, but a desire not to become part of the United States explains what British North Americans wished to avoid, not why they wanted to avoid it. Nor can one explain the union by the existence of a deeply rooted sense of colonial nationalism. By the 1860s many members of the colonial elites were developing a sense of a larger British-American culture, but this sentiment had to compete with strong local and provincial loyalties. What the vast majority of English-speaking British North Americans (and some French-speaking ones) did share, as the royal tour of 1860 revealed, was a deep loyalty to British institutions and a desire to maintain the Imperial connection. Of course, the key concern of French Canadians was the survival of their distinctive national culture, but the dominant *Bleu* faction accepted the need for a strong central government (in nineteenth-century terms) to promote economic development, to take control of the west, and to withstand the growing power of the United States.

English Canadians were also concerned about survival—the survival of a British-American community on the continent of North America in the face of an increasingly aggressive American imperialism and the gradual withdrawal of British garrisons from the continent. For English Canadians Confederation was designed to create a federal government strong enough to defend the new nation's existing boundaries, to attract immigrants from the British Isles, and to undertake a policy of expansion in the west before the region fell under American control. What was not at stake in 1864–7 was whether Canadians would remain British subjects living under the protection of the British flag. Indeed, English-Canadian confederates believed that union would ensure the survival of the British Empire on the North American continent and enable the colonists to assume a more important place in the Empire. In the words

---

[1] Phillip Buckner, 'Casting Daylight upon Magic: Deconstructing the Royal Tour of 1901 to Canada', in Carl Bridge and Kent Fedorowich, (eds), *The British World: Diaspora, Culture and Identity* (London, 2003) and Phillip Buckner, 'The Invention of Tradition? The Royal Tours of 1860 and 1901 to Canada', in Colin M. Coates, (ed.), *Majesty in Canada: Essays on the Role of Royalty* (Toronto, 2006), pp. 18–43.

of a youthful Charles Tupper in 1860, Confederation held out the hope that 'British America, stretching from Atlantic to the Pacific, would in a few years exhibit to the world a great and powerful organization, with British institutions, British sympathies, and British feelings, bound indissolubly to the throne of England'.[2] Although the anti-confederates disagreed with the terms of union, they were as committed to the preservation of the Imperial connection as were their opponents. One of the most consistent arguments used against the Quebec Resolutions was that a flawed union would lead to a premature and unwanted independence.

Canadians (as they all became in 1867) considered Imperial support crucial if the new Dominion was to expand its authority 'from sea unto sea'. Even though Canada resented the concessions that had to be made to the United States to secure the Treaty of Washington in 1871, Prime Minister Sir John A. Macdonald understood that, if he had gone to Washington representing Canada rather than as part of a British delegation, he would have done even less well in any negotiations. Without Imperial support the Canadian government might not have been able to purchase the Hudson's Bay Company's territories in 1869, would have had great difficulty in suppressing the first north-west rebellion in 1870, could not have embarked upon building a transcontinental railway at such great speed during the 1870s and 1880s, and would probably have faced greater resistance from the Aboriginal nations of western Canada to the extension of Canadian authority. For the rest of the nineteenth century Britain remained the major source of Canada's investment capital, the major market for its exports, and the major source of immigrants.

To those Imperial historians who see the grant of responsible government as simply a move from formal to informal methods of imperial control, the close economic relationship between Britain and Canada after Confederation confirms that Canada remained a British dependency and Canadians 'the ideal prefabricated collaborators'.[3] But to describe the members of the Canadian political and economic elites as collaborators is fundamentally misleading since it implies that the initiative for the policies that were pursued in British North America came from Britain (either from the Colonial Office or from some nebulous group of gentlemanly capitalists). Yet Confederation did not take place because the Imperial government supported it; Confederation took place because the British North Americans wanted it. The Imperial government could have made union impossible by opposing Confederation; it could not create a union that the colonists did not want. At the London Conference of 1866 the British government was able to persuade the colonial delegates to make some

---

[2] Quoted in Phillip Buckner, 'Sir Charles Tupper', in *Dictionary of Canadian Biography*, vol. XIV (Toronto, 1998), p. 1016.

[3] Ronald Robinson, 'Non-European Foundations of European Imperialism: Sketch for a Theory of Collaboration', in R. Owen and B. Sutcliffe, (eds), *Studies in the Theory of Imperialism* (London, 1972), p. 124.

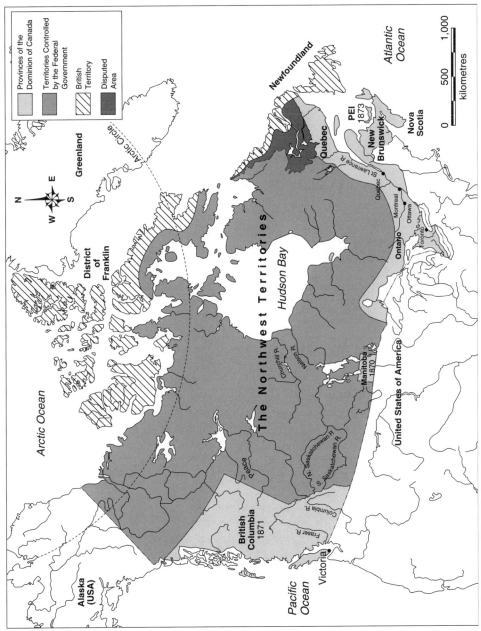

Map 4. Canada 1873

Provinces of the
Dominion of Canada

Territories Controlled
by the Federal
Government

British
Territory

Disputed
Area

Greenland

Arctic Circle

N
W E
S

District
of
Franklin

Arctic Ocean

Newfoundland

Atlantic
Ocean

PEI
1873

Quebec

New
Brunswick

Nova
Scotia

St Lawrence R.

Quebec

Montreal

Ottawa

Ontario

Toronto

The Northwest Territories

Hudson Bay

Churchill R.

Nelson R.

Manitoba
1870

N. Saskatchewan R.

S. Saskatchewan R.

Peace

Columbia R.

United States of America

British
Columbia
1871

Fraser R.

Alaska
(USA)

Victoria

Pacific
Ocean

0   500   1,000
kilometres

minor amendments to the scheme of union, but the British North America Act was essentially made-in-Canada and rubberstamped by the Imperial Parliament. Canada did not purchase the Hudson's Bay Company's territories and it did not build the CPR at the behest of either the British government or of British capitalists but because Canada had its own imperial dream.

Even before Confederation the British North American colonies were already functioning under a system of responsible government that left the Imperial authorities with little real influence in their internal affairs. The right to veto colonial legislation had largely been abandoned long before the Colonial Laws Validity Act of 1865 established that the self-governing colonies had the right to pass laws repugnant to the laws of the United Kingdom. In theory the Parliament of the United Kingdom could pass legislation affecting the British North American colonies. In practice it had long been accepted that this was a power that could only be used in an emergency, and after 1867 it was inconceivable that the Parliament of the United Kingdom would pass any Act dealing with the domestic affairs of Canada without the consent of the Canadian Parliament. Although in certain areas—such as the terms upon which money could be borrowed in London—the Imperial government and metropolitan capitalists could establish the rules of the game, even in these cases there was a process of constant negotiation, and the Canadians determined the rules which British investors in Canada, British exporters to Canada, and British immigrants had to follow. In 1879 the National Policy aroused nearly as much anger among British manufacturers as had the first colonial protective tariffs in 1858–9 but fewer formal protests because the right of the colonials to design their own tariffs had already been conceded. British capital, British technology, and British immigrants were welcomed because they brought benefits to Canadians in the form of a transportation infrastructure, plants that employed Canadian labour, a rising standard of living, and an increasingly dynamic Canadian middle class.[4] The benefits to Canada of these transfers far outweighed the advantages to Britain. Indeed, part of the reason why Canadians were able to focus their resources on programmes of internal development was that their defence costs were marginal so long as they lived under the protective umbrella of the British Empire.

Central to the way Canadians viewed the Imperial connection was the belief that communities of Britons overseas had an inherent right to self-government. Of course, Canadians recognized that there was an inequality in status between the Parliament of the United Kingdom and the Parliament of Canada, though it was an inequality that they believed would diminish over time as Canada grew in population and wealth. In the meantime they were prepared to leave

---

[4] Robert Kubicek, 'Economic Power at the Periphery: Canada, Australia and South Africa, 1850–1914', in Raymond E. Dumett, (ed.), *Gentlemanly Capitalism and British Imperialism: The New Debate on Empire* (Harlow, 1999), pp. 113–26.

the conduct of foreign policy and the responsibility for Imperial defence in the hands of the Imperial government. But the Canadian government did seek a voice in the negotiation of Imperial treaties affecting Canada by creating the position of High Commissioner in 1880 and appointing a series of powerful and influential politicians to the post. Recognizing the growing importance of the self-governing colonies, the British government began to hold periodic conferences. Though the British government set the agenda at these conferences, it could not coerce the colonies into adopting policies they did not want. At the first Colonial Conference in 1887, while the Australians were persuaded to make an annual contribution to the Royal Navy, the Canadians were not. In 1897 the Colonial Secretary, Joseph Chamberlain, took advantage of Queen Victoria's golden jubilee to hold a conference to discuss ways of creating stronger Imperial institutions. From Chamberlain's perspective the results were disappointing. The Canadian Prime Minister, Sir Wilfrid Laurier, vetoed any new Imperial structures and agreed only that conferences might be held on an ad hoc basis as need arose.

Some Canadians were discontented with Canada's subordinate status within the Imperial system. A few were even prepared to advocate that Canada should become an independent nation. But the operative word is few. Even in French Canada there was considerable sympathy for the British Empire, particularly among the conservative Catholic elite that dominated French-Canadian politics. Though disillusioned by the South African War, most French-Canadian nationalists remained content with the *status quo ante bellum*. In English Canada there was a small republican movement but its spiritual leader, Goldwin Smith, and indeed many of his followers, were recent migrants from the United Kingdom. Their republicanism was yet another British import.[5] Among native-born Canadians of British ancestry, republicanism attracted scant support, because it was associated with annexation to the United States. Many Canadians did want reciprocity with the United States—even unrestricted reciprocity if that is all they could get. But to accuse those Liberals who supported the policy of unrestricted reciprocity of 'veiled treason', as John A. Macdonald did in 1891, was an unfair—even if successful—political tactic. Like Macdonald the vast majority of English-Canadian Liberals had been born and intended to die British subjects. In the first Liberal budget of 1897, the Liberals sought to remove any doubts about their loyalty by introducing a form of Imperial preference on British imports.

More appealing than independence to some English Canadians was the goal of closer union with the United Kingdom. How many is difficult to establish since Imperial federation was a vague concept with a variety of meanings. Canadian membership in the Imperial Federation League was never large—a few hundred at its peak. Those who did support some form of Imperial federation used to

5 Wade A. Henry, 'Republicanism and British Identity in English Canada, 1864–1917', in Colin M. Coates, (ed.), *Imperial Canada, 1867–1917* (Edinburgh, 1997).

be seen in Canadian historiography as 'bad' Canadians, insufficiently committed to the creation of a Canadian nation-state and condemned for their obsequious deference to Imperial authority and British culture. Carl Berger's *The Sense of Power* destroyed this stereotype, arguing that Canadian imperialists were also Canadian nationalists.[6] Berger's book unleashed a debate that has continued to the present over whether Canadian imperialists can really be considered 'authentic' Canadian nationalists. In the end this is bound to be a barren debate because it assumes that there is such a thing as the 'essential' Canadian national identity. But collective identities are never entirely coherent and they evolve and change over time. Canadian nationalism today takes a variety of forms but none of those forms bears much relationship to the forms they took over a century ago. In any event it was always misleading to exaggerate the differences between the Imperial federationists and their opponents. Virtually all English Canadians in the late nineteenth century were enthusiastic imperialists and virtually all hoped that Canada could play a more important role in Imperial affairs (even if they objected to any kind of formal union). As John Kendle pointed out a long time ago, there is a danger in making 'an essentially fluid and flexible debate in which there was considerable overlap of ideas and individuals appear as a straightforward clash between two well-defined points of view'.[7]

Prior to Confederation, the majority of the English-speaking population of British North America were British immigrants or their offspring, with roots in British North America that did not go back more than one or at most two generations, and they considered themselves as Britons living abroad.[8] Even the majority of those English Canadians whose forebears had come to Canada as part of the pre-1815 migrations from the United States had redefined themselves as overseas Britons, frequently seeking to show through the construction of family genealogies that the roots of their American ancestors lay in Britain. The English-speaking inhabitants of British North America also identified themselves as Nova Scotians or New Brunswickers or Upper or Lower Canadians, but no one ever thought of these as national identities. Only the French-speaking population of the United Province of Canada used a term—*Canadien*—that implied a sense of belonging to a distinct national culture. English-speaking colonists did call themselves British Americans, but this description emphasized their identity as British subjects living in America. Inevitably, however, the desire to build a transcontinental state led to the belief that there was a distinct 'Canadian Nationality'. By the end of the nineteenth century, there were few native-born

---

[6] Carl Berger, *The Sense of Power: Studies in the Ideas of Canadian Imperialism, 1867–1914* (Toronto, 1970).

[7] John Edward Kendle, *The Colonial and Imperial Conferences, 1897–1911* (London, 1969), p. 217.

[8] See P. A. Buckner, 'Making British North America British, 1815–1860', in C. C. Eldridge, (ed.), *Kith and Kin: Canada, Britain and the United States from the Revolution to the Cold War* (Cardiff, 1997), pp. 11–44.

English Canadians who did not describe themselves as Canadians. To some extent this reflected the desire of English Canadians to put an end to the notion that they were lesser Britons. Most believed that the Imperial relationship would gradually be transformed into an alliance of British nations, equal in status and working together cooperatively. While in London in 1901, George W. Ross, the Liberal Premier of Ontario and a committed imperialist, pointed out that Canada had little to gain from Imperial federation since it would mean 'the sacrifice of some of the elements or privileges of self-government which we now possess'. But he insisted that Canadians were prepared 'bear their share in the burdens, in the battles, and in the struggle for imperial unity' provided that they were treated as 'partners in the British Empire'.[9]

Edward Said once wrote that it was the colonized's 'acceptance of subordination—whether through a positive sense of common interest with the parent state, or through the inability to conceive of any alternative—which made empire durable'.[10] The point is an important one—that Imperial authority ultimately rested on a substantial degree of colonial consent. But to place all of the colonies of the British Empire on the same footing is quite misleading. English Canadians did not think of themselves as the 'colonized' any more than the British minority in India did. Canadian imperialism has often been seen as an anti-modernist creed, supported by those who were frightened by the rise of industrial society, and there were Canadian imperialists who thought this way. But for most English Canadians imperialism was the road to the future, as it provided Canada with the resources to gain access to the most modern technology and to state-of-the-art transportation systems. When Canadians sought to advertise Canada abroad, they did not send illustrations of the Canadian wilderness but pictures of trains and people clearing the land as part of the march of British civilization around the globe. The majority of English Canadians proudly identified themselves as Britons or (more commonly) Britishers. Whether they had been born in the motherland or in a British colony, they saw Canada as a British nation, part of a Greater Britain extending around the globe.

In one sense British colonists, no matter where they settled, did accept a degree of cultural subordination. They frequently remembered an idealized Britain that they referred to in affectionate terms as the 'mother country' or as 'home' (even if they had never been there). They copied British legal and constitutional forms, avidly consumed British goods and British culture, and sometimes pathetically craved metropolitan respect. But there were distinct limits to their admiration for all things British. The colonists recognized that many British institutions had to be greatly modified or even jettisoned in a new environment. Primogeniture was quickly abandoned and the legal system, while based on the British principles

---

[9] *Addresses Delivered by Hon. G. W. Ross during his Recent Visit to England . . .* (n.p., 1901), pp. 2, 6.
[10] Edward W. Said, *Cultural Imperialism* (London, 1993), p. 11.

and structures, soon began to diverge in a wide range of ways from British practice. The Church of England was forced to abandon its desire to become an established church. When designing their constitution at Quebec in 1864, Canadians borrowed (reluctantly perhaps) a number of ideas from their American neighbours, creating a federal system for which there was no parallel in Britain and establishing an appointed second chamber to represent sectional interests. When designing public lands policy in the Canadian West and gold-mining legislation in the Yukon, the Canadian government normally drew upon United States models. Running alongside the mimetic impulse was an equally strong desire to show that Canada was not just a part of Greater Britain, but that it was in some ways a Better Britain, with a less rigid class structure and an education system more open to talent than that of the mother country. By emphasizing their frontier spirit or their northern character, by using the imagery of the beaver and the maple leaf, and by appropriating parts of Aboriginal culture such as the canoe and sports like lacrosse, native-born English Canadians sought to indicate that they were British, but not merely British. They found it offensive when recent migrants from the British Isles compared their new home unfavourably to their old. Canadians wished to be British, but on their own terms and in their own way: to create 'New Britains, not unworthy of the old'.[11]

By 1901 the only area of policy still in the hands of the Imperial government was foreign policy but even here the British government could not compel Canada to contribute men or money to support the decisions it took. Although the whole Empire was theoretically at war when Britain was at war, Canada did not have to participate, as the crisis in the Sudan in 1884 showed, when Macdonald refused to send Canadian troops to assist in the rescue of General Gordon (although, as during the Crimean War, the British government was allowed to recruit volunteers for service overseas in Imperial units). Indeed, during the first three decades of Confederation, Canadians were unlikely to give their consent to participation in external wars since they were engaged in their own imperial war against the Indigenous peoples of western Canada. From the Canadian perspective, western expansion would add more to the wealth of the Empire than expansion into Africa, and the CPR was as much an Imperial highway as any of the railroads built in India. In the first stage of western expansion the government of Canada needed Imperial troops to curb the resistance at the Red River in 1869–70 from the Métis, descendants of mixed marriages between French and British fur traders and Indigenous women. Out of weakness the Canadian government was forced to concede many of the Métis' demands, but in 1873 the North West Mounted Police (NWMP), a paramilitary force loosely modelled upon the Royal Irish Constabulary, was created to assert Canadian authority in the west. Even though many of the officers and men were

---

[11] Agnes Maule Machar, 'Canada for the Laureate', printed in George W. Ross, (ed.), *Patriotic Recitations and Arbor Days Exercises* (Toronto, 1893), p. 53.

recruited in Britain, the Mounties quickly became the stuff of legend in English Canada. In 1897 a small delegation of Mounties accompanied the much larger militia contingent sent to represent Canada at Queen Victoria's diamond jubilee. There were complaints that the Canadian militia were not easily recognized as Canadians whereas the Mounties in their distinctive hats and red coats were identifiably Canadian. Ironically with the west largely pacified by 1900, there were discussions in Ottawa over whether a federal police force was still necessary, and it was only the publicity generated by the NWMP's participation in the South African War which saved them from extinction and turned them into the Royal North West Mounted Police. Increasingly the RNWMP represented Canada at coronations, royal weddings, and other Imperial ceremonies in London.

The NWMP arrived in the west just at the moment when resistance from Canada's Indigenous peoples was undermined by the disappearance of the buffalo. Reluctantly the native leadership agreed to a series of one-sided treaties, surrendering their Aboriginal title for food and supplies, and the Mounties were able to contain the small number of native peoples who refused to sign a treaty. However, when a second Métis rebellion broke out in the north-west in 1885, the Canadian government was forced to call upon the Canadian militia, which travelled west on the CPR to defeat the rebels at Batoche. This was Canada's first national war, for the rebellion brought together men from across Canada in defence of the Canadian state. When the North-West Field Force returned from the campaign, they were given a rapturous welcome across Canada. Canadian historians now prefer to interpret the 1885 rebellion as a civil war but that was not how it was seen at the time. English Canadians (and initially French Canadians) viewed the Métis as an Aboriginal 'other'. English-Canadian newspapers compared the Canadian campaign against Riel to the recent British campaigns in Egypt and the Sudan. In the House of Commons Macdonald even described Louis Riel as 'a kind of half-breed Mahdi'.[12]

Not only do such references show that Canadians believed that they were doing their bit as empire builders in western Canada but they also destroy the myth that Canadians lacked interest in the wider Empire. This was a myth in 1854 when the government of the United Province of Canada allowed an Imperial regiment to be recruited in Upper Canada for the Crimea. It was a myth in 1857 for Canadian newspapers were full of reports of the atrocities committed during the Indian Mutiny and of the heroism of British troops. It was also a myth in 1884. Even though Macdonald was not prepared to send Canadian troops to assist in the rescue of General Gordon, there could have been few Canadians who did not know how Gordon died and who did not blame Mahdi (and probably

---

[12] Brien Brothman, 'Surveying Imperialism: The English-Canadian Press and British Imperial Conduct in Africa, 1880–1885', Ph.D. thesis (Laval, 1989), pp. 320, 322; Paul James Maroney, 'The "Peaceable Kingdom" Reconsidered: War and Culture in English Canada, 1884–1914', Ph.D. thesis (Queen's University, 1996), chap. 1.

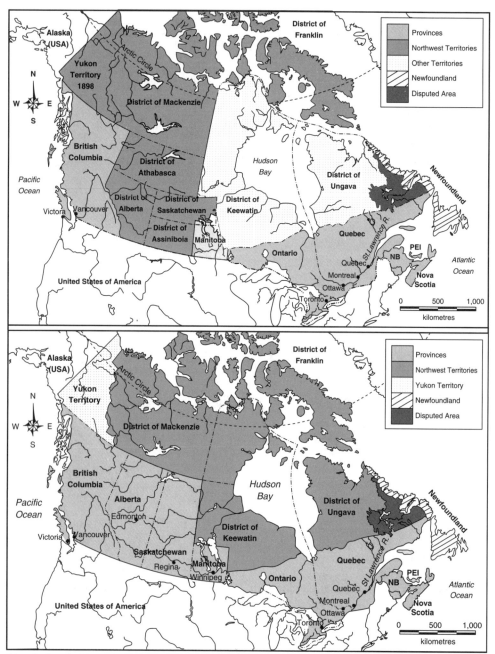

Map 5. Canada in 1898 (top) and 1905 (bottom).

Gladstone) for his death. English Canadians took pride in British victories over 'lesser breeds' in Africa and Asia and even Dominion Day celebrations usually had an imperial tone. The celebrations in Saint John, New Brunswick, on 1 July 1899 concluded with a re-enactment of the 'Taking of Omdurman'.[13] In *The Place British North Americans Have Won in History* (1866) Henry J. Morgan pointed out that the first soldier to win a Victoria Cross had been a boy from Toronto killed during the Charge of the Light Brigade, and in his *Canadians in the Imperial Naval and Military Service Abroad* (1891) J. Hampden Burnham listed with pride the substantial number of Canadians who held high rank in the Imperial army and navy, many of them products of the Royal Military College at Kingston. There were many other Canadians who achieved no great fame but whose exploits were followed by relatives, friends, and neighbours in the communities they left behind. Canadians drew no distinction between those who served the Empire at home and abroad. Veterans of the Fenian Raids and the North-West Rebellion marched alongside veterans of the Crimean War and the Indian Mutiny (whether they had been born in Canada or had simply retired there) in Decoration Day ceremonies, held annually in a number of Canadian cities by the 1890s. After 1900 they would be joined by an even larger number of Canadian veterans of the South African War, who would meet annually to celebrate Paardeberg Day.

They were not the only Canadians to serve the Empire overseas. Canadian churches were caught up in the missionary enthusiasm that swept the Anglo-American world in the late nineteenth century. It is simplistic to describe missionaries as agents of the Imperial government, but most missionaries did believe that the Empire was a force promoting British culture and Christian civilization and defined their mission in imperial terms. The first Canadian missions were among Canada's Indigenous peoples, but the Canadian churches began to send missionaries overseas in the 1840s. Confederation enabled the Canadian churches to organize more effectively and by 1900 all of them had substantial missions overseas. In numerous Canadian churches, both Catholic and Protestant, funds were raised to support missionary activities and sermons were preached extolling the sacrifices made by missionaries in the field. Missionary accounts became popular reading. Some missionaries became martyrs; others returned to receive honorary degrees and to play an active and important part in Canadian society. Canadian missionaries who had served in southern Africa helped to drum up anti-Boer sentiment and enthusiasm for Canadian participation in the South African War.

Though most missionaries were male, women were active in organizing the bake sales and the harvest suppers that raised the funds to support missionary activity overseas and in 1870 the Baptists in Canso, Nova Scotia, formed the first separate women's organization to promote overseas missions. Women in the

---

[13] *Official Programme of Dominion Day Celebration* (Saint John, 1899).

other Protestant churches soon followed and women's denominational missionary societies formed by far the largest national women's organizations right up to the First World War.[14] Perhaps not all missionaries and their supporters would have agreed with the Presbyterian missionary Dr Maggie O'Hara, who declared that her three great enthusiasms were the Presbyterian Church, Queen's University, and the British Empire (or at least not with the first two), but missionary activity overseas brought home to hundreds of thousands of Canadian men and women the reality of belonging to a global empire and strengthened their belief that the Empire was doing God's work at home and abroad.

Although Confederation accelerated the creation of denominational churches that were national in scope and that defined themselves in Canadian terms, the Protestant churches (and the Irish Catholic churches in English Canada) continued to recruit ministers in Britain and retained close ties with the 'mother' churches in Britain. A steady stream of Canadian clerics made their way across the Atlantic to attend synods or just to visit the birthplace of their denomination. They were not alone. During the late nineteenth century the Atlantic was shrinking as steamships made the passage ever faster, cheaper, and safer. A growing number of immigrants were able to return home temporarily to visit the families and friends they had left behind. The immigrants' children came to visit the homeland they had heard so much about or branches of the family whom they had never met. As the Canadian economy was transformed by industrialization, a growing number of wealthy and ambitious Canadian merchants and businessmen also migrated to the mother country, particularly to the large urban centres, and a number of prominent Canadian politicians, such as the native-born Sir Charles Tupper and the Scottish-born Lord Strathcona (who had spent all of his adult life in Canada), would retire in Britain. So did Lady Macdonald after Sir John A.'s death in 1891. Other Canadians were attracted by the cultural opportunities, particularly in the metropolis. The Canadian-born Emma Albani sang frequently at Covent Garden and the Canadian-born exotic dancer Maud Allen was well known to a slightly different audience.

Some British immigrants returned because Canada had not lived up to their hopes or out of simple homesickness. Others crossed the Atlantic repeatedly in search of better opportunities. The journalist Arthur Hawkes criss-crossed the Atlantic nineteen times before finally settling in Toronto.[15] Although a large number of British immigrants moved on to the United States, close to a quarter of a million became permanent residents of Canada between 1871 and 1901. The new immigrants were drawn primarily from Britain's urban centres and by 1901 all of Canada's major cities contained a substantial British-born minority.

[14] Ruth Compton Brouwer, *New Women for God: Canadian Presbyterian Women and Foreign Missions, 1876–1914* (Toronto, 1990), pp. 4–5, 22, 193; Myra Rutherdale, *Women and the White Man's God: Gender and Race in the Canadian Mission Field* (Vancouver, 2002), pp. xxi, 29.
[15] *The British News of Canada* (Montreal and London), 30 Mar. 1912.

Beginning in 1854, the cost of postage from Canada to Britain fell dramatically and the introduction of the penny post at the end of the century, an initiative of the Canadian Postmaster General, Sir William Mulock, and increasing literacy on both side of the Atlantic meant that it was much easier than in the past for immigrants to maintain contact with family back in Britain.

By the late nineteenth century the British government had abandoned any direct involvement in promoting emigration, although in 1886 it did establish an Emigrant Information Office to encourage those considering migration to go to the British colonies overseas. The Canadian government contributed by subsidizing a flood of propaganda that downplayed the difficulties facing emigrants and emphasized Canada's Britishness. The British North American colonies had been represented individually at the Crystal Palace Exhibition in London in 1851 and at the International Exhibition of 1862 but Canada was especially well represented at the Colonial and Indian Exhibition of 1886. The Canadian government contributed $300,000 and arranged for over 17,000 Canadian exhibits. Most of the exhibits were of Canadian agricultural produce, timber products, minerals, and manufactured goods, designed to show that Canada was a land of abundance and promise. But there was also a substantial exhibit of educational materials, of books about Canada or by Canadians, of Canadian newspapers and photographs, and of oil paintings of Canadian scenes. Special excursions were arranged for visitors from outside London and reduced rates for workingmen, and over 5.5 million people visited the Exhibition. The Exhibition helped to create a sense within Britain of the growing importance of the colonies to Britain and led to increased sales in Britain of everything from Canadian apples to Canadian organs and harvesters. It was also covered extensively in the Canadian press, and played its part in strengthening Canadians' sense of belonging to a vast and prosperous empire.[16] Its success led to a host of publications dealing with the resources of Greater Britain, to the creation of the Imperial Institute, and to exhibitions at Edinburgh in 1886 and Glasgow in 1888 and 1901 that promoted closer links with Scottish communities overseas.

The Canadian government also encouraged British organizations to see Canada and its resources for themselves. In 1884 the Canadian government gave the British Association a $25,000 subsidy, as well as reduced steamship fares and free travel on all government railways. Nearly 1,000 members of the Association and their dependants travelled to Montreal and some of the party went as far as the Rockies. They returned impressed by the spectacle of 'Anglo-Saxon, British-Canadian enterprise spreading itself over the surface of this vast country'.[17] Many networks bridged the Atlantic. A number of Canadian doctors had trained in

[16] E. A. Heaman, *The Inglorious Arts of Peace: Exhibitions in Canadian Society in the Nineteenth Century* (Toronto, 1999), pp. 190–210.
[17] A. L. Richardson, *Report of the Visit of the British Association to the Canadian North-West* (Winnipeg, 1884), p. 36.

Britain and remained members of the British Medical Association. Canadian lawyers not only studied British texts but many of them visited London, a few to appear before the Judicial Committee of the Privy Council, others to attend specialized conferences, many simply for inspiration. Canadian scientists and engineers frequently belonged to the British Association for the Advancement of Science, which held its annual meeting in Toronto in 1897. A small number of Canadians went to Britain for their education at Oxford, Cambridge, or Edinburgh, and Canadian schools (particularly private schools) and universities continued to recruit their staff in Britain. A substantial number of Canadian journalists began their careers in Britain and a number who began their careers in Canada would end them working in Britain. After the completion of the transatlantic cable, Canadian newspapers could draw more easily upon British papers for their international stories. Of course, they also drew information from American sources, but even a cursory glance at the editorial pages reveals that most Canadian newspapers in 1901 wished to promote a British-Canadian sense of identity and shaped their reports accordingly.

British culture also crossed the Atlantic. Britons at home and abroad not only sang from the same hymn books but the same popular songs. The 1887 and 1897 silver and diamond jubilee celebrations spawned a host of music hall songs that became popular across Canada and British composers like Sir Alexander Campbell Mackenzie toured Canada to promote sales of their compositions. There was not a military or brass band in English Canada that did not know 'Soldiers of the Queen' and the 'British Grenadiers'. Many organists in Canada had trained in Britain, including Dr Charles Harris who emigrated to Ottawa in 1880 and organized choir tours, festivals, and concerts, making music (according to the London *Times*) 'an effective link of empire'.[18] During the late nineteenth century literate Canadians (and an increasing number of Canadians—especially English Canadians—were literate) read Dickens, Scott, Tennyson, and Shakespeare. They also read Rider Haggard's adventure stories, Arthur Conan Doyle's mystery stories, and Rudyard Kipling's poetry, all of which contained a thinly disguised imperial message.

American popular culture was also growing stronger in Canada, and Canadians were more likely to go to live performances of American vaudeville and American circuses than to the theatre to see touring British actors like Henry Irving. Partly because they faced the constant threat of American cultural domination, English Canadians believed that a national literature should be 'patriotic and ameliorative' and that 'in cultural affairs, nationhood would be achieved only by transplanting the most admirable traditions of the Old World to the New'.[19] The history, the literature, and the poetry that young Canadians studied in school

---

[18] Jeffrey Richards, *Imperialism and Music* (Manchester, 2001), pp. 41, 138, 338, 454.
[19] Carole Gerson, *A Purer Taste: The Writing and Reading of Fiction in English in Nineteenth-Century Canada* (Toronto, 1989), p. 154.

were largely British, although with a substantial proportion of works written by Canadians who drew upon British models. By the end of the century Canadians were also engaged in recovering their own history. Local historical societies flourished and a host of publications poured out—all of them extolling Canada's past and future as a British nation. The first Canadian Club was founded in 1894 and branches quickly spread across the country. But while the Canadian Clubs were concerned to develop Canadian symbols, history, and literature, they were also firmly committed to the preservation of the Imperial connection. Across the country efforts were made to commemorate British Canada's heroes, both old and new. The exploits of Imperial heroes like Nelson, Wellington, and Livingston were as well known in Canada as in Britain. But Canadians also wished to commemorate the heroes of the War of 1812–14—Sir Isaac Brock, Sir John Harvey, Laura Secord, even Tecumseh. Shortly after his death, the first major monuments to Sir John A. Macdonald were unveiled both in Westminster Abbey and in Canada. Who and what was commemorated varied from region to region. Naturally Wolfe took pride of place among English Canadians living in Quebec. In Ontario emphasis was placed on the defence of Canada during the War of 1812–14 and the rebellions of 1837, and in both Ontario and New Brunswick there was a revival of interest in commemorating the arrival and sacrifices of the Loyalists and the defence of those provinces against the Fenians in the 1860s. In Nova Scotia it was the war at sea in 1812–14 that was remembered. But everywhere except in French Canada the emphasis was on the pride that Canadians could take in their Imperial past.[20]

Many of the historical societies had very clear missionary objectives. The Women's Canadian Historical Society of Toronto, formed in 1895, was designed to 'foster a knowledge of Canadian history among those belonging to other nationalities, who make their homes on Canadian soil and thus become citizens of the British Empire'.[21] Clementina Fessenden used the Ontario Historical Society as the base from which she launched the campaign that made Empire Day a national holiday. Much of this activity was orchestrated by conservative upper-class women, but many of the women involved in promoting Canadian history—like Anne Curzon and Matilda Edgar—were also active members of the National Council of Women and promoters of women's rights. Undeniably the national mythology that these men and women promoted excluded many Canadians, but it was a mythology widely shared in English Canada by the majority of those who were, or who could invent a claim to be, of British origin and/or culture. Imperial ideology was not simply the tool that the Canadian upper classes used to defend hierarchy; it was central to the way men and

---

[20] C. J. Taylor, *Negotiating the Past: The Making of Canada's National Historic Parks and Sites* (Montreal and Kingston, 1990); Colin M. Coates and Cecilia Morgan, *Heroines and History: Representations of Madelaine de Verchères and Laura Secord* (Toronto, 2002).

[21] Donald A. Wright, 'The Professionalization of History in English Canada to the 1950s', Ph.D. thesis (University of Ottawa, 1999), p. 32.

women of all classes in English Canada (with remarkably few exceptions) viewed themselves—as members of an Imperial race whose institutions and culture were superior to all others. Their imagined community was Canada but Canada was itself part of a larger imagined community—the British Empire.

At the head of both imagined communities was Queen Victoria. Celebrations of the monarch's birthday and other royal anniversaries can be traced back to the very beginnings of colonial settlement, but prior to the 1850s they tended to be rather formal, officially sponsored events. The 1860 royal visit undoubtedly strengthened popular monarchism in Canada but even more important was the expansion of literacy and the popular press. By the end of the century Canada had nearly 1,000 daily and weekly newspapers. In English Canada (and to a lesser degree in French Canada) these newspapers carried regularly reports about royal marriages, deaths, and other ceremonial functions. The enthusiasm shown across English Canada for Victoria's silver jubilee celebrations in 1887 and the even more elaborate diamond jubilee celebrations in 1897 did not emerge out of a vacuum. Nor did the widespread expression of grief that followed the Queen's death in 1901 and the enthusiastic welcome given to her grandson during the 1901 royal tour. The newspapers helped to create this enthusiasm but they were also responding to it, for they recognized that enthusiasm for the monarchy sold papers.

British migrants to Canada were aware that they were moving to a society very different from the one they were leaving. Indeed, most were moving because the new society seemed to offer greater opportunities than the old. But they were not going to an entirely strange and alien land, for the institutions and the cultural environment that they found in English Canada were sufficiently familiar that many immigrants felt that they were moving from one British community to another. Even within the United Kingdom there existed a multiplicity of British identities, reflecting the national, regional, and even local characteristics of the British population and also class and gender differences. Some of these identities were more easily transferred across the Atlantic than others. English miners in British Columbia and Scottish miners in Cape Breton settled in sufficient numbers that they were able to transplant a shared working-class culture.[22] But even in these communities, some of the miners were drawn from different parts of the British Isles and over time there was bound to be a degree of ethnic fade. Indeed, most English, Scottish, and Protestant Irish immigrants became more British overseas than they had felt themselves to be at home, since they rarely settled in ethnic enclaves and intermarriage between the different Protestant groups was common. Irish Catholics were a partial exception to this generalization since Irish Catholics usually married Irish Catholics. Moreover, the debate over the right of Catholics to send their children to separate schools

---

[22] John Douglas Belshaw, *Colonization and Community: The Vancouver Island Coalfield and the Making of the British Columbian Working Class* (Montreal and Kingston, 2002).

exacerbated Protestant–Catholic tensions. But by the late nineteenth century most Irish Catholics in Canada were native born and increasingly their views on Imperial questions were little different from those of the other British groups, particularly since a majority of Canadians were in favour of home rule for Ireland, a measure unanimously endorsed by the Canadian Parliament in 1882. Irish Catholic Canadians would prove only slightly less enthusiastic than other British Canadians in their desire to support Britain during the South African War.[23]

The late nineteenth century did see a proliferation of ethnic-based organizations. St Andrew's and Caledonian societies, Robbie Burns clubs, and branches of the Sons of Scotland were found right across Canada in 1901. The Irish also had their ethnic associations, although with separate societies for Catholics and Protestants, and branches of the Sons (and Maids) of England and St George societies spread across the country. Ethnic societies were in one sense divisive since they encouraged people to retain distinct ethnic identities, but they also served to break down local and regional differences, weakening the divisions between Highland and Lowland Scots and between emigrants from the north and south of England. Moreover, all the major ethnic associations came together at times of public celebration, to march on Dominion Day or on Queen Victoria's birthday, on all these occasions waving Union Jacks and singing 'God Save the Queen' and thus publicly declaring a shared British identity. Some organizations had already begun to lose their original ethnic bias. The largest and most important voluntary society in late nineteenth-century Canada was the Orange Order to which at its peak nearly a third of all English-speaking Protestant adult males belonged. Although originally a fraternal organization imported from Ireland by Irish Protestant emigrants, by the end of the century the Orange Order had long since outgrown its Irish ethnic roots, although its goal remained to keep Canada Protestant and British.

There is, of course, nothing strange about individuals holding multiple allegiances, particularly within a large, multicultural empire. Although Scotland had lost its independence in 1707, a sense of Scottish national identity persisted. Most Scottish nationalists were prepared to define themselves as British, so long as Scottishness was given a wide stage for self-expression and a status overseas approximating that of Englishness within the Empire.[24] Irish Protestants also felt no sense of conflict between their sense of Irishness and their commitment to the Union. Only among Irish Catholics did Unionist nationalism have limited appeal, but the solution most Irish Catholics demanded in the late nineteenth century was a degree of home rule similar to that already possessed by Canada. Although these older national identities persisted within Canada,

---

[23] Mark G. McGowan, *The Waning of the Green: Catholics, the Irish, and Identity in Toronto, 1887–1922* (Montreal and Kingston, 1999).

[24] John Mackenzie, 'A Scottish Empire? The Scottish Diaspora and Interactive Identities', in Tom Brooking and Jennie Coleman, (eds), *The Heather and the Fern: Scottish Migration and New Zealand Settlement* (Dunedin, 2003).

they were gradually subsumed within a larger sense of Canadian identity. English Canadians, however, continued to see themselves as British as well as Canadian. This was not merely a matter of switching hats as need dictated, because for most English Canadians their British and Canadian identities were so completely interwoven that one could not be disentangled from the other. In their minds to be Canadian was to be British. Britishness was an ambiguous concept that defies precise definition. For many Canadians, it implied a code of behaviour and a cultural identity that could be acquired given time and commitment, which is why English-Canadian nationalists placed such great emphasis on a public school system that could absorb minority groups and how they justified repressive laws aimed at the destruction of non-British cultural practices. But even those who subscribed to a cultural definition of Britishness tended to see limits to who could be assimilated. To be British was to be 'white'. Like Britishness itself, 'white' was a socially constructed category that could be extended to include those one wished to assimilate or constricted to exclude those one did not, but there was little opposition to the introduction of laws restricting 'Oriental' emigration, which were first introduced in the 1880s. By the end of the century the sense of Canada as a racial community was becoming stronger in English Canada, as it was elsewhere in the Empire. Within Canada the British majority had no doubt that history and destiny were on their side and that they would predominate over all other racial groups, including the French Canadians.

English Canadians did want distinct national symbols that could represent Canada, but these symbols had also to contain some recognition of Canada's British identity. There was a flag debate in 1900 but it revolved around whether the Union Jack or the Red Ensign should fly from government buildings—a debate won by those who supported the flying of the Union Jack on the grounds that the Union Jack was as much the birthright of Britons overseas as Britons in the mother country. When the Duke of Cornwall toured Canada in 1901, he heard 'O Canada' only in French Canada. Throughout English Canada he was greeted with 'God Save the King' and 'Rule Britannia' but also with 'The Maple Leaf Forever', a Canadian patriotic song written by a Scottish emigrant, which had become English Canada's unofficial national anthem and which stressed that the British flag and a British identity had been 'planted firm' on 'Canada's fair domain'.

Participation in the South African War expressed English Canada's growing desire to become more active in the larger Imperial world. While there were no important Canadian interests at stake in South Africa, English Canadians saw the Empire as threatened, sympathized with the plight of the English-speaking minority in the Transvaal, and viewed the Boers as aggressors. Only a handful of English Canadians doubted that Britain's cause was just and not many more opposed the decision to allow Canadian volunteers to be recruited to serve in South Africa as part of a Canadian contingent. English Canadians celebrated with enthusiasm the relief of Kimberley, Ladysmith, and Mafeking and swelled with pride when the Canadian contingent distinguished itself at the battle of Paardeberg. 'Marching to Pretoria' would be sung by generations of young Canadian boys who joined the Canadian branches of the Boy Scout movement, created by Robert Baden-Powell, one of the Imperial 'heroes' to emerge from the South African War. Another hero was the youthful Winston Churchill who undertook his first—but not last—tour of Canada in 1901. But Canada also had its home-grown heroes: Sam Steele, one of the many Mounties who enlisted, and Trooper L. W. R. Mulloy who lost the sight of both eyes and toured the country making patriotic speeches. English-Canadian women wrote patriotic books and verse about the war, raised funds for the war effort, and knitted socks for the 'boys' overseas. When the government called for women volunteers to go to South Africa as teachers (to educate the Boers in British values), over 1,000 volunteered for the forty posts available. In February 1900 Canadian women also formed the Federation of the British Daughters of the Empire, renamed the Imperial Order Daughters of the Empire in 1901, which within a decade had 137 chapters across Canada.[25]

In 1901, Sanford Evans wrote that both 'British Imperialism' in Canada and 'the other great element in national life, Canadianism' have been 'strengthened' because of the war.[26] Other observers noted the same phenomenon. When the Duke of Cornwall toured Canada in 1901, everywhere in English Canada he was greeted by the same message: the desire of English Canadians to create 'a Canadian nation, yet one thoroughly loyal to the British Throne and devoted to the maintenance of those principles on which British institutions are based'.[27] In the 1860s English-Canadian enthusiasm for the Empire may have been tied to a sense of insecurity on a continent dominated by the United States. But by 1901 the American–Canadian boundary had been firmly established (except in Alaska) and the notion that English Canadians and Americans shared the same Anglo-Saxon racial heritage was popular on both sides of the border.[28] A less intense anti-Americanism (though one that could still flare up over issues like the Alaska Boundary dispute) was, however, not a sign that English Canadians were becoming more American and desired continental union but a sign of their self-confidence that they had created the infrastructure for a national community that could resist absorption into the United States. Part of the reason for this self-confidence was that English Canadians felt more integrated into the British Empire than ever before and they no longer feared for the survival of the British Empire on the North American continent. On Dominion Day

[25] Phillip Buckner, 'Canada', in David Omissi and Andrew Thompson, (eds), *The Impact of the South African War* (Houndmills, 2002).

[26] W. Sanford Evans, *The Canadian Contingent and Canadian Imperialism* (Toronto, 1901), p. 328.

[27] *Daily News-Advertiser* (Vancouver), 3 Oct. 1901.

[28] Edward P. Kohn, *This Kindred People: Canadian–American Relations and the Anglo-Saxon Idea, 1895–1903* (Montreal and Kingston, 2004).

in 1891, John Schultz pointed out that he kept two pictures—'garlanded with Maple Leaves'—on his mantelpiece: one of the Queen and the other of the Fathers of Confederation. For Schultz the picture of the Queen symbolized that Canadians were 'heirs, equally with those who live in the British Isles of the glory and traditions of the British Empire'. But the picture of the Fathers of Confederation symbolized that Canadians also had a national identity within the Empire that they were equally determined to preserve.[29] By 1901 one could still find Canadians who believed that 'You can not have two nations in one nation; and if the British Empire is to be one nation, we must not talk of Canadian nationality, or South African nationality'.[30] But Sir John Thompson reflected the voice of the English-Canadian majority when he declared in 1893 that 'every man who is a Canadian at heart feels that this country ought to be a nation, will be a nation and, please God, we shall keep it a nation; but, sir, we do not desire it should be a separate nation'.[31]

[29] John Schultz, 'The Greatness of our Heritage', in *Dominion Day, 1901. Winnipeg Public Schools* (Winnipeg, 1901).

[30] Quoted in Margaret A. Banks, *Sir John George Bourinot, Victorian Canadian* (Montreal and Kingston, 2001), p. 84.

[31] John Castell Hopkins, *Life and Work of the Rt. Hon. Sir John Thompson* (Brantford, 1895), p. 394.

SELECT BIBLIOGRAPHY

CARL BERGER, *The Sense of Power: Studies in the Ideas of Canadian Imperialism, 1867–1914* (Toronto, 1970).

PHILLIP BUCKNER, 'Canada', in David Omissi and Andrew Thompson, (eds), *The Impact of the South African War* (Houndmills, 2002).

LISA CHILTON, *Agents of Empire: British Female Migration to Canad and Australia, 1860s–1930* (Toronto, 2007).

E. A. HEAMEN, *The Inglorious Arts of Peace: Exhibitions in Canadian Society in the Nineteenth Century* (Toronto, 1999).

GED MARTIN, *Britain and the Origins of Canadian Confederation, 1837–1867* (Basingstoke, 1995).

MYRA RUTHERDALE, *Women and the White Man's God: Gender and Race in the Canadian Mission Field* (Vancouver, 2002).

PETER B. WAITE, *Canada, 1874–1896: Arduous Destiny* (Toronto, 1970).

5

Canada and the 'Third British Empire', 1901–1939

John Herd Thompson

On Saturday, 2 February 1901, a parade of men followed the Union Jack through the snow-covered streets of the mining and smelting town of Greenwood, British Columbia, to mourn Victoria, their departed Queen. The town's women and children watched from sidewalks and balconies as the police and volunteer firemen, the mayor and council, clergymen, the Board of Trade, half a dozen fraternal organizations, the Trades and Labour Council, the Western Federation of Miners, workers from other unions, and a group of American citizens marched past. The town's Chinese residents took their place at the rear of the procession; when the parade ended, they stood at the back of the estimated 1,000 people who packed into the local auditorium to take vicarious part in their sovereign's funeral, happening 6,000 miles away in London.[1] Given Greenwood's population of 1,200, this large and diverse crowd suggests the overwhelming Canadian outpouring of grief at Victoria's passing. Variations of Greenwood's ceremony took place 'everywhere throughout Canada'. Victoria's death, wrote journalist J. Castell Hopkins, 'awakened a feeling of sorrow, of sympathy and of Imperial sentiment such as Canada had never felt before'.[2]

If these tributes to the departed Queen were its most vivid demonstration, 'Imperial sentiment' manifested itself in myriad forms among late Victorian and Edwardian Canadians. In September and October 1901, crowds responded passionately as the Duke and Duchess of Cornwall and York—the future King George V and Queen Mary—crossed the country on the 'all-Red route' of the Canadian Pacific Railway. At those towns where their specially built royal train passed without even a whistle stop, ordinary people stood at whatever hour on station platforms to wave Union Jacks.[3] In May 1904, Scottish travel writer

---

[1] *Greenwood Weekly Times,* 31 Jan. and 7 Feb. 1901; photograph of the procession in the National Archives of Canada, PA–51380.

[2] 'Canada and the Crown', *Morang's Annual Register, 1901,* pp. 213, 216.

[3] Phillip Buckner, 'Casting Daylight upon Magic: Deconstructing the Royal Tour of 1901 to Canada', in Carl Bridge and Kent Fedorowich, (eds), *The British World: Diaspora, Culture and Identity* (London, 2003), pp. 158–89.

John Foster Fraser found that Empire Day, launched in Ontario in 1896, was celebrated in English-language schools across the country, and that in Canada 'youngsters were taught patriotism as they were taught how to spell'. Fraser found the Union Jack ubiquitous in every Canadian city 'very much more than in an English town'. Nothing could match Toronto, 'the most ultra-British city on earth . . . Englishmen suffering from a laxity in loyalty should hasten to Toronto, where they can be so impregnated with patriotism that they will want to wear shirt fronts made of the Union Jack.'[4]

It is difficult for present-day historians to be certain what this ubiquitous 'Imperial sentiment' meant. Typically they interpret imperialism as an embryonic form of 'colonial nationalism', echoing the title of Richard Jebb's *Studies in Colonial Nationalism* (1905). Douglas Cole offers a more complex (and more satisfactory) explanation that distinguishes between *nationalism*, 'loyalty to an ethnic nation', and *patriotism*, 'loyalty to a political state'. He argues that 'all Canadians . . . were patriotic toward their own country, some felt a patriotism to Britain and the Empire, and most felt a personal loyalty to the Crown'. But many English-speaking Canadians 'possessed, at the same time, a fully developed Britannic nationalism—a pan-national creed reaching far beyond Canada's boundaries . . . to the larger Britannic or pan-Anglo Saxon nation'.[5] These English-speaking Canadians (who would have called themselves *British* Canadians) seem to have been perfectly comfortable with more than one identity, and could describe themselves as Canadian and as British (or 'Britons', or 'Britishers') in consecutive sentences—sometimes in the same sentence. Sir Wilfrid Laurier spoke, for example, of Canadians' 'conscious pride' in their 'Canadian British citizenship'.[6] Pauline Johnson, Canada's most popular poet, expressed this in a verse that many young Canadians learned by heart:

> The Dutch may have their Holland, the Spaniard have his Spain.
> The Yankee to the south of us, must south of us remain.
> For not a man dare lift a hand, against the men who brag,
> That they were born in Canada, beneath the British flag.[7]

Ronald Hyam points out that among British observers and policy makers 'Pessimism was . . . an all-pervasive and quintessential characteristic of Edwardian thinking about the Empire'.[8] There was general satisfaction that the settlement colonies had made substantial military contributions to the South African War, but considerable uncertainty about whether the Dominions would make such

---

[4] John Foster Fraser, *Canada as it Is* (London, 1905), pp. 22–3, 40–2.

[5] Douglas Cole, 'The Problem of "Nationalism" and "Imperialism" in British Settlement Colonies', *Journal of British Studies*, 10 (1971), pp. 162–4, 174, 178–9.

[6] Canada, House of Commons, *Debates 1902* (hereafter *CHCD*), 14 Feb. 1902, p. 39.

[7] Johnson, *Canadian Born* (Toronto, 1903).

[8] Hyam, 'The British Empire in the Edwardian Era', in Judith M. Brown and W. Roger Louis, (eds), *The Oxford History of the British Empire*, vol. IV: *The Twentieth Century* (hereafter *OHBE*) (Oxford, 1999), p. 50.

contributions in future. John Foster Fraser's warning was widely quoted: 'England must not look to the Dominion to do the same thing again. . . . Canada will be a free agent, whether she helps Britain or not. If she wants to she will; if she doesn't she won't.' It seemed a paradox: 'the spirit of Imperialism is in the Dominion', but 'Canada has moved towards independence, with the slimmest tie to Great Britain'.[9]

Formal constitutional ties to Britain were indeed slim. Canada for all practical purposes governed itself domestically. Britain theoretically controlled Canada's external policies, but, as the war in South Africa demonstrated, Canada made its own decisions about the extent to which it would participate in British international initiatives. The Crown was the most obvious connection to Britain. Victoria's death initiated five months of discussion about amending the royal title to acknowledge the vast changes in the Empire during her long reign. The British Cabinet rejected a Canadian proposal that Canada be named specifically in Edward VII's title, and the Canadian government protested against Colonial Secretary Joseph Chamberlain's proposal that the colonies be included with the phrase 'King . . . of Greater Britain beyond the Seas'. In the end, Edward was designated 'King . . . of the British Dominions beyond the Seas'.[10] The British Cabinet appointed the Crown's representative in Canada, the Governor-General; but the Governor-General, quipped a journalist, had less real political power than 'a saloon keeper or ward boss in the civic politics of the United States'.[11]

Despite the Canadian contingent in South Africa, the military dimension of Canada's relationship with Britain had also become less central in the new century. The Canadian fear of US aggression that had once cemented Imperial ties dissipated considerably after British and American sabre rattling during the Venezuela crisis in 1895 ended without war.[12] Canadians continued to 'regard Americans as a bragging, corrupt, boodle-hunting, nigger-lynching crowd of barbarians', wrote John Foster Fraser in the crude racist idiom of the period, but they no longer feared a barbarian invasion.[13] Although British strategic planners viewed war with the United States as 'improbable', they secretly conceded that a successful defence of Canada was impossible; First Sea Lord Sir John Fisher privately suggested that Britain 'not spend one man or one pound in the defence of Canada'. Britain thus continued the strategic withdrawal from Canada that had begun in 1871; in 1906, the last British garrisons withdrew from Halifax and Esquimalt, replaced by troops from Canada's minuscule army.[14]

---

[9] Fraser, *Canada as it Is*, pp. 246, 266–7.
[10] 'Canada and the Royal Titles', *Canadian Annual Review* (hereafter *CAR*)(1901), pp. 230–2.
[11] Agnes C. Laut, *The Canadian Commonwealth* (Indianapolis, 1915), p. 44.
[12] Norman Penlington, *Canada and Imperialism, 1896–1899* (Toronto, 1965).
[13] Fraser, *Canada as it Is*, p. 41.
[14] Fisher quoted in Samuel F. Wells, Jr., 'British Strategic Withdrawal from the Western Hemisphere', *Canadian Historical Review* (hereafter *CHR*), 49 (1968), p. 348.

Canada's economic relationship with Britain remained of great significance, for British investors provided much of the capital for the development of the infrastructure of its resource economy. Canada also depended on British consumers as a market for many of its exports. Canadian consumers, however, despite professions of admiration for British products, bought relatively few British-manufactured goods. The Laurier government, in a brilliant political stroke that neutralized Conservative accusations of Liberal disloyalty, reduced Canada's 'National Policy' protective tariff toward Britain in 1897–8, and maintained a higher tariff against the United States. This so-called 'Imperial preference', however, did not dramatically increase British exports to Canada; measured by value, Canadians continued to import three times as much from the United States as they did from Britain.

These constitutional, military, and economic connections with Canada were among the many intra-imperial bonds that Joseph Chamberlain attempted to tighten in his eight years (1895–1903) as Secretary of State for the Colonies.[15] In the hoary liberal nationalist account that forms part of Canada's creation myth, Canada becomes 'the thorn in the lion's paw' as heroic Liberal Prime Minister Wilfrid Laurier (1896–1911) relentlessly defends his country's autonomy from the evil designs of Imperial arch villain Chamberlain. As with all myths, there is a grain of truth; as befitted the senior Dominion that never failed to celebrate its seniority, Canada did in fact lead a wider Dominion resistance. Laurier rebuffed Chamberlain's attempts at closer unity at the 1897 and 1902 Colonial Conferences. He repeated his performance for Chamberlain's successors at conferences in 1907 and 1911, which were designated 'Imperial' rather than merely 'Colonial'. Laurier's behaviour at these conferences was always courtly, and his resistance to Imperial consolidation was passive or passive-aggressive, however much private fury it aroused among the constructive imperialists. Laurier did not overtly refuse Imperial commitment; instead, he temporized. Asked in 1902 for a financial contribution to the Royal Navy, he responded that Canada was 'contemplating the establishment of a local naval force'. Laurier 'contemplated' until 1910 before establishing a 'tin pot' Royal Canadian Navy by purchasing two ageing British cruisers. 'I would rather do business with a cad who knows his own mind,' grumbled Chamberlain in frustration.[16]

Chamberlain's irritation is understandable, because Laurier sent him so many mixed messages. Knighted in 1897, *Sir* Wilfrid said at the ceremony that it was 'the proudest moment of my life'. Laurier was unmoved by ethnic-based Britannic nationalism, but he espoused what a biographer has called an

---

[15] John Eddy and Deryck Schreuder provide a splendid summary of 'Imperial initiatives and Dominion responses' in the introduction to Eddy and Schreuder, (eds), *The Rise of Colonial Nationalism: Australia, New Zealand, Canada, and South Africa First Assert their Nationalities, 1880–1914* (Sydney, 1988).

[16] Jacques Monet, 'Canadians, *Canadiens* and Colonial Nationalism, 1896–1914: The Thorn in the Lion's Paw', ibid., pp. 160–91.

'intellectual imperialism' based on a profound and genuine admiration for British political institutions and ideals.[17] Reflecting upon the royal tour of 1901, Laurier remembered his own youthful debate about 'whether monarchical government or republican government was the preferable'. Now, he concluded, 'all such discussions have become obsolete. . . . We, in Canada, have the blessing of living under British monarchical institutions, and we appreciate them to the full.'[18]

Whatever his personal views, Laurier (or any Canadian Prime Minister) had to be cautious about Imperial centralization, for appearing subservient to Britain carried a heavy political price. French Canadians, who made up a third of Canada's population, watched warily for any signs of acquiescence. Canada's most outspoken anti-imperialist was Henri Bourassa, a former backbencher who left Laurier's Liberal Party to protest sending a Canadian contingent to South Africa.[19] Until the conscription crisis during the First World War, outright anti-imperialists like Bourassa were remarkably few in French Canada, but English Canada's imperial zeal was absent. While the premiers of the six primarily English-speaking provinces eagerly journeyed to London to attend King Edward's coronation, Quebec dispatched Provincial Treasurer H. T. Duffy as its representative.[20] In 1906, J. A. Hobson found 'no disloyalty, active or latent, to the British Empire' in Quebec.[21] Indeed, the prevalent elite French-Canadian discourse credited the British connection for creating a political context in which French-Canadian Roman Catholics had been able to flourish. In 1908 the Archbishop of Montreal told a congress in London's Albert Hall that to 'stand up in the heart of the Empire and openly speak of my faith . . . under the fullest protection of the British flag, has been to me supreme happiness. Always I have spoken beneath two flags, the Union Jack symbolizing our loyalty; the Papal flag symbolizing our faith.'[22] When the Honourable Adélard Turgeon welcomed the Prince of Wales back to open the Quebec tercentenary celebrations in 1908, he praised the 'British liberty which had allowed national dualism to thrive' in Canada.[23]

Canada's Irish Catholic minority shared a similar appreciation of 'the liberties received by Canadians under the British flag', and had moved away from its anti-British heritage, a process that Mark McGowan has called 'The Waning of the Green'. By 1900, the Irish Catholic weekly *Catholic Record* went so far as to describe Canada as 'the chief jewel that adorns the Imperial crown'. This did not mean that Canada's Irish Catholics had suddenly joined Irish Protestants

---

[17] Blair Neatby, 'Laurier and Imperialism', in Carl Berger, (ed.), *Imperial Relations in the Age of Laurier* (Toronto, 1969), pp. 1–9.

[18] *CHCD*, 14 Feb. 1902, p. 39.

[19] Henri Bourassa, *Great Britain and Canada* (Montreal, 1902), p. 4.

[20] *CAR* (1902), pp. 98–106.   [21] J. A. Hobson, *Canada To-day* (London, 1906), p. 57.

[22] Archbishop quoted in *CAR* (1908), p. 580.

[23] Turgeon quoted in H. V. Nelles, *The Art of Nation-Building: Pageantry and Spectacle at Quebec's Tercentenary* (Toronto, 1999), p. 27.

as avid Britannic nationalists—most of them praised Laurier's resistance to the 'new imperialism'—but it eliminated them as potential anti-imperialists.[24] Only a handful of articulate critics spoke out against Empire in English-speaking Canada, most notably Toronto professor Goldwin Smith and Winnipeg (after 1904, Ottawa) lawyer J. S. Ewart, who urged in the *Kingdom of Canada* (1908) that Canada 'say to the British connection "Adieu"', with an outright declaration of independence. Neither man had any organized following or links to his French-Canadian counterparts.

Most of Canada's self-proclaimed imperialists, however, no matter how high they waved the Union Jack, showed strikingly little genuine enthusiasm for concrete projects to consolidate the Empire. When J. A. Hobson interviewed Manitoba's Conservative Premier R. P. Roblin in 1905, he discovered that 'neither he nor any other public man [in Canada] with whom I conversed is really favorable to any strengthening of the political bonds with Great Britain'.[25] As devout a protectionist as an imperialist, Roblin also dismissed proposals to unify the Empire economically through tariff reform. In this, he mirrored Canadian businessmen's hostility to Chamberlain's vision that Canada should eschew manufacturing and serve instead as the 'granary of Empire'. An economy without a manufacturing base would be a 'blighted destiny' for Canada, the economist Adam Shortt protested in the *Imperial Preferential Tariff from a Canadian Point of View* (1904).[26] Laurier's passive resistance to a more centralized Empire, it would seem, reflected the real outlook of most Canadians, even many of the most vociferous Britannic nationalists. As John Eddy and Deryck Schreuder put it, 'settler affiliations to the British Empire were surely both obvious and real, yet also more *conditional* with each passing year'.[27]

British visitors regularly expressed concern that Canadians were being culturally 'Americanized'. In 1907, US sociologist Samuel E. Moffett described *The Americanization of Canada* with an air of satisfaction. That 'baseball is becoming the national game of Canada instead of cricket' and that Canadian newspapers spelled 'labor' and 'armor' without the letter 'u' was proof that 'The English speaking Canadians . . . are already Americans without knowing it.' Moffett concluded that Canada would soon be absorbed into the United States.[28] Others reached very different conclusions. French sociologist André Siegfried recognized 'American ideas, habits, and tendencies', but found these superficial: 'at bottom, by taste and tradition, English Canadians are very English still'.[29] Siegfried might

[24] Mark McGowan, *The Waning of the Green: Catholics, the Irish and Identity in Toronto, 1887–1922* (Montreal and Kingston, 1999), pp. 202–9.

[25] Hobson, *Canada To-day*, p. 22.

[26] Shortt reproduced in Carl Berger, (ed.), *Imperialism and Nationalism, 1884–1914: A Conflict in Canadian Thought* (Toronto, 1969), pp. 79–81.

[27] Eddy and Schreuder, *Colonial Nationalism*, p. 33.

[28] Samuel E. Moffett, *The Americanization of Canada* (Toronto, 1972), pp. 9, 97, 109, 114.

[29] André Siegfried, *The Race Question in Canada* (London, 1907), pp. 95–103.

have added Scottish, Irish, and Welsh, for between 1901 and 1921, 752,000 immigrants came to Canada from the British Isles, three times as many as from the United States.[30]

After the Alaska Boundary decision of 1903, however, there was widespread Canadian complaint about British management of Canada's diplomatic relationship with the United States. British strategic need for US goodwill had led to a bilateral agreement that a commission of six 'impartial' jurists would resolve the disputed boundary. President Theodore Roosevelt chose three outspoken partisans as the US commissioners, and the two commissioners chosen by Canada were equally committed to the Canadian position. Lord Alverstone, appointed by the British Cabinet as the third British representative, voted with the Americans to support the US territorial claim. Dispassionate assessment of the evidence suggests that Lord Alverstone would have been remiss to find otherwise. In Canada, however, the decision spurred simultaneous anti-Americanism and resentment against British authority. To protect itself against the 'very grasping' United States, Laurier announced in the Commons, 'it is important that we should ask the British Parliament for more extensive power'.[31] Laurier never made a formal request for such power, but the years that followed saw the gradual emergence of de facto direct relations between Ottawa and Washington, with only minimal British supervision. The process scarcely amounted to a Canadian declaration of independence, since at each stage Canada had British cooperation. Indeed, the impetus for the establishment of a tiny Canadian Department of External Affairs in 1909 came from British Ambassador James Bryce in Washington, who complained that Canadian–American relations tied up three-quarters of the embassy's attention, and demanded 'a sort of Foreign Office' in Ottawa to coordinate Canadian affairs in Washington.[32]

The white racism that was a universal feature of Britannic nationalism in the settlement colonies led to more acerbic conflict between Britain and Canada over migration from India and Japan. Indians as British subjects theoretically had a right to migrate to other Empire destinations; after the 1902 Anglo-Japanese agreement, Japan became Britain's Pacific ally, vital to British strategy in the Far East. Avner Offer exaggerates only slightly when he argues that excluding these migrants 'forced Australia and Canada into a foreign policy of their own, in the name of popular sovereignty and nationhood'.[33] In 1908, the Laurier government sent a cabinet minister to Japan to negotiate a 'Gentleman's Agreement' in which the Japanese promised that no more than 400 Japanese migrants each year would

---

[30] Stephen Constantine, 'Migrants and Settlers', *OHBE* vol. IV, p. 167.

[31] *CHCD*, 23 Oct. 1903, pp. 14812–17.

[32] Bryce quoted in John Hilliker, *Canada's Department of External Affairs* (Montreal, 1990), pp. 30–4. See also Peter Neary, 'Grey, Bryce, and the Settlement of Canadian–American Differences, 1905–1911', *CHR*, 49 (1968), pp. 357–80.

[33] Avner Offer, '"Pacific Rim" Societies: Asian Labour and White Nationalism', in Eddy and Schreuder, *Colonial Nationalism*, pp. 227–47.

embark for Canada. In 1910, Canada checked immigration from India with a law that required migrants to travel from their homelands by a 'continuous voyage'; no steamship company sold 'through' tickets from India to Canada.[34] In 1914, however, 376 Sikhs sailed directly to Vancouver on the Japanese ship *Komagata Maru* to test the law. The India Office pressed for their admission, but Canada refused to bend; only twenty-two passengers who had previously resided in Canada were allowed to land. The *Komagata Maru* lay at anchor for two months until the ship and its passengers were escorted out of the harbour by the cruiser HMCS *Rainbow*—one half of Canada's tiny navy.[35]

Naval defence played a role in the defeat of the Laurier government in 1911. Laurier had made clear that if 'the naval supremacy of the Empire were challenged . . . we must aid England with all our force', but his policy—a small Canadian navy that would cooperate with the Royal Navy in wartime—was too imperial for French Canada, and not imperial enough for Britannic nationalists.[36] The naval debate eroded Laurier's support in Quebec, and set the stage for a bitter general election fought on the issue of Imperial loyalty. The Laurier government had negotiated a reciprocal trade agreement that removed tariffs on the natural products that Canada exported to the United States, but left most Canadian tariffs on manufactured goods in place, including the 'Imperial preference'. Nonetheless, manufacturers denounced reciprocity as a threat that would (the language is significant) simultaneously doom 'Canadian autonomy' and 'weaken the ties which bind Canada to the Empire'. Bankrolled by these manufacturers, the Conservatives led by Robert Borden made the election a choice between 'the Union Jack and British connection as opposed to the Stars and Stripes and Yankee domination'.[37] Henri Bourassa's newspaper *Le Devoir* offered the French-Canadian variant, pointedly asking if Quebec would enjoy the same religious and linguistic guarantees if it became a state of the American union.[38] The Conservatives' loyalty campaign won the party a comfortable majority in the House of Commons, but the reciprocity debate was more than electoral America bashing. The long-term effect of the agreement would have been essentially similar to that of Chamberlain's 1902 plan for an Imperial *Zollverein*: Canada would have remained a producer of primary products, with a limited manufacturing sector, but with the United States rather than Britain as its metropole. The Canadian capitalists and politicians who opposed reciprocity believed that—in Robert Borden's words—Canada's 'marvellous

---

[34] R. C. Brown and Ramsay Cook, *Canada, 1896–1921: A Nation Transformed* (Toronto, 1974), pp. 70–1.

[35] Hugh Johnston, *The Voyage of the Komagata Maru: The Sikh Challenge to Canada's Colour Bar* (Delhi, 1979).

[36] Neatby, 'Laurier and Imperialism', p. 7.

[37] Manufacturers and Borden quoted in W. M. Baker, 'A Case Study of Anti-Americanism in English-Speaking Canada: The Election Campaign of 1911', *CHR*, 51 (1970), pp. 432, 435.

[38] *Le Devoir*, 1 Feb. 1911, p. 2.

material resources' destined the country for 'the highest position within this mighty Empire'. They were determined that within a British world system, Canada need not be relegated to a peripheral position as Britain's 'hewer of wood and drawer of water'.[39]

Despite their undoubtedly sincere professions of imperial unity, the new Conservative government brought Canada little closer to Empire in any institutional sense. Borden immediately dashed any hopes of British tariff reformers that he would forge economic links; his business supporters were adamant that Imperial preference not be increased. Conservative naval policy contained both a bill to provide a financial contribution to the Royal Navy, and a proposal to expand the Royal Canadian Navy, but the former did not pass the Upper House of Parliament, the Senate, and the latter never reached the order paper. Borden repeatedly insisted that expanded responsibility for Imperial naval defence would entitle Canada 'to a greater voice in the councils of Empire' to shape foreign policy, but his attempts to negotiate such a voice with Britain's Liberal Cabinet were rebuffed or answered with token gestures. Borden often expounded a new vision of Canada as a mediator in the Anglo-American relationship, a 'voice . . . for harmony and not for discord between our Empire and the great republic'. [40] There is no evidence that either the British Foreign Office or the US Department of State took any notice of his presumption.

Like the rest of the Empire, Canada entered the world war automatically with King George V's declaration. As did the other Dominions, however, it determined the scope of its contribution. Throughout the conflict, Canadian farm families, fishers, and industrial workers sustained the British war effort. Canadian flour, beef, pork, and salmon fed soldiers and British civilians. By 1917, coordinated through an Imperial Munitions Board directed by Canadian businessman Sir Joseph Flavelle, Canada's factories provided one-third of the munitions the British armies used on the Western Front. In those 'Flanders Fields', Canada also paid a heavy price in blood for the Allied victory. As the war coagulated into horrific stalemate, the Canadian Expeditionary Force, the initial Dominion troops to arrive in France, grew to five divisions by 1918. First engaged at the second Battle of Ypres in April 1915, where they held against a terrible new German weapon, poisonous chlorine gas, the Canadians fought at Festubert and Givenchy, in the craters at Saint-Eloi, at Mont Sorrel, and in the disastrous offensive along the Somme between June and October 1916. After the catastrophe on the Somme, Field Marshal Douglas Haig concluded that infantry battalions from the Dominions were the British army's most effective shock troops. In 1917, the four divisions of the Canadian Corps attacked Vimy

[39] Simon Potter, 'The Significance of the Canadian–American Reciprocity Proposals of 1911', *Historical Journal*, 47 (2004), pp. 81–100; John Herd Thompson and Stephen J. Randall, *Ambivalent Allies: Canada and the United States* (Athens, Ga., 2002), pp. 86–92.

[40] Robert Craig Brown: *Robert Laird Borden: A Biography*, vol. I: *1854–1914* (Toronto, 1975), pp. 231–45.

Ridge in April, Hill 70 in August, and Passchendaele in October. In 1918, they spearheaded the massive hundred-day counteroffensive that concluded on 11 November with the Armistice.[41]

Victory cost Canada more than the 61,000 dead servicemen and women, and the 173,000 wounded. The domestic stress caused by the war almost literally tore the Dominion apart. In August 1914, there had been widespread national agreement with opposition leader Sir Wilfrid Laurier's promise that Canada was 'Ready, aye, ready' to 'answer to the call of duty'. Initial conceptions of Canada's part in the war were built on this notion of duty to 'Mother Britain'. For a majority of English Canadians, however, the notion that Canada fought as a dutiful offspring of Empire soon gave way to a concept of a crusade for democracy and civilization, in which Canada became Britain's ally rather than a colony. Canada fought, a Canadian journalist attempted to explain to a US audience, out of 'loyalty to an ideal, not to a dynasty, nor to a country. She loves Britain because Britain stands for that ideal.' Canada's destiny, Agnes Laut went on, was to become 'a democratized edition of a Greater Britain Overseas.'[42] Most English Canadians came to share this vision; virtually no French Canadians could.[43] When Sir Robert Borden's government pledged Canada, with a population of fewer than 8,000,000, to maintain an army of 500,000 men in Flanders, his commitment led to military conscription, to a Union Government to impose it, and to a bitter wartime election that split Canada largely along French–English lines. Attempting to enforce conscription led to riots in Quebec at Easter, 1918. Troops from Ontario fired on a crowd that was pelting them with snowballs, killing four civilians.

Historians of Canada almost unanimously echo Carl Berger's conclusion that Canadian imperialism 'was a casualty of the First World War'.[44] There can be no doubt that, to most French Canadians, the war represented the humiliating process through which English Canada had compelled conscription; French Canada's pre-war indifference to Empire turned into apprehension of its potential military burden. For English Canadians war left a more complex legacy, however. First, historians have argued, pride in the role of the Canadian Corps in the Allied victory (although that contribution found little place in British official histories) laid the cornerstone of independent Canadian nationhood. They cite the assault on Vimy Ridge universally to symbolize 'the fact that the Great War was also Canada's war of independence even if it was fought at

---

[41] Robert Holland, 'The British Empire and the Great War, 1914–1918', *OHBE* IV, pp. 114–37; Desmond Morton, *A Military History of Canada* (Toronto, 1992), pp. 130–65.

[42] Laut, *The Canadian Commonwealth*, pp. 109–10.

[43] This argument is developed in John Herd Thompson, *The Harvests of War: The Prairie West, 1914–1918* (Toronto, 1978); Matthew Bray, 'Fighting as an Ally: The English-Canadian Patriotic Response to the Great War', *CHR* 64 (1980), pp. 141–68; and Ian Hugh Maclean Miller, *Our Glory & our Grief: Torontonians and the Great War* (Toronto, 2002).

[44] Carl Berger, *The Sense of Power: Studies in the Ideas of Canadian Imperialism, 1867–1914* (Toronto, 1970), pp. 5, 264.

Britain's side against a common enemy'.[45] Second, they have contended, the war taught Canadians that 'death and futility, not glory and civilization, were the hallmarks of imperialism'. Although 'a sentimental attachment to Britain would continue . . . the Empire was an anachronistic term'.[46]

Neither central argument of this 'death of Canadian imperialism' interpretation—that war bred nationalism and that post-war disillusionment was widespread in Canada—stands recent close examination. In his case study of the post-war attitudes of officers who served in the Canadian Corps, Patrick H. Brennan finds them 'intensely loyal to the concept of Empire and the inherent British character of Canada', and argues that these men 'saw the Dominion's future inextricably linked to the maintenance of a strong imperial link'. They 'had no difficulty reconciling what on the surface might appear to be two allegiances'.[47] In *Death So Noble*, Jonathan Vance concludes that Canadian artists, writers, and intellectuals escaped the bitter post-war cynicism that drowned their counterparts in Britain and in the US 'lost generation'. Vance describes 'a legacy, not of despair, aimlessness, and futility, but of promise, [and] certainty . . . that the war had been a just one, fought to defend Christianity and Western civilization'.[48] In the English-Canadian mind, the relationship with Britain had indeed evolved. At the beginning of the century, they had anthropomorphized Britain as the parent and Canada as the eldest child, or Britain as the stern older brother with Canada as the rambunctious youngster. During and after the Great War, the Empire became instead a 'sisterhood of free nations under one King'. President Franklin Roosevelt put it exactly this way in a less quoted sentence of his famous speech in Kingston, Ontario, in August 1938: 'Canada is part of the sisterhood of the British Empire.' Dominion status was thus 'a distinctive blend of national status and Imperial identity', and Canadians saw themselves as central to the creation of what John Darwin calls 'A Third British Empire'.[49] There was delight in Canada when the Anglo-Irish Treaty of 1921 made the Irish Free State a Dominion. 'We welcome Ireland into that great sisterhood of nations', editorialized the *Catholic Record*, 'to which she yet may render service as joyous and as loyally as does the Dominion of Canada.'[50]

Canada's leaders were at the centre of the constitutional transformation of the British Empire that began in 1917 with Sir Robert Borden's Resolution IX

---

[45] Morton, *Military History of Canada*, p. 145.

[46] R. G. Moyles and Doug Owram, *Imperial Dreams and Colonial Realities: British Views of Canada, 1880–1914* (Toronto, 1988), pp. 238–41.

[47] Patrick H. Brennan, 'The Other Battle: Imperialist vs. Nationalist Sentiments among Senior Officers of the Canadian Corps', in P. A. Buckner and R. Douglas Francis, (eds), *Rediscovering the British World* (Calgary, 2005).

[48] Jonathan Vance, *Death So Noble: Meaning, Memory, and the First World War* (Vancouver, 1997), pp. 266–7.

[49] John Darwin, 'A Third British Empire? The Dominion Idea in Imperial Politics', in *OHBE*, vol. IV, p. 71.

[50] *Catholic Record* quoted in McGowan, *Waning of the Green*, p. 201.

at the Imperial Ministers' Conference, that the Dominions were 'autonomous nations of an Imperial Commonwealth' with the right 'to an adequate voice in foreign policy'. The transformation concluded in 1931 with the Statute of Westminster. Older Canadian accounts interpret this trajectory in two phases, a period of 'tentative centralization' between 1917 and 1922, during the Conservative prime ministerships of Robert Borden and Arthur Meighen, followed by 'decentralization' from 1923 until 1926 with Liberal William Lyon Mackenzie King in office in Ottawa.[51] Modern interpretations suggest that attempts to centralize the Empire existed only in Dominion imaginations, and that centralization failed (or was never really attempted) because neither the Dominions nor the British government wanted it. The one example of coordination, the Dominion prime ministers' participation as part of a 'British Empire delegation' in the 1919 Peace Conference, was largely ceremonial. Visions of a common Imperial foreign policy vanished at the first post-war Imperial Conference, in June 1921. Arthur Meighen successfully opposed renewal of the Anglo-Japanese naval alliance lest it damage relations with the USA, even though Australia and New Zealand wanted it to be renewed. (A Liberal MP from Quebec praised Meighen for his 'manly stand' against 'the blandishments of the imperialists'.[52]) Mackenzie King, who succeeded Meighen in 1922, took great pride in fighting off Imperial advances. As Philip Wigley has pointed out, however, 'at no point had his predecessors committed the country to imperial policies beyond the immediate sanction of the Dominion government'. Wigley and other historians have also made clear that, however much the Colonial Office might muse about Imperial unity, the Foreign Office 'had little patience for collective policy making', and was delighted to be rid of any need to take the Dominions' perspectives into account.[53]

The one difficult moment in an otherwise serene progression came in 1922, when Colonial Secretary Winston Churchill attempted to manipulate the Dominions to commit contingents to a looming confrontation with Turkey by leaking his request for troops to the press. English-Canadian newspapers responded exactly as Churchill expected; the Toronto *Globe*'s headline read 'British Lion Calls Cubs to Face the Beast of Asia'. Mackenzie King, justifiably outraged, announced that Canada would commit no troops without the approval of the Canadian Parliament, and the crisis blew over before Parliament reconvened. South Africa and Australia behaved similarly. British Foreign Secretary Lord Curzon thus had no reason to invite the Dominions to help make peace with Turkey, and King was delighted not to be invited. In the shadow of this 'Chanak Crisis', the Imperial Conference of 1923 roughed in the outlines of the new British

---

[51] R. McGregor Dawson, *The Development of Dominion Status, 1900–1936* (London, 1937).

[52] Liberal MP C. G. Power in *CHCD*, 26 Mar. 1923, p. 1535.

[53] Philip Wigley, *Canada and the Transition to Commonwealth: British–Canadian Relations, 1917–1926* (Cambridge, 1977), pp. 3–4.

Empire. King played Laurier, insisted that the Conference was not a 'Cabinet shaping policy for the British Empire', and refused any advance commitments to support British policies. Curzon refused to play Chamberlain, however, and offered no proposals for a centralized Empire, for neither Curzon nor anyone else in the Foreign Office wanted Dominion partners in diplomacy. The Empire that emerged from the conference was perhaps not decentralized enough for the leaders of South Africa or the Irish Free State, and perhaps a little too decentralized for those of Australia and New Zealand, but it suited both Curzon and King.

Lord Balfour's Report after the subsequent conference of 1926 defined the Dominions as 'autonomous communities within the British Empire'. To confirm this autonomy, Canada created legations in Paris, Tokyo, and (most importantly) Washington. But the words 'embassy' and 'ambassador' were avoided deliberately to make clear that 'autonomy' did not mean 'a parting of the ways' with the Empire. The 'Minister' to the United States, Vincent Massey, was an ardent Anglophile who was announced to a bemused President Coolidge by his full title: 'His Britannic Majesty's Envoy Extraordinary and Minister Plenipotentiary to represent the interests of the Dominion of Canada'. The British government almost simultaneously appointed a High Commissioner to Ottawa, so that the Governor-General could serve exclusively as Canada's head of state and not as Britain's representative; Britain also renounced the Governor-General's long unused power to disallow and reserve Canadian legislation. In 1931, the Statute of Westminster completed Canada's constitutional autonomy, with two significant exceptions: judicial appeals to the Privy Council continued and the power to amend the British North America Act remained with the British Parliament. This significant Imperial constitutional authority remained in London not because Britain wanted to retain it, but because of disagreements between the provinces and the Dominion government. The provinces had more confidence in the Judicial Committee of the Privy Council than in the Supreme Court of Canada: 'Men far removed from the battlefield are better qualified to pass an impartial judgment,' Quebec Premier Louis-Alexandre Taschereau explained.[54]

Taschereau's remark and Massey's ornate title suggest the ambiguity of 'autonomy'. Americans found this apparent incongruity incomprehensible. In a series of lectures, University of Toronto historian George M. Wrong struggled to explicate 'The Place of Canada in the British Empire' to a US audience. The 'paradox of the British nations', he explained, was that 'the more they become separate . . . the more they hold together'. He himself was 'a Briton, [and] a Canadian' because 'it never occurred to the average Canadian . . . that he could not remain both'.[55] Wrong, like most Canadians, felt no contradictions among

[54] John Herd Thompson with Allen Seager, *Canada, 1922–1939: Decades of Discord* (Toronto, 1985), pp. 46–9, 136–7.
[55] George M. Wrong, *The United States and Canada: A Political Study* (New York, 1921), pp. 133, 140–1, 167, 190–1.

being British, Canadian, and living next door to the United States. Elites in Britain and in Canada nonetheless continued to agonize about what Governor General Lord Willingdon described as 'the dangers to the British Empire' from the 'process of peaceful penetration' of Canada by American mass culture: movies, magazines, radio broadcasts, and sport.[56] The large team of social scientists who surveyed Canadian attitudes between 1932 and 1934 for *Canada and her Great Neighbor* (research funded by a US foundation, and published in the United States) concluded that worries about 'Americanization' were groundless. Despite mass culture—perhaps because of it—they found that Canadians remained hypercritical of the United States; US movies, magazines, and radio broadcasts only confirmed the negative stereotypes that they already held of Americans. Some Canadians expressed 'a strong consciousness of kinship with the American nation', but their 'acknowledged loyalties are to Canada and Great Britain'. S. D. Clark, the sociologist who studied 'Imperial Sentiment and Dual Loyalty', concluded that 'imperial and national patriotism reinforce one another and are quick to present a common front to North Americanism'. Most interviewees in Alberta (supposedly the most 'American' province) held 'a deep attachment to British institutions', and thought that 'Canada should "work out her own destiny" guided by the British tradition of values in government, law, and public morality'.[57]

If the United States dominated popular culture after 1920, Britain remained, as it had always been, the ultimate arbiter of Canadian tastes in serious music, art, drama, and dance. In their flights of fancy, Canadian creators of high culture imagined, in Vancouver poet A. M. Stephen's words, that 'even as the culture of Athens was superseded [by Rome] . . . so will the centres of culture move from the British Isles to the Dominions'.[58] Governors-General remained the country's most important patrons of the arts, and each tried to leave a cultural legacy. Lord Willingdon established the Willingdon Arts Competitions in Music, Literature, Painting, and Sculpture in 1928, and Lord Bessborough founded the Dominion Drama Festival in 1932. British experts came to Canada not only to display their own work, but also to instruct Canadians. Dramatist Sir Barry Jackson lectured to theatre groups in 1929, toured in 1931 with his own company, adjudicated the Dominion Drama Festival, and presented the Sir Barry Jackson Challenge Trophy for the best original play written by a Canadian. Scottish filmmaker John Grierson created the National Film Board, which became Canada's most internationally recognized cultural institution. British expatriates saw themselves as launching Canadians, not imposing British styles upon them. The career of Englishman Eric Brown, curator of the National Gallery of Canada from

[56] Willingdon to Stanley Baldwin, cited in Norman Hillmer, 'Anglo-Canadian Relations, 1926–1937', Ph.D. thesis (Cambridge University, 1974), p. 92.
[57] H. F. Angus, (ed.), *Canada and her Great Neighbor: Sociological Surveys of Opinions and Attitudes in Canada Concerning the United States* (Toronto, 1938), pp. 116, 231.
[58] Thompson with Seager, *Canada, 1922–1939*, pp. 158–92, Stephen quoted p. 161.

1910 until 1939, offers revealing insight on the intersection of national and imperial identities. Brown helped establish the Group of Seven, impressionist landscape artists whose paintings Canadians still regard as the quintessence of their national identity on canvas. Brown made sure that the Group's work was well represented at the 1924 Empire Exhibition at Wembley, and this validation in Britain confirmed the seven self-styled iconoclasts as the dominant force in Canadian art.[59]

However much Canada's 'imagined community' (to use Benedict Anderson's much-quoted term) had been reimagined since the Victorian era, two things remained constant: the United States remained the principal 'Other' against which Canadians defined themselves, and 'Britishness' remained indispensable to new versions of 'Canadian-ness'. A researcher for the *Canada and her Great Neighbor* project who examined Maritime newspapers noted how editorials often contrasted favourable British examples to negative American ones. As but one example, a story 'with gruesome detail' of the lynching of an African American was 'first greedily devoured by the Halifax or St. John reader, and then made a text in his local newspaper to remind him how it is only the old country inheritance that has preserved Canada from sinking to this level'. Being Canadian required feeling morally superior to the United States, and as political economist Henry Angus observed, 'In endeavoring to maintain a sense of superiority, it is a great help to be able to count British virtues as well as Canadian.'[60]

Identities, of course, are never stationary. In the 1920s and 1930s, a new concept of Canada as a 'mosaic' of diverse ethno-cultural groups became, in Ian McKay's words, 'the governing metaphor of the new post-colonial liberal nationalism that gradually overshadowed many Canadians' earlier identification with Britain'. Canadians negotiated this celebration of difference within a continuing discourse of Britishness, however. The 'mosaic' did not so much 'overshadow . . . earlier identification with Britain', as MacKay argues,[61] as it was constructed upon a new emphasis on a new imagined multicultural British Empire, composed of diverse peoples with multiple loyalties and identities, that could be held up both as symbol and as legitimization for Canadian diversity. The mosaic thus made space within the British-Canadian 'imagined community' for those Canadians without British Isles ancestry. 'That formula of "unity in diversity"', wrote Université de Montréal economist Edouard Montpetit in 1934, 'is certainly, in an increasing degree, the hallmark of the British Commonwealth of Nations.'[62] John Murray Gibbon's *Canadian Mosaic* (1938), the foundational text of the mosaic metaphor, quoted approvingly Governor-General

---

[59] Maria Tippett, *Making Culture: English-Canadian Institutions and the Arts before the Massey Commission* (Toronto, 1990), passim.

[60] Angus, *Canada and her Great Neighbor*, pp. 168, 248.

[61] Ian McKay, *The Quest of the Folk: Antimodernism and Cultural Selection in Twentieth Century Nova Scotia* (Montreal and Kingston, 1994), p. 57.

[62] Montpetit, 'French Canada', in *Canada and her Great Neighbor*, p. 34.

Lord Tweedsmuir's admonition to Ukrainian Canadians to 'remember your old Ukrainian traditions', and the reciprocal thanks that the Governor-General received for the 'opportunity for our cultural development. . . we Canadian Ukrainians have found under the British Crown'. There remained no doubt, however, that the most important tiles in the mosaic were those from the British Isles. Gibbon dedicated his book to the Imperial Order Daughters of the Empire, and lauded the IODE for 'helping to cement this Canadian Mosaic'. He lavished praise upon the Order's 'Official ceremonies of welcome', held when immigrants were naturalized to 'impress upon New Canadians of foreign birth the privileges and duties of British citizenship'.[63]

The 1930s saw the conspicuous adoption of British symbols and discourse by non-British British subjects. Union Jacks and protestations of loyalty to the Crown became ubiquitous in newspaper reports of Ukrainian, Czech, and Polish celebrations. In 1938, under the Union Jack and the flag of Poland, Manitoba Lieutenant-Governor W. J. Tupper and his wife led the Mazurka Grand March at the Polish Springtime Festival at Winnipeg's Royal Alexandra Hotel.[64] In Dresden, Ontario, 1,500 Czechoslovakians paraded to celebrate 'Dozenky' (a harvest festival) 'led by a Czech band, clad in their native costumes, and headed by the Union Jack'.[65] British Canadians consciously and willingly incorporated such 'New Canadians' into public commemorations of Britishness. In Manitoba, the Polish Falcon Society joined the Orange Lodge and the Sons of England in the official ceremonies to mark George VI's coronation; the highlight of the concert was the Ukrainian National Choir singing Kipling's 'Land of our Birth'![66] There were millions of such Canadians, wrote journalist M. G. O'Leary, 'who do not know the call of the blood', but who 'revere the Crown and Empire, which believes. . . in human diversity, diversity of races, of creeds, of ancient faiths and loyalties'.[67] It is easy to document the manipulation of British symbols by 'New Canadians', but much more difficult to know what those symbols meant to them. It would seem, however, that the curricular focus in English language schools on 'commitment to Canada's British traditions, and pride in Canada's membership in the British Empire' had succeeded at least on a superficial level.[68]

The inter-war period became the apex of Canadian affection for the Crown, a sense of intimacy built in part by radio. The Canadian Broadcasting Corporation was, in Prime Minister Bennett's words, 'a dependable link in a chain of Empire communication', and King George V turned out to be an extraordinarily effective

---

[63] Gibbon, *Canadian Mosaic: The Making of a Northern Nation* (Toronto, 1938), pp. 305–7, 414–17; see also Katie Pickles, *Female Imperialism and National Identity: Imperial Order Daughters of the Empire* (Manchester, 2002), pp. 91–107.

[64] *Winnipeg Tribune*, 22 Apr. 1938.   [65] Toronto *Globe*, 18 Aug. 1938.

[66] Archives of Manitoba, John Bracken Papers, 'Coronation—12 May 1937', file 1084.

[67] O'Leary, 'The Sovereign Ideal', *Maclean's*, 15 May 1939, p. 5.

[68] Ken Osborne, 'Public Schooling and Citizenship Education in Canada', *Canadian Ethnic Studies*, 32 (2000), p. 14.

broadcaster.[69] The King's annual Empire Day and Christmas messages, which began in 1932 with a script written by Rudyard Kipling, were among Canada's highest-rated programmes. An otherwise unsentimental academic gushed after the broadcast of George V's 1935 silver jubilee that 'An emotional moment in the life of the Empire had been intensified and vitalized to serve, the cause of national patriotism, or of Imperial brotherhood.' Live CBC radio coverage took Canadian listeners to George V's funeral, and to Edward VIII's abdication. Some 2 million Canadians rose before dawn on 12 May 1937 to listen to George VI's coronation. Even better, these events also attracted large US audiences; 'many Canadians rejoiced in the idea that those of their American friends who chose could listen' to the 'unique quality to a British broadcast', and understand that no American movie star or sports celebrity could rival 'the majestic symbolism of the Crown'.[70]

Royal visitors crossed the Atlantic more often than they had before 1914, but not so often as to make their tours any less majestic. After his spectacularly successful national tour in 1919, Edward, Prince of Wales, made other trips to Canada in 1923, 1924, and in 1927 for the diamond jubilee of Confederation. Edward's abdication left the monarchy as institution undamaged; Canadian subjects universally blamed Mrs Simpson, the wicked American, for debauching their monarch. George VI and his wife Queen Elizabeth personified royal family values, which mattered, especially in Quebec. Every provincial legislature moved a unanimous Loyal Address to the new sovereign, but only the Quebec Assembly specifically extended 'the assurance of our fidelity to . . . Our Gracious Sovereign the Queen, and to their Royal Highnesses, the Princesses Elizabeth and Margaret Rose'. King George VI's visit—the first to Canada by a reigning monarch—outshone all previous (and subsequent) royal tours. Three million adoring Canadian subjects—almost a third of the population—greeted the King and Queen Elizabeth as they visited all nine provinces over four weeks in May and June 1939. Packed crowds attended formal events, or watched their motorcades through cities and towns; in the countryside, families waited beside the railway tracks, scrubbed and dressed in their Sunday clothes, to glimpse the blue and gold painted Royal Special as it flashed by. On tour, the members of the royal family spoke a discourse reshaped to reflect a new Empire, and to accommodate Canadian sensibilities. Edward, Prince of Wales, continually identified himself as 'Canadian', an identity that he seemed to prove by buying a ranch in Alberta. Asked during the 1939 tour if she were English or Scottish, Queen Elizabeth replied that 'Since we reached Quebec, I've been a Canadian'. On his two visits to Canada in 1901 and 1908, the future George V had grumbled about speaking in French. In 1939, George VI spoke commendable French on the platform, to the astonishment of French Canadians used to English-Canadian public men

---

[69] 'Imperial Radio Chain Visioned by Bennett', Toronto *Globe*, 19 May 1932, p. 1.
[70] Henry Angus, 'Radio Broadcasting', in *Canada and her Great Neighbor*, pp. 141–3.

to whom *bonjour* was an effort. Elizabeth was fluent. She thanked graciously every prepubescent *Canadienne* who presented her with a bouquet, and chatted in French for a quarter of an hour with the Dionne quintuplets and their parents. During a brief visit to the United States, George VI reminded Americans repeatedly that he was Canada's King as well as Britain's. To emphasize this, his photo-op at the New York World's Fair took place at the Canadian pavilion.[71]

The remarkable success of royal tours, however, could not conceal the much more limited success of inter-war attempts to expand the limited economic infrastructure of Empire. Canada's Conservative Prime Minister R. B. Bennett (1930–5), eager to lessen Canadian dependence on US markets and to restore the Depression-ravaged Canadian economy, won agreement for an Imperial Economic Conference to take place in Ottawa in July and August 1932. The President of the Canadian Chamber of Commerce, W. L. McGregor, boasted that the conference would contradict those Americans 'who imagined that the British Empire was a dead horse'. Bennett promised that it would 'lay the foundation of a new economic Empire in which Canada is destined to play a part of ever-increasing importance'.[72] Once the delegates assembled, however, the professions of Imperial goodwill that were cheap at the cocktail parties were dearly bought at the bargaining table. The British government wanted Imperial free trade, but Canada and the other Dominions preferred to maintain their high tariffs against countries outside the Empire, and to extend Imperial preferences within it. The mean-spirited haggling at Ottawa, Lord Beaverbrook grumbled, 'would have been discreditable . . . between none-too-friendly foreign powers'. The preferential system eventually agreed upon did modestly increase trade between Britain and the Dominions, and did reduce Canadian trade with the United States. It did not, however, 'knit the nations of the British Commonwealth more closely together than ever before, both politically and economically', as Bennett and Canadian businessmen had boldly predicted.[73]

Nor did Canada and the other Dominions find with Britain institutional answers to the thorny questions of Imperial defence. The question of military support for Britain remained the most sensitive imperial subject. Mackenzie King spoke for most Canadians when he offered the Imperial Conference of 1923 no 'blank cheque' for Imperial defence. 'Our attitude is not one of unconditional isolation, nor is it one of unconditional intervention', although he promised that 'if a great call of duty comes, Canada will respond'. The Canadian government, however, would decide when that duty had arrived; by 1925, both

---

[71] Quebec Address in *CAR* (1937–8), p. 222; Edward in *CAR* (1919), p. 284; Elizabeth quoted in Robert Stamp, *Kings, Queens and Canadians* (Markham, 1987), p. 228.

[72] 'Americans Warned that Empire Trade is Goal of Canada', *Toronto Globe*, 19 May 1932, pp. 1, 3.

[73] See accounts in Thompson with Seager, *Canada, 1922–1939*, pp. 219–21 and P. J. Cain and A. G. Hopkins, *British Imperialism: Crisis and Deconstruction, 1941–1990* (London, 1993), pp. 85–7, 139–40.

the Liberals and the Conservatives had promised to seek parliamentary approval before sending troops overseas. R. B. Bennett effused Imperial rhetoric, but in practice, his guiding principle was 'That man is the best Britisher who is the best Canadian'; he ignored any British attempt to prod Canada to greater military effort. Like the other Dominions and the Dominions Office, Canada preferred (in R. F. Holland's words) the 'misty rhetoric' of the League of Nations 'because it kept actual commitments to a minimum'.[74] After the 1935 Italian invasion of Ethiopia demonstrated the League's futility as an agent of collective security (a futility to which Britain and all the Dominions save New Zealand made important contributions) the Empire-Commonwealth huddled together to seek shelter from the gathering European storm. At the Imperial Conference held after George VI's coronation in 1937, Mackenzie King spoke loudest of the Dominion leaders to endorse Neville Chamberlain's policy of appeasement. King continued to drag his feet on cooperative Commonwealth defence programmes, but by 1939, his government had increased defence expenditure almost fivefold over 1935.

King never doubted that Canada would fight with Britain in a major European war initiated by fascist aggression. This 'was a self-evident national duty', he recorded in his diary in September 1938. He quietly assured Dominions Secretary Malcolm MacDonald of this belief, but did not make his conviction public until March 1939, when Hitler seized the remainder of Czechoslovakia. Then he told the Commons with uncharacteristic passion that, were Britain attacked and 'bombers raining death on London, I have no doubt what the decision of the Canadian people and parliament would be. We would regard it as an act of aggression, menacing freedom in all parts of the British Commonwealth.'[75] Virtually all English Canadians agreed. King brought most French Canadians into this consensus with a pledge that no one would be conscripted to fight overseas. Unlike Australia and New Zealand, Canada was absent from the King's declaration of war on 3 September 1939. Although Canadians had already decided on their country's course, King was careful to demonstrate that Canada had made the decision on its own. A brief parliamentary debate culminated with an overwhelming majority (there were only four nays) for the war with Germany that George VI declared on behalf of the Dominion of Canada on 10 September 1939. Historians continue to debate whether English-speaking Canada went to war for Imperial solidarity or to fight fascism. Like the question whether English Canadians were 'Canadian' or 'British', this poses a false dichotomy. In 1939, defending the Empire-Commonwealth and defending democracy welded into one objective, just as they had been during the Great War. Unlike 1914, however, the 'cub of the lion' allegory had vanished. The war editorial of the

[74] R. F. Holland, *Britain and the Commonwealth Alliance, 1918–1939* (London, 1981), p. 173.
[75] J. L. Granatstein and Robert Bothwell, ' "A Self-Evident National Duty": Canadian Foreign Policy, 1935–1939', *Journal of Imperial and Commonwealth History*, 3 (1975), p. 222.

Sarnia Observer reflected the prevalent dialogue: 'this country has taken the step expected of it by its own people first of all and by other sister nations within the Empire. Canada is a democracy that is not afraid to fight for democracy . . . until Hitlerism and all that it means is destroyed.'[76]

---

[76] *Sarnia Observer*, cited in Terry Copp, 'Ontario 1939: The Decision for War', *Ontario History*, 86/3 (Sept. 1994), p. 274.

SELECT BIBLIOGRAPHY

CARL BERGER, *The Sense of Power: Studies in the Ideas of Canadian Imperialism, 1867–1914* (Toronto, 1970).

R. C. BROWN and RAMSAY COOK, *Canada, 1896–1921: A Nation Transformed* (Toronto, 1974).

DOUGLAS COLE, 'The Problem of "Nationalism" and "Imperialism" in British Settlement Colonies', *Journal of British Studies*, 10 (1971), p. 160–82.

JOHN EDDY and DERYCK SCHREUDER, *The Rise of Colonial Nationalism: Australia, New Zealand, Canada, and South Africa First Assert their Nationalities, 1880–1914* (Sydney, 1988).

R. G. MOYLES and DOUG OWRAM, *Imperial Dreams and Colonial Realities: British Views of Canada, 1880–1914* (Toronto, 1988).

H. V. NELLES, *The Art of Nation-Building: Pageantry and Spectacle at Quebec's Tercentenary* (Toronto, 1999).

JOHN HERD THOMPSON with ALLEN SEAGER, *Canada, 1922–1939: Decades of Discord* (Toronto, 1985).

PHILIP WIGLEY, *Canada and the Transition to Commonwealth: British–Canadian Relations, 1917–1926* (Cambridge, 1977).

6

Canada and the End of Empire, 1939–1982

Phillip Buckner

Why did Canadians go to war in 1939? The simple answer is that they fought for Britain. But this answer does not explain the commitment that English Canadians made to the war effort. In 1914, when Canada was automatically at war, the British born formed almost half of the Canadian forces (and over half of those who volunteered). By 1939 around 5 per cent of Canadians were British born and many of them were quite elderly. Most Canadians of British origin were native born and their British roots were increasingly remote. Yet they formed a disproportionate number of those who volunteered to serve in the Canadian armed forces during the Second World War. No Canadian vital interests were immediately at stake in 1939. America had already replaced Britain as Canada's major source of capital investment, it provided Canada with the bulk of its imports, and it was the chief market for Canadian exports. The movies that English Canadians watched, the radio programmes they listened to, the popular fiction they read, and the sports they played were largely American in origin. This does not mean that English Canadians identified themselves as Americans, for English Canadians in 1939 had a distinct sense of their own national identity. They were, however, proud that Canada was a part of the British Empire, which they saw as a progressive institution embodying liberal values and extending the benefits of British civilization around the world. In 1942 J. L. Ilsley, the Minister of Finance, proclaimed: 'I represent people whose ancestors for the most part left the British Isles centuries ago, people whose loyalty to the British empire, whose belief in the British empire and its institutions are deep-seated' and who 'would consider it their duty to defend what they call the British empire . . . in any part of the world in which the continued existence of the empire was in peril'.[1]

It is often assumed that the First World War had shaken the commitment of Canadians to the Empire. Yet during the inter-war years the Canadian Legion continued to 'promote loyalty to the Empire and to Canada' and by 1939 close to 400,000 veterans occupied key positions throughout Canadian society, in

---

[1] Quoted in J. L. Granatstein and Peter Neary, *The Good Fight: Canadians and World War II* (Toronto, 1995), p. 225.

the learned professions, the universities, the churches, the media, the business community, and in the political parties and the civil service.[2] Only a small minority of the veterans opposed Canada's decision to enter the Second World War at Britain's side. Of course, only a handful of the veterans of the First World War served in the Second, but like the veterans, younger English Canadians had grown up in an education system and a broader political culture that glorified the Empire. It is easy to dismiss English-Canadian attitudes as a form of retarded colonialism, but English Canadians did not view Canada as a mere colony of Britain. They saw Canada as an 'independent partner nation' in what Mackenzie King called a 'Cooperative Commonwealth'.[3] Thus for many Canadians the decision by Canada to issue its own declaration of war against Germany on 10 September 1939—a week after Britain—was of great symbolic significance. Whether Canadians fully grasped in 1939 the evil that they were confronting in Nazi Germany is unlikely. Certainly they did not show much concern for the Jews of Europe who found Canada's borders closed to them. But English Canadians were not entirely unaware of what was happening in Europe and although their reaction to the outbreak of war was instinctive, it was based upon more than simply a sense of kith and kin with the British in the 'mother country'. Above all, it reflected a sense of shared Imperial values and citizenship.

With the fall of France in the summer of 1940 Canada became the second largest Allied power until Russia entered the war in June 1941. English Canadians responded with a determination to fight on whatever the cost. Over 85 per cent of the 1,086,771 men and women who served in the Canadian armed forces in the Second World War were volunteers. Just under 250,000 Canadians served in the Royal Canadian Air Force, which suffered heavy casualties during the bombing raids on Germany. Another 106,000 served in the Royal Canadian Navy and escorted convoys across the North Atlantic. But a substantial majority of those who enlisted served in the army. Initially the Canadian army suffered limited casualties since most Canadians were based in camps in Britain. On 8 December 1941 the Canadian government did agree to send 1,973 men and two nursing sisters to Hong Kong, which almost immediately fell to the Japanese; 290 Canadians were killed and the rest became prisoners. A second disaster ensued in August 1942 when 4,963 Canadians took part in a raid on Dieppe: over 1,400 were killed or wounded and nearly 2,000 captured. However misguided Canadian participation in these debacles may appear in retrospect, it would be wrong to assume that either event led to disillusionment in English Canada, where enlistments and commitment to the war effort remained high. In July 1943, part of the Canadian army was sent to Italy and in June 1944 the Canadians landed in Normandy, at Juno Beach. As the casualties mounted, so

---

[2] See Phillip Buckner, 'The Long Goodbye: English Canadians and the British World', in Phillip Buckner and R. Douglas Francis, (eds), *Rediscovering the British World* (Calgary, 2005), pp. 195–6.
[3] C. P. Stacey, *Canada and the Age of Conflict* vol. II (Toronto, 1982), p.14.

did the determination of English Canadians, even if it meant recruiting a large number of women into the labour force to increase the production of war materials and conscription to increase the supply of men for the armed forces.

In order to secure French-Canadian support for the war effort, in a Quebec provincial election in 1939 King had promised that there would be no conscription for overseas service. In January 1940 the Liberals won a federal election and King hoped that Canada's major contribution to the war could be limited to economic support and the British Commonwealth Air Training Plan, which was based in Canada. But the fall of much of continental Europe, Dunkirk, and the Battle of Britain inevitably led to the rapid expansion of the Canadian armed forces. King was compelled by English-Canadian public opinion to introduce conscription for home service under the National Resources Mobilization Act of June 1940, to hold a national plebiscite in April 1942 to allow him to replace his 'no conscription' promise with a commitment to 'conscription if necessary, but not necessarily conscription', and finally in 1944 to introduce conscription for overseas service. As in 1917 much of the pressure in English Canada was generated by the belief that French Canadians were not doing their share. More French Canadians joined the Canadian military in the Second World War than in the First, but French Canadians from Quebec were still dramatically under-represented among the volunteers serving overseas. They saw the war as England's war—not Canada's—and they voted overwhelmingly against conscription in the 1942 plebiscite. The Conscription Crisis of 1944 was not as severe as in 1917, partly because King retained the support of the majority of Quebec federal MPs for what was clearly a reluctant decision on his part. But many younger French-Canadian nationalists were enraged by King's betrayal of his promise—a promise made to Quebec. Among Quebec's intellectuals the legacy of conscription would cast a long shadow and it destroyed any lingering sympathy for the British connection among the generation of French-Canadian politicians that would come to power (federally and provincially) in the 1960s.

It is more difficult to assess the reaction of Canada's other ethnic groups to the demands of the war. People of German origin formed the largest ethnic group in Canada after the British and the French. During the First World War discrimination against German Canadians had led to bitter divisions, especially in the Kitchener–Waterloo area in Ontario. By 1939, however, the majority of 'Germans' had been in Canada for several generations and most had little sense of being German (even if the Canadian census insisted on identifying them as such). The Canadian-born A. L. Burt was defined as German because his grandfather had been born in Württemberg, but Burt studied at Oxford under H. E. Egerton, the first Beit Professor of Colonial History, served in a tank battalion in the First World War, and taught at the University of Alberta (1913–30) and then the University of Minnesota (1930–57). Burt was 'proud of the Anglo-Saxon cultural tradition in which he was reared' and in the 1950s wrote a very sympathetic history of the British Empire-Commonwealth.[4] Because his grandfather had emigrated from the Grand Duchy of Baden to Upper Canada in the 1850s, John Diefenbaker was also defined as German, even though he spoke no German and had no interest in his German roots. Diefenbaker enlisted in the Canadian Expeditionary Force in the First World War and enthusiastically endorsed Canada's participation in the Second. By 1939 even the German community in Kitchener–Waterloo was less divided over the war, since their ties with Germany had been weakened in 1914–18 and had never been fully restored. In the Second World War anti-German sentiment in Canada was more limited than in the First, partly because of the recognition that there was little sympathy for National Socialism among German Canadians. Only 800 German Canadians (out of over 400,000) were interned, as were 700 Italian Canadians (out of 112,000), the leaders of the Canadian Communist Party, and a small number of left-wing Ukrainians. But, in general, the federal government sought to minimize tensions with people of European origin and to encourage participation in the war effort, with a considerable degree of success.

This was not the case with Japanese Canadians. Despite no real evidence of subversion, the federal government yielded to pressure from public opinion in British Columbia, where almost 95 per cent of Canadians of Japanese origin lived, and evacuated all those of Japanese origin (including the Canadian born) to camps in the interior of British Columbia and the Prairies. At the end of the war the federal government sought to deport a number of Japanese Canadians against their wishes. In fact, the war did little to undermine English-Canadian (and French-Canadian) prejudice against those whose skin was a different colour. In 1947 when Canada reopened its doors to immigrants it did not remove the barriers against Asians, and even the 1952 Immigration Act was designed not to cast 'too wide an ethnic or racial net'.[5] For most English Canadians Britishness was still identified with a white skin.

Recent historiography in Canada has tended to interpret the Second World War as rupturing the Imperial relationship. Great stress is laid on the disputes between the British and Canadian governments during the war over how the Canadian forces should be used and the inevitable tensions between British and Canadian officers in the field. But whatever intergovernmental tensions there had been during the war, the Canadian veterans who had served in Europe did not come home harbouring anti-British sentiment. Walter Thompson, who had served in the Royal Canadian Air Force, was in Britain when the war ended. He joined a huge crowd 'which began with one voice to sing "Land of Hope and Glory, Mother of the Free". I came to attention in military fashion. Tears were

---

[4] Lewis H. Thomas, *The Renaissance of Canadian History: A Biography of A. L. Burt* (Toronto, 1975), pp. 5, 7, 16, 132.

[5] Harold Troper, 'Canada's Immigration Policy since 1945', *International Journal*, 48 (1993), p. 262.

running down my cheeks . . .'[6] Nearly 500,000 Canadians spent time—in some case several years—stationed in Britain. A few chose to remain after the war, including Billy Butlin, who came to Britain with the Canadian army and stayed to establish a chain of holiday camps. Most returned to Canada, nearly 45,000 of them with British wives. The wartime experience of the Canadians 'made them more consciously Canadian than they had been before; but their particular experience in England brought them close to the British people and gave a new reality to the "commonwealth connection"'. The legacy of the war was 'a network of affectionate transatlantic connections' and a sense of 'something like family feeling'.[7]

Despite 42,092 Canadian dead, the Second World War was seen by most English Canadians as a 'good war', a successful defence of freedom and liberal values against the evils of totalitarianism and fascism. Surveys taken during the war revealed that most volunteers believed that they were fighting in a just cause. The volunteers strongly supported conscription and even some form of post-war military service for Canadian youth. At the end of the First World War hundreds of memorials had been erected across Canada, listing the names of those who had fallen in defence of King and Country. At the end of the Second World War the names of the dead were simply added to the existing memorials, thus creating a sense of continuity between the two world wars. Armistice Day ceremonies reinforced this sense of continuity, as did the Canadian Legion to which many veterans of both world wars belonged. In Britain, the 'public memory' of the Second World War was used to reinforce the myth of the British as a unique 'Island race'. This myth helped the 'British' people to construct 'a new sense of a socially cohesive British identity', one that cast post-war immigrants to Britain, particularly black and Asian immigrants, as the foreign 'other'.[8] But it did not exclude kith and kin in the white Dominions. Indeed, most Canadian veterans shared this interpretation of the war, particularly since very few Canadians had fought outside Europe. The defence of Britain inevitably dominated public attention for much of the war, and both in Canada and in Britain great emphasis was laid in the post-war media on the significant part that Canadians had played in defending and supplying the mother country.

The million Canadian men and women who had served in Canada's armed forces had a substantial impact, particularly in English Canada, after the war. In 1946–7 veterans formed nearly half of the 80,000 students in Canadian universities and their number remained high until 1950–1.[9] During the 1950s

---

[6] Walter P. Thompson, *Lancaster to Berlin* (Winslow, 1977).

[7] C. P. Stacey and Barbara M. Wilson, *The Half-Million: The Canadians in Britain, 1939–1946* (Toronto, 1987), pp. 92, 174, 178–9.

[8] Paul Ward, *Britishness since 1870* (London, 2004), pp. 123–4.

[9] Peter Neary, 'Canadian universities and Canadian Veterans of World War II', in Peter Neary and J. L. Granatstein, (eds), *The Veterans Charter and Post-World War Two Canada* (Montreal and Kingston, 1998).

and into the 1960s veterans inevitably formed a significant proportion of the faculty at most English-Canadian universities. The only veterans to become Prime Minister were Diefenbaker and Lester Pearson (both veterans of the First World War), but a substantial number became cabinet ministers and MPs. Moreover, legion halls across the country—particularly in the smaller towns in English Canada—remained an important part of the social life of many veterans, where they gathered to reminisce and sing patriotic songs like 'Rule Britannia' and 'The Maple Leaf Forever'. The veterans were not united in their opinions but most continued to view the war as a defining experience that had unified the 'British people' in a just cause.

These sentiments were not confined to those who served in the armed forces. In 1940 the Ontario Minister of Education declared that the war being fought was a 'recognition of the essential oneness of the Empire'.[10] An aged Charles G. D. Roberts stressed in a 1940 poem: 'This, this is Britain, bulwark of our breed, . . . Smite her, and we are smitten, wound her, we bleed'.[11] This sense of comradeship with 'kith and kin' in the mother country was reinforced by wartime propaganda, both that produced in Canada by Canadian Broadcasting Corporation (CBC) radio and the National Film Board and the radio reports and newsreels imported from Britain. It was absorbed not just by the male civilian labour force but by the female relatives of men serving overseas, by the (mainly English-Canadian) women who enlisted to serve in the military and who replaced men in the domestic economy, and by the hundreds of thousands of women who did volunteer work. The membership of the Imperial Order Daughters of the Empire (IODE) soared to over 50,000; 60,000 volunteers belonging to the United Church Women's committees knitted socks and sweaters and 50,000 volunteers from the Catholic Women's League provided 6 million cigarettes for the troops. Canadians joined 4,000 registered charities engaged in supporting the war effort and bought $12.5 billion worth of Victory bonds. Jeff Keshen points out that there was considerable substance to the image of the war 'as a conflict uniting people in a common and noble cause'.[12] This was particularly true in English Canada. Indeed, by increasing interregional mobility as men and women moved across the country as part of the military or in search of jobs, the war helped to weaken regional differences and created an even stronger sense of national identity throughout English Canada that would persist into the post-war period. Intertwined with this sense of national identity was a sense of being part of an extended British community that had joined together to win the war.

Many English Canadians remained resentful that French Canadians had not supported the war as enthusiastically as they had, a resentment that would

---

[10] Hon. Duncan McArthur, *Education and the Empire*, lecture to the Empire Club of Canada, 28 Nov. 1940.

[11] Charles G. D. Roberts, *Canada Speaks of Britain!* (Toronto, 1941).

[12] Jeff Keshen, *Saints, Sinners, and Soldiers: Canada's Second World War* (Vancouver, 2004), pp. 23–5, 40, 47.

lead to periodic outbursts of anti-Quebec sentiment. Moreover, while CBC programmes during the war like *Canadians All* emphasized the loyalty and commitment of Canadians of European origin, they failed to alter the prejudices and the ethnocentrism of English Canadians.[13] At the end of the war English Canadians enthusiastically supported immigration from the British Isles, but only grudgingly welcomed refugees and displaced persons (pejoratively referred to as DPs). In 1946 nearly 30 per cent of Canadians wanted to close the door to all further immigration. In both English Canada and among French Canadians in Quebec the war reinforced a sense of ethnic solidarity, which Hugh MacLennan captured in his 1945 novel *Two Solitudes*.

Of course, the war also accelerated the integration of Canada and the United States. The Ogdensburg Agreement of August 1940 created the Permanent Joint Board on Defence and the Hyde Park Agreement of April 1941 encouraged closer economic ties with the United States. At the end of the war the Mackenzie King government almost negotiated a sweeping free trade agreement with the United States but drew back at the last moment. Nonetheless, over the next decade Canada would benefit from the growth of the American economy, while investment and trade with Britain would shrink. By 1957 over 70 per cent of Canadian imports came from the United States, just over 9 per cent from the United Kingdom. Moreover, Canadians were enthusiastic cold warriors. They echoed the anti-communist rhetoric of the Americans and willingly entered the Korean War. Until the 1960s there was little criticism of American leadership of the 'Free World'. The United States was now the dominant partner in what Churchill described as an alliance of the English-speaking peoples, but Britain retained its Empire and post-war British governments believed that Britain in an informal alliance with the 'old' Dominions could continue to act like a world power. So did many Canadians. Like the other Dominions, Canada now had a vastly expanded Department of External Affairs and was no longer prepared simply to respond to British initiatives, and Canadian diplomats played an active role in the creation of the United Nations and the North Atlantic Treaty Organization. But while they accepted United States leadership in the Cold War, they also believed in the continuing value of the British Commonwealth, partly as a counterpoise to the growing dominance of the United States.

In 1947 the British Empire shrank dramatically with the independence of India, Pakistan, Sri Lanka, and Burma and the departure of the Republic of Ireland. But India, Pakistan, and Sri Lanka remained members of an expanded British Commonwealth of Nations. The collapse of the Indian Empire and the departure of Ireland had been predicted even before the war and there was no immediate threat of any further disintegration. Canadian officials approved of

---

[13] William R. Young, 'Chauvinism and Canadianism: Canadian Ethnic Groups and the Failure of Wartime Information', in Norman Hillmer et al., (eds), *On Guard for Thee: War, Ethnicity, and the Canadian State, 1939–45* (Ottawa, 1988).

the decision to give the south Asian colonies independence. Less enthusiastically, they also agreed in 1949 to allow India to become a republic that recognized the King only as head of the Commonwealth. After 1948 the British Commonwealth of Nations was described in British documents as the Commonwealth of Nations and in the 1970s became simply the Commonwealth.[14] This resulted in some minor technical changes, such as the long overdue renaming of Empire Day as Commonwealth Day. But many English Canadians continued to refer to the Commonwealth as the British Commonwealth and their fundamental attitudes towards it did not change. In September 1949 the Royal Institute of International Relations held a conference on Commonwealth Relations at Bigwin Inn, Ontario. The discussions, Frank Soward reported, were 'stormy' but they 'strengthened that sense of family relationship which has made the Commonwealth greater than the sum of its parts and a champion of freedom in this troubled world'.[15] Between mid-1948 and 1960 only a handful of colonies attained independence. Most Canadians—like most Britons—did not see the Empire as an unhealthy anachronism but believed that it demonstrated the superiority of the British way of life and brought benefits to people who had not yet reached a sufficient level of political and economic maturity to be given independence. They did not sympathize with discrimination on the basis of 'race', which is why Diefenbaker was not prepared to allow South Africa to rejoin the Commonwealth after it became a republic unless it abandoned apartheid. But even on the left there does not appear to have been substantial criticism of the slow pace of decolonization until the 1960s. Many of those—like Frank Underhill—who had been critical of Canada's participation in the Empire in the inter-war years were converted to the value of the new Commonwealth, and Canadian diplomats found the reinvented Commonwealth a useful tool for giving Canada influence in the emerging 'third world'. Nonetheless, Canadian interest in Africa and Asia steadily declined (along with Canadian missionary activity) after 1945. What increasingly concerned Canadians was not Canada's relationship with the broader Commonwealth but the nature of their relationship with Great Britain.

In the immediate post-war period most English Canadians did not feel that they had to choose between being Canadian and remaining British. In *This Nation Called Canada* David B. Harkness accepted that the war had led to 'our self-realization as a Canadian people' and he called for the dropping of the word Dominion to describe the 'nation' of Canada. But he also believed that 'Canada is a British nation and proposes to continue to be a British nation'.[16] Post-war surveys showed that most Canadians wanted their own 'national' flag but the one that most English Canadians wanted was the Red Ensign (or some variant

[14] Hector Mackenzie, 'An Old Dominion and the New Commonwealth: Canadian Policy on the Question of India's Membership, 1947–49', *Journal of Imperial and Commonwealth History*, 27 (1999), pp. 82–112.

[15] F. H. Soward, *The Adaptable Commonwealth* (London, 1950), pp. 226–7, 266.

[16] David B. Harkness, *This Nation Called Canada* (Toronto, 1945), pp. 23, 11, 56.

of it). In 1945 a parliamentary committee, established to consider the design of a national flag, received 2,695 submissions, but the flag preferred by Mackenzie King was the Canadian Red Ensign with a large gold maple leaf replacing Canada's coat of arms. This would probably have become the Canadian flag (just as the Blue Ensign became Australia's flag in 1950) except for the opposition of the Quebec legislature, which unanimously passed a motion against a flag bearing 'foreign' (i.e. British) symbols, and a revolt of Quebec federal MPs against any version of the Red Ensign.[17] The King government therefore abandoned the effort to create a Canadian flag. It did, however, respond to the desire of many Canadians to be able to define themselves as Canadian citizens by introducing the 1946 Canadian Citizenship Act. Among those who welcomed the bill was John Diefenbaker, but the terms in which he defined his Canadian identity are important. Canada, he declared, 'means a citizenship which maintains in this part of North America the great heritage of British peoples everywhere in the world'.[18] Under the terms of the Act Canadian citizens remained British subjects. Fifty years later, the author of the Act, Paul Martin, Sr, claimed that he would have liked to end this anomaly but that if he had tried to do so, the bill would have been defeated.[19] Since the Liberals had a majority in Parliament, clearly many English-Canadian Liberals supported Diefenbaker's position or believed that their constituents did. Over the next few years the Liberals made few other formal changes in the constitutional relationship with Britain. In 1949 appeals to the Judicial Committee of the Privy Council were ended and the Canadian Parliament was enabled to amend the parts of the British North America Act dealing with federal responsibilities. In 1952 Vincent Massey, a prominent Liberal, became Canada's first native-born Governor-General.

In 1952 the Canadian Parliament also officially bestowed the title of Queen of Canada on Queen Elizabeth on her accession to the throne. The royal family had emerged from the war more popular than ever and in the 1950s television provided an effective means of allowing British subjects everywhere to participate vicariously in royal ceremonials. Princess Elizabeth's wedding, the funeral of her father, the birth of her children, and especially her elaborate coronation ceremony on 2 June 1953 were all major events in the Dominions. Millions of Canadians watched the coronation on television. Indeed, the promised broadcast of the coronation led to a larger demand for TV sets than the retailers were able to meet.[20] In 1951 Princess Elizabeth made her first cross-Canada tour. She returned as Queen briefly in 1957 to open the Canadian Parliament and in 1959

[17] Blair Fraser, *The Search for Identity* (Toronto, 1967), pp. 238–9; Peter Stursberg, *Lester Pearson and the Dream of Unity* (Toronto, 1978), p. 154.

[18] Canada, House of Commons, *Debates 1946*, vol. I, pp. 510–14.

[19] Paul Martin, 'Citizenship and the People's World', in William Kaplan, (ed.), *Belonging: The Meaning and Future of Canadian Citizenship* (Montreal and Kingston, 1993), p. 74.

[20] Paul Rutherford, *When Television Was Young: Primetime Canada, 1952–1967* (Toronto, 1990), p. 50.

on a longer visit to open the St Lawrence Seaway and to make the last great trans-Canada tour. These visits (and those of lesser members of the royal family) were covered extensively in the Canadian media. In 1957 the National Film Board used the royal tour to explore the role of the monarchy in a constitutional democracy, producing a film called *The Sceptre and the Mace*, which was used for educational purposes not only in Canada but throughout the Commonwealth. In 1959 it produced another documentary entitled *Royal River* which was shown in cinemas across Canada. The CBC employed 900 people and spent $500,000 covering the 1959 tour. The costs of the 1959 tour did generate controversy, but the crowds welcoming the Queen were enormous, especially in Ontario and the west. The Diefenbaker government tried to stress that the Queen was visiting Canada as Queen of Canada, although this distinction was probably lost on most Canadians as long as 'God Save the Queen' was the national anthem and the Union Jack (or more accurately the Union Flag) was Canada's national flag.[21] Winston Churchill was another British figure greatly admired in Canada and his funeral in 1965 was also viewed on television by many Canadians. Charles Lynch, the Canadian journalist, declared that 'we accepted Churchill as one of us. He was an authentic Canadian hero—he became and will remain part of our native story'—and so he would as long as the Canadian story was also a British story.[22]

The ethnic composition of Canada was changing in the post-war period, but one must be careful not to accelerate the decline of the British-Canadian majority. By 1941, for the first time, the proportion of the population defined by the Canadian census as of British origin fell to just under 50 per cent. Nonetheless, since the vast majority of the 30 per cent of people of French Canadian ethnicity were concentrated in one province, outside Quebec people of British origin still formed a majority of the population. This was particularly the case in Canada's urban centres: 80 per cent of the residents of Toronto were British in origin, 75 per cent of Vancouver residents, and even most Prairie cities had substantial British majorities. Over the next three decades 3 million immigrants entered Canada. But the British formed the largest single group of migrants, well over 900,000 or about 28 per cent of the total. The British influx was particularly heavy just after the war, over 600,000 arriving between 1945 and 1957. Ontario received about 55 per cent of the British immigrants, Quebec (in reality Montreal) about 15 per cent, the Prairies and British Columbia most of the rest. The British immigrant stream included a substantial number of professional, managerial, and skilled workers and they quickly rose to positions of authority in business, in a rapidly expanding civil service, in the teaching and

[21] Phillip Buckner, 'The Last Great Royal Tour: Queen Elizabeth's 1959 Tour to Canada', in Phillip Buckner, (ed.), *Canada and the End of Empire* (Vancouver, 2004).
[22] John Ramsden, *Man of the Century: Winston Churchill and his Legend since 1945* (London, 2002), pp. 373–93, 411.

nursing professions, and in the Canadian unions. There were, of course, tensions, but the British perceived themselves and were perceived by the English-Canadian communities in which they settled as part of the dominant ethnic culture. As British subjects they had all the rights of citizens, including the right to the vote, regardless of whether they became Canadian citizens (and some did not for many years).[23]

As the *Ottawa Journal* pointed out in 1944 in a debate over 'How British is Canada', census data provide a crude way of measuring the British influence. The *Journal* did its own impressionistic survey of the Canadian House of Commons to show that of the 179 non-French-Canadian MPs only ten could not be identified as British by origin.[24] After 1945 there was a slow growth in the number of MPs from western Canada of other ethnic origins, but their ethnic origins were frequently mixed, like John Diefenbaker's (whose mother was Scottish), and many of them shared Diefenbaker's sentiments about the British connection. These MPs were largely drawn from ethnic communities that had been established before 1914 in rural areas in western Canada. They had studied in English-language schools, where the curriculum had been defined by provincial governments controlled by the British-Canadian majority. Since most schools were locally funded and the teachers locally selected, the schools in the rural communities were not as coercive as is often assumed and the lessons were frequently shaped so as not to offend local community values. But most immigrants wanted their children to be accepted by the host community and to succeed within it. It is not surprising that as the Liberal Party in the 1960s sought to accommodate French-Canadian nationalism by espousing biculturalism and (somewhat less enthusiastically) multiculturalism it lost much of its support in the west, for the western cultural minorities had already paid the price of assimilation and for many of their descendants multiculturalism was 'an affront to their history'.[25]

Nor should one assume that all of the newer European immigrants who flooded into Canada after 1945 were opposed to the vision of Canada as a British nation. Even in the 1930s many English-Canadian intellectuals had argued that cultural assimilation was less important than economic and political assimilation and that loyalty to the Crown and to British institutions did not have to mean abandoning all aspects of one's ancestral culture.[26] The image of the Canadian mosaic was popularized by the western Canadian historian

[23] Freda Hawkins, 'Migration as a Factor in Anglo-Canadian Relations', in Peter Lyon, (ed.), *Britain and Canada: Survey of a Changing Relationship* (London, 1976).

[24] See James G. Allen, *Editorial Opinion on the Contemporary British Commonwealth and Empire* (Boulder, Colo., 1946), pp. 521–2.

[25] David E. Smith, 'Political Culture in the West', in David E. Bercuson and Phillip A. Buckner, (eds), *Eastern and Western Perspectives* (Toronto, 1981), p. 173.

[26] Barry Ferguson, 'British-Canadian Intellectuals, Ukrainian Immigrants, and Canadian National Identity', in Lubomyr Luciuk and Stella Hryniuk, (eds), *Canada's Ukrainians: Negotiating an Identity* (Toronto, 1991).

W. L. Morton in his 1961 study of *The Canadian Identity*. Indeed, the Crown served a dual purpose. For British Canadians it was a symbol of Canada's British identity. But for many non-British Canadians it symbolized that one could become a loyal subject without having to renounce one's ethnic origins. Some post-war immigrants (including some British immigrants) felt that it was time to abandon the legacies and symbolism of Empire. But many 'New Canadians', particularly those who had emigrated from countries 'behind the Iron Curtain', were enthusiastic monarchists. Robert Baldanai, an Italian-Canadian MP from Fort William, even declared 'as a non-Anglo Saxon' that 'the non-Anglo Saxons are more keen about the Queen than the Anglo Saxons'.[27]

A limited degree of tolerance for cultural diversity, primarily within the home and at ethnic festivals, did not mean any commitment to the creation of a multicultural society. Except in French-language schools in Quebec (which focused on French Canada's distinctive identity), the schools system in all the provinces in the 1950s emphasized that Canada had derived its political system, its cultural traditions, and its values from Britain. Most English-Canadian intellectuals accepted that Canada had two founding peoples, but they held stereotypical views of French-Canadian culture, which they viewed as backward and confined essentially to Quebec. It was assumed that Aboriginal peoples were part of a dying race and that immigrants would accept Canada's British identity, even if they retained residual elements of their culture. The sense of Canada as a British community was reinforced on Victoria Day, Dominion Day, and Armistice Day, all of which served as occasions on which to celebrate Canada's British origins.

Anglophilia in Canada was particularly strong at the elite level. Indeed, there was a tradition of importing prominent British figures to head Canada's cultural institutions. John Grierson became the head of the National Film Board in 1939, Celia Franca of Britain's Sadler's Wells became director of the National Ballet in 1951, Tyrone Guthrie was imported in 1953 to establish the Shakespearian Festival in Stratford, Ontario, and Peter Dwyer became director of the Canada Council for the Arts. The Stratford festival was largely the brainchild of Tom Patterson, a veteran who supposedly fell in love with the theatre and opera while serving in Britain and Italy. In fact, Patterson never got to Italy (nor even to Shakespeare's birthplace in England). A fourth-generation Upper Canadian, he had begun promoting a Shakespearian festival even before the war. The roots of the festival were thus local, not imported, and reflected the sense that Patterson and others had of Canada as a British community and of British culture as part of their intellectual heritage. In 1949–51 the Royal Commission on National Development in the Arts, Letters, and Sciences, chaired by Vincent Massey, produced a Report that also reflected this view. Fifty years later it is easy to dismiss Massey as a servile colonial, and the Massey

---

[27] Buckner, 'The Last Great Royal Tour', pp. 87–8.

Report as reflecting Canada's continued colonial subservience to Britain. But this does Massey and the Report a disservice. Massey 'saw Britain, not as a model to be aped and obeyed by servile colonials, but as a legitimate source of social and political traditions which made Canada a distinctive society in North America'.[28] Nor did Massey want simply to recreate British culture. In the 1961 Romanes Lecture in Oxford Massey proclaimed: 'Our eighteen million people, our gifts of nature, our productivity, our technology, these are largely wasted unless we make something distinctively Canadian in North America.'[29] Massey was an elitist and a bit of a snob but he was a Canadian elitist and a Canadian snob.

Indeed, Canadians had little respect for those Canadians who acted like colonials. One of the unhappier imports from Britain was Alan Jarvis, who in 1955 became director of the National Gallery of Canada. Though Canadian born, Jarvis had gone to Oxford as a Rhodes Scholar, during the war served as private secretary to Sir Stafford Cripps, and then remained in Britain where he achieved a modest reputation as a sculptor, author, and administrator. Upon his return to Canada after fourteen years in Britain he 'talked incessantly of Britain and British artists, and in a brittle mid-Atlantic accent that made him sound like a naval officer in a wartime English movie'. Jarvis was increasingly out of touch with the Canadian art world and he was dismissed from his position in 1959. But he remained a fixture on the Ottawa cultural scene, speaking constantly 'of "K. Clark" and Henry Moore and Margot Fonteyn and dear Noel. The more he drank, the more he reverted to London in 1950.' There was, the Canadian art critic Robert Fulford noted, 'something pathetic about Alan's affair with everything British'.[30]

The majority of Canada's diplomats were also Anglophiles. London remained 'the premier diplomatic post in the Canadian service' and from 1946 to 1949 and again from 1952 to 1957 it was filled by Norman A. Robertson. Robertson found his position frustrating, since the British had a tendency not to consult Canada unless a direct Canadian interest was involved. Nonetheless, Canada's relationship with Britain remained 'cordial and intimate', at least till the Suez crisis of 1956. Robertson sought to warn the British government against precipitous action against Egypt but Prime Minister Louis St Laurent and Secretary of State for External Affairs Lester B. Pearson were caught off guard and appalled when Britain and France invaded Egypt and seized control of the Suez Canal. The crisis had a considerable impact on Anglo-Canadian relations, on both sides of the Atlantic. Even a committed Anglophile like Robertson lost 'confidence in British judgment and good sense' and a feeling of betrayal in Britain lingered on after the crisis was resolved (partly by Pearson's diplomatic efforts at the

---

[28] Paul Litt, *The Muses, the Masses, and the Massey Commission* (Toronto, 1992), p. 115.
[29] Rt. Hon. Vincent Massey, *Canadians and their Commonwealth* (Oxford, 1961), p. 4.
[30] Robert Fulford, *Best Seat in the House: Memoirs of a Lucky Man* (Toronto, 1988), pp. 112–13.

United Nations).[31] But to some extent the breach was healed at Bermuda in April 1957 when the new British Prime Minister Harold Macmillan met with St Laurent and Pearson. Ironically it was English-Canadian public opinion that did not forgive the St Laurent government for failing to support Britain in a time of crisis. In 1957 John Diefenbaker and the Conservatives campaigned on a policy of restoring good relations with Britain, and in Ontario and the Maritimes this appeal helped to bring about the defeat of the Liberals and the election of Diefenbaker as Prime Minister, first with a minority government and after 1958 with the largest majority in Canadian history.

Only a few days after taking office in 1957 Diefenbaker went to London to attend a meeting of Commonwealth prime ministers. Shortly after the meeting he announced his intention to divert 15 per cent of Canada's imports from the United States to Great Britain. This was an impossible goal, although the Commonwealth economic conference, held at Diefenbaker's request in Montreal in September 1958, did lead to some very limited agreements and the British share of Canadian imports rose to a new but not lasting high of 10.7 per cent in 1960. The 1958 Conference also led to the Commonwealth scholarship and fellowship plan, which Diefenbaker strongly promoted as a means of binding the Commonwealth together. But these successes were offset by tensions over the decision of the United Kingdom to apply for entry into the European Economic Community (EEC) in 1961. Although Britain's entry was eventually vetoed by France and Britain did not enter the European Union until 1973, Anglo-Canadian trade continued to decline, and by the end of the 1960s the United Kingdom accounted for only 5 per cent of Canada's imports and 9 per cent of its exports. Diefenbaker had viewed with some alarm Britain's attempt to negotiate its way into Europe in the early 1960s, but by the end of the decade the Trudeau government viewed the prospect with comparative equanimity.[32]

Diefenbaker also antagonized Macmillan at the Commonwealth Prime Ministers' Meeting in March 1961 when he refused to compromise on the wording of a declaration condemning apartheid. But while the relationship between Diefenbaker and Macmillan steadily deteriorated, the degree of the antagonism was not revealed to the public. During these years the two Prime Ministers made frequent appearances in each other's capital, a steady stream of ministers crossed the Atlantic in both directions, and there were good relations between Canadian and British civil servants. As transatlantic air travel became easier, a host of professional organizations (parliamentary, academic, press, educational, legal) began to organize more regular transatlantic meetings, and organizations like the Royal Commonwealth society and the English-Speaking Union were active in

---

[31] John Hilliker and Greg Donaghy, 'Canadian Relations with the United Kingdom at the End of Empire', in Buckner, (ed.), *Canada and the End of Empire*, pp. 25–31.

[32] Bruce Muirhead, 'Customs Valuations and Other Irritants: The Continuing Decline of Anglo-Canadian Trade in the 1960s', ibid.

both countries. The general public also began to travel as never before and a number of charter companies were established to meet the demand for cheaper transatlantic flights. The number of Canadian students studying in Britain and of British students studying in Canada reached new levels, thanks partly to the Commonwealth scholarship programme. Teacher exchanges became more frequent. Many British immigrants went home to visit relatives left behind, many veterans returned to visit places where they had been stationed during the war, and many native-born Canadians came to explore their ancestral roots. In 1957 the CBC became one of the founding members of the British Commonwealth International Newsfilm Agency in order to have access to news independent of American sources, and many Canadian newspapers and magazines carried regular reports on events in Britain. The irony of this period is that despite the chilly relations between the British and Canadian governments, there was 'growing contact at all levels between the peoples of Britain and Canada'.[33] Moreover, Diefenbaker remained convinced that the Commonwealth was an important counterweight to the United States, especially as his relationship with the new American President, John F. Kennedy, deteriorated. The elections of 1962 and 1963 revolved around the question of American–Canadian relations and in 1963 the Conservative minority government was replaced by a Liberal minority government headed by Lester Pearson.

Perhaps reflecting the tensions between Ottawa and Washington, most polls showed growing sentiment for remaining within the Commonwealth in the early 1960s. Yet there was no disguising the fact that as the winds of change swept across Africa, the Empire was coming to an end. As Britain withdrew from its remaining colonial possessions, its international weight was visibly declining and the application to the EEC seemed to symbolize a turning away from Empire towards a more limited role within Europe. Under these circumstances Canada had little choice but to readjust its relationship with both Britain and the United States. But this is too simple an explanation for the fundamental shift in English-Canadian attitudes that took place in the 1960s in what José Igartua has described as English Canada's 'Quiet Revolution'.[34] In the 1960s Arnold Smith, a Canadian who became the first Secretary General of the Commonwealth, sought to convince Julius Nyerere, President of Tanganyika, not to withdraw from the Commonwealth over Rhodesia because 'we in Canada believe we invented it and that it is at least as much ours as the British—and we would take withdrawal as a personal affront'.[35] In reality, Canada and the other white-settlement Dominions did not have the same sense of commitment to the rapidly expanding and

[33] Lord Garner of Chiddingly, 'Britain and Canada in the 1940s and 1950s', in Lyon, (ed.), *Britain and Canada*, pp. 101–3.

[34] José E. Igartua, *The Other Quiet Revolution: National Identities in English Canada, 1945–71* (Vancouver, 2006).

[35] Quoted in W. David McIntyre, *The Significance of the Commonwealth, 1965–90* (Christchurch, 1991), p. 56.

predominantly non-white Commonwealth as they had had to the old. Lester Pearson made this clear in his first meeting as Prime Minister with a number of high-ranking American officials on 22 May 1963. According to the American memorandum of the conversation, 'Pearson frankly stated that the British Empire and Commonwealth, as it had previously existed, was in rapid dissolution by the emergence of colonial entities into independent states, and that the advent of African Commonwealth states doomed the Commonwealth system.' Pearson hoped that Canada could maintain some kind of special relationship with the United Kingdom, Australia, New Zealand, and perhaps with India, but he did not see the emerging multicultural Commonwealth as of great significance in defining Canada's place in the world.[36] For many English Canadians the Commonwealth was no longer 'British' enough to retain their emotional loyalty.

After 1947 Canadian citizenship was open to anyone who fulfilled the residency requirements and was prepared to take an oath of loyalty to the Crown. But alongside this civic definition of nationalism was an older sense of ethnic identity that stressed that authentic Canadians were British. Until the 1960s a majority of English Canadians still thought of Canada as a British country with a special relationship with the United Kingdom, despite Suez and despite Britain's attempt to enter the EEC. But Canada's population grew from 14 million in 1951 to over 21.5 million in 1971; three-quarters of the increase was caused by the baby boom and by 1966 nearly half the population was under 24. Most of this new population was based in the cities; over 2.5 million people lived in Montreal in 1966 and nearly 2.3 million in Toronto. Because of the rapid influx of immigrants into the cities they no longer possessed the same ethnic tone. The Orangemen still marched on the 12th of July but the Orange parades were becoming smaller and attracted less notice. The Orange Order, the Imperial Order Daughters of the Empire, even the Boy Scout movement were products of an earlier era, whose membership was ageing. All of them went into decline, in the case of the Orange Order and the IODE rapid decline, in the 1960s. It was perhaps not inappropriate that John A. Macdonald was the first and John Diefenbaker the last Prime Minister to belong to the Orange Order.

For older English Canadians every step in the gradual unravelling of Britishness in Canada brought with it voices of dissent. At each juncture there were sections of the community who felt that something important was being taken from them. But these sentiments had less and less resonance among younger Canadians, who had only a limited (if any) memory of the Second World War. In the 1950s young Canadians—particularly young English Canadians—grew up in an age of unprecedented prosperity, in suburbs that mushroomed across the country, and they completed high school and entered university in record numbers. They

---

[36] Gordon T. Stewart, ' "An Objective of US Foreign Policy since the Founding of the Republic": The United States and the End of Empire in Canada', in Buckner, (ed.), *Canada and the End of Empire*, pp. 96, 114.

were not as religious as their parents and grandparents and all the mainstream Protestant churches lost membership. The post-war generation watched American television shows, read American comic books, and went to American movies. A small stream of Canadian cultural figures continued to gravitate to London, but New York and Hollywood were the new meccas for younger English-Canadian writers, performers, and artists. This did not turn all Canadians into transplanted Americans, for at the level of everyday life Canadians had evolved a distinct and resilient national culture.[37] Indeed, support for joining the United States dropped significantly during the 1950s and anti-Americanism grew much stronger in the 1960s, particularly among Canadian university students, the Canadian cultural community, and Canadian socialists and Marxists who began to talk about American imperialism. But the cultural distance between Canada and Britain was continually growing. When the Beatles gained recognition in Canada in the 1960s—as part of the so-called 'British invasion'—it was through the filter of the *Ed Sullivan Show*. For the generation of English Canadians born during and after the Second World War, Britain was an increasingly remote place with a lower standard of living and an undesirable class system. The schools system taught them to admire British culture and British institutions but they did not think of themselves as British. Armistice Day and Dominion Day and Victoria Day held little meaning to them (except as public holidays) and they did not stand when 'God Save the Queen' was played in cinemas because they really did not identify it as Canada's national anthem. During the flag debate in 1964 Tommy Douglas, the first leader of the New Democratic Party, admitted that while he had great affection for the Red Ensign, 'my children couldn't care less whether the Union Jack' was on Canada's flag. Douglas and many other English Canadians had come to believe that a new flag must respect their children's views and reflect the future, not the past.[38]

The immediate catalyst for change came from Quebec, where the Quiet Revolution in the early 1960s unleashed a rapidly growing separatist movement whose intellectual leadership called for the liberation of Quebec from its status as a colony of first Britain and then English Canada. Lester Pearson's response was to appoint the Royal Commission on Bilingualism and Biculturalism to examine French-Canadian grievances and to attempt to remove the symbols of colonialism to which French Canadians objected. In 1964 Pearson announced to the Canadian Legion that his government was going to produce legislation creating a Canadian flag. Most (but certainly not all) veterans responded by demanding that the new flag be the Canadian Red Ensign. But Pearson recognized that Quebec would never be happy with a flag that had the Union Jack as part of the design and thus began one of the longest and most bitter

---

[37] Allan Smith, 'English Canadian Cultural History: Towards a Different Telling of a Much Told Tale', in Peter Easingwood et al., *Probing Canadian Culture* (Augsburg, 1991).

[38] Stursberg, *Lester Pearson and the Dream of Unity*, p. 163.

debates in the history of the Canadian Parliament. The struggle has sometimes
been presented as a struggle between those who were still colonial in their hearts
and authentic nationalists. But it was really a struggle between two groups of
Canadian nationalists, those who believed that Canada was and ought to be
a British nation and those who believed that Canada ought to redefine itself
with symbols with which Canadians of all ethnic origins—particularly French
Canadians—could identify. The former group probably still formed a slight
majority in English Canada, albeit a shrinking one. Moreover, for the first time
the issue of Canada's connection with Britain became a defining issue in party
politics. Since Confederation the Conservatives had repeatedly sought to cast
themselves as the party loyal to the Imperial connection. But English-Canadian
Liberals had always denied the charge of disloyalty. Although Liberals might differ
over the impact of reciprocity with the United States or over the extent to which
Canada should be automatically bound to follow British leadership in foreign
policy, most English-Canadian Liberals until the 1960s were as committed to the
British connection as their opponents. On occasion they even used the loyalty cry
themselves. 'Keep Canada British. Destroy Houde's Drew. God Save the King'
was the headline in one Liberal paper in Ontario in the 1950s.[39] The Liberal
Party was reborn during its years in opposition after 1957. Half of its support
after 1958 came from Quebec and in 1962 and 1963 its appeal in English Canada
was to younger and better-educated voters in urban constituencies, whose loyalty
to the British connection was waning, and to 'new' Canadians.

The adoption of the new Canadian flag in 1964 marked the end of the
period when it was common for English Canadians to refer to Canada as a
British nation, but the new flag did not pacify Quebec and it did not give
Pearson the majority government he had hoped for. In 1965 Diefenbaker swept
the Maritimes and the Prairies and carried many rural seats in Ontario (which
adopted the Red Ensign with a provincial coat of arms as its provincial flag).
Diefenbaker warned that Canada's other British traditions were in danger. To
an extent he was right. In 1964 the Queen was booed on a visit to Quebec and
Pearson did consider turning Canada into a republic with a Canadian head of
state, leaving the Queen merely as head of the Commonwealth, but he dared
not act upon the idea. In 1967, however, the Canadian Parliament did approve
'O Canada' as Canada's national anthem, although it was not officially adopted
until 1980. During the elaborate centennial celebrations of 1967 lip-service was
paid to the importance of Canada's membership of the Commonwealth, but the
emphasis of the celebrations was on the creation of a new national identity, not
on Canada's British roots.

Pierre Elliott Trudeau, who became Prime Minister in 1968, had little interest
in the Commonwealth and was only reluctantly persuaded to attend the 1968
Commonwealth Prime Ministers' Conference. During the Trudeau years the

[39] Quoted in Paul Rutherford, *The Making of the Mass Media* (Toronto, 1978), p. 106.

remaining symbols of Canada's imperial past were discarded one by one. The Royal Mail became Canada Post, the Royal Canadian Navy and the Royal Canadian Air Force were amalgamated with the army into the Canadian Armed Forces, Dominion Day became Canada Day, and the 'Dominion Government' became the 'Government of Canada'. In 1976 a revised citizenship Act ended the privileged status of British subjects in Canada, while changes in the immigration rules ended the favouritism previously shown to British applicants. One anomaly remained. Although since 1949 the Canadian Parliament could modify those sections of the British North America Act dealing with federal responsibilities, various attempts to find a constitutional amending formula to which the provinces would agree had failed. In 1980 Trudeau acted unilaterally and sought to impose his own constitutional formula. In 1981, under pressure from the Supreme Court of Canada, the Trudeau government negotiated an agreement with nine of the provinces. Quebec and Canada's First Nations both appealed to the British Parliament against patriation on these terms, but in vain since the British government could see no reason to interfere in what was purely an internal Canadian matter. In 1982 the British North America Act became the 'Constitution Act, 1867'. Ironically, at a special ceremony held to mark the patriation of the constitution, the Constitution Act was signed by Elizabeth II, Canada's Queen but also the only remaining symbol of Canada's Imperial past.

Many Canadians of British origin, particularly those who lived in small towns and rural communities and whose roots in Canada stretched back several (in some cases many) generations, were dismayed by this process of de-dominionization. A few intellectuals also spoke out the process and against the increasing integration of Canada and the United States. In 1964 W. L. Morton proclaimed: 'Canada is at a crossroads. Either we go forward in the community that has come into being over three and a half centuries . . . or we disappear as Canada and as Canadians.'[40] George Grant argued in *Lament for a Nation* (1965) that Canada was doomed to become part of the American empire and Donald Creighton blamed the Liberals for leading Canadians down the wrong path in *Canada's First Century* (1970) and *The Forked Road: Canada, 1939–1957* (1974). These sentiments were not exclusively expressed by conservatives. Eugene Forsey, a lifelong socialist, declared: 'I feel that there is nothing ahead of me, when I retire, but to walk down the hill to the British High Commission and ask for asylum, because there will be no recognizable Canada left for me to live in.'[41] A number of Canada's prominent literary figures, like Robertson Davies, Northrop Frye, and Malcolm Ross, shared this sense of loss, though not necessarily the virulent anti-Americanism of Grant and Creighton. Born in different parts of Canada, all

[40] Quoted in Philip Massolin, *Canadian Intellectuals, the Tory Tradition and the Challenge of Modernity, 1939–70* (Toronto, 2001), p. 263.

[41] Eugene Forsey, 'Concepts of Federalism: Some Canadian Aspects', in Gordon Hawkins (ed.), *Concepts of Federalism* (Toronto, 1965), p. 22.

of these men had roots in Canada that stretched back at least two generations, they had all grown up in communities that were predominantly British, and they had all been born before 1919 and in most cases before the First World War. They were out of touch with the Canada that was coming into being in the 1960s and 1970s. Yet even some of those English Canadians who accepted the need to end the Imperial tie and to redefine Canada's national identity were a little nostalgic. 'I grew up in a country', Robert Fulford declared, 'of which my own children have seldom heard, a place nobody speaks about now, "the Dominion of Canada".'[42]

---

[42] Robert Fulford, 'A Post-Modern Dominion', in Kaplan, *Belonging*, p. 117.

SELECT BIBLIOGRAPHY

PHILLIP BUCKNER, ed., *Canada and the End of Empire* (Vancouver, 2004).

——— 'The Long Goodbye: English Canadians and the British World', in Phillip Buckner and R. Douglas Francis, eds., *Rediscovering the British World* (Calgary, 2005).

J. L. GRANATSTEIN, *How Britain's Weakness Forced Canada into the Arms of the United States* (Toronto, 1989).

NORMAN HILLMER and J. L. GRANATSTEIN, *Canada and the World to the 1990s* (Toronto, 1994).

JOSÉ E. IGARTUA, *The Other Quiet Revolution: National Identities in English Canada, 1945–71* (Vancouver, 2006).

WILLIAM KAPLAN, ed., *Belonging: The Meaning and Future of Canadian Citizenship* (Montreal, 1993).

PHILIP MASSOLIN, *Canadian Intellectuals, the Tory Tradition and the Challenge of Modernity, 1939–70* (Toronto, 2001).

C. P. STACEY and BARBARA M. WILSON, *The Half-Million: The Canadians in Britain, 1939–1945* (Toronto, 1987).

7

Status without Stature: Newfoundland, 1869–1949

James K. Hiller

Newfoundland—whose territory included both the island and Labrador—was the smallest of the colonies of settlement (in terms of population) to become a self-governing dominion. Its society, culture, and politics were in many ways similar to the other British North American colonies, but unlike its neighbours, it chose not to join the Canadian Confederation. Newfoundland's experiment with independence gave it a distinct and in some ways unique history, and certainly provided the Imperial government with a series of unusual problems.

The rejection of Confederation in the 1869 general election was so overwhelming that the word 'confederate' became a political slur, and Confederation ceased to be a subject of rational debate, at least in public. Ottawa and London were not perturbed. Neither had tried to influence the election, and both probably assumed that Newfoundland would confederate sooner rather than later. The colony was seen as unimportant, yet it was potentially problematic. Because of its small population it was not a significant market for British or Canadian goods, and Newfoundland's main export, salt codfish, was sold in the Caribbean (where it competed with the Canadian product) and southern Europe. Nor did it attract immigrants; indeed, significant migration to Newfoundland, almost exclusively from south-western England and south-eastern Ireland, had ended by the 1830s. So long as Newfoundland was British, and there was no chance of that changing, its decision had little immediate impact.

But Newfoundland's independence denied Canada full control over the east coast fisheries, and therefore complicated Canada's relations with the United States. Reciprocity involved bargaining over the fisheries, and for diplomatic purposes it was convenient to treat British North America as a single unit. Newfoundland initially acquiesced in this approach, but by the 1880s was becoming impatient. In addition, both Canada and Newfoundland were subject to the 1818 Anglo-American fisheries convention, and they could differ over questions of interpretation and enforcement.

'The affairs of Newfoundland, except where they are insignificant, are imperial', noted Sir Robert Herbert, Permanent Undersecretary at the Colonial Office, in 1890.[1] He was referring not to the convention with the United States, but to the so-called 'French Treaty Shore question', which dominated relations between Newfoundland and Downing Street in the nineteenth century. French fishing rights at Newfoundland dated back to the Treaty of Utrecht (1713), when France recognized British sovereignty over the island, with the condition that French fishermen could continue to use part of the coast in season. In addition, the islands of St Pierre and Miquelon had been ceded in 1763 as a base for French vessels fishing on the offshore banks. By the 1860s, the French fishery on the Treaty Shore between Cape St John and Cape Ray was in decline, while the French bank fishery was on the verge of major expansion. Both fisheries caused significant tensions.

France claimed an exclusive right of fishery on the Treaty Shore, and held that British subjects who settled there did so not by right but by French permission, and that French authorities could regulate how they fished and where they built their houses. In season, the Shore was French, patrolled by a French naval squadron. The British government, uncertain about what rights the French actually possessed, acquiesced in this abnormal state of affairs until the 1850s, but had to deal with increasingly vocal protests from St John's, where it was held that Newfoundlanders had every right to fish on the Shore concurrently with the French, and could settle and do whatever they wanted there, so long as the French fishery was not disturbed. The British interpretation, as it eventually emerged, fell between these extremes. Colonial governments were also concerned about St Pierre and the French offshore fishery, because it encouraged large-scale smuggling along the island's south coast linked to the sale of bait to French banking vessels, and produced fish which, by the 1880s, was competing seriously with Newfoundland exports in European markets. The injury was intensified by the fact that the French fisheries were generously subsidized.

In short, the sovereignty of the colonial government, and its ability to exploit and regulate its major resource, was significantly (and uniquely) limited by treaties arranged before the country even received colonial status in 1825. The British view was that when Newfoundlanders had requested first representative (1832) and then responsible (1855) government, they had done so understanding that such limitations would exist. In any event, the Imperial government insisted that Imperial treaty obligations had to be upheld, no matter what Newfoundlanders might think or want. As the Colonial Secretary, Lord Carnarvon, put it in 1875, 'the power of self-government . . . and the responsibility of the local administration, are necessarily and distinctly limited by the fact that the affairs of the Colony are complicated by the existence of a difficult question as to which

---

[1] Minute, 21 Jan. 1890, London, National Archives, C[olonial] O[ffice] 194/212, p. 625.

Her Majesty's Government has to deal with a foreign power'.[2] This attitude was much resented in the colony and, not surprisingly, the French question became a patriotic touchstone. Any politician who discussed compromise did so at his peril.

The dispute helped foster a mentality of victimization, and provided a scapegoat for a variety of failings. The St John's *Daily News* argued on 13 June 1898 that so long as 'the most fertile half of the Island is to a certain extent under French domination . . . we have not Home Rule, we cannot . . . so long as there is a dual authority in any part of the island'. Thus, as the then Premier, Robert Bond, said in 1900, the colony's backwardness was 'a national disgrace to England', and Newfoundlanders had no need to be ashamed, 'for we could not alter it one iota. We have been handicapped in the march of progress by imperial interdiction on the one hand, and French aggression on the other, and have thus been subjected to the imputation of an inferiority we neither merit nor feel.'[3] This argument fitted into a nationalist view of Newfoundland history which had emerged after 1815 and fast became orthodoxy. Hardy Newfoundlanders had always had to struggle against imperial indifference and hostility, symbolized by the West Country merchants, fishing admirals, and naval governors who had collectively managed the eighteenth-century migratory fishery, opposed the growth of settlement, and harassed the settlers. There followed the burden imposed by the ancient treaties. Lord Salisbury once referred to Newfoundland as 'the sport of historic errors'.[4] In the colony, significantly, the phrase became 'sport of historic *misfortune*'. Newfoundlanders had 'never had a break in the 450 years of our history', said a politician in 1947,[5] and the tradition lives on. These resentments, however, coexisted with pride in being part of the British Empire, 'loyal to the backbone', as a newspaper put it in 1865.[6]

A central issue was the administrative competence of the colonial government on the Treaty Shore, where it had no presence whatsoever. The Colonial Office moved with extreme caution, eventually allowing the appointment of magistrates (1878) and the enfranchisement of settlers (1882) over strenuous French protests. But land and other such grants were hedged about with conditions, and local fisheries legislation was largely inapplicable, since the French insisted on extraterritoriality. When a railway was built across the island in the 1890s, the western terminus had to be sited beyond the French limits. In the 1880s, colonial politicians lost patience with the gradual, step-by-step

---

   [2] Carnarvon to Governor Hill, 27 Sept. 1875, CO 194/190, p. 206.

   [3] Robert Bond in Assembly debate, 10 Mar. 1900, cited in *Evening Herald* (St John's), 19 Mar. 1900.

   [4] *Parliamentary Debates* (Lords), Third Series, CCCLI, 19 Mar. 1891, col. 1411.

   [5] J. R. Smallwood speaking in the National Convention, 22 May 1947, cited in James K. Hiller and Michael F. Harrington, (eds), *The Newfoundland National Convention, 1946–1948: Debates and Papers* (Montreal, 1995), vol. I, p. 572.

   [6] *The Patriot*, 18 July 1865.

approach and adopted an aggressive, confrontational policy, which irritated both London and Ottawa. In essence, the colonial government decided to attack the French offshore fishery by placing an embargo on the export of bait from Newfoundland's south coast. This would, it was hoped, reduce both the French catch and market competition. At the same time, given the expiry of the fishery clauses of the Treaty of Washington (1874), the government proposed to allow American banking vessels access to bait, in return for free entry of Newfoundland products into the United States—an independent reciprocity treaty. Canada objected to a potential breach in the hitherto united front on reciprocity, and the Imperial government to legislation that France would obviously interpret as yet another hostile British action. Nevertheless, the Bait Act was eventually allowed and, as feared, it precipitated a major crisis.

Though French banking vessels adapted to the changed circumstances, the Act was deeply resented. French authorities became determined to hold onto the Treaty Shore, and to enforce their interpretation of French rights. As part of this initiative, they encouraged the development of a lobster fishery, which was not as innocuous as it sounds. The Newfoundland government held that since the treaties only mentioned 'fish', the French were not entitled to catch lobsters, let alone can them; to which the French retorted that they were entitled to take any type of fish or crustacean, and to process them as they saw fit. This disagreement escalated because the Imperial government in 1890 insisted that the commodores of the British and French naval squadrons should regulate the Treaty Shore lobster fishery under an Anglo-French *modus vivendi* pending arbitration. It was then discovered that Imperial legislation authorizing the enforcement of the treaties had lapsed, and when the British commodore forcibly closed a Newfoundland-owned lobster cannery in St George's Bay, the owner sued him for trespass. The Imperial government's actions caused great indignation in the colony. Talks in London on a general Treaty Shore settlement ended in deadlock, and the colonial government refused to provide statutory authority for naval officers. Salisbury concluded that the only solution was Imperial legislation. Britain was 'bound by Treaty obligations to the French which we must fulfil', he told the Cabinet; and 'we run a considerable risk by not fulfilling them', since irresponsible behaviour on the Shore could lead to an international incident. 'It is needless to say that all the risks of war are with us.'[7] Thus enforcement legislation would be put through Parliament, and French rights would be defined by arbitration, if necessary without the colony's consent. The Imperial bill was introduced into the House of Lords in mid-March 1891.

In Newfoundland, the legislation was immediately christened 'the Coercion Bill'—'I fear that we have a Trans Atlantic Ireland of a lower type on hand', sniffed the Governor[8]—and the legislature dispatched a delegation to London,

---

[7] Salisbury, cabinet paper on 'Newfoundland', 21 Nov. 1890, Cabinet Office 37/28, p. 9082.
[8] Governor O'Brien to Knutsford, private, 28 Mar. 1891, CO 194/218, p. 344.

where a deal was worked out. The colony agreed to pass temporary enforcement legislation, and the Premier, Sir William Whiteway, negotiated the terms of permanent legislation. The arbitration was postponed *sine die*, since France refused to participate until convinced that an award would be implemented. Whiteway's enforcement bill was controversial and unpopular. It split his party, and was defeated in the 1892 session. Facing an election, and with the immediate crisis over, Salisbury decided not to revive the Imperial bill.

In the meantime, a tussle had been developing with Canada. Not only had Newfoundland begun to regulate the sale of bait to Canadian vessels, but it had quietly sent a delegate to Washington to explore the possibility of an independent reciprocity treaty. This was done with the permission of the Imperial government, to make partial amends for browbeating the colony over the French question, and to encourage cooperation. Unexpectedly, the Newfoundland delegate, Robert Bond, managed in 1890 to negotiate a draft convention behind the back of the British Ambassador. The Canadian government furiously and successfully lobbied against ratification, and the Newfoundland government was in its turn incensed. Lord Knutsford, the Colonial Secretary, pointed out that 'the leave to negotiate does not carry with it an obligation or an engagement to sanction the arrangement when made',[9] but the Assembly was unimpressed, and characterized the failure to ratify the convention as a hostile act calculated 'to permanently disturb the loyalty for which the Colony has . . . been remarkable'.[10] In March, Canadian vessels were denied bait licences. The Canadian government demanded imperial intervention, while privately raising the possibility of Confederation.

During the winter of 1891/2 a tariff war developed between Newfoundland and Canada, which ended only when the Canadian government threatened to make things difficult for Newfoundlanders fishing in Canadian waters. A conference between the two governments took place in Halifax in November 1892. It was anticlimactic. The Newfoundlanders were unwilling to discuss Confederation, and the Canadians refused to make any concessions. For the moment Canada had Newfoundland pinned down. The latter could not refuse bait to Canadian fishermen, could not impose discriminatory tariffs, and apparently could not bargain with the United States without Canadian permission. Newfoundland might have, theoretically, the same status as Canada; but the conference confirmed that it certainly did not have the same stature. 'It would appear', wrote Whiteway, 'that Her Majesty's Government, whilst conferring upon this Colony a constitution, would desire to withhold from it those constitutional rights which are part and parcel of . . . that constitution. If this Colony is to be made wholly subservient to Canada . . . it would be well that we should know it.'[11]

---

[9] *Parliamentary Debates* (Lords), 17 Feb. 1891, Third Series, CCCL, pp. 819–20.
[10] *Evening Telegram* (St John's), 14 Feb. 1891.
[11] Whiteway to Governor O'Brien, 4 May 1892, in O'Brien to Knutsford, conf., 30 May 1892, CO 194/221, p. 285.

Lack of stature was further demonstrated by the Colonial Office's handling of Newfoundland domestic issues during the 1890s. Officials had experienced enormous frustrations dealing with the colony, which they saw as an anomalous imperial nuisance—as an Ireland which had unfortunately been granted home rule, with a political elite perceived as being parochial, incompetent, corrupt, and often unreasonable in its dealings with the Imperial government. Thus, when the colony's two private banks suspended payment in December 1894, precipitating a financial crisis which might bankrupt the government, the Colonial Office decided against intervention. Bankruptcy would have advantages: the Imperial government could step in as receiver, and decide whether Newfoundland should become a crown colony administered from London, or a Canadian province. In any event, responsible government would be over. The Newfoundland government judged Confederation to be the lesser evil, and sent a delegation to Ottawa. However, since its victory over reciprocity, the Canadian government had lost interest in bringing Newfoundland into Confederation, and was in any case wary of taking responsibility for the French Treaty Shore. Even so, terms might have been agreed had the Conservative federal government been less parsimonious, and the Imperial government willing to provide a dowry. Negotiations collapsed and, to the dismay of the Colonial Office, the colony managed to raise loans that ensured its survival.

Tensions between the colony and the Imperial government revived in the early twentieth century during the premiership of Robert Bond, a nationalist anti-confederate who, more than any other Newfoundland political leader, was preoccupied by the colony's status within the Empire. By 1900, when he took office, France and Britain were beginning to explore the possibility of rapprochement, and the settlement of the Treaty Shore issue was seen as an essential part of the package. To make Bond more flexible, Joseph Chamberlain, the Colonial Secretary, decided that Newfoundland should be allowed to try once more to obtain reciprocity. Canada objected, but, Chamberlain acidly noted, 'Sir W. Laurier who is so strong an adherent of Home Rule that he must pay special attention to Mr. Redmond, cannot complain if the principle of Home Rule is followed in the case of N[ew]f[oun]dland'.[12]

The ploy had positive and negative consequences. In November 1902, Bond and John Hay, the American Secretary of State, signed a draft reciprocity treaty. Though Chamberlain was annoyed that, *inter alia*, the treaty granted the United States most favoured nation status, meaning that Newfoundland could not grant an imperial preference, official chagrin was tempered by the knowledge that the treaty faced a rough time in the Senate. For his part, Bond proved to be reasonably cooperative on a settlement with France. The 1904 convention provided that France would give up its ancient fishing rights, but retain a concurrent seasonal fishery within the former limits, though landing on the coast was forbidden. The

---

[12] Minute by Chamberlain, 7 Jan. 1902, CO 194/248.

British government agreed to compensate the owners of French establishments, and, reluctantly, added territorial concessions in West Africa. The agreement was welcomed in the colony. 'This island', declaimed Bond, 'which some of us love so dearly despite its backwardness, its isolation, its ruggedness, physical and climatic, may henceforth be hailed not only as our native land, but our own land, freed from every foreign claim, and the blasting influence of foreign oppression—ours in entirety—solely ours.'[13]

The unwelcome repercussions of the US treaty followed its effective rejection by the Senate in 1905. The Bond government unwisely decided to respond by harassing American fishermen in Newfoundland waters by applying a strict (and contentious) interpretation of the 1818 convention, and by using the Bait Act and a new Foreign Fishing Vessels Act to curtail American participation in the winter herring fishery. When restrictions were imposed in October 1905, the United States government issued a formal protest, and the British government immediately intervened: Newfoundland herring would not be allowed to disrupt Anglo-American relations. Bond was prevented from enforcing his policy, and in 1906 the Imperial government unilaterally imposed a *modus vivendi* pending an arbitration on the interpretation of the 1818 convention. This was followed by an Imperial Order-in-Council (1907) forbidding any seizures or arrests of American vessels. Such actions were heavy-handed. Bond claimed they constituted 'a menace to Responsible Government in the Colonies',[14] and justifiably wondered whether London would have treated a more important colony in this way. But he received little more than sympathy at the 1907 Colonial Conference, and at home the dispute failed to rouse patriotic enthusiasm. The Imperial government had shown once more that the implementation of international treaties, and British foreign policy as a whole, took precedence over Newfoundland's ambitions. It was some compensation that the award of the Hague Tribunal in 1911 substantially upheld the British—that is, Canadian and Newfoundland—arguments concerning the interpretation of the 1818 convention, and the amenability of American fishermen to local law. But by that time reciprocity was dead and Bond was no longer Prime Minister. With his political exit, the end of both the French and American fishery questions, and the defeat of reciprocity, Newfoundland's relations with Britain settled into a drab normality that persisted until August 1914.

For all the quarrels with the Imperial government, Newfoundlanders had always seen themselves as loyal members of a great Empire. A British Society existed from 1834, and the Orange Order, which arrived in 1863, at its peak had 190 lodges. The first overseas company of the Church Lads' Brigade was formed in St John's in 1892. The first colonial Royal Naval Reserve contingent followed in 1900. The Boy Scouts and the Imperial Order Daughters of the Empire

---

[13] Speech in Assembly, reported in *Evening Telegram*, 22 Apr. 1904.
[14] Quoted in *Evening Telegram*, 10 Sept. 1907.

appeared in 1910, and the Legion of Frontiersmen the next year. Royal tours to North America always stopped in St John's, and Imperial honours were prized. Roman Catholics of Irish ancestry displayed their imperialism less stridently than Protestants, perhaps, but the loyal toast was drunk at Benevolent Irish Society dinners and both groups were able in 1897 to celebrate with enthusiasm the Queen's jubilee and the 400th anniversary of John Cabot's voyage. Indeed, the main oration at the Cabot ceremonies was given by the Roman Catholic Bishop, who claimed that Cabot had discovered and given to Britain 'the New World, her first and most ancient and most loyal colony, the brightest gem in her crown, the foundation of her future greatness'.[15] Loyalty to the British Empire was an important element in a Newfoundland identity which, by the late nineteenth century, though primarily among the elites, was beginning to transcend ethnic and religious divisions. Governor Sir Ralph Williams commented in 1911 that Newfoundland was 'untainted by American ways', and 'untouched by the dream of individual Empire held by so large a section of those of the great Dominion. It is British to the core . . . bound to the mother country far less by ties of interest than by ties of affection.'[16]

Given this background, there was no question in 1914 that the colony would contribute whatever it could to the war. Unusually, the Governor, Sir Walter Davidson (fresh from the Seychelles), played a prominent role. He became chairman of the Newfoundland Patriotic Association, a non-denominational, non-partisan body that functioned as an unofficial war ministry until 1917. For a while, this unique expedient worked. The newly formed Newfoundland Regiment fought honourably at Gallipoli and on the Western Front. Other Newfoundlanders served in the Royal Navy and as foresters in Scotland. The regiment suffered particularly appalling losses at Beaumont Hamel on 1 July 1916, the first day of the Battle of the Somme. This failed offensive almost immediately achieved iconic status, as an expression of Newfoundlanders' inherent qualities and their Imperial loyalty. Since 1917, 1 July has been observed as Memorial Day, Newfoundland's own day of remembrance.

As was the case elsewhere, initial unity and enthusiasm began to crack as the war continued. Profiteering scandals and the conscription issue doomed the Patriotic Association, and a pro-conscriptionist national government took over. Its Prime Minister, Sir Edward Morris, was present at meetings of the Imperial War Cabinet and the Imperial War Conference, clear evidence that Newfoundland was accepted as a Dominion, equal in status to the other self-governing members of the Empire.

This was the apogee of Newfoundland's role in Imperial affairs, and at the Paris Peace Conference the fragility of the country's position was clearly

---

[15] Quoted in Jiří Smrz, 'Cabot 400: The 1897 St. John's Celebrations', *Newfoundland Studies*, 12/1 (1996), p. 24.
[16] Williams to Harcourt, conf., 24 Apr. 1911. CO 194/283, p. 158.

exposed. Manoeuvring between the objections of the United States to separate Dominion representation, and the justifiable expectations of the Dominions themselves, Lloyd George decided to sacrifice the claims of Newfoundland, the least influential Dominion, in order to obtain representation for the others and for India. Newfoundland found itself sidelined, excluded from the list of signatories of the Versailles Treaty, and also from the list of original members of the League of Nations. There could not have been a clearer demonstration of the gap between status and stature which had always characterized Newfoundland's relations with Britain, and of its subordinate place in the Imperial hierarchy.

There was surprisingly little fuss in a Newfoundland beset by political discord and economic and financial crises. It formally adopted the style 'Dominion' in 1918,[17] and appointed a High Commissioner. Its Prime Ministers continued to attend Imperial conferences. But Newfoundland never applied for League membership, and voluntarily allowed its foreign relations to be handled by the Imperial government. As a result, the Foreign Office decided that while Newfoundland might be a member of the Commonwealth for internal purposes, it had no separate international status. As an official noted in 1923, 'There are two types of British Dominion status: the major type, as exists in Canada etc. . . . and the minor of which hitherto Newfoundland has been unique.'[18]

This was an instance in which the Great War did not mark a 'coming of age', a stage in the progress from colony to nation. There was great pride in the accomplishments of the Royal Newfoundland Regiment, as it was known from 1917, and impressive memorials were raised in Europe and at home. The image of the 'fighting Newfoundlander' certainly entered the nationalist pantheon, but it has never been argued that the war forged a national identity. That already existed. Rather, the war left a sad legacy of loss, instability, and debt, and 'has been seen increasingly as a senseless slaughter that crippled the country's future'.[19] In effect, Newfoundlanders turned in on themselves. Preoccupied with their country's dismal economic and financial state, politicians in the 1920s had little interest in international and Imperial affairs. At the 1926 Imperial Conference, the Prime Minister stated that he attended 'as the representative of what we much prefer to call Britain's oldest Colony rather than Britain's youngest Dominion':

We represent such a very small number of people that we do not expect to have very much to say on Imperial matters . . . The message I would bring from Newfoundland

---

[17] This was not the legal title. The permanent letters patent and Governor's instructions (both 1876), which used the terms 'Colony' and 'Island', were not amended.

[18] Addam, minute of 3 Jan. 1923, quoted in William C. Gilmore, *Newfoundland and Dominion Status: The External Affairs Competence and International Law Status of Newfoundland, 1855–1934* (Toronto, 1988), p. 102.

[19] Jerry Bannister, 'Making History: Cultural Memory in Twentieth-Century Newfoundland', *Newfoundland Studies*, 18/2 (2002), p. 189, n. 5.

to-day is that we are entirely satisfied with the status under which we exist and we do not even require to be consulted as to questions of foreign policy.[20]

In 1931, when the draft Statute of Westminster came before the legislature, the government was initially prepared to accede to it. However, public opinion was opposed, and there was much talk about the need to strengthen rather than loosen ties with Britain: 'Let the Oldest Colony once more take the lead in showing staunch and unswerving fealty in act as well as in word of mouth to Britain's Crown.'[21] The result was that Newfoundland exercised 'the New Zealand option' and requested that sections 2 to 6 of the statute should not apply until appropriate local legislation was passed.

The Depression intensified Newfoundland's already desperate situation, and by 1932 the government was unable to continue full payments on a public debt of approximately $100 million, one-third representing the cost of the Great War. Notice of partial default caused alarm in Ottawa and London, and financial assistance was provided while an Imperial royal commission investigated the situation. The Newfoundland Royal Commission, chaired by Baron Amulree, reported in November 1933. Its central recommendation had been scripted by a Whitehall bureaucracy genuinely concerned about the impact that default by a Dominion might have on the financial markets, and anxious for a quick solution. Moreover, the Canadian government had made it abundantly clear that it would not provide financial assistance, and was not interested in Newfoundland becoming a province. The solution was that the Newfoundland debt would be rescheduled, and guaranteed by the British government—in effect, a disguised default. But since financial intervention was incompatible with Dominion status, responsible government would have to be suspended, and replaced by government by an appointed Commission. The rationale minimized the impact of the Depression, bypassed the cost of the Great War, and emphasized alleged misgovernment, corruption, and financial extravagance. This reflected at least some of the evidence collected in Newfoundland, but also a bureaucratic mind-set which mistrusted and disliked local politics and politicians.

On the basis of the report, intervention could be presented to the British Parliament as benign and constructive imperialism—the rehabilitation of an Imperial prodigal. In Newfoundland, the Amulree recommendations were greeted, on the whole, with relief and gratitude. Demoralized by years of economic and financial difficulty, most Newfoundlanders were prepared to accept the apparent failure of independence. With almost indecent haste, without negotiation or hesitation, the government dutifully rammed through the legislature an address requesting the suspension of responsible government. In February 1934 a Commission of three Newfoundlanders and three British officials, chaired by the Governor, took over the administration of what had become constitutionally a colony, though still

[20] W. S. Monroe, quoted in Gilmore, *Dominion Status*, 104.
[21] *Evening Telegram*, 13 Mar. 1931.

legally a Dominion. The Commission, which had full legislative and executive powers, was to remain in place, the legislation specified, until the country was again self-supporting, and there was a request from the people for constitutional change.

The period of Commission government was a unique experiment in Imperial administration. In the rush to avoid default, however, the experiment had not been adequately thought through. It was unclear, for instance, how much freedom of action the Commission was to be allowed, and how far it could implement a programme of reconstruction and reform. In time, the Dominions Office made clear that it exercised supervisory control, and that what it wanted in Newfoundland was 'progress with economy and without adverse publicity'.[22] In short, costs were to be controlled, and the local elites, which had strongly supported the establishment of the Commission, accommodated. However, given the persistence of the Depression, balanced budgets proved unattainable, and controversy could not always be avoided. By the late 1930s the Commission was widely unpopular, mainly because it was secretive, and had failed to fulfil the inflated expectations which had accompanied its inauguration. Its achievements were real, but unspectacular, necessary, and largely bureaucratic—among them the reorganization of the civil service, tax reform, improvements in health and education, and the encouragement of modernization in the fishing industry. Most Newfoundlanders could see little improvement over the situation in 1934, and it is likely that the Dominions Office would have had to reform the Commission system, had not war intervened.

The war brought prosperity and full employment. American and Canadian forces built large military bases both on the island and in Labrador, whose interior boundary, long disputed with Canada, had been finally established in 1927 by the Judicial Committee of the Privy Council. The construction boom eventually waned, but the economy in general did well, and Newfoundlanders also found work on the mainland, and served in the Canadian and British armed forces. There was widespread unhappiness over the destroyers-for-bases agreement (1941), which gave the United States government ninety-nine-year leases and virtual sovereignty over its base areas, but the Commission had no option but to concur. Overall, the people of Newfoundland and Labrador had higher disposable incomes than ever before, and the government generated a surplus large enough to enable it to make interest-free loans to the United Kingdom. There was no question that the country was again self-supporting, and that direct rule had to end after the war.

The events that followed have generated an extensive literature and a controversy which lasts to this day. The British and Canadian governments agreed in 1945 that their common aim would be to bring Newfoundland into Confederation.

[22] Peter Neary, *Newfoundland in the North Atlantic World, 1929–1949* (Montreal, 1988), p. 105.

Britain had always favoured this option and, in this first phase of decolonization, wanted to be free of responsibility for Newfoundland. The war had changed Canada's attitude. There was not a great deal of enthusiasm for the acquisition of another Maritime province—as Newfoundland was perceived—but officials now recognized that Canada had essential long-term interests in the region. There was concern about supposedly growing American influence and the security of the Atlantic coast, and considerable value was placed on Labrador's economic potential. Only Newfoundlanders themselves could bring about the end result, and in 1946 they were assumed to be largely anti-confederate. Thus the Dominions Office arranged for the election of a National Convention to consider the country's financial and economic condition, and recommend forms of future government to be placed on a referendum ballot. The Convention met between September 1946 and January 1948, sent delegations to London (where the reception was deliberately frosty) and Ottawa, and finally recommended that the referendum choice should be between a return to responsible government and a continuation of the Commission. It rejected a motion to include Confederation. The Dominions Office overturned the recommendation and placed Confederation on the ballot anyway—an intervention which fuelled well-founded anti-confederate suspicions that the deck had been stacked from the outset. Indeed, there were many who felt betrayed by the mother country to whom they had so often protested their loyalty; where now was British fair play? There followed two bitterly contested referenda, and Confederation—presented by its supporters as 'British Union'—finally emerged with 52 per cent of the vote. It was enough for London and Ottawa. The Terms of Union were settled in December 1948; and on 31 March 1949 the Dominion of Newfoundland became a Canadian province. Its flag (until 1980) continued to be the Union Jack.

The social and economic impact of the Depression and the Second World War had allowed Confederation to become a realistic constitutional option. Many Newfoundlanders were nervous about resuming independence, fearing another collapse and the loss of the higher standard of living to which they had become accustomed. And it was the war that made Canada genuinely interested in the proposition, which had not been the case before 1939. Arguably, Newfoundland might have been well advised to have joined Canada in the 1860s and preserve, like the Maritime provinces, 'a shabby dignity'.[23] But Newfoundlanders believed then that they had the resources to underpin a separate existence. The years that followed had shown that prosperity was elusive, and that independence was costly. In the end, a vulnerable and narrowly based economy was unable to sustain a public debt that largely represented two 'national' projects—railway building and the Great War. And in the end, too, the Britain with which Newfoundlanders had always identified, seeing themselves as the most loyal members of the Empire,

[23] David G. Alexander, *Atlantic Canada and Confederation: Essays in Canadian Political Economy* (Toronto, 1983), p. 74.

became determined to end what it had long seen as an imperial anomaly—a small, relatively unimportant, and precarious colony which nevertheless was entitled to the trappings of responsible government and Dominion status. Becoming a province ended that anomaly, but in substituting Ottawa for London, Newfoundland had not found a solution to its inherent problems, and became inevitably involved in a different but similar (and continual) process of defining the relationship between a peripheral province and an imperial heartland.

SELECT BIBLIOGRAPHY

WILLIAM C. GILMORE, *Newfoundland and Dominion Status* (Toronto, 1988).

JAMES HILLER and PETER NEARY, (eds), *Newfoundland in the Nineteenth and Twentieth Centuries: Essays in Interpretation* (Toronto, 1980).

———— , (eds), *Twentieth-Century Newfoundland: Explorations* (St John's, 1994).

PETER NEARY, *Newfoundland in the North Atlantic World, 1929–1949* (Montreal and Kingston, 1988).

S. J. R. NOEL, *Politics in Newfoundland* (Toronto, 1971).

F. F. THOMPSON, *The French Shore Problem in Newfoundland: An Imperial Study* (Toronto, 1961).

8

British Migration and British America, 1783–1867

Elizabeth Jane Errington

In 1818, a contributor to the Edinburgh *Scotsman* was astounded at 'the extraordinary emigration from all quarters of the Old World' to the New. 'It is impossible', the author commented, 'to look at the vast multitude, of all conditions and professions, who are throwing up their prospects in their native country . . . without a sensation of wonder.' The *Scotsman* posited that once trade and industry revived after more than a generation of war, the people would be content to stay at home. In the meantime, this was 'a spectacle without parallel since the time of the Crusades'.[1] For John Gemmill of Glasgow, a 46-year-old stonemason and father of nine, the promise of peace was not enough. In 1821, unemployment and economic uncertainty continued to run high in Scotland, and many regions of Ireland and England, and Gemmill was one of over 15,000 British nationals who left home that year to make a new life for themselves in America. Although over the next few years the 'extraordinary emigration' did seem to dissipate, by the end of the decade, the numbers of migrants again began to rise sharply. When the young English author Catherine Parr Traill and her husband and half-pay officer Thomas boarded the *Laurel* at Liverpool in 1832 bound for Upper Canada, they were two of over 100,000 who left Great Britain and Ireland that year. Between 1815 and the mid-1860s, it is estimated that almost 5 million Irish, English, Scots, and Welsh packed up their goods and made their way to North America and Australasia.[2]

The destination of choice was the former Thirteen Colonies, now the United States of America. But after 1815, a steady stream, and in some years a majority, of British and Irish migrants consciously chose to settle in the northern half of the continent (see Table 8.1). By the time of Confederation in 1867, the Empire in North America had been transformed from a number of scattered

---

[1] Quoted in *Kingston Gazette*, 8 Sept. 1818.

[2] For a discussion of the problems with emigration statistics for the period, see Donald Harmon Akenson, *The Irish in Ontario: A Study in Rural History* (Kingston and Montreal, 1984), pp. 14–15.

Table 8.1. Departures from ports in Great Britain and Ireland and arrivals in North America, 1815–1860

| Years | Total number of departures[a] | Destination as Percentage of Total | | |
		British North America	USA	Combined total
1815–19	96,000	55	45	100
1820–4	95,500	70	27	97
1825–9	120,400	49.5	46	95.5
1830–4	380,600	59	37	96
1835–9	285,900	34	52	86
1840–4	454,700	37.5	49	86.5
1845–9	1,012,000	25	68	93
1850–4	1,839,700	11.5	71	82.5
1855–9	657,800	8	60	68

[a] Numbers are approximations.

Source: Modified from N. H. Carrier and J. R. Jeffery, *External Migration: A Study of the Available Statistics, 1815–1950* (London, 1953), p. 96.

Imperial outposts that, at the beginning of the century, had been British in name but, with the exception of Quebec, decidedly American in their peoples and practices, into increasingly mature British settler societies. In 1867, about 60 per cent of Canadians were of British origin.[3] Many of them continued to identify themselves as English, or Irish, or Scots, or Welsh, and maintained close ties with communities on the other side of the Atlantic; but colonists also increasingly identified themselves as British and claimed membership in an Empire that spanned the globe.

The story of the remarkable migration and the resulting transformation of British America after the bitter civil war of 1776–83 rested on a number of complex and interwoven realities. Overarching, but most often not directing this development, were London's periodic concerns for the security of the North American Empire and its changing policies with respect to emigration. By the 1820s, individual colonies began to set their own agendas and to assert their particular interests in the matter. At the centre of the story, though, were the thousands of Britons who either alone, or more often in the company of family and friends, actually left home and made their way to British North America. At times, Imperial, colonial, and personal interests and concerns reinforced each other, and individuals and families emigrated as a result of state encouragement and support. Much of the time, however, London and colonial centres disagreed, often sharply, on who should be encouraged to settle in North America and how best to do this; and people often left home and settled with no regard for, and sometimes in defiance of, official policies.

[3] *Royal Commission on Bilingualism and Biculturalism*, vol. IV, table A-4, p. 248.

What contemporaries in Great Britain and Ireland characterized as a 'tide' of emigration initially seemed but a resumption of the eighteenth-century phenomena that had been interrupted first by the American Revolution and then by the long war with France. But much had changed since thousands of migrants had made their way to North America in the 1760s and 1770s. As a consequence of the American Revolution, the British presence on the continent was significantly diminished. In 1783, the North American Empire was dominated by the sprawling interior colony of Quebec, with its largely Catholic and French-speaking population. A few Scots and American merchants had established themselves in Montreal, and along the Atlantic coast the Aboriginal population was beginning to be outnumbered by an assortment of Yankee Planters, French-speaking Acadians, 'foreign' Protestants, and, in Newfoundland, Irish and English fishers. The west was largely uncharted territory, officially the domain of the Hudson's Bay Company but primarily the home of Aboriginal peoples who periodically traded with the handful of Scottish, English, and American fur traders who lived and worked in the interior. A distinctly British presence was only really apparent in the garrison communities—Halifax, Quebec, and, to a lesser degree, Cataraqui (soon to be called Kingston) and Niagara on the north shore of Lake Ontario.

During the first few years after the American Revolution, the need to secure a presence on the continent and to meet the Crown's obligations to those subjects of the Thirteen Colonies who had remained loyal to Great Britain came together and led to the reconstitution of the Empire. Even before the Treaty of Paris was signed in 1783, London began to make preparations to relocate tens of thousands of American Loyalists to Nova Scotia and Quebec. Governor General Frederic Haldimand negotiated land transfers with the Mississauga in the area that would become southern Ontario; survey crews from Halifax and Quebec began to mark out concessions and lots for settlement; and contracts were let to provision the new arrivals.

The 35,000 or so Loyalists who arrived in Nova Scotia had high expectations. They had lost their homes, their livelihood, and often their families as a result of the war. They expected not only an asylum and compensation for their losses but also confirmation that their loyalty had not been in vain. But when the flotillas carrying disbanded militiamen and their families, and groups of unassociated Loyalists, landed at Halifax, Port Roseway (soon renamed Shelburne) on the south shore of Nova Scotia, and at the mouth of the St John River in the Bay of Fundy, authorities there were still scrambling to prepare for the influx. Tensions mounted as the Loyalists, living in tents, rough huts, or ships' holds, had to wait for land and had difficulties finding work. Many resented the resident population who, they argued, had not suffered the privations of war and exile. They also resented the apparent ineptness of colonial authorities. Moreover, members of this heterogeneous group had little in common but 'the experience of exile'. Soon after their arrival, racial tensions between disbanded soldiers in Shelburne and black Loyalists living in nearby Birchtown erupted into violence when white settlers charged that their neighbours were underbidding them for work. White Loyalists also fought among themselves about what kind of communities they should plant in their new homes.[4]

Within a year of peace, Nova Scotia was partitioned. In the new colony of New Brunswick, with its predominantly Loyalist population of artisans, labourers, and small farmers camped at the mouth of the St John River, community leaders set to work to establish an agricultural society that would be 'the envy of the American states'—one that rested on landed privilege and hierarchical notions of order and respectability.[5] In the refashioned Nova Scotia, although a few Loyalists were integrated into Halifax society, most faced significant challenges eking a living from the poor soil or finding work and adjusting to their new homes. Black Loyalists, many of whom had joined the Royal Standard in response to promises of freedom and land, found themselves in particular difficulties. Slavery was still recognized in Nova Scotia and racial discrimination was generally condoned. Black Loyalists were the last to be resettled and many received no land at all. Not surprisingly, nearly half of them eagerly accepted a plan in 1792 to relocate to Sierra Leone. By 1800, a growing number of white Loyalists too had become discouraged and left the region in search of better opportunities. Some of them made their way west to the new colony of Upper Canada.[6]

Originally, the 'upper country' or the region along the north shore of the upper St Lawrence River and Lakes Ontario and Erie had been intended as a refuge for members of the Iroquois Confederacy who had allied themselves with the British during the war. This plan was revised in 1783–4. Two tracts of land, along the Grand River and on the north shore of Lake Ontario, were reserved for the Mohawk and other Aboriginal allies; the rest was made available to members of provincial regiments who had taken part in the bitter conflict on the New York frontier and to those who had fled to Quebec and Niagara during and just after the war, all told between 6,000 and 8,000 refugees.[7] Grants were initially allocated by provincial corps and former officers were placed in charge. Pressure from the emerging Loyalist elite, who soon chafed at living in a colony governed by civil law from Quebec, led to the partitioning of Quebec in 1791. A year later, former British officer and veteran of the Revolution John Graves Simcoe arrived

[4] Graeme Wynn, 'A Region of Scattered Settlements and Bounded Possibilities: Northeastern America, 1775–1800', *Canadian Geographer*, 31 (1987), p. 321.

[5] Ann Gorman Condon, *The Envy of the American States: The Loyalists of New Brunswick* (Fredericton, 1984).

[6] James Walker, *The Black Loyalists: The Search for a Promised Land in Nova Scotia and Sierra Leone, 1783–1870* (New York, 1976); Neil MacKinnon, *This Unfriendly Soil: The Loyalist Experience in Nova Scotia* (Montreal and Kingston, 1986).

[7] Elizabeth Jane Errington, 'The Loyalists', in *The Oxford Companion to Canadian History* (Oxford, 2004), pp. 368–9.

in the new colony of Upper Canada determined to mould this frontier into, in his words, 'a little Britain' in the wilderness.[8]

The exodus of the Loyalists from the United States was only the beginning of a generation of migrations within and to British America. Within a few years of their arrival, many disgruntled, bitter, or homesick Loyalists returned 'home' to the United States. After 1792, between 15,000 and 20,000 restless American settlers began to make their way north to take up land in Upper Canada; another thousand or so settled in what would become the Eastern Townships of Quebec.[9] The already heterogeneous population of the Maritime colonies was soon augmented by the arrival of migrants from the British Isles. Despite official prohibitions, English and Irish fishermen and their families began to settle in growing numbers along the coast of Newfoundland. At the beginning of the nineteenth century, a few hundred Scots Highlanders arrived to take tenancies in Prince Edward Island, offered by Lord Selkirk, an avid supporter of British colonization in the New World. In 1812, Selkirk also organized and sponsored a small party of Highlanders who trekked from Hudson Bay to begin a new settlement at the Red River (near present-day Winnipeg). By 1812, about 17,000 Gaelic-speaking Scots had also taken up land and established businesses in eastern Nova Scotia and Cape Breton; other Highland families had joined kin and former neighbours who had fled north after the Revolution and settled in Glengarry County, in eastern Upper Canada.[10]

Knitting these diverse and restless populations into recognizably 'British' colonies posed no easy task for the colonial and imperial authorities. Although the official language was English, French continued to be the working language for most in Quebec, and Gaelic, German, Dutch, and various Aboriginal dialects were regularly heard in other settlements throughout British America. The new colonists also adhered to a wide variety of faiths. There were Scots and Irish Catholics. Many Planters and Loyalists were Congregationalists; others joined Anglican churches or attended Methodist meeting houses. In addition to small congregations of Presbyterians, there were also vibrant communities of Baptists in Nova Scotia and New Brunswick, a legacy of the revival sparked by Henry Alline in the 1770s. The religious landscape was particularly diverse in Upper Canada. In addition to what might be considered mainstream denominations, including increasing numbers of American Methodists, communities of Quakers,

---

[8] Jane Errington, *The Lion, the Eagle and Upper Canada* (Montreal and Kingston, 1985), pp. 20–1.

[9] Peter Marshall, 'Americans in Upper Canada, 1791–1812: "Late Loyalists" or Early Immigrants', in Barbara J. Messamore, ed., *Canadian Migration Patterns from Britain and North America* (Ottawa, 2004), pp. 33–4.

[10] J. M. Bumsted, *The People's Clearances: Highland Emigration to British North America, 1770–1815* (Winnipeg, 1982); Marianne McLean, *The People of Glengarry: Highlands in Transition, 1745–1820* (Montreal and Kingston, 1991).

Mennonites, and various pacifist sects like the Tunkers were drawn to the colony by Lieutenant-Governor Simcoe's promise of exemption from military service.

Colonial leaders were determined to avoid the problems that had given rise to revolution in 1776. The Church of England, with its rational theology and emphasis on hierarchy and stability, was given a privileged status throughout the colonies. At the same time, political authority was firmly vested in the Crown. Although all the colonies had elected Assemblies, their power were firmly checked by appointed Councils made up of carefully chosen colonial gentlemen of property and standing. Not surprisingly, rank-and-file Loyalists often resisted attempts to curtail their participation in colonial affairs; they also pressed forward their own interests as small farmers, craftsmen, and labourers. In the most 'loyal' colony of New Brunswick, for example, much of the population vigorously opposed attempts to create a landed aristocracy; and, as late as 1812, the colonial elite still struggled to control a people determined to recreate the political, social, and religious world of the former Thirteen Colonies. In Upper Canada, Imperial appointees met significant opposition from both the Loyalist leadership and American settlers to Simcoe's plans to plant Old World institutions on the frontier.[11]

Perhaps the greatest impediment to Imperial aspirations was, as Graeme Wynn has cogently argued, the scattered nature of colonial settlement. Until the War of 1812, 'the reach of colonial institutions was limited', and most of the time, settlers who lived in isolated communities strung out along the major waterways were preoccupied with clearing the land, working the fishing grounds, or labouring in the bush.[12] Colonists' understanding of who they were and what they were doing did not rest on some abstract notion of the Empire or membership in a particular colonial society. Rather, it remained rooted in the worlds they had left behind. Recently arrived Scottish, Irish, Welsh, and English emigrants sought support and solace from communities on the other side of the Atlantic, relationships that were strengthened by the periodic arrival of kin and former neighbours. For most new settlers, however, 'home' was in the United States. Soon after the Revolution, even the most ardent Loyalists began to visit family and old friends south of the border; Upper Canadians attended meetings led by preachers from New York; and a vibrant trade developed between farmers and merchants in the United States and British America. Indeed, throughout the first generation of post-revolutionary settlement, the British colonies in North America remained integral parts of communities that spanned the international border. It was only among colonial leaders, a few merchants who were tied to the Atlantic economy, and members of the garrisons that there was a sense of being part of a British world that was centred in London.

[11] David Bell, *Early Loyalist Saint John: The Origins of New Brunswick Politics, 1783–1786* (Fredericton, 1983); Errington, *The Lion, the Eagle and Upper Canada*, pp. 20–54.
[12] Wynn, 'A Region of Scattered Settlements', p. 337.

Authorities in both London and the colonies were conscious of the precari-
ousness of Britain's hold on the northern half of the continent, and when war
broke out with the United States in 1812, many predicted that Upper Canada
would quickly succumb to the enemy. Although such fears were unfounded, even
before the war was over London began to lay plans to better secure its colonies.
Military spending was to be increased and British subjects would be encouraged
to 'people' the colonies to help form a physical bulwark against future American
incursions. When hostilities in North America ceased in 1815, London officially
closed colonial borders to American settlers. In July of the same year, Parliament
recruited and paid the passage from Glasgow of almost 2,000 Scottish farmers,
labourers, and former soldiers who were given land on the Imperial frontier of
Upper Canada. Planting military settlements was expensive, however, and even
though subsequent parties of emigrants were co-sponsored by private benefactors,
reports of the difficulties new settlers encountered led many in Britain to question
the benefits of the colonization programme. The government was also roundly
criticized for abrogating official policy that, for half a century, had attempted
to discourage emigration altogether. Although the Colonial Office insisted that
its sponsorship scheme was intended only to direct those already planning to
emigrate to go to British America instead of to the United States, many in Britain
were alarmed that so many apparently industrious farmers and skilled craftsmen
were leaving the country.[13]

The question of what role, if any, Parliament should take in assisting or directing emigration and in promoting colonization was the subject of considerable
debate in both Great Britain and the colonies in the years after the end of the
Napoleonic Wars. Agricultural reform and industrialization brought national
prosperity; but the new economy also fostered growing unease and unrest among
all manner of people threatened by the accelerating pace of change. Throughout
the 1820s, while Britons publicly debated how best to cope with the difficulties
faced by unemployed labourers and displaced farmers, economists warned that
the redundant population was placing an increasing strain on national and
local resources and endangering the peace and future 'prosperity of the mother
country'.[14] In 1823 and again in 1825, the Colonial Office sponsored the
departure and resettlement in Upper Canada of parties of Irish Catholic farmers
who had been particularly hard hit by deteriorating economic circumstances.
Subsequent reports from the colony about the success of the Peter Robinson
expeditions were, at best, mixed. When the Select Committee on Emigration,
chaired by enthusiast Wilmot Horton, recommended in 1827–8 that Parliament
adopt a national scheme of emigration and colonization to help alleviate distress
at home and simultaneously strengthen the colonies, many remained sceptical.
Some argued strenuously that 'there was abundant room within these Kingdoms

---

[13] Helen Cowan, *British Emigration to British North America* (Toronto, 1961), p. 77.
[14] *Observer* (London), 14 Oct. 1827.

for the exertion of profitable labours'.[15] Others, in and out of Parliament, suggested that to encourage a Briton 'to disregard the feelings of home, cross the ocean and bury himself in the wilderness' was cruel and unjust.[16] In the end, the Committee's recommendations were rejected and, to the disappointment of many who had hoped to benefit from continued parliamentary assistance, it was decided to leave emigration 'to the enterprise of private and associated speculators'[17] and to the decision of individual Britons. The most Parliament would do was to continue to regulate the American trade in such a way that emigrants would be encouraged to proceed to the British colonies and not to the United States.

The new Passenger Act of 1817 set the standard. In response to pressure from shipping interests, the Act significantly eased regulations concerning the number of passengers British ships could carry on an Atlantic crossing. Restrictions were further reduced throughout the 1820s, and as the cost of passage to colonial ports decreased, an increasing proportion of emigrants leaving British ports landed at Quebec and Saint John. Despite warnings that conditions on board ships were becoming deplorable, the Passenger Act was suspended altogether in 1827. The results were disastrous. Reports from the colonies of an unprecedented number of shipwrecks and of emigrants arriving ill and starving convinced London to assume some responsibility for emigrants' welfare. The Passenger Act of 1828 included detailed regulations concerning the accommodation and provisioning required on all ships carrying emigrants, measures that were strengthened throughout the next decade. Enforcement of the regulations was, however, haphazard. Although Parliament appointed a few agents and customs officers in British and colonial ports to oversee the trade, A. C. Buchanan, a Lower Canadian shipping agent and London's man in Quebec, noted in his annual reports that many ships' masters ignored the regulations with impunity.[18]

Parliament's decision not to subsidize emigration directly did not preclude other agencies from offering financial assistance to prospective migrants. In a calculated attempt to keep the poor rates from rising exponentially, a few parishes in the south of England began, in the mid-1820s, to send local paupers to America. In 1831 and 1832, the peak years of parish assistance, it was reported that over 10,000 such emigrants landed in Quebec, about 10 per cent of all arrivals. Among them were members of the first contingent organized by the Petworth Committee, sponsored by Lord Egremont of Sussex.[19] The new Poor Law of 1834 officially regulated these efforts and for the rest of the decade and

[15] 'Emigration', *Blackwood's Edinburgh Review* (May 1828), p. 617.
[16] 'Mr. Wilmot Horton and Emigration', ibid. (Feb. 1828) p. 192.
[17] 'Bandana on Emigration', ibid. (Sept. 1826), p. 470.
[18] Oliver MacDonagh, *A Pattern of Government Growth, 1800–60: The Passenger Acts and their Enforcement* (London, 1961), chap. 4.
[19] Wendy Cameron et al., *Assisted Emigration to Upper Canada: The Petworth Project, 1832–38* (Montreal and Kingston, 2000), p. 21.

into the 1840s, a small but steady stream of 'parish' emigrants disembarked at Quebec and Saint John. British newspapers also regularly printed announcements of private associations whose express purpose was to 'enable the poor', members of the labouring classes, or groups of artisans or mechanics to emigrate. In parts of Scotland, Ireland, and England, organizations for relief of manufacturing workers, the Children's Friends Society, local committees of emigration, and some landlords, including the Earl of Breadalbane of Scotland and Lord Mount Cashel of Ireland, sponsored individuals or parties of local residents bound for British America.[20] Colonists were often alarmed by the arrival of so many apparently poor emigrants. They also resented Imperial policies that seemed to encourage the emigration of people who were 'unaccustomed and frequently unfit for the kinds of labour in demand in the colonies'.[21] In the end, only about 10 per cent of Britons who arrived in British America between 1815 and the mid-1860s depended on the state or private organizations to cover the cost of the journey and at least some of these migrants could afford the passage but were determined to save their limited capital to use in their new homes.[22]

Imperial policies concerning emigration were often closely tied to colonial land policies. As they had done with the Loyalists, after 1815 the Colonial Office provided disbanded soldiers and their families with land; half-pay officer emigrants also continued to receive their annual stipends and this injected much needed capital into colonial economies. London was increasingly unwilling, however, to subsidize settlement directly. Edward Gibbon Wakefield and other Imperial strategists persuasively argued that it was best for both the colonies and Great Britain that emigrants cover their own costs of settlement. This created a conundrum for those concerned about the future of the colonies. British America, and particularly Upper Canada, with its large tracts of 'empty' land, needed settlers. Certainly, 'capitalists, regularly bred farmers, active master craftsmen, in short our middle class of society' were preferred;[23] but promoters also promised that anyone with 'the hardy habits of the peasant'—labourers, farmers, and artisans—could acquire land and independence on the frontier.[24] Starting a farm was, however, expensive, and given the continuing attraction of the United States, settlers had to be enticed to stay in British America. Private land companies were among the first to address this issue. The Canada Company, founded in Upper Canada in 1826, and a decade later, the British American Company of Lower Canada and the New Brunswick and Nova Scotia Land Company, purchased Crown land and began to offer new arrivals

---

[20] Michael Vance, 'The Politics of Emigration: Scotland and Assisted Emigration to Upper Canada, 1815–1826', in T. M. Devine, (ed.), *Scottish Emigration and Scottish Society* (Edinburgh, 1992), pp. 37–60.

[21] *Views of Canada and the Colonists by a Four Years Resident* (Edinburgh, 1844), p. 247.

[22] Cameron, *Assisted Emigration*, p. 21.

[23] 'Emigration to Canada', in *Chambers Information for the People* (Edinburgh, 1835), p. 3.

[24] 'MacGregor's British America', *Blackwood's Edinburgh Review* (June 1832), p. 927.

lots at good prices. The Canada Company was the most successful of the three and provided clients with a host of other services including forwarding mail and remittances home to fund other would-be migrants. The efforts of private entrepreneurs to attract settlers were intermittently supplemented by various colonial programmes. With the reluctant compliance of London, Sir John Colbourne, Lieutenant Governor of Upper Canada from 1828 to 1835, established a network of agents to assist emigrants and made Crown and reserve land available on easy terms of repayment. When news of the rebellions and continued civil unrest in 1837–8 in the Canadas brought emigration to all of British America to a virtual halt, the Upper Canadian legislature attempted to revive the trade by sending its own agent, Thomas Rolph, to the British Isles to reassure Britons that the colony was safe. By the time that the flow of migrants resumed in 1841–2, direct colonial intervention in the trade or in subsidizing settlement had ceased.

Emigrants who landed at Quebec, Halifax, or Saint John bewildered, tired, and often ill and without funds did receive some short-term assistance from local residents. Prompted by a mixture of Christian benevolence and fear of disorder, leading colonists began after 1815 to establish a myriad of local aid and benevolent organizations to provide 'strangers in distress' with provisions, temporary shelter, and advice. As the number of emigrants increased, however, the resources of these privately funded societies were soon strained to the breaking point and, in the early 1830s, communities began to petition colonial legislatures for financial support. The outbreak of cholera in 1832 required extraordinary measures. To arrest the spread of the highly infectious disease, colonial authorities built quarantine stations at Grosse Isle just outside Quebec City, at Halifax, and at Partridge Island, near Saint John, and emigrants were required to pass an increasingly stringent health inspection before proceeding on. Temporary and then permanent Boards of Health were also established at ports of entry and centres along the St Lawrence and the Great Lakes to inspect and quarantine those infected. By the time cholera broke out again in 1834, and was followed by outbreaks of typhus and typhoid that periodically plagued emigrant arrivals to the 1860s, colonial governments and municipal leaders had a rudimentary system in place to protect the local populations. Its limitations were all too apparent in 1847, however, when shiploads of Irish migrants fleeing the famines arrived exhausted, hungry, and ill. Local and colonial resources were overwhelmed and to forestall any repetition of this, in 1848 and 1849, colonial authorities effectively closed the borders to further famine emigrants.[25] The question of funding such programmes was a constant irritant between London and the colonies. A new emigrant tax, imposed by London in 1834, went some way to defraying the costs but British Americans absorbed most of the financial burden themselves.

[25] Cecil J. Houston and William J. Smyth, *Irish Emigration and Canadian Settlement* (Toronto, 1990), pp. 27–8.

Imperial polices and state assistance, whether from London, individual parishes or communities, or from the colonies themselves, undoubtedly encouraged many Britons to make their way to the colonies in North America. But by the mid-1820s, emigration had also become a part of national life in Great Britain and Ireland. A growing number of travellers' accounts and settlers' stories presented the British public with information on a host of possible destinations and emigrants' guides offered encouragement. National and local newspapers regularly carried reports of parties leaving home for America and Australia and often included news 'from the colonies'. The discourse of emigration and Empire, which by the 1850s had even begun to extol the virtues of life in the most distant British American colony, British Columbia, was an ever present hum in the background as individuals and families considered their options. Most who left home for the colonies were not, as some sceptics at the time charged, swept up in the 'fever' or infected by the American 'mania'. The vast majority of them expected to pay their own way and everyone knew that this could be a life-altering decision. Many prospective emigrants carefully read and probably reread such popular journals as *Chambers Information for the People* or *Counsel for Emigrants* or one of the other guides and settlers' accounts that offered detailed commentary and advice. Beginning in the 1830s, they attended emigration meetings and listened to colonial promoters extol the virtues of one particular destination over another. Most then carefully weighed information gained from the public record with personal reports received from kin, former neighbours, or even distant acquaintances who were already settled in the New World before making their decision. [26]

It is impossible to determine with any certainty why some English, Irish, Scots, and Welsh chose to migrate while many of their neighbours, friends, and often immediate family members decided to stay at home. Scholars frequently consider emigration within a national framework and suggest that Britons left home because they were Scottish, or English, or Irish. Yet as Bruce Elliott has argued, 'factors such as trade cycles, the impact of war, industrialization, and the agrarian revolution affected different localities and regions . . . in different ways, to differing extents, and with varying chronologies and impacted upon social classes differently'.[27] A better way to unpack motivation is to examine it within the context of particular communities and regions. Family dynamics and personal circumstances (a recent marriage or a death in the family, for example), or the opportunity to leave home in the company of kin or friends, also often played a part in an individual's decision. Moreover, as Marjory Harper persuasively argues, 'private encouragement and practical assistance from family, friends, and

---

[26] Elizabeth Jane Errington, *Emigrant Worlds and Transatlantic Communities* (Montreal and Kingston, 2007).
[27] Bruce Elliott, 'Regional Patterns of English Immigration', in Messamore, (ed.), *Canadian Migration Patterns*.

community' who were already settled in the New World 'were of inestimable and enduring importance in stimulating secondary migration and directing patterns of settlement'.[28]

This was particularly true of Scottish families who were among the first to resume the transatlantic crossing after the Napoleonic Wars. Those parties from the Highlands and the Glasgow region who were able to take advantage of the short-lived government sponsorship programme marked the beginning of an exodus of Scottish farmers, crofters, and labourers for whom British America, and not the United States, was the preferred destination. Families from the Highlands chartered vessels, gathered provisions, and set off for the colonies to join friends, and to grasp the opportunities regularly extolled in local newspapers. Many of these often extended kin groups were propelled by landlord-directed agricultural reforms that led to, among other things, the clearances in the Highlands. In the 1830s and 1840s, others fled famine and the potato blight. Most Highlanders were not destitute when they left home and they could afford the cost of passage and provisions. This often took all their financial resources, however, and by the time they arrived in the colonies, they had few funds. Lowlanders too were attracted to the imperial frontier by the availability of land and by commercial opportunities opening up in colonial centres.[29] Scottish merchants had long been involved in the North American fur trade and merchants in Glasgow and Aberdeen were intimately tied to houses in Montreal, Quebec, Halifax, and Saint John. In many ways, the Scottish emigrant trade in the post-1815 period was an extension of already well-established trading connections in fish and timber. To many Scots, British America was very much part of a Scottish Empire.[30]

By mid-century, Scottish migrants and their children were well represented in colonial communities from the shores of Nova Scotia to the valley of the Red River. In Cape Breton and in parts of Nova Scotia, many lived in relatively isolated communities that often resembled those of home. After 1815, however, most Scottish emigrants made their way to Upper Canada, where they had the greatest opportunity to own their own farms. Some were induced by land companies or assistance from landlords to settle in the Eastern Townships and New Brunswick and a few Scottish labourers, who had initially been recruited as servants of the Hudson's Bay Company, retired with their Aboriginal or 'mixed blood' Métis families to the small community at Red River.

Often not so visible, but certainly greater in numbers, were colonists of Irish origin. The wars of Napoleon had only slowed this migration; when trade with North America resumed, an increasing proportion of those travelling steerage on returning timber and merchant ships were Irish. Between 1815 and 1845, the

---

[28] Marjory Harper, 'British Migration and the Peopling of the Empire', in Andrew Porter, (ed.), *The Oxford History of the British Empire*, vol. III: *The Nineteenth Century* (Oxford, 1999), pp. 79–80.

[29] Malcom Gray, 'The Cause of Scottish Emigration, 1750–1914: Enduring Influences and Changing Circumstances', in Devine, (ed.), *Scottish Emigration*.

[30] T. M. Devine, *Scotland's Empire, 1600–1815* (London, 2003).

exodus was dominated by Protestant farmers, artisans, and labourers and their families who moved to the colonies to take up land as a 'strategy of heirship' and, as the century unfolded, to join family members and friends who had gone before. As a number of Canadian scholars have persuasively illustrated, these were people of some financial means who were not 'pushed' from their homes but made a conscious decision that life in the colonies offered them better opportunities for the future.[31] By the late 1820s, the decreasing cost of the transatlantic passage also encouraged a growing number of young, usually single Catholic labourers and artisans to make their way to the New World. Although most were bound for the United States and British America was but another stop on a journey that had taken them from home to England or Scotland and then across the Atlantic, between 1820 and 1845 approximately one-third of Irish Catholic migrants stayed in the colonies. Initially most took work as day labourers or domestics, or joined gangs of workers harvesting timber or digging canals in New Brunswick and Upper and Lower Canada,[32] but many eventually managed to continue their journey from the bush or colonial cities and towns to the countryside. At the time of Confederation, approximately 58 per cent of British Americans were of Irish descent, a majority of them Protestants, and farming was their most common occupation.[33]

As Cecil Houston and William Smyth conclude, the pre-famine era was 'definitive in the formation of Canadian Irish communities'. The arrival in 1847 of over 100,000 destitute and miserable emigrants who were fleeing the famine was nonetheless alarming at the time. Not only were colonial resources stretched to the breaking point, but this seemed to confirm colonists' fears that British America had become a dumping ground for the Empire's unwashed and unwanted. But more than 60 per cent of these new arrivals proceeded south and joined their countrymen in the United States; the rest gravitated to already existing Irish Catholic communities in various colonial cities, including Quebec, Montreal, and Toronto. Although they faced significant financial challenges, within a generation the children of the famine emigrants were relatively well established.[34] To the colonists' relief, the 1847 famine migration was an aberration. The following year, of the 25,000 Irish migrants who landed in British America, almost two-thirds of them were really bound for the United States.[35]

Welsh and English migrants were often lost amidst the panoply of peoples who came to British America between 1815 and 1860. Shortly after the war, a

---

[31] Bruce Elliott, *Irish Migrants in the Canadas: A New Approach* (Montreal, 1988), p. 7; Catharine Anne Wilson, *A New Lease on Life: Landlords and Tenants & Immigrants in Ireland and Canada* (Montreal and Kingston, 1994); Houston and Smyth, *Irish Emigration*, pp. 21–2.

[32] Houston and Smyth, *Irish Emigration*, pp. 26–27.

[33] Akenson, *The Irish in Ontario*, pp. 337–8.

[34] Sherry Olson and Patricia Thorton, 'The Challenge of the Irish Catholic Community in Nineteenth-Century Montreal', *Social History/Histoire sociale*, 35 (2002), pp. 331–62.

[35] Houston and Smyth, *Irish Emigration*, p. 26.

few small parties of Welsh families arrived in Nova Scotia and New Brunswick; a steady stream of Yorkshire families joined relatives in the Maritime colonies and, after 1820, others made their way to Upper Canada. Labourers from the West Country (and from Ireland) also reopened the connection to St John's and small seaport communities in Newfoundland. It was not until the 1830s, with the initiation of various parish programmes, that the English really 'discovered' British America and, in subsequent years, sponsored emigrants were often followed by family members and former neighbours. When seen in terms of total numbers, however, it was not until well into the 1840s that the 'tide' of English migration began to turn north from the United States, and by then, a few adventurous souls had begun to make the long voyage to Victoria and mainland British Columbia.[36]

The English were nonetheless relatively well represented among the small but highly coveted numbers of 'gentlemen' emigrants who settled in British America after 1815. Attempts by colonial leaders to entice British and Irish men of capital to come to the colonies were not particularly successful; between 1815 and 1867, the vast majority of emigrants had only limited means and many relied on family and friends to help cover their costs. Those few half-pay officers and gentlemen emigrants who did arrive soon gained access to the halls of powers, however, and they reinforced the efforts of provincial leaders to inculcate 'British' manners and morals into the wider colonial societies.

By the time of Confederation, the settlement of hundreds of thousands of emigrants from the British Isles had transformed the Empire in North America. Even with the significant outmigration that, by 1850, included young French Canadians who journeyed to New England and the midwest of the United States to find work and land, once scattered frontier communities had become increasingly mature settler societies. Most colonists were now British in origin as well as name and even in the once exclusively French, Catholic colony of Quebec, over 20 per cent of the population was of British descent. Throughout the other colonies, the language of business and of the hearth was English; once isolated communities were now linked by well-travelled roads and networks of state authority that included institutions that had been established, in part, to meet the pressures posed by emigrants' arrival. Houses of Industry took in the unemployed; jails and new penitentiaries incarcerated and tried to reform the wayward; hospitals cared for the indigent ill; local orphanages took children into care; and common public schools tried to promote good citizenship. In some parts of the 'older' colonies (Nova Scotia and New Brunswick in particular), where there was little vacant arable land by 1840, the pre-industrial, traditional rural economy was giving way to market capitalism. Even in Upper Canada, which received most of the post-war

[36] Alan G. Brunger, 'The Geographical Context of English Assisted Emigration to Upper Canada in the Early Nineteenth Century', *British Journal of Canadian Studies*, 16/1 (2003), pp. 7–31.

migrants, by mid-century new arrivals were forced to take up marginal and reserved land.

What some have termed a 'golden age' of colonial development came at significant cost to the original Aboriginal populations. European assumptions that untilled 'waste land' was just waiting for the axe and the plough and British laws of private property and trespass increasingly clashed with First Nations' use of the environment. Cleared land, farm fences, indiscriminate hunting, and overfishing exerted growing pressure on traditional ways of life. In Upper Canada, the original inhabitants were increasingly marginalized as authorities sold tracts of designated Indian lands to prospective farmers and ignored white squatters who encroached on Aboriginal territories. At the same time, the efforts of Methodists, Anglicans, and Catholics to convert and civilize their 'red' brothers often divided Aboriginal communities and reshaped cultural beliefs and practices.[37]

To many emigrants, the very presence of Aboriginal peoples in the Canadas and the Maritimes was a romantic anachronism. British America was, by definition, a white settler society. While colonial authorities and Christian missionaries pursued a policy of assimilation, most travellers and colonists assumed that this 'degenerate race' was doomed to extinction. White settlers living in the western reaches of the continent had a more difficult time sustaining such attitudes. Until well after Confederation, English-speaking, white colonists at Red River were very much a minority population among French- and English-speaking Métis and First Nations residents. In Victoria and British Columbia, miners, traders, and the few settlers were surrounded by dynamic communities of Aboriginal peoples who, although often devastated by European disease and contact with traders, were not soon going to disappear. When Chinese labourers from California and Hong Kong were enticed to the area by promises of gold in the 1850s, and black American migrants arrived looking for land and work, anxious white settlers determinedly asserted their 'natural' claim to the land and its resources.[38]

Victorian assumptions about racial differences also influenced how white colonists in Upper Canada and Nova Scotia viewed the arrival of black settlers from the United States. After 1800, the practice of slavery declined rapidly in British America; but when about 2,000 free black American refugees arrived in Halifax after the War of 1812, they had considerable difficulties gaining land and finding work. About 400 left immediately for New Brunswick; the rest gradually found a place for themselves in Nova Scotia. Nonetheless, until Confederation, black colonists and Aboriginal people continued to inhabit the lowest rungs of

[37] L. F. S. Upton, 'The Origins of Canadian Indian Policy', *Journal of Canadian Studies*, 84 (1973), pp. 51–61.
[38] Adele Perry, *On the Edge of Empire: Gender, Race and the Making of British Columbia, 1849–1871* (Toronto, 2001).

the social and economic order in the region.[39] The arrival in south-western Upper Canada after 1830 of growing numbers of fugitive slaves and free black migrants from the United States in search of land, employment, and a better future for their families also created some concern. Support for the anti-slavery campaign was generally high throughout British America and many white colonists welcomed the new arrivals; others, however, demanded segregated schools and separate places of worship, and were reluctant to engage black colonists for anything but menial employment. Black immigrants were themselves divided about whether it was better to maintain segregated communities or to try to integrate fully into the host community. When the Civil War erupted in 1861, almost 20 per cent of the approximately 20,000 black Upper Canadians returned home, disillusioned with their experiences under British rule. The rest, including members of the small black community in British Columbia, tenaciously proclaimed their citizenship in the Empire.[40]

The debates about whether black migrants were appropriate settlers highlighted the varied assumptions that white, British emigrants brought with them about the society they hoped to build in the New World. Certainly, some Britons left home to escape an untenable personal situation or familial or community obligations. More than a few men emigrated as a way to end their marriage. Many young, and some older, single or unattached women emigrated in an attempt to maintain or assert their independence; and a few British 'gentlewomen in distress', skilled tradeswomen, and teachers found ready markets for their skills in the colonies (as some of their sisters did in Australia).[41] But most new arrivals to British America did not want to sever ties with kin and community. They left home in the company of family members; and they maintained connections with and often continued to rely, financially and emotionally, on those they had left behind as they established themselves in the New World.

As emigrants gradually became colonists and settled into their new lives, they continued to nurture links to 'home'. Identifying oneself as Scottish, or English, or Irish, could offer a sense of security and community in a strange land. Colonial churches, for example, frequently reflected the congregations' religious beliefs and their ethnicity. As resources permitted, Irish Catholics, Scots Presbyterians, Highland Catholics, or English or Irish Anglicans built their own places of worship and took part in the familiar liturgy surrounded by their countrymen and women. Sometimes, congregations petitioned former landlords,

---

[39] Harvey Amani Whitfield, ' "We Can Do as We Like Here": An Analysis of Self Assertion and Agency among Black Refugees in Halifax Nova Scotia, 1813–1821', *Acadiensis*, 32/1 (2002), pp. 29–49.

[40] Michael Wane, 'The Black Population of Canada West on the Eve of the American Civil War: A Reassessment Based on the Manuscript Census of 1861', *Social History/Histoire sociale*, 28 (1995), pp. 465–85.

[41] Elizabeth Jane Errington, ' "Information Wanted": Women Emigrants in a Trans-Atlantic World', in Phillip Buckner and R. Douglas Francis, (eds), *Canada and the British World: Culture, Migration, and Identity* (Vancouver, 2006).

or synods, or other religious organizations at home for assistance; at other times, they called on their neighbours to join them in a building campaign. Church establishments in Britain responded to the growth in colonial congregations by sending missionaries from home. The Society for the Propagation of the Gospel, based in London, supported Anglican churches on the frontier; the Glasgow Colonial Society, founded in 1825, aggressively recruited ministers to serve the Church of Scotland in British America. The arrival of British Methodist missionaries to Upper Canada after 1820 sparked fierce competition with their American counterparts. The Catholic Church, which continued to dominate religious life in Quebec, established separate dioceses to meet the needs of the growing number of Scottish and Irish Catholic settlers in the Maritimes and Upper Canada. Even at mid-century, as congregational life in the colonies began to be increasingly shaped by denominational affiliation, religious-ethnic identities remained strong.

Many new arrivals and their children and grandchildren found a continuing connection to 'home' through one of the many ethnic organizations that flourished in the colonies. Local branches of the St Andrew's and St George's societies and the Orange Lodge had been active in British American centres since the beginning of the century. By 1830, the Hibernian Society, the Celtic Society, the Highland Society, and the St Patrick's Society (among others) also held regular meetings, hosted dinners and lectures, and organized national days of celebration. Members often met emigrants at the docks and offered newly arrived countrymen shelter and assistance; ethnic associations also provided emigrants with a social and economic network that helped ease their way into the community. A number of associations consciously reaffirmed their national identity by gathering donations to relieve distress at home. More often, they supported local projects—a lending library or the local mechanics' institute, for example. Most importantly, however, fraternal, ethnic organizations offered members fellowship and community.

One of the most active ethnic associations was the Irish-based Orange Lodge. It first appeared in British America soon after its founding in Ulster in 1794, and by the mid-nineteenth century, there were branches in communities from Newfoundland to British Columbia. To an Irish Protestant emigrant, a local lodge 'was a ready-made introduction into the new society' and many simply transferred their membership from home. At convivial monthly or fortnightly meetings, members renewed associations and made new contacts. At the annual celebration of 12 July, lodges from throughout a neighbourhood would come together to celebrate, to march, and to reaffirm their commitment to a Protestant future. The Order had a definite ideological agenda and, as Cecil Houston and William Smyth note, it 'constituted a steadfast and staunch garrison, defending the monarch and parliamentary traditions of imperial Britain'.[42] By the 1840s, membership in the Orange Order had opened up well beyond its original Irish

---

[42] Houston and Smyth, *Irish Emigration*, p. 183.

roots and had become an 'indigenous social movement' that was often at the centre of the social and political life of the community.[43]

Members of the Orange Lodge periodically took their defence of the Crown and their community to the streets. In Upper Canada, where the Order was particularly strong, elections in the 1830s and 1840s often ended in pitched battles as Orangemen defended their vision of a Protestant, loyal society—and Conservative candidates—with their votes and their clubs. With the arrival of growing numbers of Irish Catholic migrants in the 1840s, religious tensions in many communities grew and in the 1840s, Orangemen in Saint John and Woodstock, New Brunswick, often confronted apparently 'unruly' Irish Catholics during St Patrick's Day parades, with the tacit approval of community leaders.[44] Throughout the 1850s, Toronto, sometimes known as 'the Belfast of Canada', was rocked by sectarian skirmishes on 12 July and 17 March. For those Irish Catholic British Americans who were already well established in the colonies, the emergence of militant anti-Catholicism was alarming. Many tried to distance themselves from the raucous behaviour that seemed to characterize life in Irish, working-class enclaves in Halifax, St John, Montreal, Toronto, and other colonial centres. The appearance in Toronto in 1859 of a branch of the Irish Revolutionary Brotherhood, commonly known as the Fenians, further divided the Irish community. The Fenian Brotherhood provided hundreds of young, Irish, working-class men with fellowship, entertainment, and a cause—home rule in Ireland. To many of its members, the Fenian Brotherhood was but another ethnic organization that offered members a sense of community in an alien world. But many in the Irish Catholic community were alienated by the Fenians' anti-British rhetoric and the radical actions of a few of their members. They also feared the Protestant backlash that such activities often provoked. When Fenians from the United States invaded the colonies in 1866, almost all Irish Canadians disavowed the movement.[45]

Although the sectarian violence that periodically rocked colonial communities often transcended ethnicity, conflicts over access to work, land, resources, and influence were often rooted and sustained by the confluence of ethnicity and class. In Quebec, for example, *Canadiens* resented the growing numbers of American, Scottish, and English migrants who monopolized valuable farmland and increasingly dominated the political life of the colony. In the 1830s and 1840s, French and Irish canal workers clashed over the right to work in Upper Canada; they also clashed with British engineers and foremen over wages and the conditions of work. Proposals to establish common schools in Newfoundland

---

[43] Scott See, 'The Orange Order and Social Violence in Mid-Nineteenth Century Saint John', *Acadiensis*, 13/1 (1983), p. 12.

[44] Gordon M. Winder, 'Trouble in the North End: The Geography of Social Violence in Saint John, 1840–1860', *Acadiensis*, 29/2 (2000), pp. 27–57.

[45] Michael Cottrell, 'St. Patrick's Day Parades in Nineteenth Century Toronto: A Study of Immigrant Adjustment and Elite Control', *Social History/Histoire sociale*, 25 (1992), pp. 57–73.

in the 1850s pitted Irish Catholic residents against the Protestant leadership, and this was part of a sustained battle conducted on various fronts between the predominately Irish Catholic labouring classes and the English-speaking Protestant merchant elite.

Yet even as colonial economies matured and, at least in urban centres, class interests began to supersede ethnicity, British Americans continued to identify with their particular national origins. The children and grandchildren of British emigrants proudly celebrated 'their' national saints' days; they attended the local 'Scotch' or 'English' or 'Irish Catholic' church; they went to meetings of their local ethnic organization and donated their time and money to causes it espoused. At the same time, residents were consciously members of their immediate communities and colonies—they were New Brunswickers, Nova Scotians, Newfoundlanders, Upper Canadians, or *Canadiens*. Many also proudly identified themselves as Britons and shared a sense of being part of an imagined 'British World'.[46] They celebrated the Queen's birthdays, prayed for the success of British soldiers in far-flung parts of the Empire, supported British missionary work to 'the heathen' in both India and the British-American west, and established and supported various benevolent organizations that had ties to associations at 'home'. Many members of the rising colonial middle classes also tried to emulate a lifestyle that mirrored that of middle-class parlours in London. It was only when colonists made the pilgrimage 'home' or entertained visitors or new settlers from the old country that they became conscious of the uniqueness of their own societies.

The 'tide' of migration to British America began to wane after 1855, and in the 1860s, the numbers of emigrants who annually passed through quarantine stations and settled in the colonies were counted in the hundreds, not the thousands. British Americans themselves continued to be a mobile lot. The sons and daughters of immigrants moved throughout the colonies, looking for work or for their own homestead; some began to make their way to Rupert's Land and the Red River valley; a few joined British cousins and friends in British Columbia. Most British-American migrants headed south, however, and although the Civil War interrupted this flow, between 1850 and Confederation outmigration to the United States far surpassed immigration into the colonies.

Great Britain was more than a sentimental anachronism on the eve of Confederation. Seventy years after the American Revolution, British America was decidedly British—in its peoples and its practices. Transatlantic communities had been institutionalized in colonial governments and in colonists' everyday lives. When civil war broke out south of the border, colonial authorities again turned to London for support and they welcomed the arrival of British soldiers sent to reinforce Imperial garrisons. Indeed, the American Civil War seemed to

---

[46] Carl Bridge and Kent Fedorowich, 'Mapping the British World', in Carl Bridge and Kent Fedorowich, (eds), *The British World: Diaspora, Culture and Identity* (London, 2003).

underline the colonies' continuing dependence on London. But when the war ended in 1865, neither London nor politicians in British America expressed any real fear about the integrity or, despite raids by American Fenians in 1866, the security of the British Empire in North America. London's primary concern was now how to disengage from the day-to-day life in the British colonies; colonial leaders were preoccupied by their efforts to knit distinct communities together into one nation. The question in 1867 was not whether British America was 'British' but how its peoples would shape their Britishness into a new nation.

SELECT BIBLIOGRAPHY

D. H. AKENSON, *The Irish in Ontario: A Study in Rural History* (Montreal and Kingston, 1984).

WENDY CAMERON et al., (eds), *English Immigrant Voices: Labourers' Letters from Upper Canada in the 1830s* (Montreal and Kingston, 2000).

HELEN I. COWAN, *British Emigration to British North America: The First Hundred Years* (Toronto, 1961).

BRUCE S. ELLIOTT, *Irish Migrants in the Canadas: A New Approach* (Montreal and Kingston, 1988).

MARJORY HARPER, *Emigration from North East Scotland*, vol. I: *Willing Exiles* (Aberdeen, 1988).

CECIL J. HOUSTON and WILLIAM J. SMYTH. *Irish Emigration and Canadian Settlement: Patterns, Links, and Letters* (Toronto, 1990).

BARBARA MESSAMORE, (ed.), *Canadian Migration Patterns: From Britain and North America* (Ottawa, 2004).

CATHERINE ANNE WILSON, *A New Lease on Life: Landlords and Tenants and Immigrants in Ireland and Canada* (Montreal and Kingston, 1994).

9

Rhetoric and Reality: British Migration to Canada, 1867–1967

Marjory Harper

In 1871, the first Confederation census reported that 16 per cent of Canada's population had been born outside the new Dominion. Following over half a century of sustained British immigration, it was not surprising that almost 84 per cent of that influx had come from the British Isles, and that the favouritism shown to British immigrants would continue until the points system was introduced in the 1960s. By the 1971 census, while the foreign born still accounted for 15 per cent of the total population, the British and Irish component had dropped to 33 per cent of immigrants. In 1871, 45 per cent of Canada's population still claimed British origins through the male line in their family.[1] In the century after Confederation the implications of these patterns of migration, as well as the motives of migrants and sponsors, generated considerable debate on both sides of the Atlantic. Among the key influences that moulded British migrants' images of Canada, the recruitment efforts of battalions of agents and the campaigns of philanthropists to incorporate Imperial colonization into their rehabilitation programmes resonated with the Whitehall policy makers' objective of populating the senior Dominion with loyal and industrious stock from the overcrowded metropole. Throughout this period the Canadian government continued to endorse the reinforcement of the country's British heritage, while periodically expressing concern that too many of the new immigrants were unfitted to serve Canada's economic needs. Meanwhile, the cultural impact of waves of predominantly English immigrants not only shaped Canadian institutions and attitudes until the late twentieth century, but also influenced non-British migrants' approaches to establishing themselves in their new homeland.

[1] See Table 9.1.

Table 9.1. Birth countries of Canada's population, 1871–1971

Year	Canada	E and W	Scot'd	Ireland	Total British	European	USA	Asiatic	Other	Total
1871	3,010,803	147,081	125,450	223,212	498,953	28,699	64,613	—	1,942	3,605,010
1881	3,721,826	169,504	115,062	185,526	478,615	39,161	77,753	—	7,455	4,324,810
1891	4,189,368	219,688	107,594	149,184	490,573	53,841	80,915	9,129	9,413	4,833,239
1901	4,671,815	203,803	83,631	101,629	421,051	125,549	127,899	23,580	1,421	5,371,315
1911	5,619,682	519,401	169,391	92,874	834,229	404,941	303,680	40,946	3,165	7,206,643
1921	6,832,224	700,442	226,481	93,301	1,065,448	459,325	374,022	53,636	3,294	8,787,949
1931	8,069,261	746,212	279,765	107,544	1,184,830	714,462	344,574	60,608	3,051	10,376,786
1941	9,487,808	635,221	234,824	86,126	1,003,769	653,705	312,473	44,443	3,512	11,505,710
1951	11,949,518	627,551	226,343	80,795	933,049	801,618	282,010	37,145	6,089	14,009,429
1961	15,393,984	662,102	244,052	92,477	1,048,491	1,437,169	283,908	57,761	16,934	18,238,247
1971	18,272,780	—	—	38,490[a]	1,103,145	1,646,025	309,640	119,430	78,800	21,568,310

[a] The Irish figure refers to Southern Ireland only. The 1971 census does not differentiate those born in other parts of the British Isles.

Source: www.statcan.ca/english/freepub/11-516-XIE/sectiona/sectiona.htm, Historical Statistics of Canada, Section A, Population and Migration, Series A29, 'Country of birth of other British-born and the foreign-born population, census dates 1871–1971'. Series A26, 'Population, Canadian, other British and foreign-born, by sex, census dates, 1871 to 1971'.

PERCEPTIONS

Although the United States absorbed the vast majority of British migrants from 1835 until 1909, even during this period it was Canada that consistently generated most publicity in the British press. By the end of the century, when doctrines of new imperialism had taken firm root and the America-bound Irish exodus had waned, Canadian opportunities were trumpeted with increasing confidence and frequency, and in 1910 Canada again became the main recipient of migrants from the British Isles. The commitment of 1920s governments to Empire settlement, coupled with the constraints of American quotas, turned the spotlight even more firmly on the Dominions and, although Australia attracted more settlers under the Empire Settlement Act of 1922, Canada remained, overall, the favourite destination of British migrants throughout the inter-war years, particularly during the heavy 1920s exodus. From 1948 the balance shifted, as migrants were wooed by Australia's energetic subsidized recruitment campaign at the same time as they were deterred by transatlantic shipping shortages, the devaluation of the pound in 1948, and restrictions in the capital that migrants could transfer to Canada.[2]

From Canada's perspective, Britain was both the prevalent and preferred source of migrants from the eighteenth century until the 1970s, but the increasing English dominance within that movement has been masked by a persistent impression on both sides of the Atlantic that Canada was a land of Celtic exiles. Although Highland Scots undoubtedly played a major part in the creation and reinforcement of Gaelic-speaking enclaves in the Maritimes and eastern Ontario for a century after 1763, even before Confederation most Scottish migrants were Lowlanders. That trend intensified over the following century, notably between the wars, when Scottish tradesmen, particularly from the recession-hit central belt, transferred both skills and radical unionism to Canada. While Scots comprised between 20 and 25 per cent of British-born migrants at each census, the Irish component dropped from 60 per cent before Confederation to 45 per cent in 1871, 30 per cent in 1891, and 11 per cent in 1911, before levelling out at a consistent 9 per cent from 1921. From 1951 (when they were first differentiated statistically) only 3 per cent of those Irish migrants were born in the Republic. The Protestant affiliations of the majority of pre-Confederation Irish immigrants persisted after 1867, particularly in southern Ontario, where the Orange Order remained an important force until the 1960s, although there were enclaves of Irish Catholicism in the Maritimes.

---

[2] N. H. Carrier and J. R. Jeffery, *External Migration: A Study of the Available Statistics, 1815–1950* (London, 1953), p. 96.

The lack of scholarly attention paid to Welsh migrants in Canada is attributable to their statistical anonymity, rapid assimilation, and preference for dispersed over clustered settlement, as well as the strong networks that developed between the industrial regions of Wales and the eastern United States. More surprising is the historiographical neglect of the English born, who grew from 29 per cent of British migrants in 1871 to 35 per cent in 1881, 45 per cent in 1891, and 48 per cent in 1901. Thereafter they accounted for between 62 and 67 per cent at each census. While evidence of regional origins is largely anecdotal, immigration agents' reports, passenger lists, and settlement surveys suggest they came from all over England, but especially from the north, with a growing urban bias that contradicted the official emphasis on rural recruitment. Scholarly indifference is attributable to the strength of the Celtic cultural legacy in Canada, coupled with an initial tendency to define the English as a founding people rather than an ethnic group. Their distinctiveness was further obscured by difficulties in identifying clear examples of English ethnicity, and the migrants' own tendency to equate Englishness with Imperial Britishness. Recently, however, English ethnicity has been sidelined from an increasing reluctance to applaud a bygone elitism, whereas those of Scottish and Irish origin have adopted the fashionable, if not always legitimate, mantle of victimhood.[3]

Migrants received mixed messages from the press on both sides of the Atlantic. For a generation after Confederation British newspapers peddled negative stereotypes of a snowbound, Indian-infested wilderness alongside alluring advertisements of a range of untapped resources and settlement opportunities. English migrants particularly found it difficult to shake off images of wayward remittance men or destitute misfits, and were occasionally compared unfavourably with Scots or even Irish. Especially in the west, according to the *Pall Mall Gazette*, 'a situation will be given to a Scot, an Irishman, a Canadian, or an American, rather than to the Englishman who is not mentally and morally acclimatised', and Keir Hardie, visiting Canada in 1907, quickly became aware of the unpopularity of the English, especially Londoners, on account of their intractability and 'inveterate habit of grumbling'.[4] The Canadian press tempered the welcome offered to skilled, affluent rural migrants with resentment against arrogant, ignorant city loafers who could not shed their class-consciousness, superiority complex, or 'antique notion' that they were 'coming to a country owned by Great Britain'.[5] Although anti-English rhetoric was limited, and the stipulation that 'No English Need Apply' may have appeared in only one Winnipeg job advertisement, some Canadians resented English settlers on the grounds of their alleged arrogance. Such cultural prejudice was often a front for

---

[3] Phillip Buckner, 'Introduction', *British Journal of Canadian Studies*, 16/1 (2003), pp. 1–6.

[4] *Pall Mall Gazette*, undated, quoted in B. Stewart, *'No English Need Apply' or, Canada, as a Field for the Emigrant* (London, 1909), pp. 82–3; *Labour Leader*, 4 Oct. 1907, p. 233.

[5] *Manitoba Free Press* (Winnipeg), 18 June 1907, quoted in Stewart, *'No English Need Apply'*, p. 80.

economic resentment that had little to do with the migrants' ethnic background
or adaptability. Official encouragement of British settlement as a means of
excluding 'the hewer of wood and drawer of water of other nations', particularly
in the west, was set against evidence that Britons were less likely to take up the
recommended occupation of farming, along with contradictory complaints from
labour unions that they undercut jobs and wages, and from employers that they
would not tolerate poor pay and conditions.[6]

Criticism of unsuitable British migrants paled into insignificance in comparison with much greater public hostility towards the oriental and central
south-eastern European influx, particularly in British Columbia and on the
prairies. Anti-oriental sentiment on the west coast provoked federal–provincial
tension, restrictive head taxes on Chinese and East Indian immigrants, and
grudging voluntary quota agreements between Canada and Japan in 1908 and
1922. Blacks were consistently discouraged though not legislated against, while
perceived European anarchists, socialists, and communists were screened out
from the 1920s to the 1960s. But acute labour needs periodically overrode
nativist prejudices, notably in the 1890s, 1920s, and 1950s, when central and
southern European agriculturists, domestics, and construction workers were
admitted at the behest of railway companies, farmers, and industrialists. Canada
actively—if not always successfully—encouraged all new arrivals to assimilate
into English-speaking Protestant Canadian society through the churches and the
state-supported public school system, upholding the Empire and its institutions
while still making provision for Catholics either in separate schools or within the
state system.

RECRUITMENT, RESCUE, AND REHABILITATION

During the century after Confederation most British migrants continued to
come to Canada independently, as individuals and in family groups. Occasional
attempts to establish large ethnic settlements, such as Saskatchewan's Barr Colony
in 1903 and Alberta's 1920s enclave of Catholic Hebrideans at Vermilion,
suffered from problems of poor planning, introspection, and isolation, and
group settlement was favoured primarily by central and eastern Europeans.[7] For
many migrants, personal letters and visits home provided a major conduit of
information, encouragement, and—frequently—remittances, while those who
could not tap into family or community networks were amply catered for by

---

[6] Stewart, *'No English Need Apply'*, p. 49; N. Kelley and M. Trebilcock, *The Making of the Mosaic: A History of Canadian Immigration Policy* (Toronto, 1998), pp. 122–3.

[7] L. Bowen, *Muddling Through: The Remarkable Story of the Barr Colonists* (Vancouver, 1992); Marjory Harper, *Emigration from Scotland between the Wars: Opportunity or Exile* (Manchester, 1998), pp. 97–108.

newspapers and guidebooks. Even more pertinent were the efforts of agents, who promoted Canada through public lectures, private interviews, and colourful publications in virtually every corner of the British Isles.

In 1867 the federal and provincial departments of agriculture were initially given concurrent responsibility for immigration, although in practice most recruitment was undertaken at the federal level. In 1896 responsibility shifted to the Department of the Interior, in 1917 to the newly created Department of Immigration and Colonization, in 1936 to Mines and Resources, and in 1950 to Citizenship and Immigration. For most of this period the primary objective was to secure farmers, agricultural labourers, and domestics, preferably from Britain, 'men of good muscle who are willing to hustle', while discouraging those of sedentary occupations.[8] Resident agents, supervised by a London headquarters, were stationed at strategic locations throughout Britain and Europe to orchestrate recruitment and inspect embarking passengers. They supervised the army of ticket agents within their districts, men who booked the passages, but who generally had no loyalty to any particular destination and who made their money on commission.

For the first thirty years after Confederation a combination of economic depression, undeveloped infrastructure, and American competition inhibited successful settlement, as migration into Canada was offset by an unprecedented haemorrhage to the United States. Over 1 million went south in the 1880s, and in 1891 the prairie population was only 250,000. In 1896, however, the determination of federal and railway agents to promote prairie settlement was tackled with renewed zeal after the election of Wilfrid Laurier's Liberal government. Clifford Sifton, appointed Minister of the Interior in 1897, was convinced of the centrality of the west to Canada's future prosperity, and he persuaded the federal government to inject $4 million into the immigration budget over the next decade. Agency work was accorded a much higher profile, as experienced farmers were sought from all over Europe. Agents in the British Isles were quick to exploit both the discomfiture of farmers in a period of agricultural depression and the renewed public interest in Canada spawned by doctrines of new imperialism. British immigrants constituted 52 per cent of arrivals in Canada between 1904 and 1914, compared with 31 per cent from the United States, the second largest supplier. Sifton's successor, Frank Oliver, was more concerned with the settlers' ethnic and cultural origins than their agricultural prowess, and in 1913 British arrivals reached 190,854, compared with 15,267 in 1896, the year when Sifton's initiative had begun.[9] These ideological priorities continued to shape policy until 1962, when, in response to the shortage of

---

[8] Hugh G. Skilling, *Canadian Representation Abroad: From Agency to Embassy* (Toronto, 1945), p. 15.

[9] Table 9.2. See also M. C. Urquhart and K. A. H. Buckley, (eds), *Historical Statistics of Canada* (Cambridge, 1965), p. 23 ('Immigrant arrivals in Canada, 1852–1960'); p. 29 ('Immigrant arrivals from the United States, 1904–1960').

Table 9.2. Outward movement from the British Isles, 1867–1950

Decade	Canada	USA	Australasia
1867–76	193,331	1,263,565	228,945
1877–86	241,481	1,353,808	389,721
1887–96	236,579	1,503,503	193,321
1897–1906	436,743	1,111,085	139,593
1907–16	1,115,418	953,314	443,314
1917–26	565,167	454,845	368,073
1927–36	230,593	196,821	158,266
1937–46[a]	58,696	53,995	29,020
1947–50	91,643	65,792	187,368

[a] Southern Ireland excluded from 1937. No returns available during the Second World War.

Source: N. H. Carrier and J. R. Jeffery, *External Migration A Study of the Available Statistics, 1815–1950* (London, 1953), pp. 95–8, table D/F/G (1).

recruits from traditional sources, ethnicity was finally eliminated as a statutory hinge of Canada's immigration policy, followed in 1967 by the introduction of a points system under which applicants were selected primarily on the basis of education and skills.

The salaried federal agents who were the linchpins in the system were chosen with careful regard to local needs and connections. William Griffith, sent from Manitoba to Bangor, North Wales, in 1897, was a Welsh-speaking native of Bangor, whose cousin controlled a syndicate of Welsh newspapers, and was therefore a key ally in the propaganda war. Henry Murray, appointed at the same time as Griffiths, but to the Glasgow office, had experience as a purser with a transatlantic shipping company, and John Maclennan, sent to the Aberdeen agency in 1907, was a Gaelic-speaking Canadian with Highland ancestry. Maclennan's appointment, which divided Scotland into two agency districts, was a reflection of Oliver's increased commitment to British migration, and was accompanied by the opening of two more offices, in Exeter and York.

The federal agents exploited every promotional tool available. Written newspaper advertising was the commonest form of blanket publicity, supplemented by posters in libraries, railway stations, and other public places. Government-sponsored pamphlets were widely circulated, and essay competitions were organized in schools, which were also presented with wall maps and promotional literature. Written advertising was reinforced by visual promotion. Canadian produce was prominently displayed at agricultural shows, as well as in the windows of the agents' city-centre offices, and travelling exhibition wagons toured the country. Lectures, on which the agents set a high premium, were generally illustrated by lantern slides, or, as technology improved, by movie films, and federal agents were joined on the lecture circuit by temporary assistants, provincial agents, and transcontinental railway company representatives. Delegations of journalists and farmers were invited to tour Canada at the federal government's expense, in the hope that they would publicize their favourable impressions after returning home, and successful settlers were brought back to their home areas to lecture on their experiences. Numerous individual interviews were conducted with interested parties, and some assiduous booking agents even accompanied recruits across the Atlantic, securing jobs for them and helping them to settle in, while simultaneously collecting fresh propaganda for their campaigns.[10]

Although there is ample evidence that agents played a constructive part in facilitating migration, frequently transforming a vague restlessness into the concrete decision to migrate, their activities did not go unchallenged. In addition to federal–provincial in-fighting and problems with lazy or over-enthusiastic booking agents, there was opposition from rival destinations, the Conservative pro-landlord press, and disappointed clients. Scottish migrant Alexander Sutherland wrote scathingly from Summerston Station, Ontario, in 1930, against disingenuous agents who 'are telling people about a country they know nothing about from actual experience. So my advice is: stay in the Old Country if you have a job at all.'[11]

While most migration was the fruit of individual and family decisions that had been shaped by private encouragement or agents' advice, charitable societies also played a persistent part in orchestrating the relocation of disadvantaged clients to purportedly greener imperial pastures. By 1886 at least forty-nine organizations sponsored the removal of children, women, and the unemployed, primarily to Canada, in the hope that such demographic engineering would simultaneously solve labour supply problems on both sides of the Atlantic, rehabilitate the destitute and distressed, and cement Imperial ties. But although many assisted emigrants continued to cross the 'golden bridge' well into the twentieth century,[12] the philosophy and practice of aided migration were clouded by controversy in donor and host countries alike.

Particular opprobrium was reserved for the shipment of almost 100,000 children from British institutions to Canada between 1870 and 1930. Many of those who came under the care of parish guardians, institutions such as the National Children's Home, or philanthropists like Thomas Barnardo, William Quarrier, Annie Macpherson, and James Fegan were orphans, but some were delinquents, while others had been abandoned or abused by their parents. Most came from urban areas and were referred to the rescue homes by poor law inspectors, clergymen, and teachers. Barnardo's, the major participant, sent

---

[10] Marjory Harper, 'Pressure and Persuasion: Canadian Agents and Scottish Emigration, *c*.1870–*c*.1930', *The Historian*, 81 (Spring 2004), pp. 17–23.

[11] *John O'Groat Journal* (Wick), 3 Aug. 1930.

[12] G. B. Smart, *Report of the Chief Inspector of British Immigrant Children and Receiving Homes for 1915–16* (Ottawa, 1917), p. 12 (Library and Archives Canada, PAAPJV 7282 C4C3).

30 per cent of its recruits to Canada between 1882 and its founder's death in 1905, while Quarrier's dispatched 35 per cent between 1872 and 1930. The philanthropists assumed that both countries would benefit from simultaneously lancing the boil of overpopulation, unemployment, and pauperism in Britain and meeting the incessant Canadian demand for cheap farm and domestic labour.[13] But 'well-planned and wisely conducted child-emigration' allegedly paid greater dividends than solving the 'perplexing problems' of the mother country and the 'most urgent needs' of the senior Dominion. Children who were relocated in rural Canada, an ocean apart from unsanitary urban environments, depraved backgrounds, or dysfunctional families, would, argued the evangelical Christians who initially spearheaded most schemes, blossom spiritually as well as econom-ically. When eugenic philosophies of racial purity replaced the evangelicals' emphasis on salvation around 1900, the migrants' perceived value as bricks of Empire became the crucial justification for their removal, with Canada being commended increasingly for its environmental more than its moral qualities.

The promoters' optimism was countered by an army of critics, who lambasted child migration schemes for dumping the youthful dregs of British slums on unwitting Canadian communities, diverting attention from the urgency of improving welfare provision at home, and uprooting children from familiar environments and sometimes even from family units. The harshest criticism emanated from Canada, where the clamour for cheap labour was tempered by public and press disgruntlement with the character and capabilities of recruits who from the start were pejoratively labelled as 'home children'. A federal report in 1888 made the inflammatory allegation that 'the majority of these children are the offal of the most depraved characters in the cities of the Old Country', urging the government to 'put its foot upon the importation into this country of that class of people'.[14] The advice was ignored, and during the economic depression of the 1890s child migrants were accused of stealing jobs, filling jails, and introducing medical and moral pollution to Canada. When a disabled Barnardo boy was murdered by his employer in 1895, the case was remarkable less for its portrayal of shocking cruelty by the employer than for the legislative backlash which aimed to restrict 'the dumping of the diseased off-scouring of the hotbeds of the hellish slumdom of England among the rising generation of this country'.[15] The eugenic argument had been turned on its head, and, despite the persistent optimism of G. Bogue Smart, Chief Inspector of British Immigrant Children, pejorative allegations about 'syphilitic paupers' with 'inherited tendencies to evil' who were 'little better than brutes' continued

[13] G. Wagner, *Barnardo* (London, 1980); S. L. Barnardo and J. Marchant, *Memoirs of the Late Dr Barnardo* (London, 1907), p. 154.

[14] Canada, House of Commons, *Journals* (1888), Report of the Agriculture and Colonisation Committee, pp. 10, 12–14.

[15] *Owen Sound Sun Times*, quoted in Kenneth Bagnell, *The Little Immigrants: The Orphans who Came to Canada* (Toronto, 1980), pp. 68–9.

to stigmatize child migrants until the schemes fizzled out in the early 1930s in the wake of three home boy suicides, further restrictive legislation, and the onset of the worldwide economic Depression.[16]

British criticism focused initially on the charge that those who sponsored child migration were spiriting away scarce farm labourers and domestics, and, in the case of the pioneer Maria Rye, feathering their own nest into the bargain. In 1869 she escorted her first party of seventy-five girls to Niagara-on-the-Lake for placement with local farmers. Five years later she was vilified in an official report by an English Local Government Board inspector, Andrew Doyle, who accused her of excessive recruitment, inadequate after-care, and financial fraud, and the Canadian authorities of laxity in inspection and educational provision.[17] In the more child-centred climate after the First World War, psychologists bewailed the dislocating effects of severing all domestic ties and sending children on a one-way ticket to an unknown destiny, while the British and Canadian authorities alike were accused of being disingenuous in publicly promoting the welfare of the emigrants while privately procuring cheap labour for Canadian farms. In the same era the schemes came under political attack from socialists who claimed that they perpetuated the inequalities of a social structure that required root and branch reform, notably through the introduction of state welfare provision. They scored a partial victory in 1925 when, following the report of a British parliamentary delegation into child migration and settlement in Canada, juvenile migration was restricted to those who had reached the school-leaving age of 14.[18]

What did the emigrants themselves think? On the one hand, the effusive and formulaic letters which pepper the annual reports of sending institutions were tailored to the expectations of sponsors who craved the oxygen of publicity. The emigrants' welfare hinged largely on fortuitous placements in sympathetic families and communities, a tall order in a culture that tended to regard them as cheap labourers or even potential delinquents. ''Doption, sir, is when folks gets a girl to work without wages', was the opinion of one child migrant in 1874.[19] Canadian receiving homes put a naive faith in written indentures that employers could easily circumvent with regard to treatment, schooling, and wages. Placement inspections were often cursory, and the homes could be oblivious to the practical perils of physical, sexual, and psychological abuse involved in sending children to unvetted, isolated situations. 'I never knew what profanity was or what a beating was until I was on that first Canadian farm', recalled former Barnardo home boy Len Russell.[20] In the 1990s, more than half a century after the last home

---

[16] P. T. Rooke and R. L. Schnell, 'Imperial Philanthropy and Colonial Response: British Juvenile Emigration to Canada, 1896–1930', *The Historian*, 46 (Nov. 1983), pp. 70–4.

[17] G. Wagner, *Children of the Empire* (London, 1982), pp. 81–97.

[18] Parliamentary Papers (PP) 1924–25, XV, Cmd. 22085, British Oversea Settlement Delegation to Canada, 1924.

[19] PP 1875, LXIII, 12, Report of the President of the Local Government Board by A. Doyle.

[20] G. H. Corbett, *Barnardo Children in Canada* (Peterborough, 1981), p. 98.

children arrived in Canada, controversy was rekindled when the plight of these most vulnerable emigrants came under intense media scrutiny, and some former home children resurrected bitter memories of suffering under brutal employers, having been unable to articulate their grievances at the time either because of their youth or for fear of reprisals.[21]

But child migration has had a misleadingly pejorative press. Huge establishments such as Barnardo's sometimes fell victim to the sheer scale of their rescue work, and the particular difficulty of implementing adequate inspection procedures. Far from being malevolent or unconcerned about the welfare of their charges, institutions were generally happy to improve their practices in the light of experience. Some retrospective memories reflect much more widespread contentment and gratitude than critics are willing to acknowledge, with one former recruit, who emigrated from Congleton in 1926 under the auspices of the National Children's Homes, endorsing both child migration in general and the much-maligned Barnardo enterprise in particular.

During my life in Canada, I have met Dr Barnardo boys and girls, and most of what I have heard from them is good. Yes, there has been the odd voice of protest, but that is par for the course. Many came to Canada with a chip on their shoulder and at the turn of the century they found life hard. . . . But what would have happened to us waifs if there had been no Homes? I am proud to be an orphan.[22]

Many children undoubtedly benefited from the fresh start in a country which they commended as 'a fine place . . . to grow big and strong in', with guardians who gave 'shelter, food, and care' when they were 'adrift in poverty and despair',[23] and a few subsequently sponsored the emigration of siblings or applied to the British orphanage for their own recruit.

Between 1922 and 1931, amid swelling public criticism of their motives and methods, the charities that sponsored child migrants were able to draw on funding provided under the Empire Settlement Act to subsidize the transatlantic passages and farm training of their charges. This rearguard attempt by the British government to promote the stability and security of the Empire allowed Britain to spend up to £3 million a year on assisted passage and settlement schemes, in partnership with Dominion governments or voluntary organizations, constituting an unprecedented departure from the long-standing official reluctance to countenance state-aided emigration. As well as breathing new financial life into established migration charities, it spawned a number of new enterprises, and

---

[21] For an analysis of the recent upsurge of interest in child migration, see Stephen Constantine, 'Children as Ancestors: Child Migrants and Identity in Canada', *British Journal of Canadian Studies*, 16/1 (2003), pp. 150–9.

[22] E. Marshall, Toronto, quoted in P. Harrison, (ed.), *The Home Children* (Winnipeg, 1979), p. 234.

[23] Stirling Council Archives, PD41/1/1, Whinwell Children's Home, Stirling, 1901 annual report; Harrison, *The Home Children*, p. 39.

within a decade, approximately 127,654 migrants—25 per cent of the British total—had come to Canada under its auspices.[24]

The best-known and most popular voluntary society, on both sides of the Atlantic, was the Salvation Army, which by 1922 advertised itself as 'the world's largest emigration agency'.[25] Founded in Britain in 1878 and established in Canada in 1882, carefully regulated Empire settlement soon became an integral part of its rescue and rehabilitation strategy. In 1904 approximately 1,500 emigrants were sent to Canada, rising to 13,000 in 1906. These 13,000 were selected from over 100,000 applicants. About 60 per cent of the migrants came from urban areas, most were aged between 20 and 30, and almost 70 per cent were male.[26] Within a month of the Armistice the Army received nearly 6,000 applications from would-be emigrants, and by 1930 it had sent out a total of 200,000 recruits, mainly to Canada, less than 1 per cent of whom, it claimed, had been deported or had returned dissatisfied.[27] Its popularity stemmed both from its range of facilities and from a closer class identity between sponsors and migrants than was the case with most voluntary societies.

The Salvation Army's pre-war campaign was directed primarily at working-class migrants who wished to escape from poverty or meagre opportunity in Britain to take up farm work or domestic service in Canada. While some were dependent on subsidies from the Army's Loan Fund, which they were expected to repay in annual instalments, the majority paid their way, using the Army's services to facilitate their ocean passage, relocation, and employment. Supervised passages were recommended not only to single women, but to the dependants of married men whom the Army had sent ahead to Canada to prepare a new home, and groups of young, unaccompanied children were also sent out to join their parents. As well as escorting 'conducted parties' of up to 200 on commercial shipping lines, from 1905 the Army also began to charter its own steamships, in which the entire accommodation was reserved for its clients. Using lists of job vacancies supplied by colleagues across Canada, Army officers operated labour bureaux on board ship, interviewing passengers and matching employers' needs to colonists' skills, so that by the time the vessel docked all those who required situations had secured them. In November 1905, in response to severe unemployment in Britain, it took the unusual step of organizing a winter sailing of several hundred selected men for whom it had secured work on lumber camps and farms in Ontario, undertaking to look after their families until they could

---

[24] Kelley and Trebilcock, *The Making of the Mosaic*, 190; D. H. Avery, *Dangerous Foreigners: European Immigrant Workers and Labour Radicalism in Canada, 1896–1932* (Toronto, 1979), p. 97.

[25] *All The World* (Oct. 1922), p. 427.

[26] *The New Settler: Being a Review of Twelve Months' Immigration Work in Connection with the Salvation Army* (Toronto, 1907), pp. 14–15: report from Brigadier T. Howell, Secretary for Immigration, Toronto, to Commissioner Coombs, 12 Jan. 1907.

[27] D. Lamb, *Empire Migration and Settlement* (London, 1935), p. 8.

afford to send for them.[28] While migrants benefited from the efficiency of an international network that escorted them every step of the way and also found them employment, the Canadian immigration authorities welcomed the Army's careful selection and supervision of recruits. In addition to the commission it received as a booking agency, the Army also received annual federal and provincial government grants to support lecturing, publishing, and administrative expenses in Britain and the care of newly arrived migrants in hostels across Canada.[29]

The British government's endorsement of the Salvation Army's migration work was reflected in the special commendation it received when the Empire Settlement Bill was promulgated in Parliament.[30] Bolstered by extra funding made available under the 1922 legislation, in the post-war era the Army concentrated first on the assisted resettlement of British war widows and their children, and subsequently on a new Boys' Scheme, whereby unemployed youths and those in blind-alley occupations could apply for assisted migration as farm labourers. Countering criticism that it was assisting the poor and potentially destitute at a time when governments on both sides of the Atlantic prioritized soldier settlement, the Army demanded that each widow supply two references from previous employers, pass a medical examination, and sign an undertaking to work as a domestic, while recruits for the Boys' Scheme underwent three months' preliminary training on an Army farm in Essex, before being shipped out to pre-arranged positions. Convinced that its reputation hinged on its distinctiveness, the Army tried to operate largely autonomously, distancing itself from the controversies engendered by some Empire settlement schemes. Nevertheless, it came into intermittent conflict with governments and organized labour over its sponsorship of allegedly 'undesirable' migrants, including industrial workers who masqueraded as agriculturists in order to secure assisted passages.[31]

Like many charitable migration societies, the Salvation Army enthusiastically advocated the relocation of suitable spinsters. Approximately 15 per cent of recruits to its women's branch before 1914 were single, unaccompanied women, and after the war it embarked on a scheme to transfer 10,000 single women, mainly to Canada, under the Empire Settlement Act's shared funding arrangements.[32] Having begun to bud in the mid-nineteenth century, female migration

[28] Salvation Army, International Emigration Office, *The Surplus* (London, 1909), pp. 43–4.

[29] National Archives of Canada, RG 76, C-10421, vol. 487, file 752538, part 1: philanthropic societies which assist immigrants to Canada, 1907–1929; M. Langfield, ' "A Chance to Bloom": Female Migration and Salvationists in Australia and Canada, 1890s to 1939', *Australian Feminist Studies*, 17 (2002), pp. 287–303.

[30] *Hansard*, CL III, 26 Apr. 1922, col. 582.

[31] When the widows' scheme was first devised in 1916, the Canadian government refused a request from Lamb for a $100,000 grant. (Langfield, 'A Chance to Bloom', p. 295). See also V. Knowles, *Strangers at our Gates. Canadian Immigration and Immigration Policy, 1540–1990* (Toronto 1992), p. 68.

[32] *Empire Reconstruction: The Work of the Salvation Army Emigration-Colonization Department, 1903–1921 and after* (London, n.d.); Langfield, 'A Chance to Bloom', p. 296.

societies blossomed for more than fifty years after 1880. The dual argument that
had spawned the earliest schemes to assist female migrants—'civilizing' the male-
dominated colonies and reducing the surplus of women in Britain—took on a
new dimension in the closing years of Victoria's reign, in response to economic
depression in Britain and the simultaneous upsurge of eugenic imperialism.
Migration, it was argued, would benefit not only working-class women, but also
educated, middle-class girls who had failed to find a husband or an acceptable
job and were struggling to maintain their lifestyles in the teeth of rising costs.
Girls who shunned domestic service were promised, somewhat disingenuously,
that competent workers who earned their own living in Canada were treated as
social equals by their employers, while those who still baulked at the idea were
assured that they could secure alternative and congenial employment as nurses,
teachers, or mothers' helps, with better prospects in the marriage market than at
home. Eugenic arguments of racial purity were music to the ears of those who
advocated middle-class female migration, allowing them to present their recruits
as 'missionaries of empire', whose function was not only to fill vacant situations,
but ultimately, and more crucially, to become the wives of British settlers and
mothers of the next colonial generation.

Although domestics were wooed by virtually all the servant-hungry settler colonies with offers of assisted passage and settlement, Canada—which
was allegedly 'in morals and sobriety superior to the Australian and African
colonies'—was accorded the most sustained and positive publicity.[33] Between
Confederation and the 1930s approximately 250,000 women, mostly British,
emigrated as household workers,[34] either independently or under the auspices
of voluntary societies, the most prominent of which was the British Women's
Emigration Association. Formed in 1884, the BWEA selected its recruits on the
principle that 'the requirements of the Empire must come before the needs of
the individual', as well as with the practical objective of solving labour supply
problems at home and abroad.[35] Girls were chaperoned throughout their travels,
given access to a passage loan fund, and, from 1901, repeatedly reminded of
their imperial duty and destiny through exhortations in the *Imperial Colonist*,
the Association's monthly magazine. In 1909 a residential training home for
'genteel' recruits was opened in Shropshire, where, for 10 shillings a week, twelve
students at a time were given a three-month course in colonial skills. Three
years later the Colonial Intelligence League—an offshoot of the BWEA created
in 1910 to find situations for refined middle-class women in order 'to keep
the British Empire for the British Race'—opened the 15-acre Princess Patricia

[33] Library and Archives Canada, RG76, C-53, vol. 44, file 1378: immigration and colonization,
BWEA, Grace Lefroy, BWEA secretary, to Sir Charles Tupper, 25 May 1894.
[34] M. Barber, 'The Women Ontario Welcomed: Immigrant Domestics for Ontario Homes,
1870–1930', *Ontario History*, 72 (Sept. 1980), p. 148.
[35] *Imperial Colonist* (Oct. 1909), p. 147.

Ranch on Lord Aberdeen's Coldstream Estate in British Columbia's Okanagan Valley.[36]

After the war the administration of female migration was restructured, with increasing government involvement on both sides of the Atlantic. In Britain the BWEA and its offshoots were amalgamated and reconstituted as the Society for the Overseas Settlement of British Women, a recognized department of the Oversea Settlement Committee with an annual Treasury grant of £5,000 and responsibility for orchestrating female migration in conjunction with the Dominions under the Empire Settlement Act. In Canada the Women's Division of the Department of Immigration and Colonization was created, largely to protect the country against an anticipated influx of undesirable settlers, with women officers stationed in both Britain and Canada to exercise control over the selection, placement, and after-care of migrants. But although Canada accounted for 80 per cent of domestics who made use of the drastically reduced ocean fares under the 1922 legislation, the overall figure of 100,000 single women assisted to the Dominions under the Empire Settlement Act fell far short of expectations and underlined the long-standing incompatibility between British supply and Dominion demand.[37]

Assisted female migration, like its juvenile counterpart, was accompanied by Canadian accusations that Britain was offloading unemployable misfits and British claims that Canada was both stealing domestic servants who were in short supply at home and holding out misleading expectations of high wages and boundless opportunities. Voluntary societies, anxious not to alienate potential subscribers by assisting the removal of women whom those subscribers wished to employ themselves, stressed that they recruited, not among those who were already in service in Britain, but from the ranks of factory and shop workers, as well as educated gentlewomen who would not deign to dirty their hands at home. Careful screening and supervision, prompt repayment of loans, and easy integration into Canadian society were all proof, they argued, of the success of their programmes, and although almost 700 British domestics were deported during the 1920s for moral misdemeanours or destitution, they constituted less than 1 per cent of the assisted British spinsters who arrived in Canada between the wars.[38] The Salvation Army was particularly careful in its selection, notwithstanding occasional mistakes, such as Mabel Pile, aged 22, who was given an assisted passage from Liverpool in November 1926, shortly after being

[36] Hon. Mrs. Norman Grosvenor, quoted in G. F. Plant, *A Survey of Voluntary Effort in Women's Empire Migration* (London, 1950), 83; Andrew Yarmie, ' "I had always wanted to farm": The Quest for Independence by English Female Emigrants at the Princess Patricia Ranch, Vernon, British Columbia, 1912–1920', *British Journal of Canadian Studies*, 16/1 (2003), pp. 102–25.

[37] J. Gothard, ' "The healthy, wholesome British domestic girl": Single Female Migration and the Empire Settlement Act, 1922–1930', in Stephen Constantine, (ed.), *Emigrants and Empire: British Settlement in the Dominions between the Wars* (Manchester, 1990), pp. 72–95.

[38] B. Roberts, *Whence They Came: Deportation from Canada, 1900–1935* (Ottawa, 1988), pp. 117–18.

convicted of theft. Following subsequent convictions for shoplifting, for which she served two terms in Toronto jail, she was deported back to Liverpool on the *Montcalm* in August 1927.[39]

WAR, DEPRESSION, AND REVIVAL

The deportation weapon, introduced in the 1906 Immigration Act, was increasingly used by Canada to expel 'undesirable' migrants. Following the influx of large numbers of charitably assisted Britons in 1907 (the consequences of an economic downturn in Britain), 70 per cent of Canada's 1,748 deportations the following year were British immigrants.[40] In 1910 the legislation was extended beyond criminals and the diseased to exclude also the destitute and those with suspect political and moral credentials. Between the wars deportation was employed to counter the negative effects of allegedly indiscriminate recruitment under the Empire Settlement Act, particularly in the Harvesters' Scheme of 1928. This 'unqualified disaster' was a rerun of the 1923 venture whereby almost 12,000 unemployed Britons had been hired by the British and Canadian governments to help bring in the prairie harvest. In 1928 8,500 hastily selected unemployed British miners were also given one-way passages under the Empire Settlement Act, in the hope that, after the harvest was over, they might find permanent work. In the event, 6,876 recruits returned home, many at the expense of the British government when Canada refused to accept responsibility for inexperienced, unwilling workers who had simply been 'attracted to a free trip across the ocean'.[41]

The First World War and its aftermath did not therefore simply herald the tranquil dawn of unprecedented government sponsorship of migration, initially through the Soldier Settlement Scheme 1919–24 and more comprehensively through its successor, the Empire Settlement Act. Far from promoting Imperial unity, these collaborative ventures often proved contentious, disappointing the hopes of both sponsors and migrants. Despite selection by Canadian officials stationed in Britain, relatively few ex-service personnel who took up the free passages offered under the Soldier Settlement Scheme were the physically fit agriculturists desired by Canada. Two-thirds were women and children, mostly war widows and orphans, while many others were men from urban-industrial backgrounds who remained in the cities, incurring the displeasure

---

[39] The National Archives, Kew, London, Dominions Office (DO) 57/39/OSO 5295, deportation file of Mabel Pile, quoted in Kent Fedorowich, 'Restocking the British World: Empire Migration and Anglo-Canadian Relations, 1919–1939', unpublished seminar paper delivered at the Research Institute of Irish and Scottish Studies, Aberdeen University, Mar. 2004.

[40] Knowles, *Strangers at our Gates*, pp. 80–1; Roberts, *Whence They Came*, p. 38. The total deportation figure relates to the fiscal year, which ended in April 1909.

[41] Kelley and Trebilcock, *The Making of the Mosaic*, p. 190.

of officials, who warned them, perhaps disingenuously, of the likelihood of unemployment and destitution.[42] Meanwhile, the British Colonial Secretary, Alfred Milner, criticized the Dominions' tendency to assess these migrants only on 'the immediate utility of their labour' rather than their 'potential value as citizens in the Dominions'.[43]

Canada's misgivings about the applicability of assisted Empire migration to land settlement were apparently vindicated when the 1931 census revealed that less than 10 per cent of migrants had taken up farming, and the British and Canadian governments blamed each other for the inadequate planning, excessive costs, dependence mentalities among the settlers, and failure to repay loans that characterized many schemes under the Empire Settlement Act. The root problem, however, was the anachronistic and misleading promotion of land settlement at a time of burgeoning urbanization and shrinking farming opportunities. It was therefore not surprising that both the quantity and quality of recruits fell far short of expectations on both sides of the Atlantic, while many migrants themselves were disillusioned at the disparity between rhetoric and reality. According to David Jones, a Welsh telephone wireman who went to Saskatchewan in 1928 as an assisted agriculturist, despite having 'never seen a farm before I came here', Canadian life was 'right opposite' to the promotional film images of 'nice summer weather' and 'men running about in motor cars'.[44]

If British settlement in the 1920s failed to reach the levels seen before the war, the Depression of the 1930s effectively ended assisted migration. Tighter entry regulations and an upsurge of deportations were followed by the abolition in 1936 of the Department of Immigration and Colonization. Total immigration plummeted from 1,230,202 in the 1920s to 158,562 in the 1930s, and although most new settlers were British and American citizens, arrivals from the British Isles declined from 245,423 to 36,560.[45] During the Second World War migration was limited but 5,500 child evacuees and 1,000 mothers were brought to Canada in 1940, before the programme was abruptly abandoned following the sinking of the SS *City of Benares* with the loss of seventy-three children. Canada also received 44,886 war brides who arrived with 21,358 children,

[42] Kent Fedorowich, 'The Assisted Emigration of British Ex-servicemen to the Dominions, 1914–1922', in Constantine, (ed.), *Emigrants and Empire*, pp. 60–4.

[43] The National Archives, CO 721/13/2491, Milner to the Duke of Devonshire, Governor-General of Canada, 1 Oct. 1920.

[44] Royal Commission on Immigration and Settlement (Saskatchewan), 1930, Archives of Saskatchewan, RG-MG, I, pp. 126–31; V, pp. 9–19; reprinted in K. H. Burley, (ed.), *The Development of Canada's Staples, 1867–1939: A Documentary Collection* (Toronto, 1970?), pp. 73–6, 82–83.

[45] *Eighth Census of Canada, 1941*, I: *General Review and Summary Tables* (Ottawa, 1960), table 25, p. 671; www.statcan.ca/english/freepub/11-516-XIE/sectiona/sectiona.htm, Historical Statistics of Canada, Section A, Population and Migration, Series A350, Immigrant Arrivals in Canada 1852–1977. Site accessed 20 Nov. 2004.

mostly between 1945 and 1947.[46] Imperial institutions such as the Imperial Order Daughters of the Empire anticipated that the war brides—94 per cent of whom were British—would reinforce Canada's British identity, and in the late twentieth century these women attracted considerable attention from oral historians. Canada provided free, one-way passages, organized by the Department of National Defence through the Canadian Wives' Bureau in Regent Street, and on arrival the women were met by Red Cross personnel who put them on special trains and sent them to their destinations, having first tried to notify husbands or in-laws of their imminent arrival. One war bride, bound for Vancouver, was struck by the different receptions given to the new arrivals:

First, there was the big city greeting, which was frightfully formal. Husbands and in-laws were behind a barricade on one side, the brides carefully herded over to and lined up on the opposite side and a brass band and dais and VIPs in the middle . . . Then there were the small community greetings, which were very informal and the most fun to watch. Everyone was relaxed and happy, especially in Quebec . . . Finally there were the whistle stops, which made for rather sad reunions. In most cases just the husband greeted the bride, and they drove off in some sturdy vehicle into the icy wastes.[47]

The culture shock and homesickness that so often accompanied the migrant experience were felt acutely by young war brides. Although en route they were introduced to luxuries of which ration-hit Britain could only dream, many were ill prepared for the life that awaited them. A few women were given the heartbreaking news that, while they were crossing the Atlantic, their husbands had been killed in action, while others had been deserted. Some wives did not recognize their men out of uniform, one recalling that, in civilian clothes, her husband looked like Al Capone.[48] Girls who had left home in the teeth of parental opposition sometimes encountered hostility from their in-laws, as well as from small Canadian communities which resented the theft of their most eligible bachelors. While most women were welcomed and integrated quickly into their new environment, some did not conform to Canadian images of refined English womanhood, while some wives found Canada disappointingly different from the idealized picture painted by their husbands. Life was particularly difficult for urban migrants who found themselves in isolated prairie locations, but even those from rural backgrounds did not always adapt easily.

If Canadian opinion was slightly ambivalent towards war brides, it was downright hostile to any idea of relaxing migration restrictions in the immediate aftermath of peace. Memories of the unemployment that had followed the First World War were coupled with continuing xenophobia and fears among young professionals that their careers, already blighted by Depression and war, would be

---

[46] G. Bilson, *The Guest Children: The Story of the British Child Evacuees Sent to Canada during World War II* (Saskatoon, 1988), pp. 10, 60; J. Hibbert, (ed.), *The War Brides* (Toronto, 1978), preface.
[47] Ibid., p. 81.   [48] Ibid. pp. 66, 87–8, 92.

further hampered by migrant competition. It soon became clear, however, that all sectors of Canada's economy were crying out for workers. While 3,000 Polish Free Army veterans and 50,000 displaced persons from Europe were brought out under bulk labour schemes to fill vacancies on farms and in the construction and extractive industries, recruitment efforts, particularly for skilled migrants, were again directed primarily at Britain. In 1947 and 1948 Ontario's Premier, George Drew, frustrated at the shipping bottleneck and European refugee influx, organized an airlift of over 7,000 Britons, to work in the province's factories, after which the federal government negotiated with Trans-Canada Airlines to fly British settlers straight out for a much lower fare than the ocean passage. Even the migrant who arrived 'with only a shilling in his pocket' was welcome, and in 1951—a year when only 31,000 of the 194,000 migrants to Canada came from Britain—a loan scheme was introduced to entice British and northern European migrants across the Atlantic.[49] But although over a third of the 2,500,000 migrants to Canada between 1945 and 1967 came from Britain, with a particular upsurge following the Suez crisis of 1956, their cultural, as well as their numerical, dominance was steadily eroded by the liberalization of migration policy in response to pressure from business and labour interests, ethnic lobby groups, and the multiracial Commonwealth forum.

The expectations and experiences of post-war migrants mirrored those of earlier generations, and are difficult to categorize objectively. While some waxed lyrical about the prosperity and boundless opportunities of Canada in comparison to the austerity of war-ravaged Britain, others claimed they had been deceived by fraudulent promises of abundant employment and a congenial environment. An engineering graduate of Edinburgh University, who foresaw few prospects in Scotland, had no difficulty in securing a well-paid post in the aircraft industry when he arrived in Ontario in 1951, and a teenager from Birmingham, who went to Toronto in a family group in 1953, welcomed both the superior living standards and the 'unstuffiness' that was so different from the 'ordered society' and 'system of predestination' that characterized life in the English Midlands.[50] An ordered society was certainly not a feature of Prince George, British Columbia, which was variously described by two female migrants in the 1950s as a cold outpost of the 'Drunken Canadian West' and a 'dump' with no suitable accommodation or decent stores, which 'even boasted they still had whorehouses'. Coming to London, Ontario, in 1948 was 'the worst mistake we'd ever made', according to the embittered wife of an accountant who had failed to secure remunerative work, but her allegations that Canada House and the British press peddled 'a load of malarkey' reveal more about her own unrealistic expectations, homesickness,

---

[49] H. Keenleyside, Minister of the Interior, speaking in 1949, quoted in J. Bruce, *After the War* (Don Mills, 1982), p. 91. See also p. 92.

[50] Ibid., pp. 140, 181.

and wounded pride than the way in which Canada was promoted in post-war Britain.[51]

BEING BRITISH IN CANADA

The British settlers who dominated migration to Canada during the century after Confederation were significant not only because of their contribution to agriculture, industry, commerce, and the professions. Of equal importance was their social and cultural impact, which in turn was integrally connected to the migrants' perceptions of their ethnicity. While few wanted to replicate conditions in their homeland, most were unwilling to sacrifice their identity on the altar of economic opportunity. Some 'basked in the glory of empire' and were perturbed that British accents, traditions, and values were not always understood or accepted.[52] For one migrant from the East End of London, 'It was a real shocker . . . as if I was in a foreign country, and here I was thinking Canada, being part of the British Empire and all that, that I would be received as a wonderful person.'[53]

Perhaps the exaggerated expectations of some migrants arose, paradoxically, from the privileged position enjoyed by the British in Canada. They came to a country of which they automatically became citizens, whose language they already spoke, and where the majority of the population—overwhelmingly except in Quebec—shared their ethnic origins and culture. Loyalty to the Empire was taken for granted among English-speaking Canadians, and the sense of a collective, pan-British identity was reflected in the large numbers, mainly of Canadian born, who volunteered for the Boer War and the two world wars. Enlistment figures were particularly high among those of Highland and Protestant Irish ancestry who—thanks to their early arrival and establishment—continued to be disproportionately represented in the Canadian elite until well into the twentieth century. Intermarriage also diluted specific ethnicities as time went on, or at least gave individuals the choice to pick and mix the ethnic groups with whom they identified. For most British migrants, the celebration of their specific origins was cosmetic rather than crucial, and their well-being did not depend on the social, spiritual, and occupational support systems offered by ethnic boarding houses, churches, Masonic lodges, and friendly societies. At the same time, however, migrants who settled in isolated monolingual enclaves or worshipped separately, like Highland Scots or Scottish and Irish Catholics, preserved their distinct

[51] Barry Broadfoot, *The Immigrant Years* (Vancouver, 1986), pp. 60–3, 179–80.
[52] R. McCormack, 'Cloth Caps and Jobs: The Ethnicity of English Immigrants in Canada, 1900–1914', in J. M. Bumsted, (ed.), *Interpreting Canada's Past*, vol. II: *After Confederation* (Toronto, 1986), p. 180.
[53] Broadfoot, *The Immigrant Years*, p. 121.

identities more successfully than those whose ethnicity was not an integral part of their lifestyle.

Woven into this overview of British migration have been recurring disparities between the expectations and experiences of sponsors and migrants alike. Throughout the nineteenth century policy makers resisted demands to subsidize migration, but when they relented in the changed circumstances of the 1920s, legislative efforts to stimulate movement failed to fulfil their potential, and were accompanied by acrimonious disputes between Britain and Canada about the calibre of recruits. Voluntary societies, with a long tradition of assisting needy migrants, were simultaneously accused of bleeding Britain of its workforce and burdening Canada with unemployable paupers, and were unable to secure enough recruits to capitalize on the funding released by the Empire Settlement Act. Sponsors who prioritized the migrants' imperial duty were often disappointed with recruits whose goal was economic betterment, while migrants blamed their problems on the misleading promises of agents and the hostility of Canadians who reminded them of 'what a huge favour Canada had done by letting us come into their country'.[54] But conflict is easier to identify than cooperation, and for the silent majority of migrants and hosts, British settlement in Canada was probably a relatively positive and enriching story of integration and mutual support.

[54] Ibid., p. 195.

SELECT BIBLIOGRAPHY

MARILYN BARBER, *Immigrant Domestic Servants in Canada* (Ottawa, 1991).

BARRY BROADFOOT, *The Immigrant Years: From Britain and Europe to Canada, 1945–1967* (Vancouver, 1986).

JENNI CALDER, *Scots in Canada* (Edinburgh, 2003).

STEPHEN CONSTANTINE, (ed.), *Emigrants and Empire: British Settlement in the Dominions between the Wars* (Manchester, 1990).

MARJORY HARPER, *Adventurers and Exiles: The Great Scottish Exodus* (London, 2003).

NINETTE KELLEY and MICHAEL TREBILCOCK, *The Making of the Mosaic: A History of Canadian Immigration Policy* (Toronto, 1998).

VALERIE KNOWLES, *Strangers at our Gates: Canadian Immigration and Immigration Policy, 1540–1990* (Toronto, 1992).

ERIC RICHARDS, *Britannia's Children: Emigration from England, Scotland, Wales and Ireland since 1600* (London, 2004).

10

French Canadians' Ambivalence to the British Empire

Colin M. Coates

Reflecting on his first visit to London in 1831, the celebrated French-Canadian historian François-Xavier Garneau expressed the profound ambivalence of a French-Canadian subject of the British Empire. He was vastly impressed by Westminster Abbey: 'I seemed to be wandering amidst the great men of my homeland, and even if I was a British subject as a result of unfortunate events, I found some consolation in those Norman princes and knights, breastplated and lying on their tombs, among the glorious memories which will always be the heritage of their nation.'[1] Owing his allegiance to Britain to the unhappy memory of the military conquest of Quebec in 1759–60, Garneau could still revel in the fact that the English had, much earlier, experienced the same fate at the hands of his own Norman ancestors. The history of French Canada and that of England were intimately connected, and the shame of the Conquest could be stilled by reflection on that longer history.

Garneau was not alone in his equivocal reaction to the British connection. Donal Lowry has recently pointed out that non-British subjects of the Empire could readily embrace belonging to the larger realm through their allegiance to the monarch.[2] While this point is well taken, it is worth emphasizing how French Canadians used the British connection in ways that provided them with as much autonomy as possible. The military integration of French Canadians into the British Empire held a number of implications beyond memories of wartime destruction. Colonists of another European empire, they spoke a language to which many Europeans imputed a higher standing than they did to English. Despite the dramatic changes which their French homeland would experience,

[1] François-Xavier Garneau, *Voyage en Angleterre et en France dans les années 1831, 1832 et 1833* (repr. Ottawa, 1968), p. 136. Throughout the chapter I have translated lengthy quotations in French into English.
[2] Donal Lowry, 'The Crown, Empire Loyalism and the Assimilation of Non-British White Subjects in the British World: An Argument against "Ethnic Determinism"', in Carl Bridge and Kent Fedorowich, (eds), *The British World: Diaspora, Culture and Identity* (London, 2003), pp. 96–120.

they retained a potential allegiance, even if this was more cultural than political, to another country. While some French Canadians loudly declaimed their allegiance to British institutions, the language of loyalty could mask a discourse of defiance.

French Canadians had many reasons to feel ambivalent about the British Empire. Throughout the period of French colonial rule, the French settlements in North America faced almost continual threat from the British, most strongly propounded by the settlers in the colonies to the south. In 1629, the Kirke brothers captured Quebec, still a tiny outpost. The Kirkes held the fort until 1632, when under the terms of the Treaty of Saint-Germain-en-Laye Quebec reverted to France. This was by no means the end of the British threat to the French colony. Sustaining the Iroquois resistance to the French throughout the second half of the seventeenth century, the Anglo-American colonists remained a steadfast menace to the small French colony, as indeed French expeditions in their turn harassed British holdings in Hudson Bay, Newfoundland, and New England.

Antipathy to the French colony was firmly established among the Protestant colonists to the south. Colonists from New England led the assaults on French outposts in the Atlantic region as well as the two large-scale, unsuccessful, expeditions that attempted to take Quebec in 1696 (Sir William Phips) and 1711 (Sir Hovenden Walker). American hostility to their distant French Catholic neighbours was evident on all occasions, and for some Anglo-American colonists, the crusade against Catholics provided a key cultural impetus that bolstered their commercial goals in supplanting the French. 'I doubt not but the cause is God's . . . for all that is dear to us in our country, our flourishing, yes, our very subsistence in it, yea our religion lyes at stake', wrote Reverend John Barnard of Marblehead, Massachusetts, in 1745 concerning the French threat: 'Cape Breton must be destroyed or we must expect to be destroyed by them.'[3]

On six occasions in the seventeenth century and with some finality in 1710, Anglo-Americans attacked the main Acadian settlement at Port Royal. The Anglo-Americans were successful in ending French control, though not all French influence, over the Acadian population in peninsular Nova Scotia. Under the terms of the 1713 Treaty of Utrecht, the French Crown ceded political control over Acadia (essentially peninsular Nova Scotia, although the boundaries remained unclear) to the British. The French Catholic population of Acadians retained their good agricultural lands on the Bay of Fundy for the next four decades. Despite the state of war which existed between the French and the British during the War of the Austrian Succession (1744–8), the Acadians managed to pursue a vigilant neutrality, providing foodstuffs for both sides and maintaining their agrarian economy. In response to the loss of Acadia, the French Crown set about fortifying Île

---

[3] Quoted in Francis D. Cogliano, 'Nil Desperandum Christo Duce: The New England Crusade against Louisbourg', *Essex Institute Historical Collections*, 128 (1992), p. 187.

Royale (Cape Breton) through the sizeable fortress of Louisbourg, protecting French fishing on the Grand Banks and shipping to the St Lawrence settlements.

The evacuation of the main French settlement in Newfoundland, Plaisance (Placentia), in 1713–14 illustrated a fundamental reality about the French colonies in North America: their political destinies lay in the hands of distant treaty makers. The fortress of Louisbourg was captured in 1745, but then restored to the French. Important as the battles may have been, the defeat of French forces in 1758 at Louisbourg and the following year at the Battle of the Plains of Abraham outside Quebec City did not, in themselves, seal the fate of the French colonies in North America. But the French victory at Sainte-Foy in 1760 and the seizure of St John's, Newfoundland, in 1762 were not accompanied by the necessary reinforcement by French ships. Authorities in Montreal surrendered in 1760, and the Terms of Cession were concluded in that year. With the Treaty of Paris (1763), France abandoned its claims to territory in northern North America, though it ensured its lucrative access to the Grand Banks fisheries, landing rights on the 'French Shore' of Newfoundland, and the small islands of St Pierre and Miquelon. The Treaty afforded the free exercise of the Catholic religion to the new British subjects, with the significant limitation that these rights were to be enjoyed 'as far as the laws of Great Britain permit'. In fact, if British laws had been literally applied in Quebec, they would not have provided much solace for Catholics. As Linda Colley points out, one of the key factors that united the different nations comprising the United Kingdom in the eighteenth century was Francophobia.[4] Following the definitive cession of Quebec to the British in 1763, the remaining French population in northern North America therefore faced an uncertain fate.

Indeed, the experience of the Acadians portended doom for the larger groups of French inhabitants of North America. Early in the Seven Years War (1754–63, in its North American theatre), authorities in the colony of Nova Scotia (as Acadia had been renamed in 1713) deported around 13,000 Acadians, scattering them among seaports on both sides of the Atlantic. The British colonial populations did not welcome these arrivals. In 1756, Massachusetts colonists petitioned their governor, to complain of 'the receiving among us so great a Number of Persons whose gross Bigotry to the Roman Catholick Religion is notorious and whose Loyalty to His Majesty Louis XV is a thing very disagreeable to us'.[5] While small numbers of Acadians settled in France, most others made painstaking efforts to regain regions in North America under French or at least Catholic control. Some 3,000 made their way to Louisiana, now under Spanish—and therefore Catholic—control, while the majority wended their way back to

---

[4] Linda Colley, *Britons: Forging the Nation, 1707–1837* (New Haven, 1992).

[5] Quoted in Naomi E. S. Griffiths, *The Contexts of Acadian History, 1686–1784* (Montreal and Kingston, 1992), p. 106.

Atlantic Canada, finding homes in the coastal regions of Nova Scotia and what were shortly to be renamed New Brunswick and Prince Edward Island.

Avoiding the deportations, about 2,000 Acadians had already streamed into the St Lawrence valley and the Gaspé Peninsula, and the local French population had many reasons to dread the British take over of the colony. In the course of war, many lives had been lost as a result of the thorough bombardment of the fortress of Quebec and the scorched-earth tactics that General James Wolfe had authorized in order to cut off provisions to the French troops within the fortress walls. British troops burned hundreds of houses and barns in the parishes near the city. What one historian has called 'l'année des Anglais' was a year of destitution and pain throughout the St Lawrence valley.[6]

Looking into the future from 1763, British authorities might have expected the relatively small French-speaking Catholic population of the St Lawrence valley (about 75,000) and Acadia (over 1,000 scattered in the region) to be effectively assimilated into an Anglo-Protestant whole. After all, by the mid-eighteenth century, about one hundred years after the British takeover of New Netherlands (New York), little was left of the Dutch culture in the region. A comparison to the contemporaneous decline in Gaelic-speaking Scotland, which had a larger population in the 1760s, or indeed the much larger Irish-speaking population of Ireland in the nineteenth century, would have predicted the difficulty in maintaining a distinctive linguistic identity. However, as elsewhere within the British Empire, the experience was different: French speakers within northern North America, like the Afrikaans-speaking population in southern Africa and the French speakers in Mauritius (both ceded to Britain in 1814), were able to maintain their culture and language.

The success (termed 'survivance' in an older French-Canadian historiography) can be attributed to a number of factors: the relative weakness of British colonial institutions, the largely autonomous French-Canadian Church, and the limited immigration of English speakers to the new areas. Officially, British authorities continued to desire the assimilation of French speakers, but they did not have the institutional means to carry out the policy. In 1828, Colonial Secretary William Huskisson declaimed in the House of Commons: 'it is still the duty and interest of this country to imbue it [Canada] with English feeling, and benefit it with English laws and institutions.'[7] Rural schools, which received some state funding, were not introduced throughout Lower Canada until the 1820s, and the language of instruction was French where the pupils spoke that language. Moreover, the high cultural status of French meant that many educated British spoke the language, and therefore much financial and government business was conducted in French. The English-speaking minority often found it easier to operate in French than to

---

[6] Gaston Deschênes, *L'Année des Anglais: la Côte-du-Sud à l'heure de la Conquête* (Sillery, 1998).

[7] Quoted in James Sturgis, 'Anglicisation as a Theme in Lower Canadian History, 1807–1843', *British Journal of Canadian Studies*, 3 (1988), p. 220.

convince French Canadians and Acadians to adopt English. The overwhelmingly rural character of Quebec and the Acadian settlements in the Maritimes provided a further cultural insulation for the French-speaking Catholic populations, just as it would do for the Gaelic-speaking Scottish immigrants in Cape Breton throughout the nineteenth century.

Like their fellow colonists, French speakers were linked to the British Empire through economic ties, participating in the fur and timber trades, selling their wheat, and later producing cheese and bacon for the urban populations of the United Kingdom. Capital flows also remained important. Railroad-building channelled funds through Montreal financiers. Britain remained a significant investor in Quebec well into the twentieth century. Until the 1960s and 1970s, Montreal remained the key financial centre of Canada, although the financial links between local financiers and distant British backers usually excluded French-Canadian entrepreneurs. However important the economic ties between French-Canadian economic endeavours and Imperial markets, institutional controls did not inexorably follow the economic links.

Helping the cause of the French-Canadian and Acadian populations was the fact of a substantial demographic increase. Much has been made of the high birth rate among French Canadians, although when one controls for rurality, the rate is not much different from other North American societies during the same time period. In any case, the French-Canadian population increased dramatically: from the 75,000 at the time of the Conquest, the population grew to around 1,000,000 by the 1850s. The vast majority of the people who claim French ancestry in Canada, some 7,000,000 French Canadians and Acadians in 2001, as well as many of those of French origin in the United States, can trace their genealogy to the French settlers during the time of New France. Beginning in the 1840s, large numbers of French Canadians emigrated to the United States, where colonies of French speakers ('petits Canadas') were established. These Franco-American groups are in decline today, but for three or four generations they remained vibrant outposts of French-Canadian culture, maintaining familial and institutional ties to the homeland in Quebec.

An older historiography overstated the difficulty of integrating Quebec into the British Empire. According to Alfred LeRoy Burt, 'it was utterly alien in language, religion, laws, political institutions, and culture. Never had the Empire swallowed anything like this. How could it be assimilated?'[8] In fact, as the autonomous legal, religious, and educational institutions of Scotland showed, integration did not require complete assimilation. Indeed, Quebec became the linchpin in developing a workable constitution for the new British North America, and its unique characteristics were central to all the attempts to revise the arrangements between the different parts of British North America.

---

[8] Alfred LeRoy Burt, *The Evolution of the British Empire and Commonwealth from the American Revolution* (Boston, 1956), p. 39.

For practical military and strategic reasons, British legislation and treaties provided varying degrees of protection for the French: the Treaty of Paris offered some limited protections, while the Quebec Act of 1774 recognized French civil law (as was done in other former French colonies such as St Lucia, and indeed as the United States would later do in Louisiana). Property rights, specifically seigneurial tenure, were thus ensured in the colony. The Quebec Act also allowed Catholics to take up civil office in Quebec at a time when Catholics were excluded from such positions in the United Kingdom. In the context of growing unrest in the colonies to the south, the Quebec Act aimed to conciliate the French-Canadian elites to the British Crown, and it proved successful in doing so. At the same time the Quebec Act contributed to a great deal of anti-Catholic hostility in the United Kingdom and the Anglo-American colonies, and added to the colonial disaffection created by the Stamp Act and the 'Coercive Acts'. Although some in Quebec agreed with the American opposition to this legislation, there was no swell of enthusiasm in response to the invitation from the Continental Congress to join the rebellion. The subsequent invasion of American rebels in 1775 received some limited popular support, particularly when cash was available for ready payment, but the religious and economic elites rallied to the British cause. The difficulties of waging a winter siege of Quebec City ensured the failure of the American invaders.

The protections of the Quebec Act did not extend to the Acadians, and Acadian (and British) Catholics had to wait until Catholic Emancipation in 1829 before they received rights already possessed by Catholics in Quebec. The Acadians were already a minority in Nova Scotia and with the arrival of the first large wave of English-speaking immigrants after the Conquest, the Loyalists, new constitutional arrangements were deemed necessary which ignored Acadian realities. Two new provinces were carved out of greater Nova Scotia and given colonial status in 1784: New Brunswick (which became the home of the majority of Acadians) and Cape Breton (until 1820 when it was reunited with Nova Scotia).

The arrival of the Loyalists also led to the Constitutional Act of 1791, which provided an institutional focus for French Canadians in Quebec, even though the larger goals of the legislation were very different. 'Canada' was divided into two sections. Lower Canada contained the majority of the French population. Upper Canada was left open to British and Anglo-American immigration, as were the Eastern Townships in southern Quebec, governed by English rather than French land tenure. By the early nineteenth century, with the better agricultural lands of Lower Canada and the eastern American states already occupied, British and Americans streamed onto the marginal soils of the Eastern Townships, as did the French whose lands in the old seigneuries of the St Lawrence valley were increasingly crowded. The Constitutional Act also created a representative Assembly, which, through a broad interpretation of property rights, would be dominated by French Canadians. Some British officials wished to limit voting privileges to those who owned their property without the restrictions imposed by seigneurial title. Such a decision would have limited the suffrage to large landowners in the countryside and wealthy city dwellers. However, a broader interpretation of landed property was adopted, which gave the voting rights to the small landholders (habitants). The franchise ensured de facto French-Canadian control over the representative Assembly. Not surprisingly, one of the first debates in the new Assembly was over the language of proceedings, and by majority vote French was recognized alongside English as an official language of the legislature. British authorities would later come to regret French-Canadian domination of the Assembly, particularly as it acquired greater powers over colonial finances.

A few French Canadians imbibed at least some elements of 'English feeling'. A small elite of Anglophile French Canadians provided a significant mediating function between the French community and the British colonial authorities. The landholding Lanaudière family provides a good, if extreme, example. Unable to activate the contacts that would have allowed them to pursue a military career in France, Charles-François de Lanaudière and his son Charles-Louis had returned to the new British colony in 1762. Charles-Louis subsequently became aide-de-camp to the Governor-General, and later received the sinecures of Surveyor General of Woods and Waters and Overseer of Highways. English author James Lambert remembered Lanaudière as 'one of the most respectable gentlemen in the colony . . . He is sincerely attached to the English government, and in his conduct, manners, [and] principles, he seems to be an Englishman.' Lanaudière's nephew concurred, remembering him as 'our English uncle, because . . . he had adopted the cold, undemonstrative manners of real English gentlemen'.[9] Among the elite landholding families, the Lanaudières were not alone in providing their support to British colonial rule.

Catholic authorities also played a key role in supporting the new British rulers of the colony. Especially in the context of revolutionary France and the tumultuous state of the Church in the homeland, religious leaders in Quebec were relieved to offer strong support for the constituted authorities. In return, local administrators ignored the secret instructions they had been given to suppress the liberties of the Catholic Church. The French Revolution led to the immigration to Lower Canada and Acadia of an important cohort of conservative Catholic priests, anxious to educate their flock on the horrors of the revolutionary experience in France.

While French-speaking inhabitants more generally had few reasons to be loyal to the British, the hand of the British state was light, and remained so well into the nineteenth century. Colonists were free of many of the direct tax burdens of their metropolitan cousins. In 1812, at a time of protests against the possible conscription of militiamen to fight the Americans, the Montreal judge

---

[9] Quoted in Yves Beauregard, 'Lanaudière, Charles-Louis', in *Dictionary of Canadian Biography*, vol. V (Toronto, 1983), pp. 791–2; Philippe Aubert de Gaspé, *Mémoires* (Montreal, 1971), p. 84.

Pierre-Louis Panet lectured the recalcitrant: 'Canadians live so happily under the British government, without taxes or imposts, protected in their religion that they may exercize freely or rather that they neglect too much, this religion which teaches you duties that you only fulfill imperfectly. For 52 years you have lived under the present government. What complaints would you dare to make against it?'[10] Indeed, for much of the history of Quebec, the fiscal impositions of the Imperial government remained small, restricted primarily to import duties. The political complaints of French-Canadian subjects, outspoken and challenging as they became, involved a desire to control those taxes raised in the colony, but were not enhanced by the crippling financial burdens that emboldened popular uprisings in places such as France. Many of the crises of the colonial period were, in fact, occasioned by overzealous British officials, such as Governor James Craig (1807–11), whose term in office came to be typified as a 'reign of terror' for his fierce opposition to French-Canadian political leaders and journalists.

The experiences of revolutionary France attracted the attention of potentially rebellious French Canadians. Certainly British authorities and visitors to the colony worried about the loyalty of the French Canadians. Travelling through the St Lawrence valley, Lord Selkirk recorded in 1803 the unhappiness among the French-Canadian population: 'There is but one opinion as to the universal disaffection of the French Canadians to the British Government . . . The postillions as they drive along are continually speaking to their horses—generally scolding—one of them ended a string of Oathes with Sacré Anglais!'[11] Some French Canadians made their hostility to the British authorities even more apparent. In 1805, the rural parishes near Montreal addressed a petition to Napoleon: 'We are ready to undertake any measures at the first sight of the French, whom we still regard as our brothers.' Well into the 1830s, a latent sympathy for the former homeland can be seen in the popularity of the first name 'Napoléon'.[12]

In the late eighteenth and early nineteenth centuries, Anglo-Protestant immigration to Quebec remained small in the French-speaking areas. These settlers flocked to unoccupied, and therefore less expensive, property in New Brunswick, Nova Scotia, Prince Edward Island, the Eastern Townships of Lower Canada, and Upper Canada. With dramatically increasing numbers after the end of the Napoleonic Wars and later in the 1840s and 1850s—some 800,000 British and Irish immigrants passed through the St Lawrence valley between 1815 and 1851—there was much unrest in the major towns of British North America, principally Quebec, sometimes spurred by the fact that immigrants brought contagious diseases like typhoid with them. Immigrants were not merely an

---

[10] Quoted in Sean Mills, 'French Canadians and the Beginning of the War of 1812: Revisiting the Lachine Riot', *Histoire sociale/Social History*, 76 (2005), p. 48.

[11] Patrick C. T. White, ed., *Lord Selkirk's Diary, 1803–1804* (Toronto, 1958), p. 217.

[12] Quoted in Claude Galarneau, *La France devant l'opinion canadienne (1760–1815)* (Quebec, 1970), pp. 272–7, 333.

economic threat to the established population, but they were a medical threat as well. The immigrants tended to settle, at least initially, in the urban centres, and the cities of Quebec and Montreal both had English-speaking majorities in the middle decades of the nineteenth century. Even if many moved on to Upper Canada or the United States, others competed, often violently, for waged jobs in shipbuilding, canal construction, or logging. A few integrated into French-Canadian society (hence the existence of clans of French-Canadian Ryans or O'Neills), but most remained outside it.

Debates over the future of French Canada took form within the contexts of British political traditions. French-Canadian leaders expounded their political views by using British parliamentary rules and appealing to the broader sense of British liberties. Advancing French-Canadian claims, *Patriote* leader Louis-Joseph Papineau wrote in 1822 that 'we were born English subjects as much as those who come to us from the banks of the Thames'. As political relations became more tense in the 1830s, Papineau's reference points were other parts of the British Empire which had analogous constitutional characteristics, such as Ireland, Malta, and Jamaica. 'A responsible local and national government for each part of the Empire . . .', he argued, 'that is what Ireland and British America demand.'[13] Papineau adopted more radical positions in the 1830s, but the themes of many of the political assemblies discussing their opposition to British policy in the heady autumn of 1837 still maintained an outwardly deferential attitude to British institutions, accusing the Imperial government of trampling on the freedoms of British subjects. A colony-wide boycott of items imported from Britain was launched to put pressure on the Imperial government, and hostilities broke out once the shipping season ended on the St Lawrence. Papineau's attitude towards the rebellions of 1837–8 was as ambivalent as many of his compatriots, and he fled the colony at the outbreak of hostilities.

In the political ferment that laid the foundation for the rebellion in 1837, invective aimed at the British monarchy more generally and the newly enthroned Queen Victoria more specifically expressed the revolutionary fervour of the time. A *Patriote* speaker in the rural parish of Nicolet decried the new monarch: 'As for the [late] king, he is nothing but a big zero to whom Canadians pay a pension . . . The proof that kings are nothing but zeros is that we are now governed by a young queen seventeen years of age.' The British government's stern reaction to French-Canadian demands for greater control over public expenditure and patronage in the colony also allowed many rebels to argue that the Imperial authority was suppressing their British liberties: 'A combined and dishonorable junction of Whigs and Tories, in a House of Commons "reformed" but in name', wrote the *Patriote* press, 'may pass Resolutions to annihilate the

[13] Quoted in Yvan Lamonde, 'Conscience coloniale et conscience internationale dans les écrits publics de Louis-Joseph Papineau', *Revue d'histoire de l'Amérique française*, 51 (1997), pp. 8, 19–20.

last remnant of Liberty left in the Colonial Legislatures.'[14] Much of the political debate involved issues of access to government patronage and appointments, a demand for insertion into the governing system, not a direct rejection of it.

In the event, small numbers of *Patriotes* organized in late November 1837 and achieved early victories, but the harsh British suppression of the rebellion isolated the supporters of radical political change. Some French Canadians had sided with the colonial authorities in any case, just as support for rebellion had extended beyond French Canadians. A second rebellion, more explicitly republican and launched from the United States in late 1838, was quickly suppressed. In those *Patriotes* who were executed for their part in the 1838 rebellions or who were exiled from the colony, later French-Canadian nationalists could identify the early leaders of their independence struggle.

One of the main achievements of the rebellions was to create new fault lines within the French-Canadian political leadership. For his part, Papineau spent eight years in exile in the United States and France. He returned to Quebec in 1845, but his political standing had been diminished, and he did not command the same following in the aftermath of the failed rebellions. A new set of politicians assumed more prominent roles, many of these men being more willing to cooperate with colonial authorities and make strategic alliances with English-speaking politicians. Lord Durham's report on the rebellions in Upper and Lower Canada restated British desires to assimilate French Canadians. In order to reduce French-Canadian autonomy, the two colonies of Upper and Lower Canada were joined in 1840 to create the United Province of Canada. While this constitutional change aimed to reduce French Canadians to a political minority, even if they remained a numerical majority at the time, it did not lead to its intended outcome. Louis-Hippolyte La Fontaine allied with Robert Baldwin in the 1840s to re-establish new political powers for French Canadians within the institutions of the newly united colony of the Canadas. Even the highly unfavourable terms of the Act of Union of 1840 could be modified to create political space for French Canadians. By 1848, not only had French been recognized again as an official language in the legislature, but the English- and French-speaking reformers had achieved a large degree of political autonomy within the Empire through the British acknowledgement of responsible government. The key moment was Governor-General Lord Elgin's acceptance of the Rebellion Losses Bill of 1849, in the face of sustained opposition from Tory members of the legislature and hostile mobs in the capital of Montreal. The backdrop of American 'Manifest Destiny' helped to focus the attention of colonial politicians on economic and political options for British North America.

It is a testament to the political skills of French-speaking politicians that the Confederation agreement of 1867 that created Canada's current constitutional

---

[14] Quotations in Allan Greer, *The Patriots and the People: The Rebellion of 1837 in Rural Lower Canada* (Toronto, 1993), pp. 191, 143–4.

framework provided substantial protection, albeit severely limited, for French-Canadian Catholics in the new country. This was primarily assured through the re-establishment of the separate jurisdiction of Quebec. Outside Quebec, the British North America Act provided little solace to French Canadians, and many Acadian leaders did not support the constitutional change. Minority-language Catholic schools were progressively suppressed outside Quebec, beginning in 1871 in New Brunswick, home to the majority of Acadians. Whatever its shortcomings, the 1867 Act had created one province where the majority would be Catholic and French. The English-speaking population of Quebec was at its highest level, reaching about 25 per cent in the 1871 census, and the British North America Act was more explicit in its protection of English-speaking minorities than French-Catholic minorities outside Quebec. But Quebec would henceforth be a province in which the political weight would be held by French-speakers, and it was guaranteed a minimal number of seats in the Canadian Parliament (sixty-five), the only province to receive such assurance. Fights over jurisdiction would prove to be a constant of Canadian constitutional history, but in the context of the 1860s, the British North America Act accorded a great deal of protection to francophones in Quebec, where the French-Canadian majority was now in control of their civil law code and educational and welfare institutions. On the day Confederation came into being, 1 July 1867, the newspaper *La Minerve* effused: 'As a distinct and separate nationality, we form a state within the state. We enjoy the full exercise of our rights and the formal recognition of our national independence.'[15]

In the aftermath of the failed rebellions, some members of the French-Canadian elite competed to proclaim greater degrees of allegiance to the broader British Empire. Too much can be made of this rhetoric, but the words do indicate what the speakers thought it politically useful to say. In 1846, Colonel Étienne-Pascal Taché claimed in the legislature of the United Canadas that 'we will never forget our allegiance till the last cannon which is shot on this continent in defense of Great Britain is fired by the hand of a French Canadian', while the venerable Marguerite de Lanaudière commented at the time of the symbolic visit of the French frigate *La Capricieuse* in 1855 that 'Our hearts belong to France, but our arms belong to England.' Later in the nineteenth century, the eccentric Conservative politician Sir Adolphe Chapleau was undoubtedly carried away with the occasion, Prime Minister Sir John A. Macdonald's fortieth anniversary banquet, when he promised eternal loyalty: 'French Canadians will be the last on the continent to sing the glorious hymn "God Save the Queen".'[16] Not all

[15] Quoted in A. I. Silver, *The French-Canadian Idea of Confederation, 1864–1900* (Toronto, 1982), p. 41.
[16] Taché, quoted in Jacques Monet, *The Last Cannon Shot: A Study of French-Canadian Nationalism, 1837–1850* (Toronto, 1969), p. 3; Lanaudière, quoted in Aubert de Gaspé, *Mémoires*, p. 40; Chapleau, quoted in Kenneth J. Munro, *The Political Career of Sir Adolphe Chapleau, Premier of Quebec, 1879–1882* (Queenston, 1992), p. 153.

French-Canadian politicians proclaimed their allegiance to the Empire in such a bold fashion, but for decades after the rebellions few expressed open hostility to the British connection. On a different social level, French-Canadian parents adopted the name 'Victoria' for their baby girls more than did parents elsewhere in the British North America and at a much higher rate than in the United Kingdom.[17] While one cannot assume that all parents were choosing the name specifically to honour the Queen (some had adopted the name following British victories at Trafalgar and Waterloo, before Victoria's birth), the choice clearly had lost the negative connotations that the Queen had inspired in 1837.

While some French Canadians proclaimed positive views of the British tie, this did not necessarily mean that all, even the elites, saw themselves as full-fledged members of the larger Empire, and in this they differed greatly from their fellow Canadians of British descent. For most French Canadians, the ties to the British Empire led only to England, if at all, and not elsewhere around the globe. Few French Canadians made careers in other parts of the Empire, although there are rare cases such as Sir Percy Girouard, Governor of Nigeria (1908–9) and Kenya (1909–12). Girouard, who was educated at the Séminaire de Trois-Rivières, had an English-speaking mother. During his time in the colonial service, his links to his French-Canadian past became increasingly tenuous, and he seldom visited Canada after the 1880s.[18] Likewise, until after the Second World War, few French Canadians made careers in the Dominion military, primarily an English-language institution. With the exception of the handful of French-Canadian men deported to the penal colony of Australia in the early nineteenth century, for crimes against property and later for participating in the rebellions of 1837–8, few French Canadians made their way to distant outposts of the Empire. Of all the deported rebels, most made the arduous return journeys home to Quebec. Catholic missionaries were a partial exception to the rule, their calling taking them in large numbers to British colonies in Africa and Asia, as well as colonies where French was an official language.

If the Empire provided few careers for French Canadians, it also offered little intellectual training. Few French Canadians chose to attend the ancient British universities, and they often felt like pioneers in doing so. Marius Barbeau, the distinguished ethnographer, became the first French-Canadian Rhodes Scholar when he registered at Oxford in 1907. Among the cohort of intellectuals who came of age in Quebec in the inter-war years, only one, the classicist Maurice Lebel, studied in England, while the majority pursued their higher degrees in France.[19] In the 1950s, Jacques Parizeau, future separatist Premier of Quebec,

---

[17] K. Schürer and L. Dillon, 'What's in a Name? Victorias in Canada and Great Britain in 1881', *Local Population Studies,* 70 (2003), p. 57.

[18] A. H. M. Kirk-Greene, 'Canada in Africa: Sir Percy Girouard, Neglected Colonial Governor', *African Affairs,* 83 (1984), pp. 207–39.

[19] Lawrence Nowry, *Man of Mana: Marius Barbeau* (Toronto, 1995), p. 68; Catherine Pomeyrols, *Les Intellectuels québécois: formation et engagements, 1919–1939* (Paris, 1996), pp. 478–9.

ignored his academic mentor's advice to go to Paris for his doctorate and instead enrolled in the London School of Economics. A meeting with an elderly major in the Indian army provided an epiphany for him, Parizeau recalled many years later: 'I realised that for people like him, those who were considered the masters in Quebec, the Sahib—the English Canadians—were, for people like him, only "damned colonials"! I tell you, this changed my views on life.'[20] Parizeau cultivated an English accent, according to his biographer, in order to intimidate English Canadians. In the case of Parizeau, it is interesting to note that a certain degree of Anglophilia, and indeed a rather pompous adoption of British forms of speech, did not instil a strong allegiance to the current constitutional formation of Canada.

Britain and the Empire were not a major part of the greater cultural world of French Canadians. Writers like Sir Walter Scott were said to have a great impact on the development of French-Canadian literature, but most other influences came through France. Even in the context of the complicated political history of France in the nineteenth century, influences continued to flow from the French-speaking world to Quebec. The publication of a history of Acadia in 1859 by the French writer Edmé Rameau de Saint Père was an important moment in the development of national identity, though less significant than the American poet Henry Wadsworth Longfellow's 'Evangeline'. When the Acadians adopted a national flag in 1884, they based their emblem on the French Tricolour. For French-Canadian writers and performers, international success was measured by their renown in France, not in the United Kingdom. One rare exception was the soprano Dame Emma Albani, a fixture at Covent Garden in the late nineteenth century; she performed throughout the Empire and was asked to sing at a private funeral service for Queen Victoria. In 1903, the influential nationalist leader Henri Bourassa spelled out the multiple loyalties of French Canadians: 'Our English compatriots . . . have nothing to fear from the double allegiance which is ours: intellectual and moral allegiance to France, political allegiance to England; because both are entirely subordinate to our exclusively Canadian patriotism.'[21]

Unlike the case in English-speaking Canada, very little immigration from francophone Europe bolstered the French population in Canada after 1760. There was little French Protestant settlement throughout Canadian history, and therefore the French in Canada remained largely Catholic, despite Protestant attempts to proselytize among them. Indeed, the Catholicism of French Canada was reinforced in the nineteenth century as male and female religious orders from Belgium and France established a presence in the country.

---

[20] Quoted in Pierre Duchesne, *Jacques Parizeau, I: Le Croisé, 1930–1970* (Montreal, 2001), p. 161.
[21] Quoted in Yvan Lamonde, 'Le Lion, le coq et la fleur de lys: l'Angleterre et la France dans la culture politique du Québec (1760–1820)', in Gérard Bouchard and Yvan Lamonde, (eds), *La Nation dans tous ses états: le Québec en comparaison* (Montreal, 1997), p. 175.

Events in France continued to garner interest among French Canadians. Some of the military experiences of France stimulated financial support, but not military volunteers. The francophile Narcisse-Henri-Édouard Faucher de Saint-Maurice recorded in the newspaper *L'Événement* in 1880 at the time of the Franco-Prussian War: 'We respect England, and we are grateful to her for having given us the most precious possession, liberty . . . But it is only France that we love with passion.'[22] For French Canadians, an alternative homeland offered cultural inspiration, but it did not demand personal military sacrifice.

French Canadians remained aloof from calls for sacrifice on behalf of the British Empire. In the late nineteenth century, no influential French Canadian joined the calls for Imperial unity. Historian Réal Bélanger has argued that Canadian Prime Minister Wilfrid Laurier awkwardly juggled British-Canadian demands for greater involvement in the Empire with French-Canadian desires for greater autonomy. He resisted calls for 'imperial unity' in much the same way as his vocal critic Henri Bourassa.[23] Desirous of protecting the autonomy that they had acquired, French Canadians, unlike British Canadians, saw little to gain from a larger imperial stage. Most French Canadians placed limits on their enthusiasm for the imperial adventures of the British Empire. In the 1850s, the Crimean War, jointly waged by Britain and France, mustered some limited financial support among French-Canadian elites, anxious to convey 'the sympathies that our former colony conserves still towards France'.[24] But no French-Canadian soldiers enlisted in the fight.

More challenging, the South African War (1899–1902) opened up a significant rift between French and British Canadians. Many British Canadians expressed their desire to aid in the suppression of Boer rebels, while among French Canadians there was sympathy for the Afrikaner linguistic and religious minority's resistance to being overwhelmed by British settlers. British Canadians wished to send troops to support the British forces, while French Canadians resisted involvement in the distant military engagement. Henri Bourassa denounced British actions, charging Colonial Secretary Joseph Chamberlain with trying to 'centralize Imperial power at the expense of colonial liberty'.[25] The political debate spilled into the streets of Montreal. In March 1900, students from McGill University celebrated victories at Ladysmith and Paardeberg by attacking French-language newspapers, too supportive, they claimed, of the Boer

[22] Narcisse-Henri-Édouard Faucher de Saint-Maurice, *Le Canada et les Canadiens-français pendant la guerre franco-prussienne* (Quebec, 1888), pp. 14–15.

[23] Réal Bélanger, 'L'Élite politique canadienne-française et l'Empire britannique: trois reflets représentatifs des perceptions canadiennes-françaises (1890–1917)', in Colin M. Coates, (ed.), *Imperial Canada, 1867–1917* (Edinburgh, 1997), pp. 122–40.

[24] Quoted in A. W. Rasporich, 'Imperial Sentiment in the Province of Canada during the Crimean War, 1854–1856', in W. L. Morton, (ed.), *The Shield of Achilles: Aspects of Canada in the Victorian Age* (Toronto, 1968), p. 151.

[25] Quoted in Carman Miller, *Painting the Map Red: Canada and the South African War, 1899–1902* (Montreal, 1993), p. 442.

position. In response, French-speaking university students marched on McGill University, waving the French flag and singing 'La Marseillaise'. The Boer War conflicts presaged the broader conflicts surrounding conscription during the First World War.

One of the key political debates in the first two decades of the twentieth century was the degree of military commitment Canada would make to Britain and the Empire. French Canadians believed that the country should focus on defending its own territory and should avoid external engagements. Nonetheless, as Europe lurched towards war in the summer of 1914, French-Canadian elites supported the move towards war and initial voluntary enlistment. But they refused to countenance enforced conscription. As the war dragged on and tens of thousands of Canadian soldiers perished in the trenches, perceptions of lower enlistment rates among French Canadians led to mounting hostility from English speakers. In the end the National Government, a war time coalition of Conservatives and Liberals that almost entirely excluded French Canadians, recommended conscription. In the ensuing riot in Quebec in April 1917, four members of the crowd were shot by military police. Later that year, in the general election, the National Government won only three seats in Quebec and lost all four Acadian constituencies in New Brunswick.

The French-Canadian response to conscription had at its core French-Canadian attitudes to their place within the British Empire, and represented one of the greatest political challenges to the Canadian Confederation to that time. In January 1918 a motion placed in front of the Quebec legislature by Joseph-Napoléon Francœur called for Quebec to consider separation from Canada. This motion may have been nothing more than a 'bluff', aimed at acquiring the attention of English-speaking Canadians. The motion was quickly withdrawn after a brief debate in the chamber, but it did illustrate the range of thought that was possible as a result of the Conscription Crisis.

For many decades, one of the key dividing lines between the two main political parties in Canada remained their attitude to the British Empire, the Conservatives having a much stronger tendency to support Imperial commitments. The 1922 Chanak Crisis illustrated why French Canadians tended to shun the party. The Conservative leader, Arthur Meighen, responded: 'Ready, aye, ready', while the more astute and careful Liberal leader William Lyon Mackenzie King refused to commit Canadian military support to the distant Turkish conflict. The Conservatives remained, in the eyes of French Canadians, the party of conscription, having proposed it in 1917 and continuing to support it in the Second World War. The issue of conscription was handled more deftly in the Second World War by the Liberal government led by Mackenzie King. Initial promises of no conscription gave way to a lengthy and staged retreat from that position by means of a national referendum in 1942. The government asked voters to release it from its earlier promise, and French speakers throughout the country resoundingly said 'no'. Even with a healthy overall majority in favour of conscription, the Canadian government still hesitated, and by the time the military draft was imposed in 1944, much of the French-Canadian hostility to the policy had been attenuated, if not dissipated.

Thus, until the 1980s, French-Canadian electoral support, with only an exceptional result in 1958, and to a lesser extent in 1930, strongly supported the Liberal Party, ensuring the party a virtual lock on power. The influential Montreal journalist Claude Ryan noted in the 1960s how the Conservative Party maintained an antagonistic stance towards French Canada: 'the Conservatives, under certain very serious historical circumstances which have divided the country several times since the beginning of the century, have not hesitated to put their attachment to the mother-country before the search for an honourable compromise with French Canada.'[26] As a result, French-Canadian politicians have found the Liberal Party a means to power, even when their political predilections may have started out in other parts of the political spectrum. Eventually, French-Canadian perspectives on many issues related to national autonomy would become the general Canadian view.

The process by which French-Canadian nationalism came to focus primarily on the future of the province of Quebec was a lengthy one. Through the first half of the twentieth century, one of the dominant forms of French-Canadian nationalism was to see an arc of French-language, Catholic settlements, concentrated in Quebec but including outposts in the Maritime provinces, northern and eastern Ontario, and extending into Manitoba, with a few isolated pockets in the more western provinces and even the United States. This sprawling archipelago was perceived as a series of islands in a larger sea that was Protestant, materialist, and English speaking. As Sylvie Lacombe argues, French-Canadian intellectuals believed that their society had a moral mission in North America.[27]

The reality of French Canada was more complex, in part because of the sizeable English-speaking Catholic population in Canada, often antagonistic to French-Canadian rights, and in part because the ideological and sociological make-up of French Canada was more complex than the image that nationalists conveyed. Nonetheless, the argument could be made that the British tradition of diversity provided support for the French-Canadian communities. Just as the United Kingdom is composed of different 'nations', so could Canada be perceived the same way, and the British institutions which protected differences within the United Kingdom could have the same effect in Canada. By the 1960s, the definition of French Canada became limited, in Quebec, to those living in the province. The sense of Acadian identity, as well as that of other francophones living outside Quebec, continued to evolve on a different plane, and the rights

---

[26] Quoted in Richard Jones, *Community in Crisis: French-Canadian Nationalism in Perspective* (Toronto, 1967), p. 25.

[27] Sylvie Lacombe, *Rencontre de deux peuples élus: comparaison des ambitions nationale et impériale au Canada entre 1896 et 1920* (Quebec, 2002).

of francophones throughout the country were encouraged by the adoption in 1969 of official bilingualism by the Canadian Parliament. But from the Quebec perspective, the hopes for the survival of a distinct francophone society in North America came to depend on the political future of the one province.

At the same time, British symbols provided a means for protesting French Canadians' position within Canada. The word 'anglais' could be applied to designate all who were not French Catholics: whether British Canadians, Irish, English, or Scots, or indeed other ethnic groups. Many French-Canadian thinkers expressed concerns over 'Anglo-Saxon' control over commerce and banking. Nonetheless, the empirical truth of external economic domination did not give expression to much meaningful anti-English sentiment in French-speaking communities; much of this resentment was instead reserved for the more immediate neighbours, Jews, who lived at least in the city of Montreal in closer proximity to the French neighbourhoods and ironically who spoke French in much higher proportions than did the English speakers. According to the fieldwork of the American sociologist Everett C. Hughes in the 1930s, 'the symbolic Jew receives the more bitter of the attacks which the French Canadians would like to make upon the English or perhaps even upon some of their own leaders and institutions'.[28]

By the 1960s, the association of Britishness and the colonialism experienced by Québécois (a term that replaced 'French Canadian' in Quebec itself) led to new reactions. For many nationalist activists in Quebec in the 1960s, the impetus behind Quebec separatism was the worldwide decolonization movement. While most nationalists understood Quebec as a colony first of English Canada, and secondarily of the United States, the debate over symbols continued to invoke Canada's ties to Britain. Queen Elizabeth's visit to Quebec City in 1964 was met with derision and hostility from nationalist youth, a contrast to the enthusiastic greetings accorded to earlier royal visits. Shouting 'Vive Elizabeth . . . Taylor', the students were beaten with nightsticks by the police, anxious to contain the unrest.[29] The terrorist group Le Front de la Libération du Québec (FLQ) saw a direct continuity between the British conquest of New France and the colonial status of Québécois in the second half of the twentieth century. A 1963 Manifesto decried 'the arrogant domination of Anglo-Saxon colonialism'.[30] Many of the objects which the FLQ attacked had British connotations: the statue of Queen Victoria in Quebec City, mailboxes with 'Royal Mail' written on them, the hotel Le Reine Elizabeth in downtown Montreal. On Victoria Day in 1963, seventy-five sticks of dynamite were exploded outside a munitions hall of the Second Regiment in Montreal. When the violence of the FLQ escalated in 1970,

---

[28] Everett C. Hughes, *French Canada in Transition* (Chicago, 1963), p. 217.
[29] J. L. Granatstein, *Canada, 1957–1967: The Years of Uncertainty and Innovation* (Toronto, 1986), p. 265.
[30] Frank Scott and Michael Oliver, eds., *Quebec States her Case* (Toronto, 1964), p. 83.

their first kidnap victim was the British Trade Commissioner James Cross, an ironic choice given the rapidly decreasing importance of British investment in Quebec by the 1960s.

Although the FLQ was clearly a fringe group, the more general French-Canadian antipathy toward symbols of British colonialism contributed to the transformation of many nation-wide Canadian symbols, from the new Canadian flag in 1964 to the adoption of the official national anthem ('O Canada', replacing 'God Save the Queen') in 1980. Exploring another connection, Québécois nationalist struggles of the last forty years have paralleled in many ways those of Scotland, and nationalists in both nations follow closely the rises and dips in their fortunes, and use each other strategically to illustrate their own political potential.

Even for those politicians most desirous of independence, such calls have always been tempered with a desire to maintain much of the institutional framework within which Quebec has developed: the parliamentary tradition, membership of the Commonwealth, and a 'sovereignty-association' relationship with the rest of Canada. In the aftermath of the first Quebec referendum on sovereignty-association in 1980, which returned a 60 per cent 'no' vote, the Canadian government, led by Quebecker Pierre Trudeau, proposed a radical change in the Canadian constitution, initiated in part to ensure that such amendments would no longer have to be passed by the Westminster Parliament. The debate over the patriation of the Canadian constitution in 1982 created an odd circumstance where the separatist provincial government in Quebec, led by René Lévesque, appealed to Westminster Members of Parliament in their attempt to block the constitutional change. In the end, the Trudeau package of constitutional reforms was passed, without Quebec officially agreeing to the new version. In this negative fashion, just as Quebec had been the pivot around which constitutional change had occurred in 1763, 1774, 1791, 1840, and 1867, the same remained true in 1982. In 1982, however, the Quebec government, the only political jurisdiction representing a majority French-speaking population in North America, itself did not agree to the redefinition of its constitutional links to the rest of the country.

With analogies to the Irish and the Afrikaners, French Canadians occupied ambiguous places within the British Empire. On the one hand, the Empire threatened assimilation into an English-speaking and Protestant world. But within the Empire, it was also possible to occupy niches where distinctive cultures could survive and even flourish, despite the threats that did exist. In the case of French Canada, astute elites, through their mastery of colonial institutions, carved out a political, geographic, and cultural space. Demographic circumstances, including a high but not extraordinary birth rate and the relatively limited immigration to French-speaking areas, confirmed French-Canadian control over certain parts of British North America. Sincere allegiance to the Empire could be strongly felt, but only by a limited fringe of the elite. For French Canadians in Quebec, more than for Acadians or other French-speaking minorities, the British Empire created an ambiguous space where a fair amount of autonomy was possible. One constant aim of French-Canadian political leaders has been to acquire the greatest degree of autonomy, ranging from responsible government within an Imperial setting, to provincial status within an overseas Dominion, to sovereignty-association with the rest of Canada.

From 1763, French Canadians have been in the world of the British Empire and Commonwealth, but they have not been 'of' the British Empire. The ability of the French-Canadian population to develop largely outside significant British cultural and ideological influences is indicative of the interstices created within the broad Empire, and the degree of success political leaders could achieve in working out their own relationship with the larger political entity.

SELECT BIBLIOGRAPHY

GÉRARD BOUCHARD, *Genèse des nations et cultures du Nouveau Monde: essai d'histoire comparée* (Montreal, 2000).

SYLVIE LACOMBE, *Rencontre de deux peuples élus: comparaison des ambitions nationale et impériale au Canada entre 1896 et 1920* (Quebec, 2002).

YVAN LAMONDE, *Histoire sociale des idées au Québec, 1760–1896* (Montreal, 2000).

PHILIP LAWSON, *The Imperial Challenge: Quebec and Britain in the Age of the American Revolution* (Montreal and Kingston, 1989).

JACQUES MONET, *The Last Cannon Shot: A Study of French-Canadian Nationalism, 1837–1850* (Toronto, 1969).

H. V. NELLES, *The Art of Nation-Building: Pageantry and Spectacle at Quebec's Tercentenary* (Toronto, 1999).

ARTHUR I. SILVER, *The French-Canadian Idea of Confederation, 1864–1900* (Toronto, 1982).

PIERRE TOUSIGNANT, 'The Integration of the Province of Quebec into the British Empire, 1763–1791', in *Dictionary of Canadian Biography*, vol. IV: *1771 to 1800* (Toronto, 1979), pp. xxxii–xlix.

11

Aboriginal People of Canada and the British Empire

Sarah Carter

At the time of the conquest of New France most of Canada was Aboriginal territory, with only a few scattered zones of contact with Europeans. The entrenchment of settler control was a protracted and uneven process and for many years settler authority was limited, fragile, and contested. Initially Aboriginal people were able to ignore, challenge, or creatively negotiate the advance of colonial rule. However, the establishment of settler dominance and privilege throughout much of Canada by the later half of the nineteenth century had severely reduced the capacity for Aboriginal resistance, resulting in a vast imbalance of power between Aboriginal people and newcomers. In settler colonies, colonial desire focused on land and its resources,[1] but although Canada shared many features with other British settler colonies, the diversity of Aboriginal people, their varied environments and resources, and the unique patterns of contact with newcomers meant that there was no single or monolithic pattern of encounter with settlers. Aboriginal land for agriculture was desired by settlers in many localities, but not in others where Aboriginal labour was necessary to extract resources, and where the land did not invite intensive settlement, as in the massive territories of the fur trade that persisted well into the twentieth century. Vast regions of Canada did not begin their British existence as colonies of settlement, as typified by Newfoundland and the territory of the Hudson's Bay Company (HBC) where land was claimed by Britain through metropolitan-based commercial interests. Nor did the Imperial government pursue a consistent, uniform policy toward the colonies of British North America; rather, there was an ad hoc set of responses to local conditions, which were in part the result of the initiatives, politics, and diplomacy of Aboriginal nations seeking to direct the structure of their relationship with the British.

---

[1] See Patrick Wolfe, 'History and Imperialism: A Century of Theory, from Marx to Postcolonialism', *American Historical Review*, 102 (1997), pp. 388–420, and Patrick Wolfe, *Settler Colonialism and the Transformation of Anthropology* (London, 1999), pp. 1–3.

After the Conquest, Aboriginal nations made it clear to the British that they did not consider their sovereignty extinguished. 'Englishman, although you have conquered the French you have not yet conquered us!' declared Ojibwa chief Minavavana at Michilimackinac.[2] The British did not initially understand the power and sovereignty of Aboriginal nations, and they tried to abandon the French practice of distributing annual presents of ammunition, firearms, and blankets. To Aboriginal nations, gifts were a symbolic reaffirmation of relations based on trade, military alliances, or peaceful coexistence. When the British failed to meet such conditions in 1763, Pontiac, an Ottawa leader, led an uprising that year which successfully persuaded the British to resume the policy of giving gifts. The British continued this policy of conciliation and annual presents until the end of the War of 1812. Indeed, the British Indian Department, created in 1755, was staffed mainly by military officers, 'able and energetic' men who established 'an enviable record of reconciling British with Indian interests [which] rested not on their capacity to coerce or command Indians but on their powers of persuasion and their observance of the traditional imperial position that relations between Britain and the Indians constituted relations between separate nations'.[3]

The Pontiac rising also demonstrated that Aboriginal nations were determined to defend their lands from intruders. The Proclamation of 1763 arose out of the need to formulate foundational principles of coexistence between Aboriginal people and settlers as land in the Ohio valley was threatened by the expansion of settlement. The Proclamation was not a unilateral declaration of the Crown's will; Aboriginal nations were active in its formulation and ratification. The result was a document that embodied competing goals and visions, as Aboriginal people were concerned with preserving their lands and sovereignty, while Britain was attempting to acquire territory and jurisdiction. The Proclamation declared that all lands forming the part of British North America that had not been ceded to or purchased by the British were to be considered 'reserved lands' for Aboriginal people. The document implied that no lands were to be taken without their consent and that their territorial integrity and decision-making power over their lands was to be respected and protected. Colonial governments were forbidden to survey or grant unceded lands, British subjects were prohibited from settling on unceded lands, and private individuals were prohibited from purchasing Indian lands. But the Proclamation also outlined a policy designed to extinguish Aboriginal rights to land, for the British had included statements that claimed 'dominion' and 'sovereignty' over lands reserved as Aboriginal territory. However, only officials of the Crown could purchase land from Aboriginal people at public meetings or assemblies. The Proclamation was presented for

---

[2] Quoted in John Borrows, 'Wampum at Niagara: The Royal Proclamation, Canadian Legal History, and Self-Government', in Michael Asch, (ed.), *Aboriginal and Treaty Rights in Canada: Essays of Law, Equality and Respect for Difference* (Vancouver, 1997), p. 157.

[3] Noel Dyck, *What is the Indian 'Problem': Tutelage and Resistance in Canadian Indian Administration* (St John's, 1991), p. 48.

affirmation to a multi-nation assembly at Niagara in 1764, where it was accepted by a number of First Nations. While the written document conveys the Crown's view of the agreement, oral sources have preserved the perspective of the First Nations people, who understood the Proclamation as Britain's solemn pledge to recognize and protect Aboriginal rights and interests.[4]

These principles became the foundation of the relationship between the British Crown and the First Nations, and they provided the procedural rules for subsequent treaty making. This approach was distinct from the one adopted in Australia, where territory was acquired by the British under the 'convenient legal fiction that by the "occupation of land belonging to no one", the doctrine of *terra nullius* applied'. Maori rights in New Zealand were enshrined in the 1840 Treaty of Waitangi, through which Britain gained sovereignty and the exclusive right to pre-empt Maori land.[5] But the principles of the proclamation were applied differently throughout the colonies of British North America. For example, although the Proclamation of 1763 was intended to apply to the Maritime colonies, it was not acted upon by the colonial governments there. The British took the view that the land rights of the Mi'kmaq and Maliseet had been extinguished first by French occupation, and then by the 1713 Treaty of Utrecht, which granted Britain title to Acadia. This was not the position taken by the Mi'kmaq and Maliseet who consistently maintained that they had only granted usage and usufruct to the French, and who did not view themselves as conquered by the British. The Mi'kmaq challenged British claims and fought for their lands with the assistance of the French, but the collapse of French power brought an end to this resistance.

Because the Maritime colonies experienced rapid and massive settlement, beginning with the arrival of the Loyalists in the late eighteenth century, a shift in the balance of power between Aboriginal people and newcomers occurred earlier there than elsewhere in British North America. The Loyalists did not feel bound by the provisions of the royal proclamation because they believed that the land was owed to them because of their loyalty to the Crown. In Nova Scotia the land base of the Mi'kmaq was greatly eroded by the nineteenth century; their game, fur, and fish stocks were much reduced, and they lacked the resources to develop an agricultural economy. No Aboriginal territorial rights were recognized except for the right to hunt and fish 'at the pleasure of the sovereign', and the Mi'kmaq had to petition the colonial government for grants to occupy their own territories. Some small, scattered areas were designated as reserves, but the land and locations were poor, and white squatters also continually invaded the reserves. In 1841 Chief Paussamigh Pemmeenauweet appealed to Queen Victoria: 'All these woods

---

[4] Borrows, 'Wampum at Niagara', pp. 161, 168.

[5] Paul Havemann, 'Comparing Indigenous Peoples' Rights in Australia, Canada and New Zealand: Some Signposts', in Paul Havemann, (ed.), *Indigenous Peoples' Rights in Australia, Canada and New Zealand* (Oxford, 2001), p. 8.

[were] once ours. Our Fathers possessed them all. Now we cannot cut a Tree to warm our wigwams in Winter unless the white Man please . . . Pity your poor Indians in Nova Scotia. White Man has taken all that was ours.'6 Queen Victoria asked the Colonial Secretary to look into the matter, but little came of the initiative. Similarly there were few concrete results from an 1859 Act designed to compel squatters to pay for the reserve land they claimed. Electing instead to defy the legislation, few squatters paid anything at all. By the mid-nineteenth century the Mi'kmaq were seen as a 'dying race', upon which expenditures for education or economic assistance would be wasted.

The Proclamation was also ignored in New Brunswick where only tiny reserves were set aside. The Proclamation was even disregarded in Cape Breton and Prince Edward Island, which had been newly acquired in 1763, and where the rationale could not be used that title had been ceded to the British before 1763. No land at all was set aside for the Aboriginal occupants of Prince Edward Island until 1859, when only a tiny grant was made on the Morell River. In 1870, Britain's Aborigines Protection Society raised the funds to purchase the offshore Lennox Island and seven Aboriginal families were settled there.7

'In the colony of Newfoundland it may therefore be stated that we have exterminated the natives.' This was the conclusion of the 1837 *Report of the Select Committee on Aborigines* that examined the impact of British settlement on the Indigenous people of the Empire.8 The last known surviving Beothuk, a woman named Shanawdithit, died in 1829 of tuberculosis in a St John's hospital. The cause of the total extinction of the Aboriginal people of Newfoundland remains the subject of much debate. The theories advanced to explain the catastrophe include the calamitous results of encroachment on their territory and competition for limited resources that led to starvation, the introduction of European diseases, the Beothuk's withdrawal into the interior, and their armed conflicts with the Mi'kmaq along with European hunters and trappers. However, there were naval officers, governors, settlers, merchants, and visitors to Newfoundland who were gravely concerned about the fate of the Beothuk, and who feared that 'the English nation, like the Spanish, may have affixed to its Character the indelible reproach of having extirpated a whole race of People'.9 But various attempts to end a cruel cycle of altercations and retaliation were ineffective.

The Aboriginal people of Quebec occupied the territories beyond the settled areas along the St Lawrence at the time of the conquest. There were also a number of Aboriginal settlements within the colony, and these were granted

6 Arthur J. Ray, *'I Have Lived Here Since the World Began': An Illustrated History of Canada's Native People* (Toronto, 1996), p. 147.

7 Olive Dickason, *Canada's First Nations: A History of Founding Peoples from Earliest Times* (Toronto, 1992), p. 232.

8 Quoted in Ingeborg Marshall, *A History and Ethnography of the Beothuk* (Montreal, 1996), pp. 227–8.

9 Quoted ibid., p. 120.

to missionary orders for the purpose of attracting people to the Catholic faith. Aboriginal land in Quebec was initially to be protected by the Proclamation of 1763, but the arrival of the Loyalists led to an abrupt change in British policy, as the greater priority became making land available quickly. Under a 1791 ordinance of the colonial government, any settler who took an oath of allegiance to the Crown could settle on Aboriginal land, and the Constitutional Act of 1791, which divided Quebec into Upper and Lower Canada, provided for free land to entice settlement. After 1791 the Aboriginal policies of Upper and Lower Canada diverged. The Proclamation was largely ignored in Lower Canada and settlers steadily advanced on arable Aboriginal land, although the Canadian Shield country to the north of the colony remained almost exclusively Aboriginal territory throughout much of the nineteenth century. Settlers encroached even on the reserved lands set aide by the religious orders, such as at Oka (Kanesatake) where the Sulpicians began to sell parcels of the reserve to settlers.

It was in Upper Canada, and then in the United Province of Canada (following the Act of Union of 1841), that the legal, legislative, economic, bureaucratic, and spatial framework designed to entrench settler dominance and privilege was first established. Upper Canada was the 'laboratory' for the policies that were eventually extended throughout much of the rest of Canada. In Upper Canada the principles of the royal proclamation were observed, or at least an 'illusion' of adhering to these principles was created, as settlement advanced on Aboriginal land.[10] Upper Canada remained vulnerable to attacks by the United States until the War of 1812, and the British Indian Department continued to nurture the support of Aboriginal allies by maintaining a nation-to-nation relationship with the self-governing Aboriginal nations. These alliances were useful for military reasons, but they also assisted in the peaceful surrender of Aboriginal lands for settlement. To accommodate the Loyalists, land cession treaties were made with the Anishinabeg (including the Ojibwas, Ottawas, and the Algonquians). The earliest of these treaties was with the Mississaugas in 1781 when a strip of land on the Niagara River was acquired in exchange for 300 suits of clothing. In the decade after 1815 alone, nearly 7 million acres of Aboriginal land were surrendered. The earliest treaties were purchases in which a single payment of cash or goods was offered, and the British regarded them as transactions in real estate through which the Crown acquired complete title to the surrendered tracts. The Aboriginal people most likely had a different conception of these agreements, not believing that the land was sold once and for all, but rather agreeing to share their land. Large councils were not always held as specified in the Proclamation, the treaties were not always fully explained, and oral promises made by the colonial authorities were later ignored.

The end of the War of 1812 marked a turning point in relations between Britain and the First Nations of Upper Canada. Courting Aboriginal support

[10] Ray, *'I Have Lived Here'*, pp. 151, 155.

for purposes of military alliances was no longer a cornerstone of British policy and officials in Britain began to lobby for an end to the costly policy of granting annual presents. In 1818 the Lords of the Treasury decided that the colonies should pay for the acquisition of land, and a system of perpetual annuities was devised to replace the lump sum payments. The annual interest payments of the purchasers of the land would fund the annuity payments, which became a feature of all treaties with the Crown. Aboriginal leaders welcomed the annual payments as a symbolic indication of an enduring partnership with the British. Aboriginal communities had been diminished through warfare, disease, and the loss of their game resources, and they became a minority population in most parts of Upper Canada because of the massive influx of Loyalists and British immigrants. Aboriginal leaders recognized the need to come to a suitable accommodation with the newcomers and to devise strategies to cope with new economic realities. In the light of their altered circumstances in the early nineteenth century, a number of Aboriginal nations of Upper Canada, such as the Mississauga of Credit River, with the assistance of missionaries, experimented with their own development initiatives and took steps to establish agriculture. Many Algonquians rapidly adopted farming after 1820, growing wheat, oats, peas, potatoes, and other crops, and often selling these products to settlers.[11] Aboriginal leaders thus sought to maintain their cultures and societies within a new agricultural context. They saw education as a key to the future, and a tool for adaptation. They wished to build a progressive partnership with the settlers that would assist them to establish a new economic foundation for their communities.[12]

Chief Superintendent of Indian Affairs Major General H. C. Darling proposed in 1828 that his department should take the lead in 'civilizing' Aboriginal people by encouraging them to settle on reserves and take up agriculture. In 1829 Lieutenant-Governor Sir James Kempt endorsed this policy, which embodied the essence of Upper Canada's Indian reserve policy. Aboriginal people were to be provided with land for their 'cultivation and support' and with 'religious improvement, education and instruction in husbandry'. They were to be given assistance in building their houses, and they would receive rations, seed, and agricultural implements.[13] In 1830 the jurisdiction over the management of Indian affairs in Upper Canada was shifted from military to civil authorities, and control was given to the Lieutenant-Governor. In Lower Canada, authority over Indian affairs remained with the military secretary. (With the Union of 1841 the

[11] E. S. Rogers and Flora Tobobondung, 'Parry Island Farmers: A Period of Change in the Way of Life of the Algonkians of Southern Ontario', in David Brez Carlisle, (ed.), *Contributions to Canadian Ethnology* (Ottawa, 1975).

[12] John S. Milloy, 'The Early Indian Acts: Development Strategy and Constitutional Change', in Ian A. L. Getty and Antoine S. Lussiter, (eds), *As Long as the Sun Shines and Water Flows: A Reader in Canadian Native Studies* (Vancouver, 1983), p. 60.

[13] R. J. Surtees, 'The Development of an Indian Reserve Policy in Canada', *Ontario History*, 61 (1969), p. 92.

two offices of the Indian Department were amalgamated and placed under the authority of the Governor-General.) While the administrative changes in Upper Canada were intended to facilitate the programme of reserves and agriculture, the establishment of reserves remained ad hoc in nature, and promises to create reserves were not part of treaty agreements until the Robinson treaties of 1850, which covered large areas of Anishinabeg land around the Great Lakes.

This change in approach to the administration of Indian affairs was due in part to pressure from the humanitarian lobby in Britain, as well as from missionaries in Canada and elsewhere in the Empire who besieged the British Parliament and the Colonial Office with complaints and criticisms about the treatment of Indigenous peoples throughout the Empire. They urged that the Aboriginal people of Canada be encouraged to become self-supporting farmers. With massive immigration to Upper Canada there were fewer areas for the Anishinabeg to retreat to, and land had to be reserved for them. However, the reserve policy and the promotion of agriculture also facilitated the transfer of Aboriginal land into white hands. Aboriginal people had to be settled in order to farm, and thus would no longer need their former much larger tracts to sustain their fishing and hunting economies.

Efforts to create model agricultural reserve communities were beset with difficulties; the grants from the British government were small and problems arose because of the decentralized nature of the Indian Department. Yet there were signs of progress. In his last dispatch as Lieutenant-Governor of Upper Canada from 1828 to 1836, Sir John Colborne wrote of the successful nature of reserve policy and the promotion of agriculture. However, Colborne's successor disagreed. Sir Francis Bond Head, Lieutenant-Governor of Upper Canada from 1836 to 1838, believed that Aboriginal people had little inclination to become farmers and saw efforts in this direction as a waste of time. He proposed instead a policy of 'removal' or segregation from European settlers. His plan was to remove the Anishinabeg from their territories and relocate them to Manitoulin Island. Head consistently defended his proposal on humanitarian grounds, arguing that 'The greatest Kindness we can perform toward these intelligent, simple-minded People, is to remove and fortify them as much as possible from all Communication with Whites.'[14] Head believed that Aboriginal people were doomed to extinction, but felt that removal would at least permit them to disappear more slowly. He ultimately managed to convince a significant number of the Mississauga to surrender their lands and relocate to Manitoulin Island.

Many officials in the Colonial Office were genuinely concerned to protect Aboriginal people against the rapacious settler governments, particularly Lord Glenelg, the Colonial Secretary from 1835 to 1839, a committed evangelical

---

[14] Theodore Binnema and Kevin Hutchings, 'The Emigrant and the Noble Savage: Sir Francis Bond Head's Romantic Approach to Aboriginal Policy in Upper Canada, 1836–1838', *Journal of Canadian Studies*, 39/1 (Winter 2005), p. 122.

Christian with close ties to the humanitarian movement. While Lord Glenelg was cautiously receptive to the plan, Head's removal scheme aroused a chorus of opposition from Aboriginal people, missionaries, and philanthropists in British North America and in Britain. Just as Head was promoting his plan, the 1837 *Report of the British Select Committee on Aboriginal Peoples* was being compiled. One of its central findings was that various colonial governments had engaged in or permitted the wholesale theft of Aboriginal lands. The report urgently called for intervention in Upper Canada 'on behalf of hapless individuals whose landed possessions, where they have been assigned to them, are daily plundered by their more enlightened white brethren'.[15] The committee concluded that Indigenous people had a legal right to their land that had to be recognized by settlers, and enforced by colonial governments. It also urged that Indigenous people be accorded the full legal rights of British subjects, and further recommended that Aboriginal policy be kept under British control rather than be transferred to colonial officials. The Aborigines Protection Society protested against Head's removal plan and the Mississauga leader and Methodist preacher the Reverend Peter Jones (also known as Kahkewaquonaby, or Sacred Feathers) met with Colonial Secretary Lord Glenelg in 1838 and explained his people's apprehensions. The 'removal' policy being pursued in the United States from 1836 fuelled these fears. When rebellion broke out in 1837 in both Canadas, some Aboriginal people once again rose to the defence of the British Crown. With this display of loyalty the objections of Aboriginal leaders to Head's plan became more difficult to ignore and his policy was abandoned.

The abandonment of Head's policy under pressure from Aboriginal leaders and their humanitarian supporters demonstrates that settler dominance and privilege remained incomplete. It thus became apparent to many settlers that further measures were needed to ensure that Aboriginal people had no power or influence in the new order. In Canada and the other British settler colonies, as in Britain, there was an increasingly democratic franchise, but this did not include Aboriginal peoples. Moreover, with the grant of responsible government there was a shift in power from Britain to the settler colonies that carried with it serious consequences for Aboriginal people.[16] By the mid-nineteenth century Aboriginal people were no longer regarded as bold warriors to be nurtured and conciliated, but as 'savages' requiring the protection and guidance of the 'civilized'. Canadian legislation of 1850, reaffirmed in the 1857 Gradual Civilization Act, represented the first direct intervention by the Canadian Assembly into Aboriginal affairs, and from that time onward the Indian Department increasingly became an aggressive and disruptive instrument of assimilation. A curious and contradictory piece of

---

[15] Quoted in Sidney L. Harring, *White Man's Law: Native People in Nineteenth-Century Canadian Jurisprudence* (Toronto, 1998), p. 25.

[16] Julie Evans, Patricia Grimshaw, David Philips, and Shurlee Swain, *Equal Subjects, Unequal Rights: Indigenous Peoples in British Settler Colonies, 1830–1910* (Manchester, 2003), p. 36.

legislation, the 1857 Gradual Civilization Act stipulated in the preamble that the measure was designed to integrate Aboriginal people into Canadian society and to remove all legal distinctions between Aboriginal people and other Canadians. Yet the Act actually established such distinctions by creating an inferior and distinct legal status for Indians as wards of the government. [17] Indians had none of the rights and powers of British subjects. They were denied the franchise. They could not buy or sell reserve land. They were not competent to sue or be sued. Held in this unique legal category, they were to be 'gradually' trained for the full responsibilities of citizenship. Before this legislation, Aboriginal males of the United Canadas who met the legal property qualifications could vote on the same terms as white settlers; thereafter they were excluded from the franchise. They had no voice or representation in government and could not run for office. They were excluded from participation in the decision-making body that drew up the discriminatory provisions to which they were subject. To qualify for enfranchisement, a male had to demonstrate that he was free of debt, could read and write in either French or English, and was of good moral character. He could be awarded full ownership of 20 hectares of reserve land, but would then cease to be an Indian and had to renounce his right to share in any communal payments. If the scheme had worked, it would have eliminated Aboriginal people's claim to special status, and the expenses associated with that status. This was the goal of the administrators of Indian affairs well into the twentieth century, but Aboriginal people typically expressed little interest in taking advantage of the enfranchisement process.

In New Zealand, by contrast, the Maori were recognized as having the rights of British subjects, and four Maori seats were allocated in the House of Representatives in 1867. Yet Maori communal land tenure prevented them from qualifying for a franchise based on individual property ownership, and the four seats they were allocated did not represent a genuine commitment to the democratic representation of the Maori. In Australia, Aboriginal people were not explicitly excluded from the franchise, but various residential qualifications and other clauses effectively disenfranchised most of them. In each of these British colonies, including Canada, 'settlers moved quickly to counter any threat, real or imagined, that indigenous peoples might pose to white hegemony in the body politic'.[18]

The Gradual Civilization Act thus disenfranchised Aboriginal people who might have qualified if they had the requisite property and made it difficult and unappealing to apply for enfranchisement. It contravened the recommendation

[17] John Tobias, 'Protection, Civilization, Assimilation: An Outline History of Canada's Indian Policy', in Getty and Lussiter, (eds), *As Long as the Sun Shines and Water Flows*, p. 42.
[18] Patricia Grimshaw, Robert Reynolds, and Shurlee Swain, 'The Paradox of "Ultra-Democratic" Government: Indigenous Civil Rights in the Nineteenth-Century New Zealand, Canada and Australia', in Diane Kirkby and Catharine Coleborne, (eds), *Law, History, Colonialism: The Reach of Empire* (Manchester, 2001), p. 78.

of the 1837 Select Committee, which had called on colonial authorities to accord the full legal rights of British subjects to Aboriginal people.[19] Following Confederation, Ontario and Manitoba specifically disqualified Indians who received annuities from the provincial franchise, and no province recognized land in common as a basis for qualification. When British Columbia entered Confederation in 1871, the Local Franchise Act was revised to exclude all Indians (and Chinese), irrespective of their economic or citizen status. Similarly, the 1886 North-West Territories Act extended the vote to all male residents in what would become Alberta and Saskatchewan but excluded Indians and aliens.

Aboriginal people campaigned for the repeal of the Gradual Civilization Act, but in 1860 authority over Indian affairs was transferred from the Colonial Office to the government of the United Province of Canada, and this decision left Aboriginal people at the mercy of the colonial legislature. Aboriginal people were not consulted at all about the transfer, nor were they consulted about the meanings and implications of Canadian Confederation in 1867. Through the British North America Act and the 1876 Indian Act, the federal government took extensive control over Aboriginal nations, their land, and their finances. Traditional forms of government were replaced by systems of government controlled by the Indian agents. The Indian Act singled out those defined as Indians for penalties and prohibitions that applied to no other Canadians. In the years to come amendments and additions were made to this repressive Act. Produce could not be sold without the permission of an Indian agent, people were prohibited from practising their religious and spiritual ceremonies, and they were compelled to send their children to residential schools.

A significant feature of the legislation later incorporated into the 1876 Indian Act was the effort to impose Euro-Canadian social organization and cultural values. The 1876 Act assumed that women were subordinate to males and derived rights from their husbands or fathers. Women were excluded from voting in band elections. They had to prove to government officials that they were of good 'moral' character before they were entitled to receive an inheritance. Upon marriage to a non-Indian, a woman lost her status as a registered Indian, as would her children, and they would not be permitted to reside on her reserve. Even if her non-Indian husband died, her status would not be affected—only remarriage to a status Indian man could reinstate her. On the other hand, white women who married Indian men, along with their children, obtained legal status as Indians, and all could reside on reserve land. Since this was much less common than Aboriginal women marrying non-Aboriginal men, this clause served to remove many women and children from Indian status, thereby reducing government spending and responsibilities.[20]

---

[19] Harring, *White Man's Law*, 24.
[20] Victoria Freeman, 'Attitudes toward "Miscegenation" in Canada, the United States, New Zealand and Australia, 1860–1914', *Native Studies Review*, 16 (2005), p. 51.

As military allies of the British, Aboriginal nations had been asked to give their loyalty to a just, paternal British monarch. Many leaders had been presented with George III medals, which were passed down in families through generations. Medals and invocations of a just monarch were also used in HBC territory from the late eighteenth century to inspire loyalty.[21] By the early nineteenth century there was a well-established tradition in Aboriginal oratory of incorporating references to the British monarchy in kinship terms. This tradition confirmed that the Aboriginal peoples were the equals of Europeans and called on the monarch's representatives to act with the honour and integrity of the Crown. Petitions were made to the monarch's representatives in British North America for the redress of grievances suffered at the hands of local legislators and settlers. Aboriginal people also travelled to England to place their concerns directly before the monarch. For example, the Ojibwa Nahnebahwequa, or Catherine Sutton, was granted an interview with Queen Victoria in the spring of 1860.[22] The 1860 royal tour of the Prince of Wales also presented an occasion for Aboriginal people to 'claim public attention, affirm their own loyalism and cultural integrity, and demand redress of political [and economic] grievances'.[23]

A legacy of the approach devised and elaborated in Upper Canada was the smug insistence that Canada's treatment of Aboriginal people was just, benevolent, and generous. 'The liberal treatment of the Indians, and the solicitude for their well-being . . . are the outgrowth of that benevolent policy which before Confederation attained its highest excellence in Upper Canada,' was how an eminent judge put it in 1885.[24] But while 'Euro-Canadians were being prepared for a fully functioning role within the empire, including local self-government, economic prosperity, and rich social and cultural lives, Indians were being prepared for a position on the margins of Canadian society, living on small reserves under the despotic control of petty local officials, deprived of their own cultures and traditions, unable to vote or to sit on any of the decision-making bodies that influenced their lives, and subject to the regular incursions of settlers'.[25]

The system devised in Upper Canada was transported throughout much of the rest of Canada by the late nineteenth century, although there were local developments and variations. In British Columbia, before the proprietary colony of Vancouver Island was created in 1849, settlers and Aboriginal people had not competed for the land. It was the fur trade that brought Aboriginal and white people together and there were only a few small zones of contact. Competition

---

[21] Sarah Carter, '"Your Great Mother across the Salt Sea": Prairie First Nations, the British Monarchy and the Vice Regal Connection to 1900', *Manitoba History*, 48 (Autumn/Winter 2004/5), pp. 34–48.

[22] Donald B. Smith, 'Nahnebahwequay (1824–1865): "Upright Woman"', in Neil Semple, (ed.), *Canadian Methodist Historical Society Papers* (Toronto, 2001), pp., 13, 74–105.

[23] Ian Radforth, 'Performance, Politics and Representation: Aboriginal People and 1860 Royal Tour of Canada', *Canadian Historical Review*, 84 (2003) p. 2.

[24] Quoted in Harring, *White Man's Law*, p. 11.   [25] Ibid., p. 12.

for land began in earnest when colonial British Columbia was created in 1858. In British Columbia the Proclamation of 1763 was disregarded and the treaty process was almost entirely circumvented. A number of treaties were made by Governor James Douglas with Vancouver Island First Nations in the 1850s and 1860s, and small reserves were set aside, but this process did not continue on the rest of the island or on the mainland. The issue of whether the land was the Crown's or whether the Crown's sovereignty was burdened by Aboriginal claims was never squarely faced. James Trutch, Chief Commissioner of Lands and Works, was the major architect of British Columbia's Aboriginal land policy in the years between Douglas's retirement in 1864 and the colony's entry into Confederation in 1871. Trutch completely sidestepped the issue of Aboriginal title and even moved to diminish the meagre reserve lands that had been set aside by the time of his appointment. People who knew next to nothing about Aboriginal people carried out their surveying in great haste, and there was no provision for protecting the boundaries of the reserves that were already established.

When British Columbia joined Confederation, responsibility for Aboriginal affairs shifted in principle from the Colonial Office to the federal government. But unlike in the North-West Territories, the provincial government of British Columbia retained control over the allocation of land. Although the Canadian government intended that treaties, fairly generous reserves, and annuities be extended to British Columbia, the British Columbia government resented the intrusions of a distant, new authority. In 1876, a joint federal-provincial Indian Reserve Commission was appointed to allocate reserves, and the treaty approach of recognizing Aboriginal title was shelved. Gilbert Sproat, a determined Indian Reserve commissioner 1878–80, hoped to continue the Douglas approach, but he was met with a chorus of protest. This was the moment in British Columbia's history when a progressive partnership between Aboriginal and non-Aboriginal people could have been forged, but Sproat's voice was drowned out and he resigned. Governor-General Lord Dufferin was outspoken in his condemnation of British Columbia's policies. Writing in 1874 to the Secretary of State for the Colonies, Dufferin declared that the honour of the Crown was at stake, as was Canada's reputation for embracing a 'just and humane policy'. However, Dufferin's appeal to London had no impact. In 1880 the federal government backed down from insisting on treaties and fairly generous reserves. By the late 1870s the federal government had acquired a considerable land base in British Columbia through the 'Railway Belt', and this was an incentive for the Dominion to accept the provincial view on Aboriginal rights and title.[26]

Aboriginal people responded to this by protesting their increasing marginalization in their homeland through letters, speeches, and petitions. They insisted that land was the priority, and not only for hunting and fishing. They also required arable land that would permit them to farm or ranch. Aboriginal leaders drew on

[26] Quoted in Harring, pp. 137, 199.

an image of a just monarch to highlight the injustices they faced, even though there were no treaties to cement that relationship. As elsewhere in Canada the protests were dismissed as the work of devious, self-interested 'outside agitators'. The Indian Act was also used to discourage any political organizing, and this was applied to residents on the reserves of British Columbia despite the fact that they had not entered into treaties.

In 1870 the Dominion of Canada acquired the territories of the HBC. From the time of its 1670 Royal Charter, the HBC had purported to assert jurisdiction over about 40 per cent of modern Canada, but this remained Aboriginal territory until the 1870 transfer. Because of its relative isolation, difficulties with transportation, and the northern climate, settlers did not begin to covet this territory until the latter part of the nineteenth century. The HBC also deliberately discouraged any settlement that might alter the environment upon which the fur trade depended. Aboriginal people were required to trap and transport furs, and to act as middlemen to more distant groups. European traders also depended on them for their geographical knowledge, map-making skills, clothing, footwear, medicines, and food.

The vast majority of the Aboriginal people of the west were only tangentially involved in the fur trade and had little to no face-to-face contact with Europeans until the late nineteenth century. In the world beyond the posts and small settlements, the HBC had little impact and no jurisdiction. The fur trade posts were sites of cultural, social, and economic interaction that created bonds between Aboriginal and non-Aboriginal people leading to accommodation and coexistence. A way of life emerged that mixed Aboriginal and European economics, diplomacy, and laws. Marriages between traders and Aboriginal women created and cemented business and kinship ties. However, some aspects of the trade were destructive. The fur trade boat brigades carried diseases such as smallpox into new areas, and these maladies decimated Aboriginal populations. The traders introduced alcohol, a drug that proved exceptionally harmful to families and communities. The fur trade also resulted in the ruthless exploitation of the fur-bearing animals of entire districts.

A large Métis population had emerged in the western interior by the early nineteenth century. The Métis were of diverse ancestries, including in particular those who had French and Aboriginal roots (they were predominantly French speaking, or they spoke 'Michif', a patois mixture of French and Aboriginal languages), and mostly English-speaking individuals of Aboriginal and English or Scottish ancestry. Some Métis were absorbed into Aboriginal communities and spoke Cree or Ojibway. Mixed-ancestry women married European traders including those of the highest ranks. However, by mid-century it became more respectable and acceptable for HBC officers to have white wives.[27] While there

---

[27] Sylvia Van Kirk, *'Many Tender Ties': Women in Fur-Trade Society, 1670–1870* (Winnipeg, 1980).

were many outposts of Métis settlement, Red River (Winnipeg) was heartland and homeland to many Métis, and it was the first community to experience the shift from trading post to settlement colony. From the late 1840s, the 'Clear Grit' Party of Canada West argued that Canada's Manifest Destiny included the absorption of Rupert's Land, and there was talk of a railway to link Canada with the Pacific coast. Since the Métis, in the majority at Red River, occupied what was to become the 'gateway' to the west, it became important to deny that the Métis actually owned the land they occupied, and to discredit their ability to bring the land and resources in question under proper production. During the 1869 negotiations between Canada and the HBC, it was useful for Canada to insist that the rightful owners of the land were the First Nations, not the HBC, since the company would then not require compensation.[28] But Canada was compelled to give the HBC a cash settlement of $1.5 million for approximately 7 million acres of 'their' lands. This was Canada's own exercise in empire building, but it also signified an important project of the British Empire, creating opportunities for 'English Lands and English Homes in the Far West'.[29]

All of these arrangements were made without consultation with the Aboriginal residents of western Canada, who were not informed of the conditions of the transfer. Preliminary surveys were undertaken to expedite the route from Canada to Red River in advance of the transfer, even though there was no effective European possession or control of the region, and Aboriginal people continued to retain sovereignty there.[30] Under the terms of the transfer the Canadian government agreed to fulfil certain conditions concerning the Indian residents, but almost no mention was made of the Métis. This constituted an astonishing absence of any acknowledgement of responsibility, since many Métis were the children of generations of HBC employees. Under the leadership of Louis Riel, the Métis of Red River, particularly those of French and Aboriginal ancestry, resisted the transfer of authority. They established a provisional government at Red River in 1869 and demanded recognition of their land rights, the right to vote for all males (including Indians), and representation in the House of Commons. They also called for bilingual institutions, denominational schools, and provincial status. A military expedition under the command of Colonel Garnet Wolseley was dispatched to suppress the Métis resistance. By the time Wolseley's force arrived there in August 1870, the resistance had ended and Riel had fled. Canada conceded a number of the Métis' demands in the Manitoba Act of 1870. One of its terms provided for the distribution of 1.4 million acres of public land to the 'Half-Breed' families. However, for reasons that are still hotly

[28] Alex J. Russell, *The Red River Country, Hudson's Bay and North-West Territories, Considered in Relation to Canada* (Ottawa, 1869), pp. 151–2.

[29] Revd J. Wagstaff, *English Lands and English Homes in the Far West: Being the Story of a Holiday Tour in Canada* (Macclesfield, 1891).

[30] Kent McNeil, 'Sovereignty on the Northern Plains: Indian, European, American and Canadian Claims', *Journal of the West*, 39/3 (Summer 2000), pp. 10–18.

debated, most of the Métis of the new province of Manitoba did not receive their land; many left and moved further west.[31] In 1885, similar concerns about land rights led to a second Métis resistance in Saskatchewan, also under the leadership of Riel. The 'rebellion' was suppressed with an enormous show of force: 5,000 men were sent to Saskatchewan under the command of Major General Frederick Middleton, a veteran of the British Empire's 'small wars'.[32] Riel was captured and hanged in November 1885. Ontario was insistent that Manitoba and the west should be developed in the image of Ontario by central Canadians, and that the Métis should be dispersed.

In the late 1860s and early 1870s, the First Nations of the west were also deeply concerned about the news that their land had been 'sold' to Canada without any consultation. In 1868 Chief Fox, a Saulteaux of the Red River area, declared to the Governor of the HBC: 'We hear that you are trying to sell our country to other people, you never bought this country from us. How is it that you want to sell what is not yours?' [33] Chief Fox was not alone in raising such points. Aboriginal leaders throughout the north-west expressed concern not only about the transfer, but also about the smallpox epidemic of 1869–70 that had decimated their numbers, the rapid disappearance of the buffalo, and the arrival of the troops at Red River. They also asked for the cattle, tools, and agricultural implements that were essential to permit them to establish agriculture. In order to protect their jurisdiction, survey and telegraph crews were prevented from coming into Aboriginal territory before treaties were negotiated. Faced with an uncertain future, the First Nations sought alliances, agreements, or treaties that would assist them to acquire economic security, assure their cultural survival, and help establish peaceful, equitable relations with the newcomers.

By 1870 the federal government had compelling reasons to enter into treaties with the First Nations. Westward expansion was seen as a national priority. Aboriginal title was to be 'removed' with as little expense as possible. There was also concern about the warfare that prevailed across the border in the American west. In the 1870s, seven treaties were concluded with the First Nations of western Canada, and the process continued to the north with Treaties 8 to 11 (a process completed in 1921). Although this was a Canadian initiative, the treaty commissioners claimed to be representatives of Queen Victoria; they said they were speaking for her and acting under her detailed instructions. Both sides drew extensively on kinship terms. At Treaty 6, for example, Lieutenant-Governor Alexander Morris said: 'You are, like me and my friends who are with me, children of the Queen. We are of the same blood, the same God

---

[31] Sarah Carter, *Aboriginal People and Colonizers of Western Canada to 1900* (Toronto, 1999), pp. 109–11.

[32] Walter Hildebrandt, *The Battle of Batoche: British Small Warfare and the Entrenched Métis* (Ottawa, 1985).

[33] *Nor'Wester*, 25 May 1868.

made us and the same Queen rules over us.'[34] Aboriginal negotiators also made references to Queen Victoria as their mother, from whom they could expect maternal generosity, sharing, and nurturance, and the treaty commissioners were addressed as 'brothers'. In drawing on kinship terms Aboriginal negotiators confirmed themselves as the equals of the whites, and not their subordinates. According to oral histories, the treaties were understood to have created an irrevocable and perpetual familial relationship with the British Crown based on concepts, principles, and laws defined in Cree as *wahkohtowin*.[35]

In each of the written treaties the First Nations agreed to 'cede, release, surrender and yield up to the Government of Canada for Her Majesty the Queen' immense tracts of land. They were promised that they could hunt and fish throughout the surrendered tracts, except on lands taken up by settlement. They were assigned reserves and given annual payments. They were promised the implements and cattle to assist them to farm or ranch, and the government agreed to provide schools. Federal negotiators initially offered only reserves and annuities; the agricultural, educational, and housing assistance were all added at the insistence of Aboriginal negotiators. The government side undoubtedly held many of the best cards during the negotiations. The written texts of the treaties were prepared well in advance of the treaty negotiations, and there was no discussion of key sections of these documents. But Aboriginal people of the west were persistent and effective in negotiating better terms, especially with regard to agricultural assistance. At Treaty 6 at Fort Carleton, the Cree secured a promise that they would be given assistance in times of pestilence or famine. During treaty talks Aboriginal negotiators drew on their own traditions of treaty making, diplomacy, ceremony, songs, dances, parade, performance, and oratory. The pipe ceremonies were particularly important in affirming the sacred nature of mutual commitments. The treaty talks also drew on traditions of diplomacy developed through relationships with the HBC and earlier trading companies.[36]

Aboriginal negotiators and the federal or Crown commissioners emerged with fundamentally different understandings of what was agreed upon at these proceedings.[37] The government interpreted the treaties as straightforward land surrenders, and this view prevailed in legal decisions made until recently. This point of view was based on the written record, but according to the oral history of Aboriginal people these were agreements to share the land and to coexist in peace as equals. The land was neither sold nor surrendered. The treaties permitted

[34] Alexander Morris, *The Treaties of Canada with the Indians* (Toronto, 1880), p. 199; see also Carter, 'Your Great Mother across the Salt Sea', p. 38.

[35] Harold Cardinal and Walter Hildebrandt, *Treaty Elders of Saskatchewan: Our Dream is That our People Will One Day be Clearly Recognized as Nations* (Calgary, 2000), p. 34.

[36] J. R. Miller, Arthur J. Ray, and Frank Touch, *Bounty and Benevolence: A History of Saskatchewan Treaties* (Montreal and Kingston, 2000), p. 25.

[37] See Treaty 7 Elders and Tribal Council, Walter Hildebrandt, Sarah Carter, and Dorothy First Rider, *The True Spirit and Original Intent of Treaty 7* (Montreal and Kingston, 1996); see also Richard T. Price, (ed.), *The Spirit of the Alberta Indian Treaties* (1979; repr. Edmonton, 1999).

the transcontinental railroad and the large-scale settlement of non-Aboriginal people. They also established the reserve system destined to dramatically restrict the social and economic independence of the First Nations, bringing them under the administration of a formidable bureaucracy. But while these treaties meant the profound diminishment of the land base, economies, and many of the basic freedoms of the First Nations, they also created treaty rights and Crown obligations that persist to this day. This is in contrast to the situation of the Aboriginal and Torres Strait Islander peoples of Australia, who have no treaty-based rights. Despite the different understanding of the meaning of the Canadian treaties, they cemented the relationship between the First Nations and the Crown, a relationship that was celebrated, renewed, and reaffirmed through the visits of vice-regal parties and members of the British royal family right up to the present. Aboriginal people of the prairies were determined to establish new economies based on farming or ranching, and their treaty partners had promised the assistance that would permit them to do so.

The last of the prairie treaties in 1877 coincided with the beginning of several years of widespread starvation, particularly among the people who had depended on the buffalo for the basic necessities of food, clothing, and shelter. Assistance to establish farming proved inadequate.[38] Reserves were not surveyed in a timely manner, and the promised seed, cattle, and implements were either not delivered, or were of such poor quality that they could not be used. When Governor-General the Marquis of Lorne visited the west in 1881, he was told that promises of assistance were unfulfilled and that the people were starving. Although Lorne promised to pass along these requests to the Canadian government and to the Queen herself, he privately held the view, common within the federal bureaucracy, that Aboriginal people were chronic complainers, unable to cope with change and desperately clinging to the 'old' ways. Aboriginal men were depicted as incapable of farming and Aboriginal women as poor housekeepers and mothers, whose alleged inattention to domestic duties was the cause of the presence of diseases such as tuberculosis.[39] Blaming Aboriginal people for their supposed inability to cope, adapt, and change became a frequent refrain, as it deflected any responsibility from the Canadian government.

There was widespread disaffection among First Nations by the time of the second 'Riel Rebellion'. Big Bear, a prominent Cree chief, attempted to organize a confederacy of the Cree that would protest treaty violations and call for a homeland where the Cree could be settled together. Cutting off rations, or a

[38] Sarah Carter, *Lost Harvests: Prairie Indian Reserve Farmers and Government Policy* (Montreal, and Kingston 1990).

[39] See Sarah Carter, *Capturing Women: The Manipulation of Cultural Imagery in Canada's Prairie West* (Montreal and Kingston, 1997) and Sarah Carter, 'Categories and Terrains of Exclusion: Constructing the "Indian Woman" in the Early Settlement Era in Western Canada', *Great Plains Quarterly*, 13 (1993), pp. 147–61.

'policy of starvation', was used to enforce adherence to government control.[40] The field force sent to suppress the 1885 Métis resistance was also used to intimidate and overwhelm the First Nations, and to incarcerate their leaders, even though the vast majority did not participate in these events. Over fifty Aboriginal men were accused of various degrees of involvement in 1885 and placed on trial; very few had legal counsel, and they understood little of the proceedings as they were all conducted in English and translators were used sparingly.[41] At Battleford barracks in November 1885, there was a mass execution of eight Aboriginal men found guilty of murder. The intention was to have a public spectacle that would convey a clear message as to who was in control.

After 1885 there was a significant shift in attitudes of settlers toward Aboriginal people. Because of local events, but also because of the increased racism of white society in Britain and throughout the Empire, there was a new determination to create and police boundaries between Aboriginal people and settlers. Aboriginal people were depicted as a menace. Travel writers and missionaries to western Canada in the late nineteenth century contributed to the project of creating an imperial frame of mind for audiences at home and abroad. Aboriginal men were singled out as unworthy custodians of the land. As missionary E. R. Young wrote, the steamboats and railroads that replaced 'rude native-made boats manned by human muscles' were 'laughing in their giant strength with derision at the puny work and crude methods they have supplanted. Their shrieks and shrill whistles have awakened the echoes amid the solitudes of centuries, and now everything in that land seems to feel the throbbing pulse of a new and active land.'[42] A point commonly made in this literature was that an Aboriginal man was not 'manly' as he was 'naturally idle—to eat, smoke and sleep is the sole end of his life; though he will travel immense distances to fish or hunt, which is the only occupation of the men'.[43] Aboriginal women were cast in a different but also highly negative light as abused and overworked drudges in their own communities, and as a source of immorality, vice, and corruption in the new white communities. Discourses of racial and social purity warning of the possible decline and pollution of the imperial race characterized English-Canadian constructions of national identity in the 1880s.[44] Aboriginal people were cast as part of a rapidly diminishing past, a people who could not survive in a new industrial or agricultural world. Ishbel

[40] John Tobias, 'Canada's Subjugation of the Plains Cree, 1879–1885', in J. R. Miller, (ed.), *Sweet Promises: A Reader on Indian–White Relations in Canada* (Toronto, 1991), pp. 212–42.

[41] 41 . Blair Stonechild and Bill Waiser, *Loyal Till Death: Indians and the North-West Rebellion* (Calgary, 1997), pp. 192–237.

[42] Quoted in Sarah Carter, 'The Missionaries' Indian: The Publications of John McDougall, John Maclean and Egerton Ryerson Young', *Prairie Forum*, 9 (1974), p. 35.

[43] Mrs Cecil Hall, *A Lady's Life on a Farm in Manitoba* (London, 1884), p. 104.

[44] Mariana Valverde, *The Age of Light, Soap and Water: Moral Reform in English Canada, 1885–1925* (Toronto, 1991); Cicely Devereux, ' "And Let Them Wash Me from This Changing World": Hugh and Ion, "The Last Best West", and Purity Discourse in 1885', *Journal of Canadian Studies*, 32/2 (Summer 1997), pp. 100–15.

Maria Gordon, Lady Aberdeen, wife of Governor-General Aberdeen, wrote in her 1893 account of her tour to the west that it was merciful for 'these poor folk that their race is yearly diminishing and that bye-and-bye all traces of their existence will have vanished'.[45] However, this grim prophecy ultimately proved incorrect.

While the direct involvement of the British Empire in the affairs of Aboriginal Canadians faded by the end of the nineteenth century, the First Nations of Canada retain to this day a 'long-standing and still vibrant sense of kinship with the Crown'.[46] In May 2005 leaders of the First Nations of Alberta expressed their indignation at being virtually left out of the itinerary for the Queen's forthcoming visit, pointing to their historic relationship with the British Crown.[47] The Union Jack is still unfurled at First Nations public ceremonies such as Treaty Days and pow-wows. The flag of the Siksika (Blackfoot) nation features a tipi fashioned out of the Union Jack, signifying their 1877 treaty and their enduring connection with the British Crown, their treaty partner. Royal and vice-regal visits continue to be used as opportunities to reconfirm the treaty relationship and until recently appeals were made directly to the British Crown against unjust treatment. In the early 1980s, delegations of Canadian Aboriginal people took their protest against a constitutional agreement that did not entrench their rights to Britain. There they lobbied the British Parliament to block the patriation of Canada's constitution. Supporters of Canada's Aboriginal people succeeded in delaying passage of the bill and the debates in both houses, where both the Commons and the Lords focused overwhelmingly on Aboriginal issues. Although the bill was ultimately passed, constituting 'another disappointing chapter in the lengthy saga of pilgrimages by Aboriginal people',[48] the 1982 Constitution Act was a major watershed—one that finally entrenched existing Aboriginal and treaty rights and ensured that those rights could not be taken away without the consent of Aboriginal peoples.

[45] Ishbel Maria Gordon, Lady Aberdeen, *Through Canada with a Kodak* (Edinburgh, 1893), pp. 202–03.
[46] J. R. Miller, 'Petitioning the Great White Mother: First Nations' Organizations and Lobbying in London', in Phillip Buckner, (ed.), *Canada and the End of Empire* (Vancouver, 2005), p. 299.
[47] *Calgary Herald*, 12 May 2005.
[48] Miller, 'Petitioning the Great White Mother', p. 315.

SELECT BIBLIOGRAPHY

SARAH CARTER, *Aboriginal People and Colonizes of Western Canada to 1900* (Toronto, 1999).

OLIVE P. DICKASON, *Canada's First Nations: A History of Founding Peoples from Earliest Times* (Toronto, 1996).

JULIE EVANS, PATRICIA GRIMSHAW, DAVID PHILIPS, and SHURLEE SWAIN, *Equal Subjects, Unequal Rights: Indigenous Peoples in British Settler Colonies, 1830–1910* (Manchester, 2003).

SIDNEY L. HARRING, *White Man's Law: Native People in Nineteenth-Century Canadian Jurisprudence* (Toronto, 1989).

J. R. MILLER, *Skyscrapers Hide the Heavens: A History of Indian–White Relations in Canada* (Toronto, 1989).

KATIE PICKLES and MYRA RUTHERDALE, (eds), *Contact Zones: Aboriginal and Settler Women om Canada's Colonial Past* (Vancouver, 2005).

A. J. RAY, *'I Have Lived Here Since the World Began': An Illustrated History of Canada's Native People* (Toronto, 1996).

BRUCE G. TRIGGER and WILCOMB E. WASHBURN, (eds), *The Cambridge History of the Native Peoples of the Americas*, 2 vols. (New York, 1996).

12

Women, Gender, and Empire

Adele Perry

In the past three decades feminist scholars have alerted readers to a two-part lapse in the historiographies of both Canada and the British Empire. The first is historians' root failure to acknowledge that the past was peopled by women as well as men: the second is their related unwillingness to acknowledge that men, like women, are gendered. In response, feminist historians of Canada and the British Empire have crafted rich and substantial histories attesting to the presence of women and the importance of gender. For all this common ground, the feminist historiography of Canada and the feminist historiography of the British Empire have had remarkably little to say to one another and have, with a couple of notable exceptions, developed separately. Bringing these two scholarships in dialogue alerts us to the basic significance of women and gender to the British Empire in Canada. It also reorients our historical vision of Empire in powerful ways. If we look for women and insist that men too are gendered subjects, we find ourselves moving away from high politics and toward the ordinary, the quotidian, and the bodily. Our views of European–Aboriginal contact, settlement, and organized imperialism all shift accordingly.

CONTACT AND COLONIALISM

In the territories that would eventually be constituted as Canada the first encounters of colonialism were imagined in gendered terms and lived in gendered ways. From the fifteenth to the nineteenth century, the gendered body served as a central and guiding metaphor for European travel and exploration throughout the world, including northern North America. The difference of Indigenous

Circumstances prevented Veronica Strong-Boag from writing this chapter with me but her encouragement and suggestions were of enormous importance. Ryan Eyford, Kurt Korneski, and Mary Kinnear all provided critical citations and sources for which I am especially grateful. This chapter has also benefited from the interventions and assistance of Kristine Alexander, Bettina Bradbury, Antoinette Burton, Lisa Chilton, Barry Ferguson, Robin Grazley, Jarett Henderson, Mary Jane McCallum, and Myra Rutherdale. The financial support of the Canada Research Chairs Programme is acknowledged with gratitude and thanks.

peoples was encapsulated in women's supposed nakedness, the physicality of their labours, and the apparent ease of their childbirth. Lands were read as virgin, barren, or fertile, but in any case female, and the capture of territories and peoples was not infrequently equated with rape and the meetings of peoples likened to marriages both good and bad. Women were actually as well as figuratively present in the 'contacts' that serve as the symbolic and sometimes literal beginnings of the British Empire in Canada. European men bargained for sex with local women at the same time as they traded for fur. Experience could teach them that women had more to offer than their bodies. Indigenous women helped provide the knowledge and technology necessary for Europeans to cross North American territory in the exploration parties that have rightly been likened to guided tours. Women's authority could come as a surprise to Europeans. British explorer Captain John Ross may have been befuddled by Inuit understandings of land and women's place in it, but he could not avoid depending on the knowledge of a woman named Iigluik. '[T]his personage', he explained in 1835, 'woman though she was, did not want a knowledge of geography.'[1]

The fur trade was similarly oiled by women's words and women's work. On the east and west coasts European traders met with women who bargained skillfully on their own behalf, and husbands who explained that no deals could be made without their wives' consent. The western Canadian fur trade depended on the labours of Indigenous women, who made moccasins, snowshoes, and pemmican, the hardy and nutritious food that literally fed the trade. As wives and partners of both European and Indigenous men, women were critical links in trade relationships and valued translators, guides, and cultural interlocutors.[2]

Women were also very much there as exploration and trade gave way to missions and settlement. From the seventeenth to the twentieth century Christian missionaries saw women as strategic entries into Aboriginal societies. Missionary women associated with the Roman Catholic Ursulines or the Methodist Women's Missionary Society were sometimes accorded a special responsibility for ministering to First Nations women. Less frequently, Indigenous women like Tsimshian Victoria Young and Elizabeth Diex, Methodist converts and preachers *par excellence*, laboured within their own communities.[3] Whoever the missionaries and whatever the denomination, missions to Aboriginal women served up a remarkably similar menu of piety, moral education, and labour designed to

---

[1] Quoted in Renee Fossett, 'Mapping Inuktut: Inuit Views of the Real World', in Jennifer S. H. Brown and Elizabeth Vibert, (eds), *Reading beyond Words: Contexts for Native History* (Peterborough, 2004), p. 118; Katie Pickles and Myra Rutherdale, (eds), *Contact Zones: Aboriginal and Settler Women in Canada's Past* (Vancouver, 2005).

[2] Sylvia Van Kirk, *'Many Tender Ties': Women in Fur Trade Society in Western Canada, 1670–1870* (Winnipeg, 1980).

[3] Carol Williams, *Framing the West: Race, Gender, and the Photographic Frontier in the Pacific Northwest* (New York, 2003), chap. 3.

recast them in the mould of respectable European femininity. Women were taught to read and, less often, to write. They were instructed in rudimentary and sometimes highly syncretic forms of Christian theology. The bulk of their days were spent doing the sewing, cleaning, cooking, and agricultural production needed to maintain missionary enterprises. Missionaries conveniently legitimized this labour as critical to transforming First Nations women into Christian wives and mothers.

Morally, socially, and sexually regulating women was a state project as well, especially after First Nations people were put under the jurisdiction of the newly formed federal government in 1867. The 1876 Indian Act sought to regulate reproduction and marriage as components of race making. It mandated that Aboriginal women would lose their status as 'Indians' if they married non-status men, as would any children they bore with them. This remained the case until 1985, when Indigenous women, using the Canadian Charter of Rights and Freedoms, forced the federal government to pass Bill C-31, which rendered laws of 'Indian status' putatively gender neutral and allowed people to apply for a sort of restorative Aboriginal status from the federal government.[4] Women are disproportionately represented among people seeking to use Bill C-31 as a means of securing recognition that they are 'Indians' in the eyes of the state, if not always in those of local Aboriginal communities. Gender defines the postcolonial as it did the colonial.

The Indian Act is the most pervasive but hardly the only way that the Canadian state sought to intervene in Aboriginal women's lives. The residential school system, begun in 1879 and persisting until the 1960s, had a highly gendered logic. The rupture between families and children upon which the residential school was premised worked to undermine the roles of mothers, grandmothers, and kin. At the schools, girls learned new ways of being female. They were kept separate from boys, assigned responsibility for domestic labour, dressed—literally as well as figuratively—in the drab garb of institutionalized female poverty, and not infrequently hired out as domestic help for local settlers. As residential schools began to close their doors in the 1960s, provincial child welfare policies, and especially practices of child removal, kept up the tradition by promising solutions to female Aboriginal poverty but delivering little more than the painful separation of Indigenous children from their kin.

Indigenous women's response to the many guises of the British Empire took a number of forms and served a number of purposes. Some historians emphasize the totality of European conversion, arguing that imperialism radically reoriented Indigenous women's roles, robbing them, in the case of the Tsimshian, of customary status and authority, or, in the case of the Huron, of the fluidity of roles women enjoyed in band-level societies. Scholars have also found that

---

[4] Janet Silman, (ed.), *Enough is Enough: Aboriginal Women Speak Out* (Toronto, 1987).

missionary and state agendas could overlap with Indigenous ones, as when high-status Indigenous and European men found common ground in controlling Aboriginal women's sexuality.[5] Others have sketched a gendered pattern of resistance, arguing that women had more to lose in accepting the British Empire and accordingly fought it more. Okanagan writer Jeanette Armstrong argues that the survival of Indigenous women and their families, kin, and communities is nothing less than defiant resistance to patriarchal imperialism. The development of an international historiography of colonialism that presses the improvisational character of lived colonial experience has led historians to stress Aboriginal women's capacity to selectively and syncretically utilize Christianity, colonial governance, and trade to enhance the power and autonomy they enjoyed within Indigenous communities and cultures. Aboriginal women could and did use the layered conduits of the Empire to their own ends. In 1860 Nahnebahwequa or Catherine Sutton, an Anishnabe woman from southern Ontario, travelled to London to plead the case of Canada's Indigenous peoples and more particularly women. Nahnebahwequa spoke to the Society for the Protection of Aborigines, the Duke of Newcastle, and Queen Victoria about land rights and the particular injustices suffered by Aboriginal women 'charged with the unpardonable sin of marrying a White Man'.[6] How to square these various findings with evidence of the persistence of Aboriginal women's poverty and disempowerment within both Canadian society and Indigenous communities remains a largely unanswered challenge.

SETTLER WOMEN AND EMPIRE

The roles the British Empire carved out for settler women were very different from those accorded to Aboriginal women. In a strictly literal sense European women were rarely part of early colonization. Land and resources brought Europe to North America, and with Europeans came the precept that catching fish, trading fur, cutting wood, and defending territorial claims was work fit for men alone, preferably young and unencumbered ones. Men thus came largely alone or at least temporarily apart from wives and families. Sometimes they found local women, but a variable mix of custom and design ensured that they would rarely find

---

[5] Jo-Anne Fiske, 'Colonization and the Decline of Women's Status: The Tsimshian Case', *Feminist Studies*, 17 (Fall 1991), pp. 509–36; Jean Barman, 'Taming Aboriginal Sexuality: Gender, Power, and Race in British Columbia, 1850–1900', *BC Studies*, 115/116 (Autumn/Winter 1997/8), pp. 237–66; Jeanette Armstrong, 'The Real Power of Aboriginal Women', in Cheryl Miller and Patricia Chuchryk, (eds), *Women of the First Nations: Power, Wisdom, and Strength* (Winnipeg, 1996); Carol Devens, *Countering Colonization: Native American Women and Great Lakes Missions, 1630–1900* (Berkeley, 1992).

[6] Celia Haig-Brown, 'Seeking Honest Justice in a Land of Strangers: Nahnebahwequa's Struggle for Justice', *Journal of Canadian Studies*, 36 (Winter 2001/2), p. 158.

European ones. After an early failed effort to bring white women to the fur trade, the Hudson's Bay Company (HBC) explicitly prohibited women from taking passage on Company ships, a rule that Orkadian Isabel Gunn famously defied by presenting herself as a man until childbirth put a stop to her career as a male fur trade labourer.[7] European women began arriving in meaningful numbers as posts and camps became more permanent communities. In Newfoundland, that transition occurred in the late eighteenth century; around the St Lawrence, Lake Ontario, and Lake Erie in the years following the American Revolution and in Rupert's Land in the early nineteenth century. British Columbia's settler society remained about two-thirds male into the closing years of the nineteenth century. In each of these places, the arrival of British women—called 'tender exotics' by one nineteenth-century fur trader—marked a new phase of imperial governance and settlement, but did not on its own bring racial exclusion and hierarchy to Britain's North American colonies.

Women's changing place within British settler-colonialism occurred within a context of intractable political conflict and regular war between settlers, Indigenous peoples, and European nations over who would control northern North America and how. Acadia came under British control in 1713 and Quebec in 1763. Some 70,000 French Canadians became British subjects. Women rarely had formal roles in the fighting that accompanied these territorial changes but they were profoundly affected by war nonetheless. Fluctuations in Quebec's birth rate are one measure of how war worked itself out on women's bodies: the highest birth rates of the late eighteenth and nineteenth centuries occurred between 1761 and 1770, once the disruption of war had finally ended.[8] The transition from an *ancien régime* society that offered considerable latitude to uncloistered religious women and widows to a capitalist one ordered alongside a private–public split meant that women would find fewer opportunities for power and self-expression in the newly British Quebec.[9] The arrival of British law, with its stricter patriarchy, compounded this change. The 1774 Quebec Act restored the French civil code, and with it a marriage law that created a community of property between husbands and wives, although administered by husbands alone. That married women in Quebec could sue, be sued, and own property in their own names distinguished them from others in Britain's Empire and was but one sign of how Canada's history as a French colony would irreparably shape its career as an English one.

Alongside hardship and strife war brought opportunities for women to expand their usual roles, albeit usually fleeting ones. Koñwatsiátsiaiéñni or Molly Brant (1736–96), a Mohawk woman and partner of a British official, was a staunch

---

[7] Sylvia Van Kirk, 'Gunn, Isabel', in *Dictionary of Canadian Biography*, vol. V (Toronto, 1983), p. 394.
[8] The Clio Collective, *Quebec Women: A History* (Toronto, 1987), p. 78.
[9] Allan Greer, *The People of New France* (Toronto, 1997), pp. 60–75.

and influential ally of Britain in the contested borderlands of what are now New York State and Ontario. She fed, assisted, and helped to arm Loyalists, passed on valuable military information, and used her authority as head of a society of Six Nations matrons to serve as a diplomat and power broker between British and the Six Nations people. Brant refused to return to American soil after the war, and lived from 1783 until her death in Kingston, attending Anglican church and holding a position of some rank among the settler community.[10]

In the longer term, war, displacement, and the social and ideological pressures that accompanied them served to retract women's roles. Women and children were a significant presence in the Loyalist migrations—between 25 and 30 per cent of the adult Loyalists who migrated to eastern Ontario were female. Like most female migrants to British North America, they usually arrived as part of family groups. Women would find that notions of female helplessness and dependence challenged by the hardships of war and exile would be reasserted with new vigour as homes and communities were re-established. The patriarchal, domestic family became both a potent metaphor for a virtuous political life and a remarkably powerful presence in ordinary people's lives in the Loyalist communities in the Canadas and the Maritimes.[11]

In British North America family defined women's work. Some women, usually unmarried, earned wages from their work as teachers, or from the trade of their businesses, most of which catered to a female clientele.[12] Most women and girls worked within the confines of their own family households, caring for kin, producing food, clothing, and household goods, and tending to crops and animals, sometimes for trade or sale on local markets. They did so under British common law that codified men's control over property and labour. Under the common law, marriage made women non-existent as legal actors, unable to manage real estate, to contract, to sue or be sued, or to claim their wages. After 1851 the law of married women's property began to change, though married women's systematic incapacity to claim land would continue to animate feminist consciousness well into the late twentieth century.[13]

However unequal, women's unpaid work was important and was acknowledged as such. British North America's economy was based in the production of primary resource and agricultural products for sale on an unstable world market and was plagued by chronic labour shortages and extreme seasonal variation.

[10] Barbara Graymont, 'Koñwatsiãtsiaiéñni', in *Dictionary of Canadian Biography*, vol. IV (Toronto, 1981), pp. 416–19.

[11] Janice Potter-MacKinnon, *While the Women Only Wept: Loyalist Refugee Women in Eastern Ontario* (Montreal and Kingston, 1993), p. xv; Ann G. Condon, 'The Family in Exile: Loyalist Social Values after the Revolution', in Margaret Conrad, (ed.), *Intimate Relations: Family and Community in Planter Nova Scotia* (Fredericton, 1995).

[12] E. Jane Errington, *Wives and Mothers, School Mistresses and Scullery Maids: Working Women in Upper Canada, 1790–1840* (Montreal and Kingston, 1995).

[13] Constance Backhouse, *Petticoats and Prejudice: Women and Law in Nineteenth-Century Canada* (Toronto, 1991), pp. 177–9.

The work of women and children was crucial in keeping vulnerable households afloat through bad years, long winters, during the slow business of clearing land for farming, when hired hands could not be found or paid, and when adult men and older sons left farms for paid work in the bush. In 1821 John Howison wrote that 'Married persons are always more comfortable, and succeed sooner, in Canada, than single men; for a wife and family, so far from being a burden there, always prove sources of wealth.'[14]

It was the work of human reproduction—pregnancy, childbirth, child rearing, and care of adult men, the disabled, the ill, and the elderly—that defined settler women's lives. In newly settled areas the relative availability of land and the relative scarcity of settler women meant that the 'late marriage pattern' of western Europe did not apply. In Canada West and East, the average age for first marriage for women was a youthful 22.4 and 23.7 years respectively.[15] If women married young, it followed that they would birth often. Shop-worn stereotypes about the prolific reproduction of French Canadians are belied by the remarkably high birth rates for all of British North America. In the mid-nineteenth century Ontario had one of the highest birth rates in the world, with completed families averaging around seven. For many women adulthood was a relentless and often dangerous cycle of pregnancy, childbirth, and breast-feeding. When Canadian birth rates began to drop sharply in the later nineteenth century, nationalists in French Canada and imperialists in English Canada mourned settler women's seeming lack of interest in repopulating Canada, whether imagined as French or English. The corollary of panic around the prospect of 'race suicide' was the feared fecundity of various racialized 'others'. The 1885 Chinese Immigration Act virtually banned the migration of Chinese women in the eugenicist fear that their fertility would imperil so-called 'white Canada'.[16] The idea that white women's reproduction was a buttress to the nation and non-white women's reproduction a threat to it was sometimes implicit and sometimes explicit, but rarely absent.

Not all household labour was family labour. Most women who worked for wages in nineteenth-century Canada did so as domestic servants, labouring within another household, often as an interlude between childhood and wifehood. Enslaved women such as Sarah Pooley, a black woman owned by the well-known Loyalist Joseph Brant, performed household duties throughout British North America. The legal status of chattel slavery was unclear in Upper Canada until the Assembly of Upper Canada, at the urging of Lieutenant-Governor

---

[14] Quoted in Marjorie Griffiths Cohen, *Women's Work, Markets, and Economic Development in Nineteenth-Century Ontario* (Toronto, 1988), p. 71.

[15] Ellen Gee, 'Marriage in Nineteenth-Century Canada', *Canadian Review of Sociology and Anthropology*, 19 (1982), pp. 311–25. Unlike Gee, my interpretation stresses the particularity of the Canadian, and especially of the western Canadian data.

[16] Vijay Agnew, *Resisting Discrimination: Women from Asia, Africa, and the Caribbean and the Women's Movement in Canada* (Toronto, 1996).

John Graves Simcoe, passed a 1793 statute mandating its eventual extinction. The public and sensational resistance of Chloe Cooley, a black woman who fought her sale and removal to the United States so vigorously that more than one man was required to restrain her, was a welcome prompt for Simcoe to do so. The legality of slavery remained ambiguous in Nova Scotia and New Brunswick, but by 1800, virtually all Canadian blacks were effectively free of slavery, if not of the racism that nourished it.[17] This was not sufficient to discourage Abolitionist journalist and editor Mary Ann Shadd Cary from promoting Canada West and its promises of 'British freedom' to African Americans.[18]

Yet Shadd Cary, as a woman and a black person, was essentially excluded from the imperial citizenship she so cherished. In the early nineteenth century property-owning women occasionally voted in the British North American colonies, usually for local governments, but this practice came under attack as reformers, demanding a new voice for colonial citizens, increasingly associated femininity and the family with the 'old' world of monarchy, despotism, and corruption from which they wished to distinguish themselves. When the French-Canadian rebels of Lower Canada exclaimed 'the Queen is a whore' and the critics of British administration in Upper Canada lambasted the 'family compact', they both borrowed the language of gender and morality to articulate their critique of the British Empire and their place in it.[19]

As reformers argued for the extension of political rights to the settler-citizen, they also defined legitimate political authority as necessarily male. In 1834 the Lower Canadian legislature passed an uncontroversial bill to formally disenfranchise women of all ranks. Prince Edward Island followed suit in 1834, as did New Brunswick in 1843, the Canadas in 1849, and Nova Scotia in 1851. The construction of the political subject as male was well entrenched by 1857, when 'An Act to encourage the Gradual Civilization of the Indian Tribes of the Canada' ensured that even the *potential* Aboriginal political subject was necessarily male.[20] The establishment of formal colonial governance was part of what Ian McKay has described as the project of 'liberal rule', and was premised on the relegation of women to the domestic and the expulsion of non-western peoples to a murky realm positioned outside and quite literally antecedent to

[17] Maureen G. Elgersman, *Unyielding Spirits: Black Women and Slavery in Early Canada and Jamaica* (New York, 1999).
[18] Mary Ann Shadd, *A Plea for Emigration or Notes of Canada West in its Moral, Social, and Political Aspect . . . For the Information of Colored Emigrants* (Detroit, 1852).
[19] Allan Greer, *The Patriots and the People: The Rebellion of 1837 in Rural Lower Canada* (Toronto, 1993); Cecilia Morgan, ' "When Bad Men Conspire, Good Men Must Unite!" Gender and Political Discourses in Upper Canada, 1820s–1830s', in Kathryn McPherson, Cecilia Morgan, and Nancy M. Forestell, (eds), *Gendered Pasts: Historical Essays in Femininity and Masculinity in Canada* (Toronto, 1999).
[20] Olive Dickinson, *Canada's First Nations: A History of Founding Peoples from Earliest Times* (Toronto, 1997), p. 225.

the rational, liberal polity.[21] The language of so-called 'universal suffrage' in Canada, as elsewhere, simultaneously witnessed the extension of political rights to increasing numbers of settler men and the juridical exclusion of women and certain groups of racialized men from the exercise of formal political power. Inequality did not simply go alongside the processes of colony building and nation building: it was built into their very bones.

But women, like people of colour, were very much a part of the Empire that systematically denied them authority. That Victoria was the symbolic head of the British Empire gave a decidedly female gloss to the enterprise of imperial expansion. In 1863, journalists in the settlement of Victoria on Vancouver Island explained that Queen Victoria, whether as 'a Christian, a ruler, a wife, or a mother', shone 'preeminently before the world as an example to her sex, having endeared herself not only to the people of her own happy Isle, but with the admiration and respect of every nation in every clime'.[22] It was an easy step beyond the monarch-as-mother to imagine colonies as children, whether contented in their subordinate status or progressing gradually to a supportive and derivative adulthood. 'Canada is yet in her exuberant youth', explained one loyalist in 1904, 'Great Britain is the Old Motherland from whose womb have come mighty peoples.'[23] Configuring the British Empire as a family presented the Empire as simultaneously communal and hierarchical. The familial image of Empire was played out in the countless rituals and ceremonies starring officials' families and wives. While British Columbia Governor James Douglas's part-Aboriginal wife, Amelia Connolly Douglas, made few official public appearances, the white wives of subsequent administrations were key to the construction of public authority in colonial British Columbia. The balls, openings, and galas organized and attended by officials' wives were not an incidental part in Empire's public trappings. That Douglas's successor Arthur Kennedy had a decorous, sociable, and racially acceptable wife and family was seen by the local elite as genuine compensation for his considerable failings as an administrator.[24]

Ritualized female display marked the forming of nations just as it did the maintenance of Empire. The nation of Canada inherited the gendered and racialized exclusions of the British colonies, and also the conspicuous displays of feminine spectacle and ritual. In 1992 Gail Cuthbert Brandt used the example of the female side of the Confederation conferences to argue against those who positioned so-called political history and so-called social history, including women's history, as competitors unable to share intellectual space or speak to each other's concerns. At Charlettown in 1864, the wife of the Lieutenant-Governor

---

[21] Ian McKay, 'The Liberal Order Framework: A Prospectus for a Reconnaissance of Canadian History', *Canadian Historical Review*, 81 (2000), pp. 617–45.

[22] 'His Majesty's Birthday', *British Colonist*, 11 May 1863.

[23] Henry C. Osborne, 'Three Imperial Topics', *The Empire Club of Canada Speeches, 1903–1904* (Toronto, 1904).

[24] 'The Governor's Lady', *British Colonist*, 21 Mar. 1864.

of Prince Edward Island and others fostered the social relationships upon which political alliances would be built. Anne Nelson Brown's interventions at the Quebec conference held later that year would earn her the title of 'mother of confederation'.[25]

Ordinary women also played a role in Empire. After the War of 1812 the 'Patriotic Young Ladies of York' presented the Third Regiment of York Militia with a special banner. The women, explained Anne Powell, were 'proud to imitate the example of the most distinguished of their sex, among the most virtuous and heroic nation who have always rejoiced in giving public testimony of their gratitude to their countrymen returning from Victory'.[26] Women's bodily presence and reproduction was, like their loyalty, registered as an imperial act. The absence or scarcity of settler women became synonymous with newness, roughness, and the fragility of Britain's presence and claims. It followed that the arrival of white women represented the British Empire's ability to remake eastern, central, and finally western and northern Canada in its name, the ascendancy of so-called British civilization, and the retreat of Indigenous societies and the fragile, plural societies associated with early colonial ventures and resource extraction.[27] 'Soe long as no there comes no women they are not fixed,' explained one observer of Newfoundland's imperial fortunes in 1684.[28]

The idea that ordinary settler women could somehow cement Britain's claims in North America motivated female migration campaigns throughout the nineteenth and twentieth centuries. Female migration was coordinated by a shifting combination of state, church, and voluntary organizations that aimed both to relieve the metropole of dependent subjects and provide Canada with wives and domestic servants. The British Women's Emigration Association, formed in 1884, sent most of their 16,000 female emigrants to Canada, and the Salvation Army brought another 15,000 single women to Canada between 1903 and the First World War. The image of the distressed gentlewoman migrant loomed large in female migration schemes from the middle of the nineteenth century onwards and was given substance by a minority who sought work as teachers and governesses. But most of the women who crossed the Atlantic as part of organized schemes were young and poor, many coming directly from institutions and most ending up in domestic service, at least temporarily. Whatever their class background these women were dubbed 'missionaries of

---

[25] Gail Cuthbert Brandt, 'National Unity and the Politics of Political History', *Canadian Historical Association Papers* (1992), pp. 3–12.

[26] Cecilia Morgan, *Public Men and Virtuous Women: The Gendered Languages of Religion and Politics in Upper Canada, 1791–1850* (Toronto, 1996), p. 39.

[27] Colin M. Coates and Cecilia Morgan, *Heroines and History: Representations of Madeleine de Verchères and Laura Secord* (Toronto, 2002); Sarah Carter, *Capturing Women: The Manipulation of Cultural Imagery in Canada's Prairie West* (Montreal and Kingston, 1997); Adele Perry, *On the Edge of Empire: Gender, Race, and the Making of British Columbia, 1849–1871* (Toronto, 2001).

[28] Captain Francis Whelan, quoted in W. Gordon Handcock, *Soe longe as there comes noe women: Origins of English Settlement in Newfoundland* (St John's, 1989), unpaginated [p. 21].

Empire' whose presence was required if Canada was to be reconstituted as British space. Ella Sykes, a representative of the Colonial Intelligence League for Educated Women, explained that support for Britain's Empire and opposition to America's was her core goal. 'It is an Imperial work to help girls of a high stamp to seek their fortunes beyond the seas—women who will care for our glorious Flag and what it signifies, who will stand for higher ideals than the worship of the "almighty dollar", and who will do their part in the land that their brothers are developing so splendidly.' These same connections between femininity, race, and reproduction were mobilized to argue that non-white women, including those from British possessions in India and the Caribbean, were a threat to the Canadian nation.[29]

ORGANIZED WOMEN FOR (AND AGAINST) EMPIRE, 1867–1919

Writing women and gender into Imperial history in Canada, as elsewhere, points us away from the formal realms of Empire—parliaments, armies, and proclamations—and toward the less formal social locations where Empire could be constituted, felt, and performed. But women were a part of imperialism's official history as well. They loomed large in the literature of Empire from the outset. Anna Jameson and the prolific Strickland sisters, Susanna Moodie and Catherine Parr Trail, gained an international reputation for their stories of settler women in the backwoods of nineteenth-century Ontario. Later on, women such as Sarah Curzon played a significant role in the writing of popular histories that offered a female perspective on Canada's Imperial past. The novel proved a particularly useful medium for women's thoughts on Canada and Empire. Works such as Sarah Jeanette Duncan's *The Imperialist*, published in 1904, explored imperialism's place in a small, central Canadian town. Nellie McClung is better remembered for her activism but was known, in her own day, as the author of popular novels such as *Sewing Seeds in Danny*. [30]

More women spoke about Empire in the classroom. The expansion of the public school system was premised on a radical feminization of teaching in the last third of the nineteenth century. By 1901, three-quarters of all teachers in Canada were women: the numbers were even higher among those who worked

---

[29] Quoted in Marilyn Barber, 'The Gentlewomen of Queen Mary's Coronation Hostel', in Barbara K. Latham and Roberta J. Pazdro, (eds), *Not Just Pin Money: Selected Essays on the History of Women's Work in British Columbia* (Victoria, 1984), p. 145; Marilyn Barber, *Immigrant Domestic Servants in Canada* (Ottawa, 1991).

[30] Cecilia Morgan, 'History, Nation, and Empire: Gender and Southern Ontario Historical Societies, 1890–1920s', *Canadian Historical Review*, 82 (2001), pp. 491–538; Misao Dean, *Practising Femininity: Domestic Realism and the Performance of Gender in Early Canadian Fiction* (Toronto, 1998); Jennifer Henderson, *Settler Feminism and Race-Making in Canada* (Toronto, 2003).

with younger children. Their work was poorly paid and, for most, a temporary interlude before marriage. It was frequently a work of Empire as well. School textbooks in British Columbia had a four-part project of describing the British Empire as a moral enterprise, fostering students' identification with Empire, presenting subject people as 'morally deficient Others', and ranking humanity in a supposedly scientific racial schema.[31] The history taught and presumably learned in these classrooms was an Imperial one that made meaningful room for female defenders of Britain—particularly the heroine of the War of 1812, Laura Secord, and First World War nurse Edith Cavell. Their names still grace English-Canadian elementary schools alongside Carnarvon, Strathcona, and Kitchener. In founding Empire Day in 1897, Canadian anti-suffragist and imperialist Clementina Fessenden would put a peculiarly English-Canadian and female mark on popular imperialism throughout the British world.

Women organized explicitly for, and less often against, British imperialism. Denominational missionary societies to promote the evangelization of non-Christian women and children were the first national women's groups in Canada, and remained the largest until the First World War, with a collective membership of around 200,000.[32] Women associated with the Presbyterian Women's Foreign Missionary Society or its Methodist or Anglican equivalents worked in northern and western Canada as well in south Asia, China, and the Caribbean. Significant numbers of Canadian women worked as missionaries, their Christianizing work paired with the practical labours of teaching, doctoring, and organizing. Missionary life provided single women with a rare opportunity for an independent career, travel, and a public persona all within the ambit of respectable bourgeois femininity. Women missionaries could be doctors, such as Canadian Margaret O'Hara who spent thirty-five happy years practising in India or Maria Storrs, an Englishwoman who lived in northern British Columbia's Peace River from 1929 to 1950, organizing Sunday schools and Girl Guides groups and having an undeniably good time.[33] More were missionary wives, whose unpaid labours were central to the operation of mission stations the globe over. Whether they worked to convert non-Christian peoples locally or globally, women missionaries saw their work as an imperial one, a concrete and

---

[31] Timothy Stanley, 'White Supremacy and the Rhetoric of Educational Indoctrination: A Canadian Case-Study', in J. A. Mangan, (ed.), *Making Imperial Mentalities: Socialisation and British Imperialism* (Manchester, 1990).

[32] Ruth Crompton Brouwer, *New Women for God: Canadian Presbyterian Women and India Missions, 1876–1914* (Toronto, 1990); Rosemary Gagan, *A Sensitive Independence: Canadian Methodist Women Missionaries in Canada and the Orient, 1881–1925* (Montreal and Kingston, 1992); Myra Rutherdale, *Women and the White Man's God: Race and Gender in a Canadian Mission Field* (Vancouver, 2002).

[33] Veronica Strong-Boag, 'The Case of Canada's Women Doctors: Feminism Constrained', in Linda Kealey, (ed.), *A Not Unreasonable Claim: Women and Reform in Canada, 1880s–1920s* (Toronto, 1979); W. L. Morton with Vera K. Fast, (eds), *God's Galloping Girl: The Peace River Diaries of Monica Storrs, 1920–1931* (Vancouver, 1979).

uniquely female manifestation of Britain's special stewardship for the 'heathen'. That female missionaries were actively supported by fund-raising, education, and community-building work at home ensured that this missionary project was not confined to mission stations.

Missionary groups would be central to the development of a national women's movement, marked most clearly by the formation of the National Council of Women of Canada (NCWC) in 1893. Pro-Empire groups would loom large in this 'parliament of women'. The Girls' Friendly Society, the Dominion Order of King's Daughters, and the Imperial Order Daughters of the Empire (IODE) all helped to move the NCWC in what Veronica Strong-Boag calls 'a conservative direction', one that was oriented toward preserving and fostering Canada's ties with Britain and Empire. It was not that no other alternatives were considered. In 1917, the NCWC affiliated with the International Council of Women, and the IODE registered their opposition to such internationalism by resigning.[34]

Formed in the heat of the South African War, the IODE boasted 50,000 members at its height during the First World War. Historians have found feminist leanings and feminist impact in their work, but they have also been struck by the IODE's willingness to work within a masculinist and didactically militaristic idiom. The IODE would be cautious about demanding the vote for women, clarifying their support for female suffrage only when it was basically a foregone conclusion, and one irreparably wedded to the cause of support for the First World War and, with it, the restriction of political rights for those identified as 'enemy aliens'.[35] The IODE 's feminist imperialism refracted unevenly through the second-hand stores they operated, socks they knitted for soldiers, and books they provided for schoolchildren. That the Victoria local was named the 'Lady Douglas Chapter' and the Gimli, Manitoba local the 'Jón Sigurðsson Chapter', and that the IODE raised funds by selling books about Québécois nationalist heroine Madeleine de Verchères suggests some of the ways that even most hyperbolic imperial voices in Canada were muted or at least complicated by local experiences of migration, *métissage*, and social formation.

The Girl Guides provide another example of a feminized and localized version of the British Empire. The first Canadian Girl Guide company was formed in 1909 during the upsurge of pro-Empire sentiment that marked the early years of the twentieth century. The Guides offered a unique configuration of recreation, female community, militarism, and imperialism. Individual Guides could earn cords, pins, bars, and badges based on the successful completion of appropriate tests in health, handicrafts, and service, each of which would be affixed to their

---

[34] Veronica Strong-Boag, *The Parliament of Women: The National Council of Women of Canada, 1893–1929* (Ottawa, 1976), p. 99.
[35] Katie Pickles, *Female Imperialism and National Identity: Imperial Order Daughters of the Empire* (Manchester, 2002), pp. 48–50.

standardized and conspicuously military uniforms. Some of the most valuable commodities offered by the Guides were the opportunities for female leadership and the chance to pursue non-traditional activities like carpentry. Time spent in the company of other girls and women was another enduring appeal of joining the Guides, and one that sometimes prompted homophobia. The Guides had an enormous impact on Canadian girls by any estimation. By 1929, there were approximately 28,700 members of the Girl Guides Association, and promoters estimated that at least 38,000 Canadian girls had come under the influence of guiding.[36]

Sentiment for and knowledge of the British Empire was disseminated alongside skills, friendship, and recreation in the Girl Guides. As Lisa Gaudet explains, the 1912 Guide handbook, *How Girls Can Help Build up the Empire*, 'heralded Canada's glorious deeds in the name of imperial unity: the taking of Fort Ogdensburg, the hard fighting at Lundy's Lane, and the suppression of Riel'. Ties of Empire were of the present as well as the past. In Toronto in 1914, Girl Guides presented papers on 'Honour, Purity, and Loyalty', 'The Imperial Guide', and 'The Flag and What it had Stood For'. They were asked to imagine themselves as 'one of the slender bands that binds the empire'. Those bands were imagined as giving the colonies, including Canada, a derivative role. The Canadian Guides modelled themselves directly on the British movement, and not until 1945 did Canadian Guides develop their own policy manual. These lessons in nation, Empire, and the place of women within them were doubly strong for the Aboriginal girls who joined Guide groups formed in residential schools or for the immigrant girls who participated in special 'ethnic' groups. A Guide from Blaine Lake, Saskatchewan, explained in 1922 that the goal was to 'Weld these races into one strong nation. Not Galician, nor Scotch, or even English, but British.'[37] The founding of the Canadian Girls in Training in 1917 was in part motivated by the conviction that the Guides were overly authoritarian, insufficiently Christian, 'too British', and not Canadian enough.[38]

The IODE and the Girl Guides were not the only models of female imperialism on offer in early twentieth-century Canada. Lady Ishbel Gordon, Countess of Aberdeen, was both wife of Canada's Governor-General and first President of the NCWC. She represented a genteel, civic-minded support for Empire,

[36] Veronica Strong-Boag, *The New Day Recalled: Lives of Girls and Women in English Canada, 1919–1939* (Toronto, 1988), p. 28; Lisa Gaudet, 'The Empire is Woman's Sphere: Organized Female Imperialism in Canada, 1880s–1920s', Ph.D. thesis (Carleton University, 2001), p. 325; Bonnie MacQueen, 'Domesticity and Discipline: The Girl Guides in British Columbia, 1910–1943', in Latham and Pazdro, (eds), *Not Just Pin Money*.

[37] Mary Jane McCallum, 'To Make Good Canadians: Girl Guiding in Indian Residential Schools', MA thesis (Trent University, 2002); 'Songs of Babylon', *Girl Guides Gazette*, quoted in Gaudet, 'The Empire is Women's Sphere', pp. 328, 327, 335.

[38] Margaret Prang, ' "The Girl God Would Have Me Be": The Canadian Girls in Training, 1915–1939', *Canadian Historical Review*, 36 (1985), p. 159.

one that nurtured the Victorian Order of Nurses, avoided strident, American-style activism, and tempered its imperialism with support for international organizations. The Canadian Women's Club combined its commitment to the British Empire with continental and European connections. Empire was yoked to explicitly feminist causes as well. Nellie McClung, English Canada's most prominent first-wave feminist and politician, meshed her maternal feminism with a firm imperialism. 'My heart', McClung explained, 'has been thrilled with what it is to be a citizen of the British empire.'[39] In feminist hands, Empire gave political ballast to a striking range of equity claims, including arguments for the passage of dower laws to protect women's interests in prairie homesteads, campaigns to restrict public access to liquor, struggles for women's right to the vote, and local efforts to improve medical, social, and legal services to children and youth. Both Empire and women would be writ large on the origins of what would later be known as the welfare state.

This was a feminist imperialism that was nourished in the particular context of modern English Canada. It meshed textbook imperial hyperbole and lived ties with Britain and other imperial possessions with genuine nationalist sentiment. Both English-Canadian nationalism and sycophantic Anglophilia coexisted alongside substantial cultural, political, and personal ties to the United States. Thus internationally inspired but 'made in Canada' groups such as the NCWC flourished beside British carbon copies like the Girl Guides, and organizations like the Woman's Christian Temperance Union that were born in the United States. The racial language of Empire was shared common ground, but it was always reshaped by the Canadian preoccupation with French–English division and by the perceived threat non-British migrants posed to Canada. This polyvocal way of seeing Canadian women's place in the world came to the fore with the campaign that began in the 1870s and blossomed in the 1910s to admit women to the formal mechanisms of political power. The suffrage movement used imperial as well as continental ties and could pair them both with the language of English-Canadian nationalism. It was drenched in racial thought. A common trope was the dubious 'foreigner' with electoral privileges contrasted with the virtuous 'Canadian' woman who was denied the right to vote.[40] The piecemeal and layered process that gave women the federal vote institutionalized these inequalities. The Military Voters Act of 1917 gave the vote to women nurses serving in the war; later that year, the Wartime Elections Act extended the franchise to wives, widows, mothers, sisters, and daughters of those who served the Canadian or British military. In 1918, the Women's Franchise Act gave the vote to women who were British subjects

---

[39] Quoted in Janice Fiamengo, 'Rediscovering our Foremothers Again: The Racial Ideas of Canada's Early Feminists, 1885–1945', *Essays on Canadian Writing*, 75 (Winter 2002), p. 7.
[40] Carol Lee Bacchi, *Liberation Deferred? The Ideas of the English-Canadian Suffragists, 1877–1918* (Toronto, 1983), pp. 50–5.

aged 21 and over. Chinese-Canadian women, like men, would be barred from the ballot box until 1947, as would the Inuit until 1950 and 'status Indians' until 1960.

Ties of Empire were practical as well as rhetorical. Canadian feminists operated in a wider, transatlantic, and transpacific world that put them in touch with activists in the metropole and in the other white settler dominions. The 1911 and 1912 Canadian tour of prominent English suffragists including Emmeline Pankhurst and Sylvia Pankhurst was credited with reviving an ailing movement for women's enfranchisement.[41] Between 1912 and 1914, Australian activists Margaret Hodge and Harriet Newcomb visited South Africa, Australia, New Zealand, and Canada, and the result was the British Dominions Woman Suffrage Union, which aspired to have enfranchised Australian and New Zealand women directly help Canadians and South Africans in their struggle for suffrage and enhance communication between Dominion and metropolitan feminists. They celebrated the grant of limited woman suffrage in Canada and Britain by renaming themselves the British Dominion Women Citizens' Union. Drawing attention to what they saw as the uniquely egalitarian character of what they called 'these Greater Britains beyond the seas', Commonwealth feminists developed a new kind of internationalism, one where white colonial women would play a significant role.[42] At other times Canadian activists used the institutions of the metropole to force change. In October 1929 the Privy Council reversed the judgment of the Supreme Court of Canada and declared that the word 'person' in Section 24 of the British North America Act meant women as well as men. From that point women would be appointed to the Canadian Senate, though, as with their elected counterparts, never in numbers comparable to men.

Historians have not always agreed about how to interpret the significance of Empire to twentieth-century feminist thought. Scholars in the 1970s and 1980s tended to celebrate the achievements of early suffrage and reform activists and downplay or even white wash their 'ideological impurities so that they might stand as icons of resistance'.[43] In the 1990s, historians argued that race and hierarchy—and by implication and sometimes explication, Empire—were at the heart of feminist practice in late nineteenth- and early twentieth-century Canada. More recent scholarship has called attention not simply to the importance of race and Empire to feminist thought and work, but to the contradictions and ambivalences that went alongside it. Veronica Strong-Boag and Carole Gerson have showed how Mohawk feminist, performer, and author Pauline Johnson proclaimed herself both 'a great daughter of the flag' and an 'Indian to the

---

[41] Catherine L. Cleverdon, *The Woman Suffrage Movement in Canada* (Toronto, 1950), p. 117.
[42] Angela Woollacott, *To Try her Fortune in London: Australian Women, Colonialism, and Modernity* (London, 2001), pp. 116–36.
[43] Fiamengo, 'Rediscovering our Foremothers', p. 1.

core'.[44] In early twentieth-century Canada where Johnson performed, published, and lived, Empire could mean many things.

Discourses of Empire were flexible but not endlessly so. Québécois nationalists registered the intimate relationship between English-Canadian nationalism and imperialism, and connected it to what they saw as threats to women's roles within the family and the French-Canadian nation.[45] While many were content to refashion Empire to different ends, other women rejected its deep imprint on English Canada. The atrocities of the South African and the First World War pointed some feminists to a pacifist politics rooted both in a belief of women's inherently peace-seeking nature and an explicit critique of militarism and the imperialism that justified and fostered it. Gertrude Richardson, Flora McDonald Denison, Violet McNaughton, and Francis Marion Beynon all argued against war and, in different ways and at times, against Empire and Canada's place in it.[46] Beynon, editor of the populist and progressive *Grain Grower's Guide*'s 'women's page' from 1912 to 1917, was as unequivocal in her anti-imperialism as others were about their imperialism. 'Being asked to harangue a company of poor defenseless school children on Empire Day on the subject of loyalty' occasioned her to reflect publicly on the hypocrisy of 'all this babel about the grand old flag'.[47] The onset of the First World War put such dissension under increased scrutiny. Beynon's job and her life were both threatened, and in 1917 she left Winnipeg for New York city. Beynon's departure registered, among other things, her disappointment with mainstream Canadian feminism's abiding ties with Empire and war, ties that grew tighter in the South African and the First World War. These ties would be challenged by organizations like the Women's International League for Peace and Freedom, which flourished in the 1920s and served as a support for later women's peace organizations, including the Voice of Women.

CHANGING WOMEN, CHANGING CANADA, CHANGING EMPIRE

The ties and sentiments of Empire did not halt precipitously after the First World War, but they did change. Organizations that represented the most

[44] Veronica Strong-Boag and Carole Gerson, *Paddling her Own Canoe: The Times and Texts of E. Pauline Johnson/Tekahionwake* (Toronto, 2000).

[45] Susan Mann Trofimenkoff, *The Dream of Nation: A Social and Intellectual History of Quebec* (Toronto, 1983).

[46] Barbara Roberts, *'Why Do Women Do Nothing to End the War?' Canadian Feminist-Pacifists and the Great War* (Ottawa, 1985).

[47] Frances M. Beynon, 'Loyalty and Political Corruption', *Grain Growers' Guide*, 3 June 1914; Kurt Korneski, 'Liberalism in Winnipeg, 1890s–1920s: Charles W. Gordon, John W. Dafoe, Minnie J. B. Campbell, and Francis M. Benyon', Ph.D. thesis (Memorial University of Newfoundland, 2004).

explicit and celebratory wedding of women and Empire faltered. A brief boost in the IODE's membership after the Second World War was an exceptional blip in a wider pattern of decline. By the 1960s the IODE was asking, 'are we dinosaurs?'[48] For women associated with the newly invigorated and largely reinvented women's movement of the 1960s and 1970s, organizations like the IODE seemed at best quaint and at worst hopelessly outdated. The imperial enthusiasts who made such an imprint on the NCW made none on the National Action Committee on the Status of Women, the national women's organization formed in 1972, though English-Canadian nationalism, pacifism, Québécois independence, Aboriginal rights, socialism, and decolonization certainly did.[49] Empire did not disappear from Canadian women's lives, but it changed the language it used and the space it occupied. Missionary women who once spoke in the language of race, civilization, and mission now cherished the idiom of international development.[50] The Girl Guides boast a still impressive membership of over 140,000 members in present-day Canada, but have traded in their focus on Empire and citizenship for one of multiculturalism, internationalism, and social service.

These changes reflect the wider fortunes of the British Empire, the substantial differences between first- and second-wave feminism, and the shifting ground of race in post-war Canada. After the Second World War Britain conclusively lost its place as the largest source of migrants to Canada. Beginning in 1962, the 'white Canada' immigration policy was dropped, eventually to be replaced by a 'points'-based system. This model tends to channel women into the 'family class' of migrants but allowed non-European peoples unprecedented access to Canada. With migrants increasingly coming from east Asia, south Asia, the Caribbean, the Middle East, and Africa, Canada became an increasingly multiracial as well as multicultural society.[51] Aboriginal populations were growing both in numbers and in visibility. From the 1960s a highly organized Indigenous rights movement insisted that Canada was, its post-war nationalist rhetoric notwithstanding, a colonizing society, and an unwelcome one. The implications of these changes for women in English Canada would become clear in the 1980s and 1990s, when many feminist organizations grappled with the thorny, painful, and often divisive question of race. Women of colour launched a powerful critique of the legacies of feminism's connections to race and Empire, arguing that the Canadian women's movement was in effect a white women's movement, and that feminists needed to integrate the experience of women of colour into their

---

[48] Quoted in Pickles, *Female Imperialism*, p. 167.

[49] Meg Luxton, 'Feminism as a Class Act: Working-Class Feminism and the Women's Movement in Canada', *Labour/Le Travail*, 48 (Fall 2001), pp. 63–88.

[50] Ruth Crompton Brouwer, *Modern Women, Modernizing Men: The Changing Missions of Three Professional Women in Asia and Africa, 1902–69* (Vancouver, 2003).

[51] Sunera Thobani, 'Closing the Nation's Doors to Immigrant Women: The Restructuring of Canadian Immigration Policy', *Atlantis*, 24/2 (Spring/Summer 2000), pp. 16–26.

analyses and acknowledge white racialization and privilege.[52] The 1992 election
of Sunera Thobani, a south Asian woman, as President of the National Action
Committee on the Status of Women, the country's largest women's group, was
symbolic of changing feminist constituencies and priorities, just as the hostility
she encountered was symbolic of how controversial these changes remained.

While the political and cultural articulations of Canadian womanhood and
the British Empire have seen major changes, some of the most quotidian yet
revealing ways that colonialism and womanhood have come together remain
much the same, sometimes disturbingly so. In 2004 Amnesty International
brought international attention to the prevalence of violence against Indigenous
women in Canada. They argued that the number of Aboriginal women found
dead or simply deemed missing indicated the profound failure of the Canadian
justice system to protect Indigenous women.[53] The story of what have become
known as the 'missing women' speaks to the persistence of the most brutal
racial inequities and gendered power relations in contemporary Canada, ones
that cannot be comprehended without due attention to the tight binds between
gender and colonialism. This is a point that is made throughout an influential
secondary scholarship on the historical connections between gender and the
British Empire.[54] For reasons that are not entirely clear, Canada has played a
conspicuously small role in this literature. Bringing its insights and questions
to bear on Canadian history suggests a point that is only seemingly simple,
and that is that we fail to understand Empire if we fail to examine how it
worked in gendered ways. It illustrates the futility of trying to simply add women
to an unreconstructed masculinist history of Empire or anything else. Seeing
women in the history of the British Empire in Canada irrevocably leads us
to a tellingly new vision of that Empire, of its history, and, by extension, of
Canada.

[52] Enakshi Dua, 'Canadian Anti-Racist Feminist Thought: Scratching the Surface of Racism',
in Dua and Angela Robertson, (eds), *Scratching the Surface: Canadian Anti-Racist Feminist Thought*
(Toronto, 1999).
[53] Amnesty International, *Stolen Sisters: A Human Rights Response to Discrimination and Violence
against Indigenous Women in Canada* (n.p., 2004).
[54] Philippa Levine, (ed.), *Gender and Empire* (Oxford, 2004).

SELECT BIBLIOGRAPHY

SARAH CARTER, *Capturing Women: The Manipulation of Cultural Imagery in Canada's
Prairie West* (Montreal and Kingston, 1997).
COLIN M. COATES and CECILIA, MORGAN, *Heroines and History: Representations of
Madeleine de Verchères and Laura Secord* (Toronto, 2002).
MARLENE EPP, FRANCA IACOVETTA, and FRANCES SWYRIPA, (eds), *Sisters and Strangers:
Immigrant, Ethnic, and Racialized Women in Canadian History* (Toronto, 2000).
KATIE PICKLES, *Female Imperialism and National Identity: Imperial Order Daughters of the
Empire* (Manchester, 2002).

KATIE PICKLES, and MYRA RUTHERDALE, (eds), *Contact Zones: Women and Colonization in Canada's Past* (Vancouver, 2005).

J. POTTER-MACKINNON, *While the Women Only Wept: Loyalist Refugee Women in Eastern Ontario* (Montreal and Kingston, 1993).

MYRA RUTHERDALE, *Women and the White Man's God: Gender and Race in the Canadian Mission Field* (Vancouver, 2002).

SYLVIA VAN KIRK, *'Many Tender Ties': Women in Fur Trade Society in Western Canada, 1670–1870* (Winnipeg, 1980).

13

Economy and Empire: Britain and Canadian Development, 1783–1971

Douglas McCalla

Imperial policies and external trade, particularly in staple products, were the heart of the traditional narrative of Canadian economic history.[1] This is a real story: its themes, strategies, events, and characters appear clearly in the correspondence among Imperial and colonial officials and politicians, in what leading business figures wrote to them about and testified to, in much emigrant and travel literature, and often in colonial legislative documents and principal newspapers such as the *Montreal Gazette*. In revisiting the story, however, it is essential to recognize that these sources did not address—indeed took for granted—much that was central to colonial economic development. It is also important, in assessing the Imperial dimensions of the development process, to distinguish between official acts of the state and the essentially private activities and strategies of individuals seeking their own livelihood and profit. Because the colonies were separate political units, with direct ties with Britain, they are often discussed individually. As has always been recognized, however, Upper and Lower Canada on the one hand and the Atlantic colonies on the other were regional economies. Although the two regions tend to be seen as essentially separate, there were parallels between them: in both, for example, the monetary system was based on the dollar, and accounts were often kept in Halifax currency, a money of account in which the dollar equalled five shillings.[2] There were also various links, some of them through Britain.

Until the 1840s, many policy makers in Britain, most British officials sent overseas, and most local leaders believed that Imperial policy was important to the development of the colonies' economies and that colonies were important

This chapter is part of a programme of research funded initially by a Killam Research Fellowship, awarded by the Canada Council, and sustained since by the Canada Research Chairs programme.

[1] See, e.g., Kenneth Norrie, Douglas Owram, and J. C. Herbert Emery, *A History of the Canadian Economy* (Toronto, 2002), e.g. pp. 54–6, 67–9, 113–14, 120–1; elsewhere, e.g. at pp. 70–4, they seek to graft another story onto staples.

[2] See A. B. McCullough, *Money and Exchange in Canada to 1900* (Toronto, 1984).

to the British economy and British power.[3] Official influence worked through many channels and levels of connection, and sometimes at cross-purposes. There were differing perspectives, interests, and strategies, both within and among such institutions as the army, navy, Colonial Office, and Treasury; and colonists, often in competition with one another in business and politics, sought to work with, influence, and at times resist all of these.[4] Policy makers' ability actually to influence production, prices, trade, and consumption was, moreover, constrained by market forces, political elements in policy determination, and costs of enforcement. There was, for example, much colonial legislation and frequent concern by Imperial authorities about money, payments, and exchange rates, but where policy defied market forces (in which the proximity of New York and Boston played a part), the latter were the more powerful.

British government policies and actions contributing to the character and the dynamics of the economies of British North America after 1783 included the Navigation Acts (which regulated shipping within the Empire, until their abolition in 1849), preferential tariffs (e.g. for timber), formal trade regulations (including some that were indirect, such as the East India Company's rights in the British tea trade), subsidization of a variety of activities including some emigration (directly by British agencies and through colonial governments), purchases (e.g. for military supplies) and investments (e.g. for defensive works) within the colonies, regulation of some kinds of economic activity (e.g. money and banking), state-based credit (e.g. for canal building), provision of services (e.g. the post office and some transportation), and Imperial enterprise (such as the Hudson's Bay Company, a private firm that embodied a public strategy). This list omits what were the most important of all Imperial actions in shaping the economy: providing military security and building fundamental institutions—property (beginning with acquisition of title to land from Aboriginal peoples), the legal system, and the colonial state itself (including its boundaries). Until well into the twentieth century, Britain handled diplomatic negotiations and supplied diplomatic representation for Canada. In a short chapter, it is not possible to address any of these subjects fully or systematically to consider the likelihood of different outcomes from different policies or no policies.

In any case, the relationships between policy and development were complex rather than simple, reciprocal rather than one way. Policies could be positive (stimuli), negative (prohibitions), and inadvertent (as when a policy aimed at something else altogether had collateral impacts). Sceptics resisted stimuli that

---

[3] See Patrick O'Brien, 'Imperialism and the Rise and Decline of the British Economy, 1688–1989', *New Left Review*, 238 (Nov.–Dec. 1999), p. 62.

[4] Phillip A. Buckner, *The Transition to Responsible Government: British Policy in British North America, 1815–1850* (Westport, Conn., 1985), pp. 22–25; Peter Baskerville, 'Imperial Agendas and "Disloyal" Collaborators: Decolonization and the John Sandfield Macdonald Ministries, 1862–1864', in David Keane and Colin Read, (eds), *Old Ontario: Essays in Honour of J. M. S. Careless* (Toronto, 1990), pp. 249–50.

did not make sense in local circumstances, watching those who did try the new to see what happened, as in the case of British efforts to foster hemp cultivation. And if incentives were strong enough, prohibitions could often be evaded.[5] Even stimuli could ultimately be negative, if they encouraged inappropriate allocation of resources.[6]

The links between economy and Empire were never more evident than after the Conquest of New France. A few *Canadien* merchants managed to obtain connections in Britain, but the heights of colonial business were quickly dominated by men coming from or who had ties in Britain, via the army supply system or the operations of British merchants. Far into the nineteenth century, transatlantic trade in all the goods that colonists bought from Britain and in the more limited range of goods they sold there was the leading business sector. Even exports to and imports from elsewhere in the world normally were financed or settled through London. To participate required credit in Britain.

At the same time, the many post-revolutionary links between Britain and the United States remind us that Britain's prominence in the colonies' economies was in part a reflection of more general leadership. Similarly, it was London's role in world finance that made it the centre of the trade cycle, whose rhythms dramatically influenced colonial patterns. Nor was British North America's attractiveness for emigrants and investments simply a function of Empire.[7] What such analytic distinctions meant to those living in the colonies is another matter. After 1815, in every colony, many people or their parents came from Britain and Ireland, the imported goods they consumed came mainly from or through Britain, and the financial system that underlay exchange in all the colonies focused there.

WAR AND THE BRITISH NORTH AMERICAN ECONOMIES, TO 1815

At its end as at the beginning, the eighteenth century was dominated by war, the quintessential imperial process. Even in periods of peace, no one could know where or when war might occur or what its immediate costs and opportunities would be. Especially during actual conflicts, Britain's need to finance its armies,

---

[5] Ross D. Fair, 'A Most Favourable Soil and Climate: Hemp Cultivation in Upper Canada, 1800–1813', *Ontario History*, 96 (2004), pp. 41–61. On smuggling, see e.g. David Murray, *Colonial Justice: Justice, Morality, and Crime in the Niagara District, 1791–1849* (Toronto, 2002), pp. 193–5.

[6] See, e.g., Graham D. Taylor and Peter A. Baskerville, *A Concise History of Business in Canada* (Toronto, 1994), pp. 109–16.

[7] But see Marjory Harper, 'British Migration and the Peopling of the Empire', in Andrew Porter, (ed.), *The Oxford History of the British Empire*, vol. III: *The Nineteenth Century* (Oxford, 1999), p. 86; and Lance E. Davis and Robert A. Huttenback, *Mammon and the Pursuit of Empire: The Economics of British Imperialism* (Cambridge, 1988), pp. 138–42.

fleet, and allies dominated the macroeconomy of prices and exchange rates. Particularly for the Atlantic region, the policies and circumstances of wartime have been seen as providing a 'hothouse beginning', creating an economy from 'artificial' origins.[8] But even there state activity was only part of the story, and not all state actions promoted development.

For Newfoundland, Imperial power underlay the negotiation and enforcement of fishing, landing, and trading rights and metropolitan merchants, notably from the west of England, helped to shape a policy that long sought to discourage settlement. In wartime, however, having a local base proved an increasingly decisive advantage for inshore fishing; and, from the mid-eighteenth century, 'slowly, informally, and without official encouragement' Newfoundland began to acquire a settled population, which by 1810 exceeded 20,000.[9] The growth of a resident fishery also contributed to an increasing focus of external commerce in the hands of resident merchants, based in St John's. Many imports came from within the Empire, including vessels and some provisions from other North American colonies, and fish were exported directly to the British West Indies, especially after 1783. But as much as 80 per cent of the fish caught by Newfoundlanders was sold beyond the Empire, in Portugal, Spain, and Italy.[10] Essentially, the fishery was part of an international, not a protected Imperial, economy.

'Not everything that happens in wartime is caused by war,' Julian Gwyn reminds us. Still, as he shows, war, defence, and the laws of trade and navigation were essential to making Halifax the leading urban centre in the region as the capital of Nova Scotia and the centre of British military activity. If Nova Scotia's links with what Gwyn calls its 'natural trading partners in New England, New York, and Pennsylvania' were now limited by both American and British policy,[11] the Navigation Acts contributed to the immediate expansion of Nova Scotia's direct trade with the British West Indies, and to the building of the schooners used in this and coastal trades. The carriage of wood, fish, and provisions southwards and of sugar, molasses, and rum northwards was conducted in locally built vessels, with local crews, by local merchants on their own account. Governed by supply factors in the Maritimes and Newfoundland and by demand there for sugar and its products, this trade would grow as local populations did.[12] A distinct issue after 1783 was whether, because American vessels were now legally excluded from British West Indies ports, an entrepôt trade could be created for Maritime

---

[8] Norrie et al., *History of the Canadian Economy*, p. 68.

[9] Margaret R. Conrad and James K. Hiller, *Atlantic Canada: A Region in the Making* (Toronto, 2001), p. 97.

[10] Shannon Ryan, *Fish out of Water: The Newfoundland Saltfish Trade, 1814–1914* (St John's, 1986), pp. 240–1.

[11] Julian Gwyn, *Excessive Expectations: Maritime Commerce and the Economic Development of Nova Scotia, 1740–1870* (Montreal and Kingston, 1998), pp. 39, 40.

[12] Eric W. Sager with Gerald E. Panting, *Maritime Capital: The Shipping Industry in Atlantic Canada, 1820–1914* (Montreal, 1990), pp. 24–9, 49–53, 82–5, 230.

merchants and fleets between the United States and the British West Indies. Geography and power limited what might be done to exploit this possibility, and American access to British ports in the Caribbean was soon restored.

In Prince Edward Island, the principal Imperial story was the system of land tenure established in 1767, which divided the island into large lots held mainly by absentee landlords. Subsequently, the system was increasingly contested. But whatever its politics, it did not prevent the development of a mainly rural economy, based on farming, fishing, wood, and shipbuilding. As people moved and as landlords themselves invested in, borrowed against, bought, and sold their claims, a property market was created that must have reflected the costs and uncertainties of the tenure system. By 1800, there were perhaps 750 families on the island; and in the next half-century, under the established tenure system, the island's population would grow at least as rapidly as comparable areas in Nova Scotia and New Brunswick. Given proximity, there must at all times have been some comparability in living standards in these adjacent areas.[13]

One of the best known of all the Imperial stories of British North American development dates the transformation and growth of New Brunswick to Napoleon's Continental System and the obstruction of Baltic timber supplies in 1806 and 1807. British firms, arguing for the strategic importance of timber, persuaded the British government to establish preferential duties in 1809 to offset the much higher costs of shipping timber across the Atlantic rather than from the Baltic. The ensuing expansion of the timber trade prompted a rapid increase in colonial shipbuilding to supply vessels for the trade, and for sale in Britain. It should be noted, however, that extraction and export of New Brunswick wood, some of it to Britain in locally built ships, had begun soon after settlement. Shipbuilders had also regularly built vessels for coastal and other trades; until 1815, indeed, most Maritime shipbuilding was for registry in the region. That New Brunswick had existed for twenty-five years and sustained a population of about 25,000 before the establishment of the timber duties is a reminder that, whatever the importance of the duties in its development, policy was only part of the process.[14]

In the St Lawrence valley, there were parallels to the New Brunswick timber trade, both in the prior existence of shipbuilding and trade in forest products and in the rapid expansion under the preferential duties. But the most striking impact of the war era was the creation (and later defence) of Upper Canada, a separate inland colony. Its initial population was 'American', but here, in contrast to inland America, the main lines of the import trade (e.g. in cotton, nails, and tea) ran directly from Britain. Farmers in both Canadas produced wheat for local

[13] J. M. Bumsted, *Land, Settlement, and Politics on Eighteenth-Century Prince Edward Island* (Kingston, 1987), pp. 8–11, 26, 45–64, 189–92.

[14] Sager with Panting, *Maritime Capital*, pp. 27–8, 45–46; Graeme Wynn, *Timber Colony: A Historical Geography of Early Nineteenth Century New Brunswick* (Toronto, 1981), pp. 11–25.

consumption and sometimes for export to Britain, the latter reaching a peak in 1802. They also produced wood products such as potash and barrel staves for export to the British Isles.[15] These trades and wider development went on for forty years before anyone anticipated a canal connection between Upper Canada and Montreal or between Lakes Erie and Ontario and for fifty years before the first such canal systems were completed. Indeed, development proceeded not just in the most accessible areas along the St Lawrence and Lake Ontario but in remoter areas, such as the Eastern Townships and above Niagara Falls.

In 1800 about 340,000 people, including Aboriginal peoples, lived in the settled parts of Britain's remaining North American colonies; of these, almost 100,000 were in the Atlantic colonies, more than 200,000 in Lower Canada, and fewer than 40,000 in Upper Canada. This was not a large figure, not much more than 2 per cent of the almost 16 million in the United Kingdom in 1801 or 6 per cent of the population of the United States, where half a dozen major states individually had larger populations.[16] A majority of the entire population was French speaking, descended from pre-Conquest settlers. Agriculture was the dominant colonial economic activity, engaging a majority of settlers. Colonists could not have lived without links to and a variety of goods from the international economy. Still, an agricultural economy provided many basic necessities: housing, heat, most food, and (in varying degrees) clothing too. In some places, fishing could provide a living even without much supporting agriculture, and more of these inputs might be purchased, often from elsewhere within the region rather than overseas. Built on family labour and investment and on local exchange of land, goods, labour, and funds, such rural economies had their own momentum, as the expansion of the French-speaking population and economy in the St Lawrence valley demonstrated. Other early examples of such development include the establishment of immigrants, such as the groups of families from Scotland and Yorkshire who came to Nova Scotia and Prince Edward Island in the early 1770s and from the 1790s; the rebirth of Acadian society; the extension of Loyalist settlements after their initial creation; and the post-1784 movement of non-Loyalists from the United States.

MERCANTILISM AND AFTER, 1815–1870

Long after 1815 renewed warfare remained a possibility. But the immediate stress was adjustment to peace, as Britain was deeply troubled by unemployment, social

[15] Fernand Ouellet, *Histoire économique et sociale du Québec, 1760–1850: structures et conjoncture* (Montreal, 1966), e.g., pp. 88–90, 130, 190, 609.
[16] Graeme Wynn and L. D. McCann, 'Maritime Canada, Late 18th Century', plate 32, and R. Cole Harris and David Wood, 'Eastern Canada in 1800', plate 68, in R. Cole Harris, (ed.), *Historical Atlas of Canada*, vol. I: *From the Beginning to 1800* (Toronto, 1987).

disruption, and severe deflation. By the early 1820s, price levels were between half and two-thirds of their peak in 1813. In the colonies, deflation and depression contributed to a renewal of indebtedness and to pressures on public finance as revenues from customs duties fell, a trend exacerbated in the Canadas by political tensions, particularly in Lower Canada. This was one (but by no means the only) reason for Britain's attempt in 1822 to reunite the Canadas. Resisted in both colonies, the legislation failed, although one crucial issue, the allocation of customs revenues (which were collected in Lower Canada on imports destined for both colonies), was addressed in separate legislation. That this left Montreal in a separate political and legal jurisdiction from much of its upriver hinterland does not appear to have hindered exchange or expansion.

By 1815, and despite the loss of British control of the American interior, the Montreal-based fur trade, in fierce competition with the Hudson's Bay Company, had been extended all the way to the Pacific. Deflation compounded the stresses of competition, and the companies finally agreed on a merger in 1821. By then, London and the remotest west were directly linked via both Hudson Bay and the St Lawrence. Indeed, after the merger, Lachine, just outside Montreal, was made the North American headquarters for the company. The merged HBC, with 900 employees and a capitalization of £400,000 in 1825, was probably the largest enterprise in British North America; it also retained its principal Imperial role, as the means by which Britain claimed much of the continent.

The fur trade clearly did not require investments in navigation above Montreal. The motivation for making such improvements was essentially military, as the British army addressed the problem of supplying forces in Upper Canada. As expansively interpreted by Colonel John By, this mission led to the Rideau Canal, which after 1832 allowed steam navigation between the two Canadas. Such British government expenditures, and those on a routine, ongoing basis, were a factor in several of the colonial economies, but they were tending everywhere to decline as a proportion of the whole of any economy.

The post-war conjuncture was the context for efforts by merchants in the largest colonies to create banks, which were founded in Montreal (1817), Quebec and Kingston (both 1818), Saint John (1820), York (1821), and Halifax (1825). A second wave of bank creation between 1832 and 1836 tripled the number of operating chartered banks in the colonies.[17] By the time the Bank of British North America, a London-based institution with a royal charter that intended to operate in all the colonies, arrived on the scene in 1837, only Prince Edward Island and Newfoundland did not already have a local banking system of considerable competitiveness. British authorities, fearing what they saw as a colonial tendency to reckless credit creation, insisted on reviewing bank charters.

---

[17] E. P. Neufeld, *The Financial System of Canada: Its Growth and Development* (Toronto, 1972), pp. 71–89.

What such regulation actually meant is not clear: on the one hand, note issues did not approach the limits set by charters, and on the other, banks still could get into trouble, as all the Upper Canadian ones later did. Banks have sometimes been seen as reinforcing dependency, through a bias to international exchange and short-term commercial lending. Certainly they reflected the shape of Canadian business and connected it to the international system, but in practice funds lent could not be so readily confined; banks represented broader credit processes and the creation of local capital. In Upper Canada, for example, bank discounts in the mid-1830s far exceeded what would have been necessary to finance actual volumes of grain and wood exports.[18]

In the post-war period, British trade policies continued to have an essentially mercantilist orientation. The timber duties were revised downward, but still gave a substantial preference to colonial timber. Exports of square timber from New Brunswick grew rapidly to about 1820, then, with the exception of a sharply higher peak in 1824–5, levelled off, though investment in export-oriented sawmilling continued to grow.[19] From Quebec, expansion was sustained into the 1840s, with timber coming from as far west as Lake St Clair. Under the combined influence of the timber duties, Navigation Acts, and free entry for colonial ships, British North America quickly became a major supplier of vessels to the British mercantile marine, supplying over 2,000,000 tons between 1815 and 1860. Initially, capital and even skilled labour came from outside the colonies, as did some wooden inputs and most of the non-timber inputs that accounted for perhaps one-third of the final cost of a vessel; some of the latter might not even be installed until after a vessel's arrival in a British port. That was the destination for most of the new ships, and many were sold there. Although this began as something of an enclave industry, it outgrew that status.[20]

The timber trade created an imbalance of capacity between east- and westbound runs, which was one factor in the sharp fall in westbound freight and passenger rates. Many emigrants, in fact, came on timber ships; but emigrant numbers did not correlate closely with the patterns of the timber trade. And once across the ocean, emigrants were not required to stay in the port or even the colony of arrival. Although much woods work involved skills that a newly arrived immigrant was unlikely to have, some doubtless found work in the woods. Most entered the larger settlement economy. Hence the emphasis on the Corn Laws in the traditional story, which imagined them as having fostered colonial agriculture. But their purpose was to sustain Britain's landed classes, not to promote colonial development. When wheat prices fell below a threshold price, all imports to Britain were barred, as happened by the early 1820s. Prices rebounded and the

[18] Douglas McCalla, *Planting the Province: The Economic History of Upper Canada, 1784–1870* (Toronto, 1993), pp. 151–3.
[19] Wynn, *Timber Colony*, pp. 34, 102, 110.
[20] Sager with Panting, *Maritime Capital*, pp. 67–8, 70, 174–6, 188, and 270–2.

tariff regime was adjusted, but even so it was not until the 1840s that colonial wheat actually had secure access to the British market and Upper Canadian wheat became a reliable export to Britain.[21] A separate story was the effort by Canadian interests to secure preferential access for Canadian flour in the British market in a form that permitted importing American wheat and grinding it into flour for export as Canadian. This objective, briefly achieved in the 1843 Canada Corn Act, was actually of little value to agricultural development in the Canadas themselves. Sufficient mills to process Upper Canadian grain already existed and more would have been built as Upper Canadian output grew. Extra capacity to mill American wheat for the British market brought no additional value to Canadian farmers and only marginal benefits to the economy they dominated.

Which of these policies mattered to colonial growth, and how much? One test was what happened when the mercantilist policies that had apparently sustained them were removed. Not only did none of what seemed to be policy-based transatlantic exchanges collapse after 1850, they all actually expanded sharply. Thus, it was after the repeal of the Corn Laws in 1846 that the Upper Canadian wheat boom of the mid-century occurred. In the timber trade, the maximum volume and value of exports to Britain, an increasing proportion of which took the form of manufactured wood rather than square timber, came later in the century, long after the last of the preference for colonial timber had expired in 1859. In shipping, the principal authorities argue that patterns in the free trade era were still 'influenced critically by state policies'. These were not British policies aimed at regulating Imperial trade and shipping, however; the passage refers to wars, American policy, and colonial tariff structures.[22] As shipbuilding continued after 1850 and vessel quality continued to rise, ships were increasingly retained on local registry under local ownership, which produced a more than tenfold increase in colonial fleets over the next thirty years, as measured by total tonnage of larger ships on registry. Building and operating these vessels was a substantial element of the economies of the principal Atlantic ports even as an ever larger proportion of voyages were on charter on non-local routes, particularly between Britain and the United States.

It is beyond the scope of this chapter to explore the extensive literature on the institutions and policies related to land: these include tenure systems; policies on disposition of land by the Crown (including, in Upper Canada, the alien question); efforts to use land to sustain government itself and such public purposes as religion and education; and the institutions and politics surrounding land speculation.[23] But as speculation itself highlights, a land market was being created; buying, selling, and renting land and claims to it were a normal part of

[21] R. M. McInnis, 'Perspectives on Canadian Agriculture 1815–1930', 1: 'The Early Ontario Wheat Staple Reconsidered', *Canadian Papers in Rural History*, 8 (1992), p. 24.

[22] Sager with Panting, *Maritime Capital*, pp. 96, 181–2.

[23] John C. Weaver, *The Great Land Rush and the Making of the Modern World, 1650–1900* (Montreal and Kingston, 2003).

the economy. By the 1850s the outcome of land-granting processes, wherever the soil allowed, had been the creation of farms, and the principal agricultural institution everywhere was the family farm.

That Upper Canada had grown without canal connections between Lake Erie and Lake Ontario or between Lake Ontario and Montreal did not call into question the widespread understanding that provincial development would be greatly enhanced by such works. Like a number of American states, therefore, Upper Canada turned in the 1830s to the British bond market. When the 1837 financial crisis broke, the colony found itself in severe financial difficulty, but it emerged with ties to two leading international merchant banking firms, Baring Brothers and Glyn, Hallifax, Mills, and Company. Following the British-imposed union of Upper and Lower Canada, the debts of the former continued as part of the public debt of the United Province of Canada, which was augmented by an Imperially guaranteed loan to permit completion of the St Lawrence canal system. By now, Canada had an independent relationship with and its own (fluctuating) reputation in the London financial market. Through such borrowing, the Canadian canal system was completed late in the 1840s.[24] Lacking so dominant and costly a project, governments in the Atlantic region borrowed much less, and locally.

Colonial leaders began to talk about railways even in the 1830s, and in the mid-1840s at least two prime Canadian projects got as far as securing promises of British financing. But the British boom collapsed before much was accomplished on the ground. Why go to London? The main reason was that the new technology originated in Britain, and railway-oriented institutions there increasingly sought overseas business. Hence American railways also looked to London. To get attention there, colonial promoters represented their projects as essentially American. In Canada the claim was to link the inland United States to the Atlantic. There were equivalent visions in the Maritimes; thus, Sir John Harvey, Lieutenant-Governor of Nova Scotia, in 1850 supported the projected European and North American (a Saint John-focused project) because it would be 'the shortest Highway between the great families of the Anglo Saxon race'.[25]

A grand strategy was necessary but scarcely sufficient. It took government guarantees and the offer of a rate of return much higher than could be obtained in Britain at the start of the 1850s to interest British financial circles in some colonial projects. In Canada, the Baldwin–Lafontaine government's 1849 Guarantee Act offered guaranteed bonds to companies that could get half of their line built; provincial government backing was later confined to what was called the Main Trunk, but municipalities could lend their credit

---

[24] Michael J. Piva, *The Borrowing Process: Public Finance in the Province of Canada, 1840–1867* (Ottawa, 1992), pp. 1–56.

[25] Quoted in A. A. den Otter, *The Philosophy of Railways: The Transcontinental Railway Idea in British North America* (Toronto, 1997), p. 73.

to other companies. Unlike the canals, which had been built mainly as state enterprises, Canadian railways were organized as private companies, formally controlled by common shareholders. Much of the actual funding was in the form of bonds, and the financiers who managed the market in them quickly became core figures in company power structures. Only the Great Western, which linked key components in the American railway network between New York and Chicago, actually generated a great deal of traffic, notably in passengers. It quickly converted much of its bonded indebtedness to common stocks and later refinanced its government-guaranteed bonds. Such success also allowed it to finance what ultimately proved to be some ruinous strategic decisions.

As in Canada, many business and political leaders in the Maritimes wanted railways. When it became clear that private capitalists, local and British, did not see a way profitably to provide them, they were financed through the state. In the 1850s, Nova Scotia and New Brunswick each borrowed about £800,000, ultimately on bonds held in England, through the same London bankers as Canadians, to finance their principal projects. These were smaller amounts, on a per capita basis, than in Canada; together Nova Scotia and New Brunswick raised not much more money than was required to build just the Victoria Bridge at Montreal. Neither Maritime railway, however, succeeded in generating much traffic.

The largest of the Canadian enterprises, the Grand Trunk Railway, was particularly notable as an Imperial project—and represented some of the worst elements of the intertwining of the colonial state and London finance.[26] With an initial board of directors including leaders of the Canadian government, George-Étienne Cartier as its lawyer, a who's who of well-connected colonials as contractors or subcontractors on sections of its line, and the engagement of principal London financiers, notably Thomas Baring and George Carr Glyn, it transformed reasonable projects to link Montreal to the sea at Portland, Maine, and to Toronto into a line intended to run to Chicago, competing across western Upper Canada with the Great Western, and with politically motivated branches to Quebec (Lévis) and another 150 miles downriver. Neither the colonial state nor the British capitalists alone could have produced the ensuing disaster, which created a private, British-controlled company weighed down with an impossibly heavy capitalization. When the true dimensions of the fiasco became clear, Canada's public credit was so engaged that the company could not be allowed to go bankrupt and then reorganize itself with a capital appropriate to its actual traffic. The result was Canada's largest business by far, owned in Britain, controlled from London, and managed in Canada, which had a long-term, high-level, sometimes incestuous, and from the company's viewpoint frequently

---

[26] D. C. M. Platt and Jeremy Adelman, 'London Merchant Bankers in the First Phase of Heavy Borrowing: The Grand Trunk Railway of Canada', *Journal of Imperial and Commonwealth History*, 18 (1990), pp. 208–27.

poisonously antagonistic relationship with the Canadian state and local business communities.

The core technology of the age, railways drew British North American colonies into more extended financial dealings in London and new levels of public debt. Yet the radically increased level of British capital investment in the colonies in the mid-1850s produced an intense burst of inflation in the colonies and coincided with the beginning of almost half a century of net emigration from the British North American colonies. In itself, that is, the short-term expenditure of large sums on colonial railways was not necessarily a spur to development. The real issue was the people, goods, and ideas that railroads moved; here they proved to be selective, enhancing economic activity and new opportunities for investment in some centres much more than others.[27] The other major new communications technology was the telegraph. Within a decade of its initial successful tests, most of eastern British North America (including Newfoundland) was connected, in part via American lines. By Confederation, the transatlantic cable had joined Britain and North America.

Railways, the public debt incurred for them (much of which had been indirect), and the financial crisis of 1857 (which slashed imports and hence tax revenues) lay behind one of the defining steps in the politics of Canada's emerging financial autonomy, Alexander Tilloch Galt's 1859 revisions of the tariff. His main need was revenue, but he also sought to meet two other objectives. One was to encourage use of the St Lawrence (and the Grand Trunk) as the main route for imports by calculating the value of goods for purposes of duty where the importer purchased the goods (which tended to favour purchases of overseas goods, for example tea, in England or other country of origin over purchases of such goods in the United States). The other was to promote local manufacturing by not taxing imported raw materials and taxing semi-finished goods at lower rates than finished goods. [28] This was, of course, not the first tariff on British manufactured goods; but its explicit protectionism prompted objections in some British circles. That it was politically effective in Canada is a reminder that local manufacturing had already come into existence, under the earlier tariff regime.

Between 1800 and 1870, the population of the area that would by 1873 be part of Canada rose to about 3.7 million (with another 170,000 in Newfoundland), or about one-eighth of the United Kingdom's population. Since 1800, there had been an almost sixfold increase in the population of Lower Canada/Quebec and about a ninefold rise in the Maritimes and Newfoundland. Over three-quarters of all Canadians lived in what now were the provinces of Quebec and Ontario. That was about the same proportion as in 1800, but the balance had shifted

---

[27] Douglas McCalla, 'Railways and the Development of Canada West, 1850–1870', in Allan Greer and Ian Radforth, (eds), *Colonial Leviathan: State Formation in Mid-Nineteenth-Century Canada* (Toronto, 1992), pp. 192–229.

[28] Ben Forster, *A Conjunction of Interests: Business, Politics, and Tariffs, 1825–1879* (Toronto, 1986), pp. 41–51; Piva, *The Borrowing Process*, pp. 146–9.

dramatically: Upper Canada/Ontario had grown from about 10 per cent to over 40 per cent of the Canadian total. Moreover, its per capita income was by a substantial margin the highest in Canada.[29] Of the British influences in its development, immigration (discussed in Errington's chapter above) was the most important.

PROTECTIONISM, INVESTMENT, AND EMPIRE, 1870–1971

For Canada, not including the west or Newfoundland, Gross National Product in 1870 totalled $383 million, or about $106 per person. Agriculture, at almost 38 per cent of GNP, was the largest sector of the Canadian economy. The other primary sectors, fisheries, forestry, mining, and furs, produced 3.5 per cent of GNP. Manufacturing and construction accounted for somewhat over 25 per cent. About one-third of the economy was represented by other sectors, principally services (such as government, financial services, transportation, and trade) and housing rents. In 1870, the United Kingdom's GNP, depending on method of calculation, was between £953 million and £1,155 million; on a per capita basis and translated into dollars at current exchange rates, that equalled between $146 and $177 per person. Thus, GNP per capita in Canada was between 60 and 73 per cent of that in the UK. An even lower proportion is indicated by Angus Maddison, whose long-term international comparative data, based on Gross Domestic Product, are used in Table 13.1; he puts Canadian GDP per capita in 1870 at just half of that in the United Kingdom.[30] Any of these figures represents a very large gap in apparent standard of living, which is unlikely to have been narrower earlier. That so many people had nevertheless moved from Britain to British North America points to the importance of variations not visible in these aggregate data.

In the century after 1871, Canada grew from 12 per cent to 40 per cent of the United Kingdom's population (Table 13.1). Meanwhile, the UK fell as a source of Canadian imports from 58 per cent to 5 per cent; as a destination for Canadian exports from 53 per cent in 1901 to 8 per cent in 1971; and as a source of foreign investment in Canada from 85 per cent in 1901 to 9 per cent

---

[29] Kris Inwood and Jim Irwin, 'Land, Income and Regional Inequality: New Estimates of Provincial Income and Growth in Canada, 1871–1891', *Acadiensis*, 31/2 (Spring 2002), p. 161.

[30] M. C. Urquhart, *Gross National Product, Canada, 1870–1926: The Derivation of the Estimates* (Kingston and Montreal, 1993), pp. 3, 11, 24, 47; C. H. Feinstein, *Statistical Tables of National Income, Expenditure and Output of the U.K. 1855–1965* (Cambridge, 1976), tables 1–3; Angus Maddison, *Monitoring the World Economy, 1820–1992*, Development Centre Studies Series (Paris, 1995), p. 23. Using these sources and purchasing power parity as the basis for comparison, another calculation puts Canadian GDP per capita at 83% of the United Kingdom's in 1870, 93% in 1900, and 140% in 1970; see Leandro Prados de la Escosura, 'International Comparisons of Real Product, 1820–1990: An Alternative Data Set', *Explorations in Economic History*, 37 (2000), pp. 24–32.

Table 13.1. Selected comparisons and relationships, Canada and the United Kingdom, 1871–1971 (all figures are percentages)

	A Population Can./UK[a]	B GDP/capita Can./UK[b]	C UK share of Canada trade Imports	D Exports	E Non-resident investment UK share
1871	12	50	58		
1901	13	60	24	53	85
1911	16	84	24	48	77
1931	23	n.a.	18	29	36
1951	28	103	10	16	19
1971	40	114	5	8	9

[a] From 1931, UK total excludes Irish Republic; figure would be 21% if it was included. Newfoundland is included in Canadian total from 1951.

[b] Nearest year: data are for 1870, 1900, 1913, 1950, 1973.

Source: A: F. H. Leacy, (ed.), *Historical Statistics of Canada* (*HSC*), (2nd edn Ottawa, 1983), A2; Basil Mitchell and Phyllis Deane, *Abstract of British Historical Statistics* (Cambridge, 1971), pp. 6–7.
B: Angus Maddison, *Monitoring the World Economy, 1820–1992*, Development Centre Studies Series (Paris, 1995), p. 23.
C: *HSC*, G397, 400, 473–7.
D: *HSC*, G390, 393, 401–7; and M. C. Urquhart and K. A. H. Buckley, (eds), *Historical Statistics of Canada* (1st edn Toronto, 1965), F334–9.
E: *HSC*, G192; 1931 entry is actually from 1930.

in 1971. The trajectory of development carried Canada from deep inferiority to Britain in terms of GDP per capita to a considerably higher level. By 1971, Maddison's data place Canada at 114 per cent of the United Kingdom. What lies outside these numbers and this narrative is the rise of the American economy. Although Canada at times grew more slowly or faster than the United States, its development more or less paralleled American growth.[31] Thus, as Canada's ties to Britain diminished relative to its ties to the United States, its standard of living grew relative to Britain's. It is not intended to argue here that one trend caused the other, just that they coincided.

After Confederation, the Imperial economic relationship (migration aside) was dominated by two established themes: investment and finance, and trade and trade policy. These can be viewed more closely through selected episodes. The first was the construction in the 1870s and 1880s of the government-owned Intercolonial Railroad to the Atlantic and the privately owned (but government-backed) Canadian Pacific Railroad to the Pacific. These were dramatic steps in nation-building terms and were represented also as vital Imperial links. Financing such lumpy, capital-intensive projects required Canadians to go to the major markets in which such funds were raised. In one influential view, that process tended to create a 'collaborating [colonial] economic elite who clung to, and

[31] Urquhart, *Gross National Product*, p. 26.

depended upon, British power and British capital'.[32] But although they needed British funds, the CPR's principals, who had much experience in the financial worlds of both New York and London, were anything but the dependent figures this phrasing implies.[33]

In the economic conjuncture of the 1870s, as prices and transport costs fell, Canadian manufacturers were under constant pressure to lower costs. International competition could be addressed, if free trade orthodoxy was ignored, by using the tariff to raise import prices sufficiently to bar competing goods from the country. The intellectual case for protection rested on the need to shelter infant industries, and on the apparent success of protection in promoting development in the United States and Germany. The practical case was pressure from Canadian business. The 1879 National Policy tariff of John A. Macdonald and Samuel Leonard Tilley thus was about building Canada alongside the United States, on the American protectionist model, but it necessarily aimed also at keeping out competing British manufactured products. Costs fell further in the 1880s, prompting another round of tariff hikes in 1887. This brought effective tariff levels to their highest point in Canadian history.[34] The trend, although not the principle of protection, began to be reversed under Wilfrid Laurier. In 1897, he sought to please low-tariff supporters and to demonstrate Imperial loyalty through partial tariff reductions that became, in 1898, a system of specifically British, then Imperial, preferences, providing a tariff rate for goods from Empire countries lower than the general level. Despite this, the United States' share of Canadian imports continued to grow.

The next episode was the Canadian boom of 1900 to 1913, a period of accelerated development whose momentum is associated especially with prairie settlement, although other factors were also vital to the investment, urbanization, and technological development of the period. By 1901 the population of the prairies exceeded 400,000, or about 8 per cent of the Canadian total; a decade later, what were now three prairie provinces had more than tripled in population, to reach 18 per cent of Canada's population. In contrast to the 1850s wheat boom, which occurred after net immigration to British North America had largely ceased, the early twentieth-century boom attracted, indeed was partly generated by, large-scale immigration.

British investors played a key role in making this boom so massive. As Christopher Platt aptly phrased it, they 'were interested . . . in capital-seeking, primary-producing, "white" countries of recent settlement/development, which could offer a good prospect of political stability, a secure and satisfactory rate of return on investment, and the probability of capital gain—[an] "egg-laying pig

---

[32] P. J. Cain and A. G. Hopkins, *British Imperialism: Innovation and Expansion, 1688–1914* (London, 1993), p. 265.

[33] Taylor and Baskerville, *Concise History*, pp. 235–6.

[34] J. Harvey Perry, *Taxes, Tariffs, & Subsidies: A History of Canadian Fiscal Development* (Toronto, 1955), vol. I, p. 69.

which produces wool and milk" '. [35] For a few years, Canada seemed to be just that, and drew a quite remarkable proportion of capital outflows from Britain. By one estimate, a net total of about £625 million in (mainly) British capital was invested in Canada between 1881 and 1913, almost two-thirds of it after 1906, when two new transcontinental railroads were under construction. In the three peak years, 1911–13, overseas capital flowing to Canada (largely from Britain) equalled almost 40 per cent of the entire net outflow of British capital.[36] Such British investment reinforced the boom, rather than initiating it. As in the 1850s, the rapid investment of so much capital had inflationary effects, notably in land values. Again the Canadian state, both the federal government and many of the provinces, readily guaranteed bonds, fostering inappropriate capital structures and many wholly unwarranted extensions to the railroad system. Although the war unexpectedly changed everything about capital markets, it only compounded a problem of railway-based public debt that Canadians had already made and that Canadian taxpayers would carry in the decades ahead.

Simultaneously, three other processes were extending the financial links between Canada and Britain. One was British direct investment, made by British companies in many areas of the Canadian economy, including mining, manufacturing, and financial services.[37] The second was the first corporate merger movement in Canada between 1909 and 1913, which created large quantities of corporate securities, especially bonds, many of which flowed to the British market, mainly through Canadian promoters.[38] The third was the creation of electrical utilities and urban transit systems, both in and beyond Canada. When 'American technology, European capital, and Canadian entrepreneurship' were combined to build hydroelectric projects in the Caribbean, Latin America, and Barcelona, it made for some dramatic stories and, for a time, some substantial individual fortunes, but it is difficult to see this part of the capital raised in London by Canadian chartered companies as having much of an impact on actual Canadian development.[39]

As the British financial system reached its apogee, Canadian financiers, utility promoters, and railway men were familiar with and active in London. So there were several Canadian businessmen on board the *Titanic*, en route from Southampton to New York when she struck an iceberg and sank off

[35] D. C. M. Platt, 'Some Drastic Revisions in the Stock and Direction of British Investment Overseas, 31 December 1913', in *The City and the Empire*, Collected Seminar Papers 35 (London, 1985), p. 18.

[36] Michael Edelstein, *Overseas Investment in the Age of High Imperialism: The United Kingdom, 1850–1914* (New York, 1982), p. 271.

[37] Donald G. Paterson, *British Direct Investment in Canada, 1890–1914: Estimates and Determinants* (Toronto, 1976).

[38] Gregory P. Marchildon, *Profits & Politics: Beaverbrook and the Gilded Age of Canadian Finance* (Toronto, 1996), pp. 146–7.

[39] Duncan McDowall, *The Light: Brazilian Traction, Light and Power Company Limited, 1899–1945* (Toronto, 1988), p. 383.

Newfoundland on 15 April 1912. Among those lost was a towering figure in the Canadian business universe, Charles Melville Hays, the American who had been general manager of the Grand Trunk Railway since 1896. He was returning from his semi-annual board meeting in London. His position and power derived from the reality that such a company could not be managed in detail from England; but he also had to account regularly to the company's suspicious British shareholders, particularly when, as in 1912, the overseas managers' expansionary strategy was urgently calling for large infusions of capital. Three years later on 7 May 1915, the *Lusitania*, en route from New York to Liverpool, was torpedoed off the Irish coast. One of those who died was Fred Stark Pearson, also an American, who was heading for England as he struggled to save the far-flung Canadian-based utility empire he had built. Hays and Pearson represented two of the major new nineteenth-century technologies and were travelling in very different institutional context from merchants a century before, but they were following a route long familiar to Canadian business travellers. That their routes ran through New York is a reminder that most of those who made the London trip were not Canadian. That the *Titanic*'s passengers included an Astor, a Guggenheim, a Strauss, and a Widener illustrates the impossibility of making the economic history of British investment in Canada in this period into a purely Imperial story.[40]

The First World War initially accentuated the downturn already under way in capital markets, to the cost not just of Canadian financiers and new transcontinental railways but of others such as prairie farmers who had bet on sustained expansion.[41] From this perspective, Canada looks highly dependent, at the end of credit chains running from Britain. But that was only part of the story. The actual strength and complexity of the Canadian economy as it had developed by 1914 quickly became evident in the extent of wartime mobilization, with a large domestically financed public debt, substantial manufactured exports (many of which were procured by a British government agency in Canada, the Imperial Munitions Board), and some capital exports. In most respects, that is, the war reflected trends already established; what it changed was Britain's international financial role, long crucial to the 'Imperial' ties between Canada and Britain.

The next Imperial economic episode arose during the Depression, as R. B. Bennett and other imperial leaders sought to promote inter-imperial trade (and to respond to the United States' dramatic upward tariff revisions of 1930). The Ottawa Conference of July and August 1932 worked out trade arrangements to give various goods preference in other Imperial markets. Supplemented by follow-up agreements, this process perhaps bolstered Britain's exports to Canada and did help to restore Britain's place as the leading destination for Canadian

---

[40] Toronto *Globe*, 16–17 Apr. 1912; 8, 10, 11 May 1915.
[41] Jeremy Adelman, 'Prairie Farm Debt and the Financial Crisis of 1914', *Canadian Historical Review*, 71 (1990), pp. 491–519.

exports.[42] The Depression and political issues of deflation and debt relief also led Bennett to establish a Canadian central bank to provide an institution with the scope and authority to manage the national money supply and international financial dealings.[43] The Bank of Canada, which began operations in 1935, was modelled on and influenced by the Bank of England, but Canada had no interest in joining the formal sterling area that Britain created in these years.

When the Second World War broke out, the Canadian government was more prepared than in 1914 to manage the industrial and financial dimensions of being a major producer, a supplier of manpower, and by 1941 a creditor to Britain (if debtor to the United States). There was even scope for intellectual cooperation with Britain, for example in the development of atomic energy. But although the war greatly strengthened Canada's economic links to Britain, it did not affect the relative strength of the two external poles for Canada, because exchanges with the United States also intensified. Moreover, many of the wartime links to Britain proved temporary; after the war, as the data for 1951 in Table 13.1 indicate, the downward trend in principal indicators quickly resumed. Wrestling with reconstruction after the war, Britain sought to limit exchanges outside the sterling area, and later began a growing reorientation to Europe. Canadian nationalists lamented many aspects of the continuing strengthening of economic relationships with the United States in the post-war period and governments sought to foster trade elsewhere, but there was, essentially, little to be done about the basic power of that attraction. On the other hand, Canadian post-war immigration policy came to reflect Canadians' growing acceptance of a more multicultural identity and responded to a demand from people from many parts of the world for access to Canada. As a result, and even as emigration from Britain slowed after a post-war surge, Canadian ties to many areas of the Empire/Commonwealth were actually enhanced. How much, and in what ways, such immigrants' links to every part of the old Empire embodied larger economic reorientations are, however, other questions.

From the perspective of some of the economic chapters in the *OHBE*, which represent the whole of what is termed the periphery as a unit, the Imperial story of the Canadian economy was part of a larger narrative of 'the overseas English-speaking natural resource economy', whose momentum 'was largely driven by the resource needs of European industrial economies'.[44] If we begin in British North America and recognize the predominance of agriculture there,

[42] D. K. Fieldhouse, 'The Metropolitan Economics of Empire', in Judith M. Brown and W. Roger Louis, (eds), *The Oxford History of the British Empire*, vol. IV: *The Twentieth Century* (Oxford, 1999), pp. 90–2, 100–3; Ian M. Drummond, *Imperial Economic Policy, 1917–1939: Studies in Expansion and Protection* (Toronto, 1974), pp. 219–421.

[43] Michael D. Bordo and Angela Redish, 'Why Did the Bank of Canada Emerge in 1935?', *Journal of Economic History*, 47 (1987), pp. 405–17.

[44] Avner Offer, 'Costs and Benefits, Prosperity and Security, 1870–1914' and B. R. Tomlinson, 'Economics and Empire: The Periphery and the Imperial Economy', in Porter, (ed.), *The Oxford History of the British Empire*, vol. III: *The Nineteenth Century*, pp. 710, 72.

we find a rather different trajectory, in which the Canadian economy was driven by a family-focused quest for land and the possibility of independence that it gave. Categorizing agriculture with natural resources obscures its differences from extractive sectors; farming and other rural production offered many choices in terms of investments, techniques, products, outputs, and markets. At least until the prairie boom, only some, often a very small part, of the return to investing in a farm typically came from the ability to grow products sold in Europe. Except for some primary manufacturing (basic processing of raw materials), Canadian manufacturing was also oriented to the domestic market. Even the creation of the Canadian financial system, beginning in the 1820s, was in part about making new centres. In the century after special Imperial preferential arrangements ended in the 1840s and 1850s, the movements of people, capital, and goods continued to have Imperial dimensions. But the essential economic relationship now was market driven, reinforced by Canadian governments' efforts to promote development through railroad building. That the grandeur of the imperial idea can be reduced in economic terms mainly to market forces should not, however, obscure the most essential part of Empire in making the new economy, which was creating the colonies, defending them, and endowing them with the basic institutions of that market economy.

SELECT BIBLIOGRAPHY

MICHAEL BLISS, *A Canadian Millionaire: The Life and Business Times of Sir Joseph Flavelle, Bart., 1858–1939* (Toronto, 1978).

DOUGLAS McCALLA, *Planting the Province: The Economic History of Upper Canada, 1784–1870* (Toronto, 1993).

GREGORY P. MARCHILDON, *Profits & Politics: Beaverbrook and the Gilded Age of Canadian Finance* (Toronto, 1996).

MICHAEL J. PIVA, *The Borrowing Process: Public Finance in the Province of Canada, 1840–1867* (Ottawa, 1992).

ERIC W. SAGER with GERALD E. PANTING, *Maritime Capital: The Shipping Industry in Atlantic Canada, 1820–1914* (Montreal and Kingston, 1990).

GRAHAM D. TAYLOR and PETER A. BASKERVILLE, *A Concise History of Business in Canada* (Toronto, 1994).

GRAEME WYNN, *Timber Colony: A Historical Geography of Early Nineteenth Century New Brunswick* (Toronto, 1981).

14

British Justice, English Law, and Canadian Legal Culture

Philip Girard

The title's distinction between British justice and English law rests on the fact that there is, strictly speaking, no such thing as 'British' law aside from the law of the United Kingdom constitution. The political fusion of England and Scotland in 1707 left Scots law, based on local custom and uncodified Roman law, largely intact. It was the English common law, not Scots law, that was received into British North America. Yet, as Mr Justice Bora Laskin noted in his introduction to *The British Tradition in Canadian Law*, use of the more embracing adjective was justified by the fact that 'the British Monarch, the British Cabinet, the British Parliament and such British courts as the House of Lords and the Judicial Committee of the Privy Council . . . have played major roles in the establishment of Canadian legal institutions and in the directions taken by Canadian law'.[1] The British North America Act 1867 declared the new Dominion to have a constitution 'similar in principle to that of the United Kingdom', but long before then it was understood that 'what are generally esteemed the most valuable portions of British law, have been transplanted into our land,—the Habeas Corpus,—the freedom of the Press—the trial by Jury—the Representative Branch of the legislature,—the viva voce examination of witnesses; all those branches of public law . . . we possess'.[2]

Laskin might have added that in the popular imagination, the evocative phrase 'British justice' summed up the legal inheritance from the mother country, and long served as a rallying cry for those opposing all manner of private or public oppressions. To quote Murdoch again, 'Let an Englishman go where he will, he carries as much of law and liberty with him as the nature of things will bear.'[3] His conjugation of 'law and liberty' illustrates an important point about the evolution of legal culture. When British North Americans thought about the British legal inheritance, they did not imagine law as merely a set of authoritative

---

[1] Bora Laskin, *The British Tradition in Canadian Law* (London, 1969), p. xiii.
[2] Beamish Murdoch, *Epitome of the Laws of Nova-Scotia*, 4 vols. (Halifax, 1832), vol. I, p. 35.
[3] Ibid., vol. II, p. 36.

rules and institutions for dispute resolution. Law included 'lived law'—a set of values, assumptions, and practices crossing the boundaries between formal and informal law, and regulating virtually every aspect of life. Community, church, and family authority were long the bulwarks of social order while formal legal institutions remained absent or underdeveloped and professional lawyers scarce. What E. P. Thompson discovered in his study of eighteenth-century England was just as true of early British North America: 'I found that the law did not keep politely to a "level" but was at *every* bloody level.'[4]

Understood in this wide-ranging way, law was constitutive of the identity of British North Americans, and not just those of British ancestry. In time, and often after a period of *métissage* where their own legal traditions mingled with those of the British, other ethnicities were gradually acculturated into the traditions of 'British justice'. Just as indigenous populations in Africa and India turned notions of British justice against their colonizers and demanded that they live up to its ideals, so in Canada, French-Canadians, native peoples, and non-British ethnic groups sometimes used it strategically. When Chinese-Canadian Gordon Won Cumyow asked the benchers of the Law Society of British Columbia to reconsider his petition to be admitted as a student-at-law in 1918, he appealed, though to no avail, 'to traditional British Justice and fairplay'.[5]

The Quebec Act of 1774 ensured the maintenance in that colony of French civil law in the form of the *coutume de Paris*, but the establishment of English public and criminal law, an English-style judicature, and common law procedures such as trial by jury gave Quebec a legal culture of mixed heritage wherein even its private law was influenced by the English common law. At first the apparent lenity and inefficiency of English criminal law was viewed by the *Canadiens* with puzzlement and disbelief, but gradually it became an accepted part of Quebec's legal culture.[6]

A constellation of factors influenced Canadian views on the role of English law in Canada: the nature of the economy, the relative strength of settlers and native peoples, changing ideas about the nature of law itself, the state of legal professionalization, and more general ideas about Canada's role in the Empire and later Commonwealth. In a vast country where settlement proceeded over a lengthy period, it is difficult to frame a periodization that will be accurate for all regions of the country at a given time. In 1880, for example, some parts of the Maritime provinces, Newfoundland, and Quebec had been

---

[4] E. P. Thompson, *The Poverty of Theory and Other Essays* (New York, 1978), p. 96.

[5] Joan Brockman, 'Exclusionary Tactics: The History of Women and Visible Minorities in the Legal Profession in British Columbia', in Hamar Foster and John McLaren, (eds), *Essays in the History of Canadian Law*, vol. VI: *British Columbia and the Yukon* (Toronto, 1995), p. 521. Only those who could vote could become lawyers, and the Chinese were denied the vote in provincial elections.

[6] Douglas Hay, 'The Meanings of the Criminal Law in Quebec, 1764–1774', in Louis A. Knafla, (ed.), *Crime and Criminal Justice in Europe and Canada* (Waterloo, 1981).

settled for one to two centuries while huge areas in the west had not yet seen Europeans. Thus in western Canada the fur trade and fishery era continues as late as the 1880s, while settlement and industrialization tend to proceed together.

FUR TRADE AND FISHERY SOCIETY, 1600–1820

The early period of the European presence in the northern half of North America reveals a preoccupation with ensuring the conditions for economic and social order, rather than implanting a justice system as such. The English common law was not a useful tool; it assumed the existence of counties, juries, sheriffs, law texts, courts, and English-speaking people, all of which were either non-existent or in short supply. One especially valuable aspect of the common law in this context was its recognition of custom—its capacity to allow groups of people to act out and make their own law.

Prior to settlement, when Aboriginal peoples played a large role in the success of the fur trade and direct competition for the land resource had not commenced, a certain synthesis of common law and native traditions emerged. One example was the recognition of Indigenous marriage rites, known as marriage 'after the custom of the country'. An old voyageur succinctly explained the requirements: 'On ne se joue pas d'une femme sauvage comme on veut . . . Un homme engagé et un bourgeois donnent des présents aux parents de la femme, pour l'avoir. . . . Il y aurait du danger d'avoir la tête cassée, si l'on prend la fille dans ce pays, sans le consentement des parents.'[7] Parental consent plus payment of a bride price (a horse, for example), accompanied by rituals such as smoking of the calumet and followed by cohabitation, sufficed to create a union recognized as binding by both sides. Although similar in its informality to the common law marriage recognized by English law before Lord Hardwicke's Act of 1753 (and Scottish law even thereafter), there was apparently no exchange of vows between the parties as required by the common law. In contrast to many other imperial outposts, intermarriage was actively promoted among men of all ranks in the North West Company in order to ensure they stayed in the area and to help cement trade ties with influential tribes. The instructions to governors of eighteenth-century Nova Scotia also encouraged the practice.[8] The official policy of the Hudson's Bay Company was against intermarriage, but its advantages were so obvious that officials on the spot were always bending the rules. The Aboriginal people also saw these marriages as prestigious and economically advantageous and in the 1780s 'the

[7] Sylvia Van Kirk, *'Many Tender Ties': Women in Fur Trade Society, 1670–1870* (Toronto, 1999).
[8] See above, Chap. 2.

English found themselves besieged with offers of wives at their inland posts'.[9] In matters of commercial relations and inter-group violence as well, English and Aboriginal traditions mingled. On the north-west frontier, '[i]n matters of homicide Britons, Canadians and Americans acted on premises borrowed more from Indian customs than from the common law', including practices of vengeance and composition.[10]

Custom did not always present such a benign face. The recognition of slavery in all the British North American colonies in the eighteenth century was based on customary practice rather than any solid foundation in statute or common law. The Articles of Capitulation signed at Montreal in 1760 stated that all 'negroes and panis [Indian slaves]' should remain 'in the possession of the French and Canadians to whom they belong', with liberty to sell them and instruct them in the Roman Catholic faith. Both slaves and free blacks arrived in Nova Scotia soon after the establishment of Halifax in 1749, but it was the revolutionary war that brought large numbers of free blacks ('black Loyalists') and slaves to the northern colonies remaining under British rule. Some 1,200 slaves arrived in Nova Scotia alone, where the coexistence of free and slave blacks led to several attempts to re-enslave individual free blacks. The status of slavery was at first upheld in the courts, but anti-slavery opinion coalesced quickly in the 1790s. Upper Canada was the only colony to abolish slavery legislatively, albeit prospectively. A 1793 statute prohibited the importation of slaves, but existing slaves were to remain so for life and their children born after the Act would be free only at 25. In Lower Canada and Nova Scotia, the highest courts did not declare slavery illegal but created legal roadblocks to the recovery of escaped slaves sufficient to negate the rights of masters; the Loyalist judges of New Brunswick were the only ones to defend the institution. Even so, well before the Imperial abolition of slavery in 1833, it had virtually disappeared in British North America.[11]

Even where relations between Europeans were involved, the common law was only one source of law among others. After the conquest of Acadia in 1710, the Governor and Council sat in a judicial capacity at Annapolis Royal (formerly Port-Royal) and applied largely French law in disputes between Acadians.[12] In

[9] Van Kirk, *Women in Fur Trade Society*, p. 43. On later attitudes to the legality of such marriages, see Constance Backhouse, *Petticoats and Prejudice: Women and Law in Nineteenth-Century Canada* (Toronto, 1991), pp. 9–28.

[10] John P. Reid, 'Principles of Vengeance: Fur Trappers, Indians, and Retaliation for Homicide in the Transboundary North American West', *Western Historical Review*, 24 (1993), p. 32; Hamar Foster, ' "The Queen's Law is Better than Yours": International Homicide in Early British Columbia', in Jim Phillips, Tina Loo, and Susan Lewthwaite, (eds), *Essays in the History of Canadian Law*, vol. V: *Crime and Criminal Justice* (Toronto, 1994).

[11] D. G. Bell, 'Slavery and the Judges of Loyalist New Brunswick', *University of New Brunswick Law Journal*, 31 (1982), pp. 9–42; Barry Cahill, '*Habeas Corpus* and Slavery in Nova Scotia: *R. v. Hecht Ex Parte Rachel*, 1798', *University of New Brunswick Law Journal*, 44 (1994), pp. 179–209.

[12] Thomas G. Barnes, "The Dayly Cry for Justice": The Juridical Failure of the Annapolis Royal Regime, 1713–1749', in Philip Girard and Jim Phillips, (eds), *Essays in the History of Canadian Law*, vol. III: *Nova Scotia* (Toronto, 1990). Barry Moody, 'Making a British Nova Scotia', in

Newfoundland, justice was administered by seasonal fishing admirals and the Royal Navy before the appointment of the first Governor and justices of the peace in 1729. Even after 1729, as Jerry Bannister argues, 'customs occupied the centre of the island's legal culture'. Custom in Newfoundland did not have to satisfy the English test of 'time immemorial' and might acquire binding force in as little as a generation.[13] Similarly, in the Hudson's Bay Company territories, Company regulations and customary practice were the principal source of law, administered under the aegis of the highly coercive English law of master and servant. In an environment where virtually all Europeans were employees or officers of the Company, there was no 'public interest' independent of the Company's interests: even criminal offences such as theft and assault were normally treated as breaches of Company law. Only three formal trials are known to have taken place before the Company Governor and his Council (without a jury) before 1790.[14] This period of 'club law' was characterized by the ever-present threat of corporal punishment administered within a highly discretionary and paternalistic regime.[15]

The informal, hybridized, and variable nature of English law in this period was principally a response to local geographic and social conditions, but it was also a function of the virtual absence of formal courts and legally trained personnel. With the advance of settlement, this informality would cease to be seen as a strength. Imperial exploitation of the land resource would require the importation of English property law and all its trappings, while successive waves of British settlers would demand the 'British justice' they conceived was their birthright. The legal traditions of the Indigenous peoples, increasingly seen as exceptional and uncivilized, would be weakened accordingly.

THE SETTLEMENT PERIOD, 1820–1880

Until 1860 Canadian Aboriginal policy was directed from the Colonial Office and on paper it was benign. As far back as the Royal Proclamation of 1763 the

John G. Reid, Maurice Basque, et al., eds., *The 'Conquest' of Acadia, 1710: Imperial, Colonial and Aboriginal Constructions* (Toronto, 2004) paints a more positive portrait of the accomplishments of the Annapolis Royal regime.

[13] Jerry Bannister, *The Rule of the Admirals: Law, Custom and Naval Government in Newfoundland, 1699–1832* (Toronto, 2003), pp. 14–17. Peter Karsten, *Between Law and Custom: 'High' and 'Low' Legal Cultures in the Lands of the British Diaspora, 1600–1900* (Cambridge, 2002).

[14] R. Baker, 'Creating Order in the Wilderness: Transplanting the English Law to Rupert's Land, 1835–51', *Law and History Review*, 17 (1999), pp. 209–46; Russell Smandych and R. Linden, 'Administering Justice without the State: A Study of the Private Justice System of the Hudson's Bay Company to 1800', *Canadian Journal of Law and Society*, 11 (1996), pp. 21–61; Douglas Hay and Paul Craven, *Masters, Servants and Magistrates in Britain and the Empire, 1562–1955* (Chapel Hill, NC, 2004).

[15] Tina Loo, *Making Law, Order, and Authority in British Columbia, 1821–1871* (Toronto, 1994), chap. 1.

Imperial government committed itself to an orderly frontier where the interests of the Indigenous peoples would be protected as settlement advanced. The gap between this ideal and the reality at the local level was enormous, and repeatedly brought to London's attention, but local pressures proved irresistible. A parliamentary inquiry in 1836 provided a 'devastating' description of the Indian situation, but its recommendations were 'largely ignored'.[16]

With the commencement of settlement one can begin to speak of the reception of English law in earnest. Each colony was eventually endowed with its own legislature and judicature, creating the potential for a diversity of laws. Distinct legal cultures developed, but with strong family resemblances. As land was acquired or wrested from the Aboriginal inhabitants, it would be improved and commodified only if its new owners were understood to possess rights over it recognized by English law. Thus the settlers were deemed to have brought the whole corpus of the English law of real property with them.

With settlers came the raw material for juries, and with the distribution of land came title disputes, so it was not long before each colony saw itself endowed with a superior court modelled on the courts of common law at Westminster Hall. Jonathan Belcher, a New Englander who had practised as a barrister in both London and Dublin, was sworn in as Chief Justice of the first of these new colonial courts, the Supreme Court of Nova Scotia, on 21 October 1754. His commission direct from the Crown, rather than from the local Governor, represented one of the earliest attempts by the Privy Council 'to gain greater control over colonial legal systems'.[17] He was followed by his counterparts in Quebec (1764), Prince Edward Island (1770), New Brunswick (1784), Newfoundland (1792), Upper Canada (1794), Vancouver Island (1853), and British Columbia (1858), the latter two colonies being merged in 1866. Appointments to the Manitoba Court of Queen's Bench (1872) and the Northwest Territories Supreme Court (1885) were made by the Canadian, not the imperial, government, after control over these areas was transferred from the Hudson's Bay Company in 1870. Prestige and emolument went to these judges, but unpaid magistrates remained the workhorses of the justice system until the twentieth century.

The reception of English law proceeded on two fronts: the importation of 'hard' law such as case law and statutes, and the transmission of 'soft' law—the values and practices associated with the law. With regard to the former, once a colony possessed a legislature it was free to set for itself a reception date after which no new statute passed in England would automatically become law in the colony. The common law as it stood on that date, including all English statutes passed prior to that date and considered suitable to conditions in the colony,

[16] Sydney L. Harring, *White Man's Law: Native People in Nineteenth-Century Canadian Jurisprudence* (Toronto, 1998), pp. 24–26.

[17] Elizabeth Mancke, 'Colonial and Imperial Contexts', in Philip Girard, J. Phillips, and B. Cahill, (eds), *The Supreme Court of Nova Scotia, 1754–2004: From Imperial Bastion to Provincial Oracle* (Toronto, 2004), p. 38.

would be in force in that colony. Thus the Assembly of newly created Upper Canada specified that '[i]n all matters of controversy relative to property and civil rights, resort shall be had to the laws of England as they stood on the 15th day of October, 1792'. The western provinces also adopted statutory reception dates, but the four Atlantic colonies relied on the common law of reception. In theory this doctrine set the date of the first legislative assembly as the reception date, but in practice matters were considerably more fluid. In Nova Scotia the legislature first met in 1758, so that British statutes enacted after that date should not have been part of Nova Scotia law. During the 1835 trial of newspaperman Joseph Howe, however, where he was indicted for libelling the magistrates of Halifax by charging them with corruption, Fox's Libel Act of 1792, which considerably ameliorated the common law of libel, was considered by all sides to be in force.

With regard to 'soft law', the cluster of ideas known as 'British justice' remained a potent element in the legal cultures of the British North American colonies. While it could be used as an ideological weapon to reinforce class relations, Canadian scholars have generally agreed with E. P. Thompson that the rhetoric of 'the free-born Englishman, with his inviolable privacy, his *habeas corpus*, his equality before the law', was also taken up by the non-elite.[18] Again, the Joseph Howe trial provides a good illustration—in conducting his own defence Howe appealed to such notions and the jury acquitted to great popular acclaim.

The English law of real property was crucial to the success of the settlement enterprise, but it diverged considerably from the parental model. Around its liberal core, English law hedged the law of property with devices allowing for the recognition of family and community interests as burdens on the individual owner. Thus the aristocracy regularly relied on entail, rendering land effectively inalienable; the law of dower overrode freedom of testation to provide support for widows; and a wide variety of community use rights might be established by prescription over privately held land. In British North America a much more liberal property regime emerged. An Imperial statute of 1732 subjected land to seizure for debts on the same basis as chattels, disallowing the exemptions and immunities permitted to landed debtors in England. In Upper Canada and the Maritime provinces the traditional tenderness of English law towards the holder of the equity of redemption (the borrower, who was often from the landed class) was replaced by a more hard-nosed, creditor-oriented process for seizing land given as security. Primogeniture was abolished and partible inheritance instituted in the eighteenth century in the Maritime provinces, and in Newfoundland and Upper Canada in the mid-nineteenth; it existed ephemerally, if at all, in the

---

[18] The quote is from E. P. Thompson, *Whigs and Hunters: The Origin of the Black Acts* (New York, 1975), pp. 263–4, as cited in Greg Marquis, 'Doing Justice to 'British Justice': Law, Ideology and Canadian Historiography', in W. Wesley Pue and Barry Wright, (eds), *Canadian Perspectives on Law and Society: Issues in Legal History* (Ottawa, 1988), p. 46. See also F. Murray Greenwood and Barry Wright, (eds), *Canadian State Trials*, vol. I: *Law, Politics and Security Measures, 1608–1837* (Toronto, 1996).

western provinces. Registry acts sought to ensure that the state of title to land in the new colonies would be publicly known, to encourage easier circulation of the land resource, and the Torrens model of state-guaranteed title registration was adopted early on in the west. Such schemes had always been resisted in England because of the desire of landed families to keep their land transactions secret.[19]

In family law too the colonies adapted the basic English inheritance to their own needs. Judicial divorce was allowed by statute in Nova Scotia and New Brunswick in the eighteenth century, and was regularly if not frequently granted throughout the next century. Only parliamentary divorce was permitted in England until the Divorce and Matrimonial Causes Act 1857—itself later considered received into the four western provinces. The common law doctrine of unity of legal personality was also breached earlier in Canada than in England. Statutes of 1851 (New Brunswick) and 1860 (Prince Edward Island) provided that all real and personal property of a married woman would be exempt from seizure for her husband's debts, while a statute of 1859 passed in Upper Canada declared married women should enjoy their own property as separate property independent of marital control.[20] These early deviations from the English model were partially inspired by colonial New England precedents in the case of divorce, and American ones in the case of marital property.

The divergence between British North America and England in the treatment of dower during this period is particularly striking. The common law of dower entitled a widow to possession of one-third of her late husband's realty for her lifetime. It also effectively required a wife to consent to all dispositions of land by her husband during marriage: failure to 'bar her dower' allowed her to assert her rights against a subsequent purchaser if she survived her husband. The English Dower Act 1833 essentially abolished dower and restored the husband's complete freedom of disposition, *inter vivos* and postmortem, over his land. Ontario and the Maritimes went in exactly the opposite direction, strengthening the rights of the doweress against the husband's creditors and mortgagees. Dower was initially abolished in the western provinces as incompatible with the new Torrens system of title registration, but restored in the form of homestead rights which were in some respects stronger than common law dower. The reforms to dower and the early matrimonial property legislation reveal a responsiveness to the needs of the agrarian small holder and an understanding of the joint efforts required by all members of farm families for economic success. While the farm wife was not considered an equal partner with her husband, her contribution was such that she deserved some form of protection. As Justice Meredith of the Ontario Court of Appeal observed in a dower case in 1895, 'what possible right can [the husband's creditors] have

---

[19] See Philip Girard, 'Land Law, Liberalism and the Agrarian Ideal: British North America, 1750–1920', in Andrew Buck, John McLaren, and Nancy Wright, (eds), *Despotic Dominion: Property Rights in British Settler Societies* (Vancouver, 2004).

[20] Constance Backhouse, 'Married Women's Property Law in Nineteenth-Century Canada', *Law and History Review*, 6 (1988), pp. 211–57.

to take from her, and possibly from her creditors, that which is often in this country a scanty share of property gained largely by her lifetime efforts?'[21]

Many other legislative departures from English law were required in the settlement period to allow the effective exploitation of timber, water, and mineral resources, and to construct a railway network on a much vaster scale than in England. In areas such as mining where there were few useful precedents from Britain, the colonies and provinces did not hesitate to learn from American and inter-colonial models. These innovations aroused little alarm in London as long as the interests of British capital were not affected. Prior to Confederation, the formal techniques of Imperial control of Canadian law were seldom exercised. Appeals to the Judicial Committee of the Privy Council were very infrequent, and the theoretical power of the Colonial Office to strike down departures from English law remained largely that. In one instance, however, where major British interests were directly imperilled by local action—the case of the threatened expropriation of the great landlords of Prince Edward Island—the imperial government expressly withheld from the island government the power to alter their interests when responsible government was granted in 1851. The matter would not be resolved finally until after the colony joined Canada in 1873, when London abandoned the proprietors.[22]

This legal creativity has been somewhat obscured by the tendency of Canadian legal historians to focus on judge-made law in the superior courts, where deference to the English example was instinctive to the point of being Pavlovian, rather than legislation. It was also purposely obscured by Canadian contemporaries, who stressed that 'the laws of the two countries are almost identical', as a Toronto correspondent asserted in a letter to the English *Law Times* in 1856.[23] If land law revealed the adaptability of the English inheritance to the needs of a geographic and social environment far different from that of the mother country, the dominant concern in the largely judge-made areas of contract and commercial law was to keep Canadian law as English as possible so as to encourage investment and facilitate trade.[24] The ordinary administration of the criminal law too remained very loyal to the English model in both procedure and substance, according to studies of both early Halifax and the Niagara District of Upper Canada.[25] During periods when the state itself has been under

[21] *Gemmill* v. *Nelligan* (1895), 26 *Ontario Reports* 307 at pp. 318–19. See generally Girard, 'Land Law'.

[22] Margaret E. McCallum, 'The Sacred Rights of Property: Title, Entitlement, and the Land Question in Nineteenth-Century Prince Edward Island', in G. Blaine Baker and Jim Phillips, (eds), *Essays in the History of Canadian Law*, vol. VIII: *In Honour of R. C. B. Risk* (Toronto, 1999). The proprietors included local residents as well as British absentees.

[23] *Law Times*, 28 (1856), p. 85.

[24] R. C. B. Risk, 'The Golden Age: The Law about the Market in Nineteenth-Century Ontario', *University of Toronto Law Journal*, 26 (1976), pp. 307–46.

[25] Jim Phillips, 'Halifax Juries in the Eighteenth Century', in Greg T. Smith et al., (eds), *Criminal Justice in the Old World and the New* (Toronto, 1998); ' "Securing Obedience to Necessary Laws":

threat, however, it has been argued that '[b]y contemporary British . . . and even pre-revolutionary American standards, British North American governments interpreted and applied the law in a relentlessly repressive fashion'.[26]

The autonomy of the Canadian judicial system from the English was tested only once in the nineteenth century, in the *cause célèbre* of fugitive slave John Anderson. The case was highly unusual, but revealing nonetheless of English attitudes towards the Canadian judiciary and Canadian law. Anderson had killed a plantation owner in Missouri in 1853 while escaping from slavery, and arrived in Windsor, Canada West, shortly thereafter. When he was arrested in 1860 at the behest of Missouri authorities seeking his extradition, the Premier of Canada West, John A. Macdonald, referred the issue to the courts in order to stall for time. The Upper Canada Court of Queen's Bench decided that Anderson was extra-ditable under the Webster–Ashburton Treaty as implemented by the Fugitive Offenders' Act of 1849. There then followed an extraordinary course of events. In January 1861 the British and Foreign Anti-Slavery Society applied to the English Court of Queen's Bench for a writ of habeas corpus directed to the sheriff at Toronto, requesting him to bring Anderson before the English court. Hearing no Canadian counsel, the English court granted the request, causing a storm of controversy in Canada. The effect of the English decision was rendered moot when a rehearing before a court in Toronto released Anderson on a technicality. Although unquestionably bad law, *Ex parte Anderson* was successfully invoked to justify the issuance of a writ of habeas corpus by an English court to Northern Rhodesia in 1957; a similar attempt directed to Northern Ireland failed in 1971.[27]

The legal profession in each of the English-speaking colonies rapidly developed its own ethos, though all eschewed the formal split between barrister and solicitor. The Law Society of Upper Canada, established in 1797, was modelled on an Inn of Court but took its educational responsibilities much more seriously than its English counterpart. The other colonies had no similar institution and relied on the apprenticeship model of education. A few sons of elite families attended the Inns of Court into the 1830s, but purely to make useful contacts, not to further their education.[28] Few British legal professionals sought their fortune in Canada aside from those appointed directly to judgeships, and those that did gained precedence only from the time of their local admission. Many British-born young men became lawyers after emigrating, however, especially in Ontario. The bar quickly became a centre of local power, and the appointment of British

---

The Criminal Law in Eighteenth Century Nova Scotia', *Nova Scotia Historical Review*, 12 (1992), pp. 87–124. Phillips characterizes any changes as 'subtle'. David Murray, *Justice, Morality and Crime in the Niagara District, 1791–1849* (Toronto, 2002).

[26] Greenwood and Wright, *Canadian State Trials*, I, p. 38. See also volume II by the same editors, *Rebellion and Invasion in the Canadas, 1837–1839* (Toronto, 2002).

[27] Patrick Brode, *The Odyssey of John Anderson* (Toronto, 1989).

[28] David G. Bell, 'Paths to Law in the Maritimes: The Bliss Brothers and their Circle', *Nova Scotia Historical Review*, 8 (1988), pp. 6–39.

candidates to Canadian judgeships was resisted early on. Thomas Strange was the last English appointee to the chief justiceship of Nova Scotia in 1789 (he departed in 1797 for the more lucrative post of Chief Justice of Madras). The appointment of an Englishman to the New Brunswick Supreme Court in 1834 was seen as 'startling' and the British government provided assurances it would not happen again. In the new colony of British Columbia, however, Chancery barrister Matthew Baillie Begbie was appointed Chief Justice in 1858. In the Maritime provinces, increasing numbers of aspiring lawyers began to attend US law schools in the second half of the nineteenth century before returning home, inspiring an appetite for a new type of legal education. In this they participated in a more general British North American trend of openness to American legal innovations after responsible government had been achieved.

EARLY INDUSTRIALIZATION AND MODERNITY, 1880–1949

The confident remoulding of the English legal inheritance during the settlement period gave way to a certain sense of inferiority as the Empire reached its zenith at the time of Victoria's diamond jubilee. The vectors of English influence increased substantially: appeals to the Judicial Committee of the Privy Council became more frequent, particularly in matters involving the interpretation of the British North America Act 1867, and aggressive English legal publishers overwhelmed the modest indigenous industry with English legal texts, often in Canadian-footnoted editions held out as normative. The summit of a career in advocacy was to argue before the Privy Council, and a small cadre of elite Canadian lawyers thus formed an influential channel for the re-transmission of the norms of English legal culture to the Canadian environment. The appointment of a token number of colonial jurists to the committee, including Lyman Poore Duff of the Supreme Court of Canada (1918), was also an attempt to tighten Imperial linkages in the legal field. The Supreme Court of Canada, created in 1875, soon found itself reduced to the status of a 'captive court', a mere detour on the way to London where the 'real answer' would be revealed. Indeed, via the *per saltum* appeal, appellants could proceed from the highest provincial court of appeal directly to the Privy Council in some cases. Through a more liberal use of knighthoods and coveted invitations to Imperial events, authorities at the Colonial Office patronized the colonial judiciary and sought to keep them loyal to Imperial ideals. A veneer of Imperial associations in turn enhanced the prestige of colonial judges on their home turf.[29]

---

[29] On the success of these strategies in Nova Scotia, see Philip Girard, 'The Supreme Court of Nova Scotia, Responsible Government, and the Quest for Legitimacy, 1850–1920', *Dalhousie Law Journal*, 17 (1994), pp. 430–57.

This shift was greatly aided by the emergence of new paradigms of law and precedent in the late nineteenth century. On both sides of the Atlantic, scholars and judges began to treat law in a more overtly 'scientific' fashion, marking the boundaries between law and politics, between jurisprudence and policy, in ever stricter fashion. Theories of interpretation took a strongly literalist turn, to the exclusion of any overt consideration of history, social context, or policy goals. In its early decisions interpreting the division of powers between the Dominion and provincial governments, the Supreme Court of Canada regularly invoked history, geography, and Canadian circumstances in trying to understand the text of the 1867 Act, but its techniques were disapproved by the Privy Council. As Sir Montague Smith said to counsel in the course of argument in *Russell* v. *The Queen* in 1882, 'I do not think there is anything so obscure in the construction of the [British North America] Act, with regard to the distribution of power, and the dominium given to the Dominion of Canada, that renders it necessary to go into the history of it'.[30] Such techniques merely allowed the decision makers to smuggle in their own policy preferences in an opaque and unaccountable way. Along with this new understanding of law went a more hard-edged view of precedent. English law had always advocated the following of previous decisions on the same point of law as a counsel of prudence, but in 1898 the Lord Chancellor declared that English courts, including the House of Lords, could not depart from their own previous decisions. In 1879 the Privy Council declared that colonial courts were bound by the decisions of the English Court of Appeal.[31]

These trends caused a certain disruption with colonial traditions, which were forgotten or ignored. Where once Westminster had been interested in Canadian precedents on married women's property law, the flow now went the other way. All the British North American colonies outside Quebec eagerly adopted the English Married Women's Property Act 1882 and repealed their own legislation. Colonies which had already fused their courts of common law and equity in the 1850s adopted the English Judicature Acts of 1873–5 which did the same thing. When new legislation was contemplated, draftsmen preferred to be able to copy existing English acts as closely as possible so as to have the benefit of English decisions interpreting their provisions. Late Victorian lawyers in Ontario disposed massively of their early Canadian legal imprints, largely to the benefit of US law school libraries.[32]

Some disruption in the *fin-de-siècle* was inevitable in the face of significant change in Canada. As a more modern, democratic, urban, and technologically oriented society emerged, Canadian law would have to change, in some cases

---

[30] As cited by John T. Saywell, *The Lawmakers: Judicial Power and the Shaping of Canadian Federalism* (Toronto, 2002), p. 73.

[31] *London Street Tramways* v. *London County Council* [1898] AC 375; *Trimble* v. *Hill* (1879) 5 AC 342.

[32] G. Blaine Baker, 'The Reconstitution of Upper Canadian Legal Thought in the Late-Victorian Empire', *Law and History Review*, 3 (1985), pp. 219–92.

radically. When land was no longer the primary source of wealth, when parish and county began to lose their status as fundamental political units, when urban conditions spawned new types of crime and poverty, the contours of the common law were no longer sufficient. Renewed recourse to the English model was justified in some sense because England was further along the trajectory of modernity than Canada. Canadian reformers seem not to have been motivated principally by such utilitarian concerns, but by the simple prestige of English models in the heyday of Empire. In some cases, however, Canada was able to adopt legal reforms that eluded the mother country. Codification of the criminal law was discussed in both countries in the nineteenth century, but only in Canada was it successful, in 1892. Three models had been in circulation, a code drafted by R. S. Wright, originally for Jamaica, one by James Fitzjames Stephen, and another by Royal Commissioners appointed in England in 1878. Stephen's code, the most authoritarian of the three, served as the basis for the Canadian Criminal Code.[33]

This colonial insecurity and deference to Imperial models was attributable in part to the unfavourable contrast that could be made between the English judiciary, then at the zenith of its reputation, and the Canadian judiciary, known to be largely the product of patronage appointments.[34] The exacting process by which the most competent English barristers were awarded the honour of Queen's Counsel, and in turn formed the exclusive talent pool from which superior court judges were appointed, had no counterpart in Canada. Federal and provincial governments lavished QCs on their supporters, such that the designation afforded no necessary indication of talent or even competence. The federal government did not restrict judicial appointments to QCs in any case, but used them to reward political supporters, to provide regional and ethno-religious representation, and to recognize the 'arrival' of various subgroups of the population. The appointment of Pierre-Amand Landry as the first Acadian member of the New Brunswick Supreme Court in 1893, for example, was heralded by his people as a triumph. In 1949, when there had still been no Jewish appointment to a superior court in Canada (the first would occur in the following year), a Canadian Jewish Congress official insisted to the Minister of Justice that 'representation on the bench may be said to be the hallmark of acceptance as citizenry of the country'.[35] The conventional labelling of judicial posts as either Protestant or Catholic, French or English, had long delayed recruitment from other ethno-religious groups. In a country as vast and varied as Canada, it is

---

[33] Desmond H. Brown, *The Genesis of the Canadian Criminal Code of 1892* (Toronto, 1989); Martin L. Friedland, 'R. S. Wright's Model Criminal Code: A Forgotten Chapter in the History of the Criminal Law', *Oxford Journal of Legal Studies*, 1 (1981), pp. 307–46.

[34] 'Privy Council Appeals', *Canada Law Journal*, 57 (1921), p. 164; 'Appeals to the Privy Council', *Canadian Law Times*, 40 (1920), p. 259.

[35] Myerson to Stuart Garson, 2 Sept. 1949, Moishe Myerson Papers, Canadian Jewish Congress Archives.

possible that the losses in merit occasioned by such practices were offset by gains in legitimacy for the institutions in question.

Within the legal profession and legal education, a complex mingling of British and American influences occurred. With the establishment of Dalhousie Law School in 1883 the first university-affiliated professional law school on the American model was established in English Canada, and it would be followed by similar institutions in New Brunswick (1892), Saskatchewan (1913), Alberta, and Manitoba (both 1914). British Columbia and Ontario would follow much later, in 1945 and 1949 respectively. This professional reform project was to be the vehicle for a larger re-commitment to the extension of British legality and civilization in Canada in the face of the social, economic, and political transformations of the early twentieth century. This movement was largely led from the Prairies and resulted in the formation of the Canadian Bar Association in 1914.[36]

The appeal of English law and the rhetoric of British justice remained strong even in the face of an emergent post-First World War Canadian nationalism, but prominent legal figures managed to straddle this divide. Legal scholar W. P. M. Kennedy (himself a Scots-Irish immigrant from Ulster) set his extensive writings on Canadian constitutional law squarely within the Imperial tradition, but also believed fervently in Canadian autonomy and pioneered graduate study in Canadian law at the University of Toronto. Lyman Duff, appointed Chief Justice of Canada in 1933 and knighted the following year, was also portrayed as symbolizing both strong ties to English and Imperial legal traditions and Canadian independence.[37] The Victoria *Daily Colonist* summed it up in 1939: 'Sir Lyman is more than a great Canadian judge. He is an Empire figure.'[38] These parallel loyalties were evident in the ceremony accompanying the laying of the cornerstone of the new building for the Supreme Court of Canada in May 1939. With the King and Queen presiding, the Minister of Justice declared that the Canadian judiciary and bar would 'remain the protagonists of British ideals, of British traditions and British justice', while 'this new temple of supreme judicial authority, symbolizing the strength of the bonds existing between Canadians and their institutions, will add to the beauty of our national Capital'.[39] Legislation providing for the ending of Privy Council appeals had been introduced, but its progress would be delayed by the war and by a subsequent reference to the courts to determine its validity.

Ironically the counter-movement against English legal hegemony was itself fed from England. The 1930s saw not an attack on the influence of English law as

---

[36] W. Wesley Pue, 'Common Law Legal Education in Canada's Age of Light, Soap and Water', in DeLloyd J. Guth and W. Wesley Pue, (eds), *Canada's Legal Inheritances* (Winnipeg, 2001).

[37] R. Blake Brown, 'The Supreme Court of Canada and Judicial Legitimacy: The Rise and Fall of Chief Justice Lyman Poore Duff', *McGill Law Journal*, 47 (2001), pp. 558–91.

[38] 22 Apr. 1939, as cited in Philip Girard, 'Duff, Sir Lyman Poore', in the *Oxford Dictionary of National Biography* (Oxford, 2004).

[39] As quoted in Brown, 'Lyman Poore Duff', p. 578.

such, but a reaction to the role of the Judicial Committee of the Privy Council as final arbiter of the Canadian constitution, and a concurrent resistance to the conservative message of Lord Hewart in his 1929 work *The New Despotism.* Hewart's attack on the administrative state as a threat to 'British liberties' was contested by British academics such as Ivor Jennings and Harold Laski, who in turn found a certain following in Canada among legal academics. One of the most influential of these was a transplanted Englishman named John Willis who, during a long teaching career at Canadian law schools, became one of the most prominent defenders of the new administrative state and of Canadian legal autonomy. The Judicial Committee's invalidating of R. B. Bennett's New Deal-style legislation in 1937 provided a target for those who, like the socialist legal academic Frank Scott, believed its members were 'too remote, too little trained in our law, too casually selected, and [with] too short a tenure' to serve as a fit court of final appeal for Canadian matters.[40]

Although the anti-Privy Council campaign rapidly gained political support in the late 1930s, it did not indicate any wider disenchantment with the perceived British character of the Canadian legal order. Even the Privy Council maintained its mystique in some quarters. When Mrs Elizabeth Campbell thought she had been swindled out of an inheritance with the connivance of the Ontario bar and judiciary, she represented herself before the Privy Council in 1930 (the first woman to do so), won her cause, and wrote a book about it.[41] It would be hard to characterize even the cadre of left- and American-leaning legal academics as anti-imperial, but they were in any case a tiny minority, with almost no support among the bar. In many ways the 1930s represented the peak of the love affair between the Canadian legal profession and the British legal tradition. The bar was dominated by 'the last patricians', Anglophilic barristers who thought no annual meeting of the Canadian Bar Association would be complete without the presence of one of the law lords. Halifax lawyer James MacGregor Stewart may well be the avatar of this group. A devoted admirer of Rudyard Kipling, he assembled the largest private collection of Kiplingiana in the world and compiled the definitive bibliography.[42] This aggressively pro-British mood alienated francophone Quebec jurists trained in the civil law. Fearing legal assimilation, leading figures such as Justice Pierre-Basile Mignault of the Supreme Court of Canada reacted defensively and insisted on the 'purity' and specificity of the Quebec civil tradition.[43]

[40] 'The Consequences of the Privy Council Decisions', *Canadian Bar Review*, 15 (1937), p. 494. R. C. B. Risk, ' "When the World was Turned Upside Down": Canadian Law Teachers in the 1930s', *Dalhousie Law Journal*, 27 (2003), pp. 1–54.

[41] Constance Backhouse and Nancy Backhouse, *The Heiress vs the Establishment: Mrs. Campbell's Campaign for Legal Justice* (Vancouver, 2004). Campbell herself had no legal training.

[42] Barry Cahill, *The Thousandth Man: A Biography of James MacGregor Stewart* (Toronto, 2000).

[43] J-G. Castel, 'Le Juge Mignault défenseur de l'intégrité du droit civil québécois', *Canadian Bar Review*, 53 (1975), p. 544.

EMPIRE TO COMMONWEALTH: POST-WAR CANADIAN LEGAL NATIONALISM, 1945–1982

In 1946 former Chief Justice Duff made his final voyage to London, aged 81, in order to hear five Canadian appeals, one of which confirmed the legality of the deportation of nearly 4,000 Japanese-Canadian citizens to Japan after the war.[44] The last formal link with the imperial legal order was snapped in 1949 with the cessation of Canadian appeals to the Judicial Committee of the Privy Council. Two years before, the Canadian Citizenship Act (which came into force on 1 January 1947) had created the status of Canadian citizen. It did not immediately replace the amorphous concept of 'British subject' that had formerly governed voting rights, immigration status, and various other rights. Rather it proclaimed that all Canadian citizens were also British subjects, an equation that did not disappear in law until 1977, and British subjects who were not Canadian citizens retained the vote until 1975. Nonetheless, the status of Canadian citizen provided an additional focus for national identity and for the assertion of individual rights in the post-war era.

Appeals to 'British justice' declined markedly as Canadians began to look south rather than east for models, and as the proportion of British immigrants diminished steadily. Anglo-Canadian legal scholars such as Horace Read, Bora Laskin, and Frank Scott called for Canadian law to be shaped more active-ly to meet Canadian needs, and demanded of the newly liberated Supreme Court of Canada that it become a final court 'of and for Canadians'. It was now 'possible for the first time', Laskin mused, 'to contemplate deviation of Canadian law from British law in all its branches'.[45] While this call for responsive law in English Canada led to a greater interest in American law, a parallel development in Quebec led to a decline in the influence of the French model. Reformers of the 1960s and 1970s looked to other jurisdic-tions, notably in Scandinavia, for models for legislative change.[46] Contradictions between these two nationalisms resulted in urgent attempts at constitutional change to try and satisfy the demands of Quebec in the wake of the Quiet Revolution.

The evolution of Canadian legal culture in the post-war period is not a simple story of American legal thought and education overwhelming the British influence. There were strong continentalist influences in the US-style professional

[44] *Co-operative Committee on Japanese Canadians* v. *Attorney General for Canada* [1947] AC 458.
[45] Bora Laskin, 'The Supreme Court of Canada: A Final Court of and for Canadians', *Canadian Bar Review*, 29 (1951), p. 1069. See also Philip Girard, *Bora Laskin: Bringing Law to Life* (Toronto, 2005).
[46] Jean-Maurice Brisson and Nicholas Kasirer, 'The Married Woman in Ascendance, the Mother Country in Retreat', in Guth and Pue, *Canada's Legal Inheritances*.

law schools, in the increasing resort to the USA for graduate work in law, in corporate and commercial law, and in labour and human rights law. Knowledge of the civil liberties decisions of the Warren Court entered the popular mind through their echoes in television dramas, and helped to fuel claims for enhanced protection of fundamental rights at home. The enactment of the Canadian Bill of Rights in 1960, applicable only to matters within federal jurisdiction, proved to be a weak response to such demands, weakly implemented by the courts. Yet British influence by no means disappeared, and remained surprisingly strong on some issues.

The principal source of British influence was the Anglophilia of the judiciary, who continued to treat the decisions of the House of Lords and the Privy Council with great deference until the 1970s, when their importance began to wane. When Chief Justice Bora Laskin gave the Bentham Lecture in London in 1976, he cautioned that 'English decisions will have to compete on merit for consideration with decisions in Canada as well as decisions elsewhere'—an approach which was already gaining ground.[47] Other factors of lesser significance were also at play. The sudden expansion of legal education in the 1960s and early 1970s required a large infusion of legal academics. Faced with a dearth of trained Canadians, numerous British and Commonwealth scholars were hired, while Americans almost never sought positions in Canadian law faculties.

On controversial subjects such as capital punishment and the treatment of homosexual offenders Canada followed Britain's lead very closely. The British Royal Commission on Capital Punishment of 1949–53 was followed by a similar one in Canada, with similar conclusions, and the British decision to distinguish between capital and non-capital murder in 1957 was followed in Canada in 1961. Even the period of trial abolition introduced in Britain in 1965 was imitated in Canada in 1967, with final abolition following in the two countries in 1969 and 1976 respectively. The 1957 Wolfenden Report, which led to decriminalization of private consensual homosexual acts in England and Wales in 1967 (though later elsewhere in the UK), was much cited in Canada. The justifications for decriminalization advanced in the 1969 Canadian parliamentary debates on the subject were 'taken straight from the Wolfenden Report'.[48]

As Canadian politicians struggled in the late 1970s to find a suitable amending formula for the constitution and thus enable its final 'patriation', the British legacy intruded in a rather surprising fashion. It had been assumed since the passage of the Statute of Westminster 1931 that the British Parliament was a mere 'legislative trustee' of the Canadian constitution; i.e. that it could not legally decline or temporize when faced with a request from the government of

---

[47] 'English Law in Canadian Courts since the Abolition of Privy Council Appeals' *Current Legal Problems*, 29 (1976), p. 25.
[48] Gary Kinsman, *The Regulation of Desire: Sexuality in Canada* (Montreal, 1987).

Canada to amend the British North America Act. When Prime Minister Pierre Trudeau's proposed constitutional reform package initially attracted the support of only two provinces, a British parliamentary committee reported that it was Parliament's duty to discern whether there was a 'sufficient level and distribution of provincial concurrence' and to refuse to comply with an 'improper' request. Although the views of the Kershaw Committee were not adopted by the British government, when a reference to the Supreme Court of Canada was sought to determine the legality of proceeding in this manner, the Court in essence agreed with the Kershaw Committee that the power of the British Parliament remained 'untrammelled' in respect of the Canadian constitution. In the end, the Court decided that the government of Canada could legally request any change it wished from Westminster, with or without provincial support, while a majority found that an unenforceable convention existed requiring 'substantial' provincial consent before such a request could be made. Subsequent negotiations resulted in the support of all provinces except Quebec for a new constitutional package embodied in the Canada Act, which would remove all traces of British power over the Canadian constitution. In the course of these events 124 chiefs of Canadian First Nations sought a declaration from the British courts that the Canada Act was invalid without the consent of the native peoples, but the English Court of Appeal conclusively rejected the argument. Any powers and responsibilities of the British Crown or government with regard to the native peoples of Canada, said Lord Justice Slade, had devolved to the government of Canada in 1867.[49]

NEW DIRECTIONS: THE CANADIAN CHARTER OF RIGHTS AND FREEDOMS AND BEYOND

On 17 April 1982 Queen Elizabeth II visited Ottawa to sign the proclamation bringing the Constitution Act 1982 (technically, a schedule to the Canada Act) into force. This Act added an entrenched Charter of Rights and Freedoms to the Canadian constitution, created a 'made-in-Canada' amending formula, and provided for the constitutional entrenchment of the existing Aboriginal and treaty rights of the Aboriginal peoples of Canada. With this backing, the courts have struggled valiantly to oblige the Canadian government to uphold the 'honour of the Crown' in its dealings with native peoples, sometimes by implementing long-dormant treaties. The constitution of Canada is declared to be the 'supreme law of Canada', and the rights and freedoms guaranteed in it are enforceable in the courts by remedies limited only by judicial creativity. It thus leans more to the American and French traditions of fundamental rights than to the parliamentary model adopted in Britain with the implementation

[49] *Manuel* v. *Attorney-General* [1982] 3 *Weekly Law Reports* 821.

of the European Convention on Human Rights. Nonetheless, the rights and freedoms protected by the Charter are declared to be subject to such 'reasonable limits prescribed by law as can be justified in a free and democratic society', thus limiting the ostensible absolutism of the fundamental rights tradition. Section 33 also allows Parliament and provincial legislatures to 'expressly declare' that an Act 'shall operate notwithstanding' the rights guaranteed in the Charter, but it has been used only a handful of times. The Constitution Act 1982 represents a distinct break with British constitutional precedents but not a rupture with the broader British legal heritage. Indeed, the legal traffic has begun to go the other way, as British courts now look to Canadian decisions on fundamental rights as they struggle to interpret the provisions of the European Convention on Human Rights. Whether the political devolution of the 1990s in the United Kingdom will inspire British courts and political actors to look at Canadian jurisprudence on federalism remains to be seen.

In the field of private law and in some discrete areas of public law, current English case law continues to be of interest to the Canadian judiciary and legal profession, but it possesses no special birthright. Few vectors of English influence remain. After the influx of the 1960s and 1970s, few British academics remain in Canadian law schools. There may well be more Canadians teaching in British law departments than the converse, and Canadian students do graduate work at British universities much less frequently than they once did. The only organization dedicated to the furtherance of Canadian–British legal ties is the Cambridge Institute for Advanced Legal Studies, founded in 1978, but its work is not widely known.

Both Canada and Britain have been drawn into continental associations—the North American Free Trade Agreement in the case of Canada, the European Union in the case of Britain—which ensure that the most common and pressing legal issues relate to interactions with the law of the rest of the bloc. Their shared legal heritage means their legal cultures will always be mutually intelligible, but their dialects will imperceptibly become more and more distinct.

SELECT BIBLIOGRAPHY

G. B. Baker, 'The Reconstitution of Upper Canadian Legal Thought in the Late-Victorian Empire', *Law and History Review*, 3 (1985), pp. 219–92.

G. Blaine Baker and Jim Phillips, (eds), *A History of Canadian Legal Thought: Collected Essays of R. C. B. Risk* (Toronto, 2006).

W. P. M. Kennedy, *The Constitution of Canada, 1534–1937: An Introduction to its Development, Law and Custom* (Toronto, 1937).

J. T. Saywell, *The Lawmakers: Judicial Power and the Shaping of Canadian Federalism* (Toronto, 2002).

David R. Williams, *Duff: A Life in the Law* (Vancouver, 1984).

Index